Pharmacological and Toxicological Screening Methods – I

A Comprehensive Guide to Preclinical Drug Evaluation, Laboratory Animal Handling, and Modern Screening Techniques for M.Pharm Students (As per PCI Syllabus)

M. Yaso Deepika, P. Naveen, A. Divya, K. Manjeera

Copyright © 2025 Yaso Deepika, Dr. Naveen, Dr. Divya, Manjeera
All Rights Reserved.

This book has been self-published with all reasonable efforts taken to make the material error-free by the author. No part of this book shall be used, reproduced in any manner whatsoever without written permission from the author, except in the case of brief quotations embodied in critical articles and reviews.

The Author of this book is solely responsible and liable for its content including but not limited to the views, representations, descriptions, statements, information, opinions and references ["Content"]. The Content of this book shall not constitute or be construed or deemed to reflect the opinion or expression of the Publisher or Editor. Neither the Publisher nor Editor endorse or approve the Content of this book or guarantee the reliability, accuracy or completeness of the Content published herein and do not make any representations or warranties of any kind, express or implied, including but not limited to the implied warranties of merchantability, fitness for a particular purpose. The Publisher and Editor shall not be liable whatsoever for any errors, omissions, whether such errors or omissions result from negligence, accident, or any other cause or claims for loss or damages of any kind, including without limitation, indirect or consequential loss or damage arising out of use, inability to use, or about the reliability, accuracy or sufficiency of the information contained in this book.

Made with ❤ on the Notion Press Platform

www.notionpress.com

AUTHORS

Ms. Deepika Mamidisetti

Assistant Professor,
Department of Pharmacology,
School of Allied Healthcare Sciences,
Malla Reddy University,
Hyderabad, Telangana – 500100, India

Dr. Naveen Pathakala

Assistant Professor,
Department of Pharmacology,
School of Pharmacy, Anurag University,
Venkatapur, Ghatkesar,
Medchal-Malkajgiri, Hyderabad – 500088, Telangana, India

Dr. Divya Amaravadi

Assistant Professor,
Department of Pharm.D,
School of Pharmacy, Anurag University,
Venkatapur, Ghatkesar,
Medchal-Malkajgiri, Hyderabad – 500088, Telangana, India

Mrs. Kuchi Manjeera, M.Pharm. (Ph.D.)

Assistant Professor,
Department of Pharmacology,
CMR College of Pharmacy,
Kandlakoya, Medchal,
Hyderabad, Telangana – 501401, India

Editor

Dr. A. Muralidhar Rao, M.Pharm., Ph.D.

Principal,
St. Mary's College of Pharmacy,
Secunderabad, Telangana, India

Published by Notion Press

Notion Press, Inc.

800, West El Camino Real #180,
California, USA 94040

Notion Press Media Pvt Ltd

#7, Red Cross Road,
Egmore, Chennai, Tamil Nadu 600008

Email ID: publish@notionpress.com

Phone Number: +91 44 46315631

Contents

Preface vii

1. Laboratory Animal Science in Preclinical Research 11
2. Preclinical Screening of Drugs Acting on the Central Nervous System (CNS) 134
3. Preclinical Screening of Drugs for Respiratory, Reproductive, and Gastrointestinal Systems 218
4. Preclinical Screening for Cardiovascular, Metabolic, and Oncology Drugs 301
5. Immunopharmacology and Alternative Methods in Preclinical Screening 361

About the Authors 423

Preface

Pharmacological and toxicological screening methods form the scientific backbone of modern drug discovery and development. Before a new therapeutic agent reaches human trials, it must undergo rigorous preclinical evaluation to assess its efficacy, safety, and mechanism of action. This book, **"Pharmacological and Toxicological Screening Methods – I,"** has been developed to provide pharmacy students and early-career researchers with a comprehensive, curriculum-aligned reference to understand and apply these preclinical methods with clarity and confidence.

The structure of the book is based on the systematic progression of topics beginning with laboratory animal science, which lays the foundation for all animal-based pharmacological research. It covers essential topics such as species selection, genetic models, handling techniques, housing standards, and ethical considerations, all in alignment with CPCSEA and OECD guidelines. The importance of humane animal treatment and adherence to the principles of the 3Rs—Replacement, Reduction, and Refinement—is emphasised throughout the text.

Each subsequent chapter focuses on organ-system-based drug screening methods, covering the central nervous system, respiratory and gastrointestinal systems, cardiovascular and metabolic disorders, oncology, and immunopharmacology. Both classical and modern in vivo and in vitro screening models are presented with sufficient theoretical background, standard procedures, and key parameters measured. The inclusion of newer genetic tools such as CRISPR-Cas9 and immunoassay-based techniques reflects current trends and regulatory expectations in pharmaceutical research.

This book is intended to serve as a self-sufficient guide for B. Pharm. and M. Pharm. students, as well as a practical aid for research scholars working in pharmacology laboratories. Detailed

PREFACE

content tables, model-specific data, and real experimental applications have been included to make the book both academically useful and practically relevant.

In compiling this text, efforts have been made to present validated methods in a clear, step-by-step manner while maintaining scientific accuracy and ethical sensitivity. It is hoped that this book will not only support examination preparation but also inspire scientific curiosity, critical thinking, and responsible laboratory practice in the next generation of pharmaceutical scientists.

Authors

01-05-2025

AUTHORS

Ms. Deepika Mamidisetti

Assistant Professor,
Department of Pharmacology,
School of Allied Healthcare Sciences,
Malla Reddy University,
Hyderabad, Telangana – 500100, India

Dr. Naveen Pathakala

Assistant Professor,
Department of Pharmacology,
School of Pharmacy, Anurag University,
Venkatapur, Ghatkesar,
Medchal-Malkajgiri, Hyderabad – 500088, Telangana, India

Dr. Divya Amaravadi

Assistant Professor,
Department of Pharm.D,
School of Pharmacy, Anurag University,
Venkatapur, Ghatkesar,
Medchal-Malkajgiri, Hyderabad – 500088, Telangana, India

Mrs. Kuchi Manjeera, M.Pharm. (Ph.D.)

Assistant Professor,
Department of Pharmacology,
CMR College of Pharmacy,
Kandlakoya, Medchal,
Hyderabad, Telangana – 501401, India

PREFACE

Editor

Dr. A. Muralidhar Rao, M.Pharm., Ph.D.

Principal,
St. Mary's College of Pharmacy,
Secunderabad, Telangana, India

Published by Notion Press

Notion Press, Inc.

800, West El Camino Real #180,
California, USA 94040

Notion Press Media Pvt Ltd

#7, Red Cross Road,
Egmore, Chennai, Tamil Nadu 600008

Email ID: publish@notionpress.com

Phone Number: +91 44 46315631

1. Laboratory Animal Science in Preclinical Research

1.1.1 Importance of Laboratory Animals in Drug Development

Laboratory animals play an essential role in the process of discovering and developing new drugs. They are considered as vital tools for evaluating the efficacy, safety, and toxicity of drug candidates before initiating clinical trials in humans. These animals provide a living system that allows researchers to study the pharmacokinetics and pharmacodynamics of drugs in a controlled environment. Through preclinical animal studies, researchers are able to assess the absorption, distribution, metabolism, and excretion (ADME) profiles of new chemical entities. Such information helps to predict how a drug will behave in the human body and provides a scientific foundation for dosage selection and risk evaluation in human trials.

One of the most important contributions of laboratory animals is their translational value in connecting experimental findings to human pharmacology and toxicology. Animal models mimic many aspects of human physiology and pathology, enabling the study of disease mechanisms and drug responses that are otherwise difficult to explore directly in human subjects. For example, rodents such as rats and mice are frequently used to model metabolic disorders, neurodegenerative conditions, cancer, and cardiovascular diseases. The use of genetically modified animals, such as knock-out or transgenic mice, further enhances the ability to investigate specific gene functions and target pathways involved in disease progression and drug action.

Preclinical testing using laboratory animals is a regulatory requirement in almost all countries before a new drug is allowed to proceed to human clinical trials. Regulatory authorities like the United States Food and Drug

Administration (FDA), the European Medicines Agency (EMA), and the Central Drugs Standard Control Organization (CDSCO) in India have made it mandatory to generate animal data for safety pharmacology, acute and chronic toxicity, reproductive toxicity, carcinogenicity, and genotoxicity studies. The Organisation for Economic Co-operation and Development (OECD) guidelines provide standardized methods for these studies to ensure reliability and reproducibility across laboratories. For instance, OECD Guideline 420 outlines the fixed-dose procedure for acute oral toxicity testing in rodents.

In India, the Committee for the Purpose of Control and Supervision of Experiments on Animals (CPCSEA) regulates the ethical use of animals for research. Researchers must obtain approval from an Institutional Animal Ethics Committee (IAEC) before conducting any study involving animals. The proposal must justify the choice of species, number of animals, and endpoints, along with adherence to the principles of the 3Rs—Replacement, Reduction, and Refinement. Furthermore, Good Laboratory Practices (GLP) as enforced by the National GLP Compliance Monitoring Authority ensure that the data generated are scientifically valid and acceptable for regulatory submissions.

The use of laboratory animals in drug development not only accelerates the process of identifying safe and effective medicines but also provides a bridge to understand human disease models in a realistic manner. It is therefore important to use animals responsibly, adhering to scientific and ethical guidelines, to maintain the integrity of biomedical research and ensure the safety of future therapeutic agents.

1.1.2 Overview of Animal Models in Pharmacology and Toxicology

Animal models serve as essential tools in pharmacological and toxicological research for simulating various physiological and pathological conditions seen in humans. These models help researchers evaluate the efficacy and safety of new drug candidates in a controlled environment before proceeding to human trials. Depending on the specific research objective, different types of animal models are employed. Disease models are used to replicate human illnesses such as diabetes, epilepsy, hypertension, or cancer in animals, allowing the study of disease progression and therapeutic interventions. Screening models are applied for rapid evaluation of the pharmacological potential of various compounds, usually at early stages of drug discovery. Predictive models are designed to forecast clinical outcomes based on animal responses, particularly in toxicology, where they help identify the likelihood of adverse effects in humans. Mechanistic models are used to understand the molecular and cellular pathways involved in drug action or toxicity, often using genetically modified animals or targeted interventions.

The selection of a suitable animal model depends on the predictivity and validity it offers in relation to human systems. Predictivity refers to the model's ability to provide results that can be translated into expected human responses. Validity can be further categorized as face validity, construct validity, and predictive validity. Face validity refers to the resemblance of symptoms in the animal model to human disease; construct validity involves similarity in the underlying biological mechanisms, while predictive validity relates to the model's ability to respond to therapeutic interventions in a manner similar to humans. For example, the streptozotocin-induced diabetic rat model has high predictive validity for studying anti-diabetic drugs because it closely mimics the insulin-deficient state observed in type 1 diabetes.

Although animal models offer many advantages in drug research, they also present certain limitations. One of the primary advantages is the ability to perform invasive and longitudinal studies that are not ethically possible in humans. Additionally, animals can be genetically modified to reflect specific human conditions, and multiple physiological parameters can be monitored simultaneously. However, no animal model can completely replicate human physiology. Species differences in metabolism, immune response, and genetic makeup often result in discrepancies between animal and human outcomes. Furthermore, the ethical concerns and cost associated with animal experimentation demand cautious planning and justification of every study.

In recent years, there has been growing emphasis on the development and validation of alternative methods such as cell cultures, organ-on-chip systems, and computational models to reduce animal usage. Nevertheless, animal models continue to play a vital role in ensuring the safe and effective development of therapeutic agents, provided they are selected and interpreted appropriately with a clear understanding of their capabilities and limitations.

1.2.1.1 Rats

Rats are one of the most widely used species in experimental pharmacology and toxicology due to their manageable size, ease of handling, well-understood physiology, and close resemblance to human metabolic and biological systems. Belonging to the species *Rattus norvegicus*, commonly referred to as the laboratory rat, they are preferred for a variety of preclinical studies ranging from behavioral assessments to chronic toxicity evaluations.

Rats are particularly valuable in pharmacokinetic and pharmacodynamic studies because their physiological systems allow for relatively accurate extrapolation of data to humans. Their large blood volume compared to mice permits multiple blood sample collections, which is crucial for time-course studies involving absorption, distribution, metabolism, and excretion of drugs. Additionally, their body weight (typically between 200–400 grams for adult Wistar rats) makes them suitable for surgical procedures and device implantation, which is often required in cardiovascular or neuroscience experiments.

There are various inbred and outbred strains of rats used in research, each with distinct characteristics. Wistar and Sprague Dawley rats are among the most commonly used outbred strains due to their docile nature, rapid growth, and reproductive efficiency. In contrast, inbred strains like Fischer 344 or Lewis rats are used when genetic uniformity is essential, such as in immunological or transplant studies.

Rats are also widely employed in disease modeling. Streptozotocin-induced diabetic rats, spontaneously hypertensive rats (SHR), and chemically-induced models of cancer are some examples. These models enable the evaluation of drug candidates in conditions that closely resemble human pathologies. Behavioral studies such as maze tests, avoidance tests, and motor coordination assessments are also performed in rats to evaluate central nervous system drug effects.

Handling rats requires skill to minimize stress and prevent injury to both the animal and handler. They are typically grasped at the base of the tail with the body supported to avoid unnecessary discomfort. Housing should comply with regulatory standards, offering adequate space, bedding material, temperature control, and access to food and water. Enrichment items such as tunnels and nesting materials help reduce stress and promote natural behaviors.

Due to their widespread acceptance in the scientific community and regulatory agencies, rats remain a cornerstone of preclinical research, offering a reliable and reproducible model for assessing the pharmacological and toxicological profiles of new therapeutic agents.

1.2.1.2 Mice

Mice, scientifically known as *Mus musculus*, are among the most commonly used laboratory animals in experimental pharmacology and toxicology due to their small size, rapid reproduction, ease of genetic manipulation, and cost-effectiveness. Their short life span and gestation period, typically about 19 to 21 days, allow for quick generation turnover and facilitate long-term studies across multiple generations. Adult mice generally weigh between 25 to 40 grams, making them suitable for experiments requiring minimal quantities of test substances.

Mice are extensively used in pharmacological studies because of their well-characterized genome and the availability of numerous genetically defined strains. Both outbred strains such as Swiss albino mice and inbred strains such as BALB/c and C57BL/6 are used depending on the study's objective. Inbred strains offer genetic uniformity, which is valuable for reducing variability in experimental outcomes, especially in immunological and oncology studies.

One of the key advantages of using mice in experimental pharmacology is the ease with which they can be genetically engineered. Transgenic mice, knock-out and knock-in models, and CRISPR-Cas9 edited lines have become invaluable for studying gene function, disease mechanisms, and drug targets. For instance, transgenic mice expressing human amyloid precursor protein are used in Alzheimer's disease research, while immune-deficient nude mice are frequently employed in xenograft models for cancer research.

Mice are also widely used for preclinical screening in areas such as analgesics, anti-inflammatory drugs, vaccines, antiepileptics, and antidepressants. Tests such as the tail-flick test, hot plate test, forced swim test, and open field test are standardized and widely accepted protocols for evaluating behavioral and pharmacodynamic effects in mice.

Handling of mice should be done with care to minimize stress and avoid injuries. Typically, they are held gently by the base of the tail or cupped with the palm, depending on the procedure. Housing conditions must include proper temperature regulation (usually 20–24°C), a 12-hour light/dark cycle, proper ventilation, and enrichment materials like nesting paper to promote natural behavior. Group housing is common for social strains, though isolation may be necessary depending on the nature of the study.

Despite their small size, mice have made significant contributions to biomedical research, including the development of vaccines, understanding of genetic diseases, and evaluation of new drug molecules. Their genetic similarity to humans, approximately 95 to 98 percent, further strengthens their relevance in translational research. Thus, mice continue to be a foundational species in the field of preclinical pharmacological and toxicological screening.

1.2.1.3 Guinea Pigs

Guinea pigs, or *Cavia porcellus*, are medium-sized rodents that have been widely used in experimental pharmacology, toxicology, and immunology due to their unique physiological and immunological characteristics. Adult guinea pigs generally weigh between 500 to 800 grams, making them larger than mice and rats, but still manageable for laboratory procedures. Their docile temperament and ease of handling make them suitable for studies requiring frequent sampling or long-term observation.

One of the primary reasons guinea pigs are used in pharmacological studies is their anatomical and physiological resemblance to humans in certain systems, particularly in respiratory and immune responses. Guinea pigs are highly sensitive to allergens and histamines, which makes them an ideal model for preclinical screening of anti-asthmatic and anti-allergic agents. The bronchoconstriction response induced by histamine or acetylcholine in guinea pigs is similar to that observed in human asthma, allowing researchers to assess the efficacy of bronchodilators and antihistamines.

In the field of immunology, guinea pigs have historically been instrumental in the development and testing of vaccines and hypersensitivity models. They possess a well-developed complement system and show delayed-type hypersensitivity reactions similar to humans. Because of these features, they are often used in tuberculosis studies and for evaluating immune responses to various antigens. Their use in vaccine potency testing and pyrogen testing also remains significant, especially in regulatory submissions.

Guinea pigs are also unique in their requirement for dietary vitamin C, as they cannot synthesize it internally, similar to humans. This trait makes them valuable in studies related to nutrition and scurvy. In toxicology, guinea pigs are employed for dermal sensitization tests and for assessing adverse skin reactions to chemical compounds.

Handling of guinea pigs requires a gentle approach, as they can be easily startled. They should be held with both hands, one supporting the chest and the other the hindquarters. Sudden movements or loud noises should be avoided to prevent stress. Their housing requires spacious cages with solid flooring, soft bedding, and sufficient ventilation. A temperature range of 18–22°C is ideal, and fresh vegetables or commercial guinea pig feed fortified with vitamin C is essential for their health.

Despite being less genetically modifiable than mice or rats, guinea pigs retain their importance in specific pharmacological and toxicological studies where their physiological traits provide closer approximations to human responses. With appropriate care, ethical consideration, and scientific justification, guinea pigs continue to serve as reliable and informative models in preclinical research.

1.2.1.4 Rabbits

Rabbits, scientifically known as *Oryctolagus cuniculus*, are commonly used in pharmacological and toxicological research due to their moderate size, calm temperament, and physiological characteristics that make them suitable for various types of preclinical evaluations. Adult rabbits typically weigh between 2 to 5 kilograms and are particularly favored for ocular studies, skin sensitivity tests, and pyrogen testing, where their larger body size and accessible anatomical structures facilitate experimental procedures.

One of the most notable applications of rabbits in experimental pharmacology is in ocular research. The anatomical and physiological similarities between rabbit and human eyes make rabbits the preferred species for evaluating ophthalmic formulations, intraocular pressure-modifying agents, and ocular irritancy potential. The Draize eye test, once a standard method for eye irritancy assessment, was initially developed using rabbits. Although alternative models are increasingly being used due to ethical concerns, rabbits still serve a role in specific ocular safety and pharmacokinetic studies.

In addition to ocular studies, rabbits are widely used for dermal toxicity testing, especially for evaluating skin irritation, corrosion, and sensitization. Their relatively hairless skin patches allow for direct application of test substances and easy observation of inflammatory or allergic responses. Rabbits are also employed in vaccine testing, particularly for potency and immunogenicity evaluation. Their robust immune response and suitability for multiple route administrations such as intravenous, subcutaneous, and intramuscular make them ideal for such studies.

Rabbits are extremely sensitive to bacterial endotoxins, which is why they are used in the pyrogen test to detect the presence of fever-inducing contaminants in injectable pharmaceutical products. This test involves measuring body temperature elevations in rabbits after administration of a test solution. While in vitro alternatives like the Limulus Amebocyte Lysate (LAL) test are now being encouraged, the rabbit pyrogen test remains a recognized method in several pharmacopeias.

When handling rabbits, proper support of the hind limbs and back is necessary to prevent spinal injuries, as their strong back legs can cause trauma if they kick while unsupported. Rabbits should be approached calmly and handled gently to minimize stress. They are best housed individually or in pairs in clean, well-ventilated cages with sufficient space to stretch and move. A temperature range of 16–22°C is suitable for their housing, and they should be provided with a diet of commercial rabbit pellets supplemented with hay and fresh vegetables.

Although their use has declined in certain areas due to the development of alternative methods and ethical considerations, rabbits continue to provide valuable information in specific domains of pharmacology, especially where their anatomical and physiological features offer distinct advantages for research applications.

1.2.1.5 Dogs

Dogs, primarily beagles, are commonly used in experimental pharmacology and toxicology due to their well-characterized physiology, manageable size, cooperative behavior, and close resemblance to certain human biological systems. Beagles are the preferred breed for laboratory use because of their gentle temperament, uniform body weight (usually between 8 to 14 kilograms), and adaptability to repeated handling and procedures. They are particularly valuable in safety pharmacology, cardiovascular studies, and chronic toxicity evaluations.

One of the most important uses of dogs in preclinical studies is in cardiovascular research. Their heart rate, blood pressure response, and electrocardiographic patterns share similarities with humans, which makes them suitable for evaluating drugs affecting the heart and vascular system. Dogs are often used in telemetry studies, where electronic devices are surgically implanted to continuously record physiological parameters such as heart rate, blood pressure, and body temperature in conscious, freely moving animals. These studies help detect drug-induced changes in cardiac rhythm, contractility, and vascular resistance.

In toxicology, dogs are widely used in sub-chronic (90-day) and chronic (6 months or longer) toxicity studies. These studies are required by regulatory agencies like the FDA and EMA to evaluate potential adverse effects of new drug candidates following repeated administration. Dogs are typically used alongside a rodent species (usually rats) in a two-species testing model. Parameters such as hematology, biochemistry, organ weights, and histopathology are assessed to determine the toxicological profile of the compound.

Dogs also play an important role in pharmacokinetic studies due to their larger blood volume, which allows for frequent and multiple sampling over extended periods. Their oral and gastrointestinal physiology is relatively similar to humans, which aids in the evaluation of drug absorption and bioavailability. Additionally, their longer lifespan compared to rodents makes them suitable for long-term safety studies and reproductive toxicity assessments.

Handling of dogs in the laboratory requires trained personnel and a calm, humane approach. Positive reinforcement techniques, including treats and gentle verbal cues, are often used to minimize stress and promote cooperation. Dogs must be housed in clean, well-ventilated kennels with appropriate temperature control, regular cleaning schedules, and access to exercise areas. Social interaction, both with humans and other dogs, is essential for their psychological well-being. Their diet should consist of nutritionally balanced commercial dog food, and fresh water should always be available.

Despite their valuable contributions to biomedical research, the use of dogs is highly regulated and must be justified with strong scientific rationale. Ethical guidelines mandate strict adherence to animal welfare standards, and alternatives must be considered wherever feasible. The use of dogs in research has declined in recent years due to the advancement of alternative models and increased regulatory emphasis on the principles of the 3Rs—Replacement, Reduction, and Refinement—but they remain indispensable in certain areas of drug development where no suitable alternatives exist.

1.2.1.6 Non-human Primates (Monkeys)

Non-human primates (NHPs), including species such as rhesus macaques (*Macaca mulatta*), cynomolgus monkeys (*Macaca fascicularis*), and baboons, are considered highly valuable in experimental pharmacology and toxicology due to their close genetic, anatomical, physiological, and behavioral similarities to humans. Their use is often reserved for advanced stages of drug development, particularly when data from lower species such as rodents or dogs are insufficient to predict human outcomes. Adult cynomolgus monkeys typically weigh between 3 to 9 kilograms, while rhesus macaques may weigh up to 12 kilograms.

The primary application of non-human primates in pharmacological research lies in the evaluation of drugs targeting complex biological systems such as the central nervous system, immune system, and reproductive system. Due to their phylogenetic proximity to humans, NHPs exhibit highly similar immune responses, brain structure, hormonal profiles, and receptor expression patterns. This makes them particularly suitable for vaccine development, neuropharmacology, reproductive toxicity studies, and biologics testing, including monoclonal antibodies and gene therapy vectors.

In the area of toxicology, NHPs are often used in non-rodent toxicity studies required by international regulatory agencies. These studies assess potential adverse effects during repeated dosing, focusing on organ toxicity, hematological changes, immune suppression or stimulation, and behavioral alterations. NHPs are also used in reproductive and developmental toxicity studies, where their menstrual cycles, gestation period, and fetal development closely parallel those of humans. Moreover, they play a crucial role in pharmacokinetic and pharmacodynamic evaluations for drugs that act on human-specific targets, especially biologic drugs that may not cross-react in lower species.

Handling non-human primates requires a high level of expertise and stringent safety protocols. They are highly intelligent and social animals, and improper handling or inadequate housing can lead to severe stress and behavioral disturbances. Positive reinforcement training is often used to facilitate procedures such as blood collection, drug administration, and health monitoring. Housing should provide environmental enrichment, such as perches, puzzle feeders, and opportunities for social interaction. Temperature, humidity, and lighting must be strictly controlled to mimic natural conditions and support physiological health.

Due to ethical concerns and their high cost, the use of NHPs is subject to strict regulatory oversight. In India, approval from the Committee for the Purpose of Control and Supervision of Experiments on Animals (CPCSEA) is mandatory, and such studies are only permitted in registered facilities with justifiable scientific rationale. Internationally, guidelines from organizations such as the National Institutes of Health (NIH), the World Health Organization (WHO), and the European Medicines Agency (EMA) emphasize the responsible use of primates, focusing on minimizing their numbers and refining experimental protocols to reduce distress.

While their use is ethically sensitive and logistically challenging, non-human primates remain indispensable in certain domains of biomedical research. Their unique translational relevance makes them a critical species for evaluating human-specific drug responses, especially when lower species models are inadequate or non-predictive.

1.2.2 Strain-Specific Characteristics and Selection Criteria

Inbred vs Outbred Strains

In experimental pharmacology and toxicology, the selection of the appropriate animal strain is a critical step that significantly influences the accuracy, reproducibility, and translational relevance of the study. Laboratory animals are broadly classified into two genetic categories: inbred and outbred strains. Each has distinct genetic characteristics and is chosen based on the nature and objective of the research.

Inbred strains are those that have been produced by continuous brother-sister mating for at least 20 consecutive generations. This process leads to genetic homogeneity, where all individuals within the strain are considered almost genetically identical. The resulting genetic uniformity helps in reducing biological variability in experimental results and allows for precise evaluation of drug effects. Inbred strains are particularly valuable in immunological, oncological, and genetic studies where consistency and reproducibility are essential. Examples of commonly used inbred strains include BALB/c and C57BL/6 mice, and Fischer 344 and Lewis rats. These strains are often selected when the aim is to study gene-environment interactions or when a defined immune background is necessary, such as in transplant rejection or autoimmune disease models.

On the other hand, outbred strains are bred to maintain maximum genetic diversity by avoiding close relative mating. These animals have greater heterozygosity, which reflects the genetic variability found in human populations. While this increases variability in experimental outcomes, it also improves the generalizability of the results to a wider biological population. Outbred strains are commonly used in pharmacokinetic, toxicological, and behavioral studies, where a more realistic representation of inter-individual variation is desirable. Examples include Swiss albino mice and Wistar or Sprague Dawley rats. These strains are typically more robust, have better reproductive performance, and are more suitable for routine screening studies where absolute genetic control is not required.

The decision to use an inbred or outbred strain depends on several factors including the objective of the study, the expected pharmacological response, and the type of statistical analysis required. Inbred strains are preferred for mechanistic studies and for developing disease models with minimal variability, whereas outbred strains are favored in exploratory and screening studies where biological diversity may mirror human populations more closely.

Understanding the genetic background of the animal strain is important not only for interpreting experimental results but also for ensuring compliance with ethical and scientific standards. Strain-specific differences in drug metabolism, immune response, and behavioral traits must be carefully considered during experimental design to avoid confounding outcomes and to enhance the reliability of data for regulatory or translational purposes.

Genetically Defined vs Conventional Strains

In laboratory animal research, animals can also be categorized based on their genetic status as genetically defined strains and conventional strains. The understanding of this distinction is essential for selecting the most appropriate model for pharmacological and toxicological studies, particularly when reproducibility and specific genetic traits are important to the study design.

Genetically defined strains refer to animals whose complete genetic background is well characterized and controlled. These include both inbred strains and genetically engineered animals such as transgenic, knock-in, and knock-out models. In genetically defined strains, the genetic variability is minimized, which ensures uniform response to experimental interventions. These animals are used when the research objective demands precise and consistent results, especially in studies involving gene function, molecular targets, immunology, or receptor-specific drug effects. Genetically defined strains are often maintained under strict breeding protocols with documented genetic lineage and are monitored for genetic drift to ensure consistency over time.

Transgenic strains, where specific genes are inserted into the genome, and knock-out strains, where specific genes are deliberately inactivated, are examples of genetically defined animals. These models are crucial for exploring the mechanisms of human diseases such as cancer, diabetes, neurodegenerative disorders, and autoimmune conditions. For instance, the ob/ob mouse model with a leptin gene mutation is widely used to study obesity and metabolic syndrome. Similarly, the NOD (non-obese diabetic) mouse is genetically defined and commonly used in type 1 diabetes research.

In contrast, conventional strains are animals that have not been genetically characterized or manipulated. These animals are typically maintained through random breeding without strict control over their genetic makeup. As a result, they possess a heterogeneous genetic background and may exhibit a broader range of physiological and behavioral traits. Conventional strains are commonly used in preliminary screening studies, acute toxicity testing, and pharmacokinetic assessments where genetic uniformity is not essential.

While conventional strains offer the advantage of being less costly and more readily available, they often produce more variable results due to genetic diversity. This variability, however, can be advantageous when simulating the diverse responses observed in human populations. On the other hand, genetically defined strains, though more expensive and sensitive to environmental changes, provide higher precision and are indispensable in hypothesis-driven research that investigates specific biological pathways or therapeutic targets.

Choosing between genetically defined and conventional strains depends on the study goals, required reproducibility, and the nature of the pharmacological or toxicological investigation. Careful consideration of these factors improves experimental design, enhances the reliability of data, and supports regulatory compliance in drug development processes.

Species and Strain Selection Based on Study Objectives

The selection of an appropriate species and strain is one of the most critical decisions in the design of pharmacological and toxicological studies. This selection must be based on scientific rationale, ethical justification, and regulatory acceptability. Different species and strains possess unique anatomical, physiological, biochemical, and behavioral characteristics, which influence how they respond to drugs or toxic substances. Therefore, the species and strain chosen should align closely with the objectives and endpoints of the study to ensure relevant, reliable, and reproducible results.

In general pharmacological screening, rodents such as mice and rats are commonly used due to their low cost, short reproductive cycle, and availability of well-characterized inbred and outbred strains. For example, Swiss albino mice or Wistar rats may be selected for preliminary toxicity, analgesic, anti-inflammatory, or behavioral studies. If the objective is to understand the mechanism of a disease or target-specific drug action, genetically defined inbred strains like BALB/c or C57BL/6 mice are often preferred because of their uniform genetic background and predictable responses.

For immunological and vaccine studies, species with a well-developed immune system such as guinea pigs or rabbits are frequently selected. Guinea pigs are particularly suitable for allergic response and hypersensitivity models, while rabbits are widely used for antibody production and pyrogen testing. In reproductive toxicity studies, rats and rabbits are most often used due to their reproductive similarities to humans and their acceptability by international regulatory authorities for segment I, II, and III reproductive studies.

In safety pharmacology and chronic toxicity studies, both a rodent and a non-rodent species are typically required. Rats are chosen as the rodent model, while dogs (usually beagles) serve as the non-rodent model due to their cardiovascular similarities to humans and their tolerance to repeated dosing. For drugs involving the central nervous system or endocrine pathways, the selection of strain must be done with caution, as strain-specific behavioral traits or hormonal profiles can influence the outcome. For instance, Lewis rats may be chosen in studies involving stress response due to their known sensitivity to stress-induced immunosuppression.

Non-human primates are selected in advanced studies when the pharmacological or toxicological profile of the test compound cannot be adequately studied in lower species due to species-specific receptor interactions or metabolic pathways. This is especially common in the development of biopharmaceuticals, monoclonal antibodies, and gene therapies.

The choice of species and strain should also consider practical aspects such as ease of handling, ethical acceptability, housing requirements, and the availability of historical control data. It is essential that all selections be scientifically justified in the experimental protocol submitted to the Institutional Animal Ethics Committee. A careful match between study objectives and the biological characteristics of the animal model enhances the credibility of the study, reduces unnecessary animal use, and improves the translatability of findings to human health.

1.2.3 Handling Techniques for Different Animals

Manual Restraint Techniques

Manual restraint is a basic but crucial technique in animal experimentation. It involves physically holding the animal in a secure and humane manner to perform routine procedures such as dosing, sample collection, or clinical observations without causing harm or undue stress. Proper restraint ensures the safety of both the animal and the handler and helps maintain the accuracy and consistency of the experimental procedure. Restraint techniques vary depending on the species, size, temperament, and the procedure being carried out.

For mice, the most common method of manual restraint is by gently holding the base of the tail and placing the animal on a rough surface such as a wire grid or towel. Once the mouse grips the surface, the handler can use the other hand to scruff the skin at the back of the neck and support the lower body using the fingers. This technique immobilizes the mouse and allows access to the oral cavity, abdomen, or limbs for injection or examination. Care should be taken not to apply excessive pressure, as mice are delicate and can easily be injured.

In the case of rats, which are larger and stronger than mice, the base of the tail is held with one hand, and the other hand is used to grasp the rat gently around the shoulders by placing the thumb and fingers behind the front limbs. The rat is then lifted and supported with the handler's arm or against the body to provide stability. This method allows for restraint during subcutaneous or intraperitoneal injections. Rats are more responsive to gentle handling and may become calm with regular handling practices.

Guinea pigs require a slightly different approach due to their short limbs and sensitivity to stress. They should never be picked up by the limbs or tail. Instead, one hand should be placed under the chest to support the front limbs, while the other hand supports the hindquarters. The guinea pig is then held close to the handler's body to provide a sense of security. Their fragile spine can be injured if mishandled, so firm yet gentle support is essential.

For rabbits, restraint should be done cautiously to avoid spinal injuries caused by their powerful hind legs. The handler should place one hand under the chest and the other supporting the hind limbs, keeping the rabbit's back curved naturally. It should be held close to the handler's body with the head tucked slightly under the arm to keep the animal calm. Sudden movements or loud noises must be avoided, as rabbits can become stressed very easily.

Dogs should be restrained using a calm and reassuring approach. Small dogs can be lifted by supporting the chest and hind limbs, while larger dogs are often restrained by placing one arm under the neck and the other behind the hind limbs or abdomen. Muzzles or collars may be used when necessary, especially during invasive procedures. Positive reinforcement with gentle voice tones and rewards can greatly improve compliance during repeated handling.

For non-human primates, manual restraint is performed only by experienced personnel. It often involves the use of training and positive reinforcement techniques, allowing the animal to voluntarily cooperate. In some cases, specially designed restraint chairs or transfer boxes are used. When manual handling is unavoidable, protective gloves and appropriate safety measures must be used to prevent bites or injuries. NHPs are intelligent and sensitive animals, and poor handling practices can result in aggression, distress, or compromised data quality.

Manual restraint should always be performed with consideration for the animal's comfort and well-being. Habituation through gentle daily handling and desensitization training can significantly reduce stress and improve handling efficiency. Proper training of laboratory personnel and adherence to institutional animal care guidelines are essential components of humane and effective manual restraint practices.

Use of Restraining Devices

Restraining devices are specialized tools designed to hold laboratory animals securely during experimental procedures where manual restraint is either impractical or may result in injury to the animal or handler. These devices help ensure safety, reduce stress, improve procedural accuracy, and allow for repeated handling in chronic studies. The choice of device depends on the species, the type of procedure, and the duration of restraint. All devices must be used with proper training, and restraint time should be kept as short as possible to avoid discomfort or distress.

For mice and rats, plastic or acrylic restrainers, often called restraint tubes or cylinders, are commonly used. These are clear tubes with adjustable ends that allow the animal to be immobilized in a comfortable position. The tail may protrude from the rear for intravenous or intraperitoneal injections. These tubes are especially useful for procedures like blood sampling, tail vein injection, or oral gavage. Animals should be introduced gently into the tube headfirst, and the openings should be adjusted to prevent excessive movement while allowing for normal breathing.

In guinea pigs and rabbits, restraining boxes made of transparent plastic or mesh may be used for blood collection, oral dosing, or eye examinations. For rabbits, specially designed "rabbit stocks" or holding frames help stabilize the body and head during procedures such as ear vein injections or ocular studies. Care must be taken to provide padding and secure positioning to avoid stress-related injuries.

Dogs may be restrained using adjustable slings, restraint tables, or padded V-troughs, depending on the nature of the procedure. For intravenous administration or blood collection, dogs may be placed in a sitting or lateral position and gently restrained using a neck collar, leash, or soft muzzles. Specialized restraint stands or tables with adjustable straps allow for safe and repeated dosing or sampling without causing discomfort. Dogs trained through positive reinforcement often require minimal restraint, especially for routine procedures.

For non-human primates, more complex and secure restraining systems are required due to their strength and potential for unpredictable behavior. Transfer boxes, squeeze-back cages, and primate restraint chairs are used under strict supervision and ethical oversight. Restraint chairs are often padded and adjustable, allowing primates to remain in a seated position while procedures such as blood draws, ophthalmic exams, or drug administration are carried out. These devices must be approved by the Institutional Animal Ethics Committee and used only when necessary, with constant monitoring of the animal's behavior and vital signs.

Across all species, the design and use of restraining devices must follow institutional guidelines and CPCSEA or international standards. The device should allow adequate ventilation, prevent hyperextension or abnormal posture, and ensure the animal's ability to breathe and thermoregulate. Prolonged restraint, if required, should be accompanied by periodic breaks, monitoring of clinical signs, and immediate intervention if signs of distress, excessive struggling, or abnormal behavior are observed.

Properly used restraining devices play an essential role in enhancing procedural consistency, minimizing variability in data, and upholding animal welfare during experimental work. However, their use should always align with the principles of humane research, emphasizing refinement of techniques to reduce discomfort and improve the overall quality of the scientific process.

Minimizing Stress and Injuries

Minimizing stress and injuries in laboratory animals is a fundamental responsibility in experimental pharmacology and toxicology. Stress not only affects the physical and psychological well-being of animals but also introduces variability into experimental data, thereby compromising the scientific validity of the study. Injuries, whether due to improper handling, housing, or restraint, can lead to pain, distress, and even mortality, violating ethical standards and potentially necessitating repetition of the experiment. Therefore, careful planning, trained personnel, and adherence to standard protocols are essential to ensure humane treatment and high-quality data generation.

One of the most effective ways to minimize stress is through proper handling techniques that are species-specific and practiced consistently. Animals should be approached calmly and gently, avoiding sudden movements or loud noises that could trigger fear responses. Frequent, gentle handling before the actual procedure helps animals become accustomed to human interaction, reducing fear and resistance. Positive handling experiences can condition animals to associate human presence with neutral or pleasant events, which in turn minimizes the need for forceful restraint.

The duration of restraint should be kept to a minimum, and animals should never be left unattended while restrained. When restraining devices are used, they should be appropriately sized, well-padded, and properly ventilated to prevent overheating, suffocation, or pressure injuries. For prolonged procedures, scheduled rest intervals should be provided, and animals should be monitored for signs of distress such as vocalization, aggression, immobility, abnormal posture, or increased respiratory rate. In case of any sign of pain or discomfort, the procedure should be paused, and veterinary advice must be sought immediately.

Housing conditions also play a critical role in stress prevention. Animals should be provided with species-appropriate enrichment materials such as nesting paper, shelters, tunnels, or chew toys to allow expression of natural behaviors. Proper temperature, humidity, lighting cycles, and noise control contribute significantly to minimizing environmental stress. Overcrowding, isolation, and frequent relocation should be avoided as they can increase aggression, anxiety, or depressive-like behaviors in social species.

During experimental procedures such as dosing or blood collection, the use of analgesics or anesthetics should be considered where applicable to reduce pain. Techniques like warming the tail for easier vein access, using smaller gauge needles, and ensuring clean and atraumatic injections can further reduce discomfort and prevent injury. Staff involved in animal handling must undergo proper training and continuous skill development to maintain high standards of animal care and research quality.

Lastly, consistent health monitoring, prompt treatment of wounds or illnesses, and careful post-procedure observation are crucial to identifying and addressing injuries early. Documentation of incidents and review of procedures help in refining methods and preventing recurrence. By implementing these measures, researchers not only uphold ethical obligations but also enhance the reliability and reproducibility of preclinical studies, ensuring both scientific and humane integrity in laboratory animal research.

1.2.4 Housing, Caging, and Environmental Controls

Cage Types, Bedding, and Enrichments

Proper housing is a fundamental requirement in laboratory animal research to ensure the health, comfort, and psychological well-being of the animals. The selection of cage types, bedding materials, and environmental enrichments must be based on the species, strain, experimental requirements, and institutional guidelines. Housing conditions directly influence animal behavior, stress levels, immune function, and metabolic activities, which in turn affect the reliability and reproducibility of experimental results.

Cages used in laboratory animal facilities are generally made of durable, non-toxic, and easy-to-clean materials such as polycarbonate, polysulfone, or stainless steel. There are two main types of cages: conventional cages and individually ventilated cages. Conventional cages are open-top enclosures that rely on room air for ventilation and are typically used in low-risk studies. Individually ventilated cages, on the other hand, are designed with a filtered air supply and exhaust system, offering better control of the microenvironment and minimizing the risk of cross-contamination. These are preferred in specific pathogen-free (SPF) or immunocompromised animal colonies.

The size and design of the cage should allow animals to express natural behaviors such as stretching, standing, climbing, or nesting. For example, mice and rats benefit from multi-level or wide-base cages, while rabbits require cages with enough height to allow upright sitting. Guinea pigs need solid floors due to their sensitive footpads, and dogs and non-human primates require enclosures with adequate space for movement and social interaction.

Bedding materials serve multiple purposes, including absorbing moisture and waste, providing insulation, and offering a substrate for natural behaviors like burrowing or nesting. Common bedding types include wood shavings, corn cob granules, paper-based materials, and sawdust. Bedding should be non-toxic, dust-free, and changed regularly to prevent ammonia buildup and respiratory irritation. For animals like guinea pigs and rabbits, soft bedding is essential to avoid skin abrasions and pressure sores.

Environmental enrichment is a critical component of humane housing, as it reduces stress, promotes natural behavior, and improves overall well-being. Enrichments can be physical (such as tunnels, shelters, or climbing structures), sensory (like scented objects or visual stimuli), nutritional (including treats or foraging materials), or social (housing animals in compatible groups). For rodents, nesting material, cardboard tubes, and running wheels are commonly used. Rabbits benefit from gnawing sticks and hiding boxes, while dogs require chew toys, human interaction, and exercise periods. Non-human primates, being highly intelligent and social, need complex enrichment items such as puzzle feeders, mirrors, and regular social engagement.

All cage types, bedding, and enrichment items should comply with national and international animal welfare regulations. In India, the Committee for the Purpose of Control and Supervision of Experiments on Animals (CPCSEA) provides specific space and enrichment recommendations for different species. Routine inspection and maintenance of cages and enrichment tools help ensure hygiene, prevent injuries, and support ethical animal care practices. When designed and managed correctly, housing systems contribute significantly to both the humane treatment of animals and the generation of scientifically valid data.

Light–Dark Cycle, Temperature, Humidity

Maintaining appropriate environmental conditions—specifically light–dark cycle, temperature, and humidity—is essential in laboratory animal housing as these factors profoundly influence animal physiology, metabolism, hormonal rhythms, and behavior. Failure to regulate these parameters can introduce variability in experimental results and may cause stress, disease susceptibility, or even mortality in sensitive species. Therefore, controlled environmental conditions are a fundamental part of Good Laboratory Practices (GLP) and animal welfare regulations.

The light–dark cycle plays a critical role in regulating the circadian rhythm of laboratory animals. Most rodents and many other species are nocturnal, meaning they are active during the dark phase. A standard light–dark cycle of 12 hours of light followed by 12 hours of darkness (12:12 LD cycle) is commonly maintained in animal facilities. Light intensity should typically range between 130 to 325 lux at the cage level during the light phase. Excessive or fluctuating light intensity, continuous illumination, or irregular light cycles can disrupt melatonin production, reproductive cycles, immune function, and behavior. In albino animals such as Swiss albino mice, exposure to high light intensity can even lead to retinal damage, so filtered lighting is often recommended.

Temperature control is equally important, as laboratory animals are sensitive to fluctuations in ambient temperature. The optimal temperature range varies slightly depending on the species. For example, mice and rats are usually housed within a range of 20 to 26°C, while guinea pigs prefer 18 to 22°C. Rabbits are more comfortable at cooler temperatures, typically between 16 and 21°C. Non-human primates require a tightly controlled temperature of around 22 to 28°C. Exposure to high temperatures can lead to heat stress, reduced fertility, and increased aggression, while low temperatures may increase metabolic demands, affect thermoregulation, and alter drug metabolism. To prevent sudden changes, the facility should be equipped with a centralized HVAC system and backup temperature monitoring devices.

Humidity levels must also be maintained within a specific range to support normal respiratory and skin functions. The generally accepted relative humidity for most laboratory species is between 30% and 70%, with an optimal range around 40% to 60%. Low humidity levels can lead to dehydration, flaky skin, and nasal irritation, especially in species like guinea pigs and rabbits. High humidity, on the other hand, may promote the growth of molds and bacteria, leading to respiratory infections and increased ammonia accumulation from waste. Regular monitoring using calibrated hygrometers and automated alarms for deviations are part of good facility management.

All these parameters—light cycle, temperature, and humidity—must be routinely recorded and maintained according to the institutional animal care protocol. In facilities registered under regulatory bodies such as CPCSEA or international accrediting organizations like AAALAC, documentation of these environmental factors is mandatory for compliance. Consistency in environmental control not only ensures the well-being of laboratory animals but also enhances the reliability and reproducibility of experimental data across studies and institutions.

Sanitation and Ventilation Requirements

Maintaining proper sanitation and ventilation in laboratory animal facilities is essential for ensuring the health and welfare of animals, minimizing the risk of infections, and maintaining the integrity of experimental results. Unsanitary conditions or poor air quality can lead to the spread of pathogens, increased animal stress, respiratory disorders, and altered physiological responses—all of which may introduce variability in data and compromise research quality. Therefore, sanitation and ventilation must follow strict guidelines laid down by institutional, national, and international regulatory bodies.

Sanitation involves regular and thorough cleaning of cages, floors, feeding equipment, water bottles, and work surfaces to prevent the accumulation of waste, food debris, and microbial contaminants. Cages should be cleaned at least once or twice per week, depending on the species and the density of animals per cage. Automatic cage washers with high-temperature cycles (typically 82°C or higher) are widely used to sterilize cages and equipment. Disinfectants such as dilute sodium hypochlorite, quaternary ammonium compounds, or phenol-based solutions may be used for surface cleaning, but care must be taken to rinse thoroughly to avoid residue that could harm animals.

Feeders and water bottles must be cleaned and autoclaved regularly to prevent contamination by algae, bacteria, or fungi. Bedding material should be changed frequently, and waste should be disposed of in compliance with institutional biosafety regulations. Staff working in the facility must wear protective clothing such as gowns, gloves, masks, and shoe covers to minimize contamination. The workflow in animal facilities should follow a unidirectional pattern—moving from clean to dirty areas—to reduce cross-contamination risks.

Ventilation plays a key role in maintaining air quality by removing heat, moisture, ammonia, and airborne pathogens. Poor ventilation can result in elevated ammonia levels from urine breakdown, which causes respiratory irritation and increases susceptibility to infections, especially in rodents. Modern animal facilities are equipped with centralized HVAC systems that maintain a steady supply of filtered air. A minimum of 10 to 15 air changes per hour (ACH) is recommended for animal rooms to ensure proper gas exchange and control of particulate matter.

In systems using individually ventilated cages (IVCs), each cage receives filtered air directly through high-efficiency particulate air (HEPA) filters. These systems not only improve air quality but also provide a barrier against cross-contamination between cages. The air pressure within animal rooms should be maintained slightly negative or positive depending on the containment level of the animals and the nature of the experiments. For example, rooms housing immunocompromised or SPF animals often have positive pressure, while rooms used for infectious disease studies have negative pressure.

All ventilation systems should be equipped with sensors and alarms to monitor temperature, humidity, pressure differentials, and filter integrity. Routine maintenance, calibration, and validation of air handling units are essential to ensure optimal performance. Logs should be maintained to record cleaning schedules, air quality data, and filter replacement dates, as required under Good Laboratory Practices (GLP) and CPCSEA guidelines.

By ensuring strict adherence to sanitation and ventilation standards, animal facilities can minimize the risk of disease, reduce experimental variability, and promote ethical and reliable scientific practices in preclinical research.

1.3.1.1 Knock-in Models

Knock-in models are a type of genetically modified animal in which a specific gene or DNA sequence is inserted into a precise location within the genome. Unlike knock-out models where a gene is disrupted or deleted, knock-in models are designed to introduce a functional gene, a mutated gene variant, or a reporter gene to study gene expression, protein function, or the effects of genetic mutations. These models are most commonly developed in mice, although recent advances in genome editing technologies have enabled the creation of knock-in models in rats, rabbits, pigs, and non-human primates.

The generation of knock-in models traditionally involves homologous recombination in embryonic stem (ES) cells. A targeting vector is constructed that contains the desired genetic sequence flanked by homologous DNA segments matching the target locus. After introduction into ES cells, successful recombination results in the integration of the foreign gene into the host genome. The modified ES cells are then injected into blastocysts, which are implanted into surrogate mothers to produce chimeric offspring. If the germline cells are affected, the genetic modification can be inherited in subsequent generations.

With the development of newer techniques such as CRISPR-Cas9, the efficiency and precision of creating knock-in models have improved significantly. CRISPR allows for site-specific insertion of genes using a guide RNA and a repair template, drastically reducing the time and cost required compared to conventional ES cell-based methods. It also permits the introduction of small insertions, such as point mutations or tags, to study specific protein interactions or disease-causing gene variants.

Knock-in models serve several important roles in pharmacological and toxicological research. They are widely used to mimic human diseases at the molecular level, especially for studying gain-of-function mutations or altered protein expression. For example, a knock-in mouse carrying the human APP gene with familial Alzheimer's disease mutations is used to investigate amyloid-beta accumulation and test anti-Alzheimer drug candidates. In cancer research, knock-in models are used to introduce oncogenes that drive tumor formation, helping scientists explore targeted therapies and molecular pathways involved in carcinogenesis.

These models also play a critical role in validating drug targets and biomarkers. By precisely controlling gene expression and mutation types, researchers can understand the direct impact of genetic alterations on disease progression and drug response. In addition, knock-in models are employed in studies involving humanized genes, where human gene sequences replace the native gene to better mimic human physiology and pharmacodynamics in animal systems.

Despite their value, knock-in models come with certain limitations. The generation process is time-consuming and costly, especially for large genes or complex modifications. There is also a risk of off-target effects or unintended consequences at the site of insertion, which may interfere with gene regulation or produce unexpected phenotypes. Therefore, careful validation using genotyping, sequencing, and phenotypic analysis is essential after model development.

Knock-in animal models represent a powerful tool in modern biomedical research. When designed and used appropriately, they provide deep insights into gene function, disease mechanisms, and therapeutic strategies, thereby bridging the gap between molecular biology and clinical pharmacology.

1.3.1.2 Knock-out Models

Knock-out models are genetically modified animals in which a specific gene has been completely inactivated or "knocked out," meaning that it is permanently deleted or disrupted so that it can no longer produce a functional protein. These models are widely used in biomedical research to study the physiological role of individual genes, understand disease mechanisms, and evaluate drug targets. The majority of knock-out animals are mice due to the availability of embryonic stem cell technology and well-established genetic tools; however, knock-out models have also been developed in rats, zebrafish, and other species.

Traditional generation of knock-out models involves homologous recombination in embryonic stem (ES) cells. A targeting vector containing a disrupted version of the gene is introduced into ES cells. These cells are then screened to identify successful recombinants, which are injected into blastocysts and implanted into surrogate mothers to produce chimeric offspring. Mating these chimeras can lead to germline transmission of the altered gene, resulting in a stable knock-out line. This process, while accurate, is time-consuming and requires specialized expertise and infrastructure.

Recent advancements in genome editing technologies, particularly CRISPR-Cas9, have revolutionized the production of knock-out models. CRISPR allows for rapid and cost-effective deletion of target genes by introducing double-strand breaks at specific genomic locations, which are then imperfectly repaired by the cell's natural repair machinery, leading to frame-shift mutations or deletions. This method can produce both constitutive and conditional knock-outs depending on the design.

Constitutive knock-outs result in gene deletion in all tissues from early development. These models are useful for studying genes with systemic effects or for understanding baseline phenotypes. However, if the gene is essential for development, it may lead to embryonic lethality. To overcome this, conditional knock-out models are used, where gene deletion occurs in specific tissues or at specific times. This is achieved using systems like Cre-loxP or FLP-FRT, where recombinase enzymes are driven by tissue-specific promoters.

Knock-out models are essential tools in pharmacology and toxicology. They help determine the role of genes involved in receptor function, metabolic pathways, ion channels, or disease susceptibility. For example, knock-out mice lacking the LDL receptor gene have been instrumental in studying hypercholesterolemia and testing anti-lipid drugs. Similarly, knock-out models for cytokines, enzymes, and drug transporters have provided critical insights into inflammation, drug metabolism, and pharmacokinetics.

These models also aid in safety evaluation by revealing off-target or unintended effects of therapeutic compounds. By observing how drugs behave in animals lacking specific receptors or enzymes, researchers can anticipate potential side effects or drug interactions in humans. Moreover, knock-out models contribute to the identification of biomarkers and companion diagnostics in precision medicine.

However, knock-out models also have limitations. The absence of a gene from birth may lead to developmental compensation by other genes, which can obscure the actual function of the target gene. Also, results observed in animals may not always be directly translatable to humans due to species-specific differences in gene function and regulation. Hence, the interpretation of knock-out data must be done cautiously, often in combination with other in vitro and in vivo models.

Despite these challenges, knock-out animals remain a cornerstone in drug discovery and biomedical research. Their ability to dissect gene function with high specificity makes them indispensable for advancing our understanding of disease biology and therapeutic development.

1.3.1.3 Conditional Models

Conditional models are a refined category of genetically modified animals in which a specific gene can be selectively activated or inactivated in particular tissues, organs, or developmental stages, rather than throughout the entire organism. These models are especially useful when global deletion of a gene leads to embryonic lethality or causes widespread systemic effects that obscure the understanding of localized biological functions. Conditional gene manipulation allows researchers to study the role of a gene in a specific context, such as in the brain, liver, or immune system, without affecting the rest of the body.

The most widely used system for creating conditional models is the Cre-loxP recombination system. In this approach, the gene of interest is flanked by loxP sites (called "floxed"), which are specific DNA sequences recognized by the Cre recombinase enzyme. When Cre recombinase is expressed in a particular tissue or at a specific time point, it excises the floxed gene segment, thereby inactivating it. The specificity of gene deletion is determined by the promoter that drives the expression of Cre recombinase. For example, using a neuron-specific promoter like *Camk2a* will result in gene deletion only in neurons.

An advanced version of this system is the inducible conditional model, such as the Cre-ERT2 system, where the activity of Cre recombinase is controlled by a drug like tamoxifen. In this system, the gene remains intact until tamoxifen is administered, which then activates the Cre enzyme and triggers gene deletion. This temporal control allows researchers to study gene function during adulthood or disease progression without affecting early development.

Conditional models are particularly valuable in pharmacology for evaluating the role of genes in organ-specific drug action, metabolism, and toxicity. For instance, liver-specific knock-out models can be used to study drug-metabolizing enzymes such as cytochrome P450 isoforms, helping in the prediction of pharmacokinetic profiles and hepatotoxicity. Similarly, brain-specific gene deletions can aid in the understanding of neurological diseases like epilepsy or Parkinson's disease and assist in the evaluation of neuroactive drugs.

In toxicological studies, conditional models help determine target-organ toxicity and off-target effects. For example, a conditional deletion of a transporter protein in the kidney can help identify nephrotoxic potential of drug candidates. These models also allow for studying disease progression in a controlled manner, such as initiating gene deletion after the establishment of a disease model, which is critical for testing therapeutic interventions in a clinically relevant time frame.

Despite their advantages, conditional models require complex breeding strategies and careful genotyping to confirm the presence of both the floxed gene and the Cre transgene. Additionally, the efficiency and specificity of Cre recombinase activity can vary depending on the promoter used and the site of gene insertion. Leakage of Cre expression or incomplete recombination may lead to inconsistent phenotypes, which must be validated with proper controls.

Overall, conditional models represent a highly sophisticated tool in biomedical research, allowing for precise dissection of gene function with spatial and temporal resolution. Their application in preclinical drug evaluation enhances the relevance and depth of experimental findings, contributing significantly to the development of safer and more effective therapeutic agents.

1.3.1.4 CRISPR-Cas9 Engineered Animals

CRISPR-Cas9 engineered animals represent a major advancement in the field of genetic engineering and have rapidly become one of the most efficient, versatile, and widely adopted tools for creating genetically modified models. CRISPR, which stands for Clustered Regularly Interspaced Short Palindromic Repeats, along with the Cas9 (CRISPR-associated protein 9) endonuclease, allows scientists to make precise, targeted modifications in the genome of laboratory animals. This system has drastically simplified the process of developing knock-out, knock-in, and conditional models compared to traditional embryonic stem cell-based methods.

The CRISPR-Cas9 system works by introducing a guide RNA (gRNA) that is complementary to a specific DNA sequence in the target gene. The Cas9 enzyme, guided by the gRNA, creates a double-strand break at the designated genomic location. The cell's natural DNA repair mechanisms then act to repair this break. If no repair template is provided, the break is often repaired by non-homologous end joining (NHEJ), which is error-prone and results in small insertions or deletions that disrupt the gene—creating a knock-out. Alternatively, if a repair template is supplied, homology-directed repair (HDR) allows for precise insertion of new genetic material—creating a knock-in.

CRISPR-Cas9 is widely used to generate engineered animals such as mice, rats, zebrafish, rabbits, pigs, and even non-human primates. Unlike older methods, CRISPR editing can be done directly in zygotes (fertilized eggs), eliminating the need for embryonic stem cells and significantly reducing the time and cost required to produce transgenic animals. With this method, researchers can generate a genetically modified animal within a single generation, which is particularly valuable for time-sensitive studies.

One of the major advantages of CRISPR-Cas9 technology is its high specificity and programmability. It allows scientists to target virtually any gene of interest with minimal off-target effects when designed carefully. Furthermore, multiple genes can be edited simultaneously, a technique known as multiplexing, which is useful for studying complex diseases involving more than one gene or for creating multi-gene humanized models.

CRISPR-Cas9 engineered animals have significant applications in pharmacology and toxicology. They are used to create disease models that mimic human conditions more accurately, such as cancer, neurodegenerative disorders, metabolic diseases, and genetic syndromes. These models help in studying disease mechanisms, testing new drug candidates, and identifying novel therapeutic targets. For example, CRISPR has been used to develop mice with precise mutations in the *TP53* gene for studying tumorigenesis or in the *Htt* gene for modeling Huntington's disease.

In toxicological studies, CRISPR is used to create animals lacking specific drug-metabolizing enzymes, transporters, or receptors to study drug interactions, metabolism, and organ-specific toxicity. It is also being explored for generating reporter animals, where fluorescent or luminescent markers are inserted at precise loci to monitor gene expression or tissue responses in real time during experiments.

Despite its vast potential, CRISPR-Cas9 technology is not without limitations. Off-target effects, mosaicism (when not all cells carry the intended mutation), and variability in gene editing efficiency can pose challenges. These risks can be minimized by using optimized guide RNAs, high-fidelity Cas9 variants, and thorough genotypic screening. Ethical concerns also exist, especially when applying CRISPR in higher animals or in germline editing, and such studies require strict regulatory oversight.

Overall, CRISPR-Cas9 engineered animals have transformed preclinical research by making genome editing faster, cheaper, and more accessible. Their precise and flexible genetic modifications have expanded the possibilities in disease modeling, drug development, and personalized medicine, making them indispensable tools in modern pharmacological and toxicological research.

1.3.2 Production Techniques

Embryonic Stem Cell Method

The embryonic stem (ES) cell method is one of the earliest and most classical techniques used for producing genetically modified animals, particularly mice. This method allows for the precise insertion, deletion, or replacement of specific genes in a controlled manner through a process known as homologous recombination. Although more recent technologies like CRISPR-Cas9 have gained popularity due to their speed and simplicity, the ES cell method remains relevant for generating complex and targeted genetic modifications, especially when creating conditional knock-in or knock-out models.

Embryonic stem cells are derived from the inner cell mass of a blastocyst, typically harvested from a mouse embryo at around 3.5 days post-fertilization. These cells are pluripotent, meaning they have the ability to differentiate into any cell type of the body, including the germline. This unique property allows researchers to introduce genetic changes into ES cells in vitro and then use these modified cells to develop a whole animal that carries the intended mutation.

The first step in this method is the design and construction of a targeting vector, which contains the desired DNA sequence flanked by homologous regions corresponding to the target gene locus. This vector may include a reporter gene (such as LacZ or GFP) or a selectable marker (such as neomycin resistance gene) to facilitate identification of successfully modified cells. The targeting vector is introduced into cultured ES cells using techniques such as electroporation or lipofection.

Once inside the ES cells, the targeting vector aligns with the matching genomic sequence, and through homologous recombination, the endogenous gene is replaced or altered with the inserted sequence. However, this process is naturally rare and inefficient, so cells must be carefully screened to identify those that have undergone successful recombination. This is typically done using polymerase chain reaction (PCR) or Southern blotting to confirm correct integration of the desired DNA segment.

The genetically modified ES cells are then injected into blastocysts harvested from a donor mouse. These blastocysts are implanted into pseudopregnant female mice, which have been hormonally prepared to support embryo implantation. The offspring born from this process are known as chimeric mice, as they contain both normal and genetically modified cells. If the modified cells contribute to the germline, these mice can be bred to produce heterozygous or homozygous genetically modified progeny that stably inherit the mutation.

The embryonic stem cell method has several advantages. It allows for precise genetic targeting with minimal off-target effects, and it supports complex modifications such as conditional alleles, large DNA insertions, and reporter gene integration. This method has been instrumental in generating valuable mouse models used in immunology, oncology, neurology, and developmental biology research.

However, the ES cell method is time-consuming, labor-intensive, and requires specialized facilities for stem cell culture, embryo manipulation, and transgenic animal breeding. The success rate also depends on the quality of the ES cell line and the efficiency of homologous recombination. Additionally, this technique is currently limited to species like mice and rats, as stable ES cell lines have not been established for many other laboratory animals.

Despite the emergence of newer genome-editing tools, the embryonic stem cell method remains a gold standard for creating sophisticated genetically modified animal models. Its ability to deliver targeted, stable, and heritable genetic alterations continues to make it a valuable tool in preclinical pharmacological and toxicological research.

DNA Microinjection

DNA microinjection is one of the earliest and most direct methods used for the production of genetically modified animals, particularly transgenic animals. It involves the injection of foreign DNA directly into the pronucleus of a fertilized egg (zygote), allowing the introduced gene to integrate into the genome and be passed on to the next generation. This method has been widely used to generate transgenic mice, and to some extent, rabbits, pigs, goats, and sheep for various biomedical and pharmaceutical research applications.

The process of DNA microinjection begins with the collection of fertilized eggs from superovulated female animals, usually mice. These eggs are carefully examined under a high-powered microscope to identify the male and female pronuclei, which appear as two distinct nuclei within the zygote before the first cell division. A fine glass micropipette is then used to inject the DNA solution into the male pronucleus, which is typically larger and easier to access.

The DNA used for injection consists of the gene of interest along with a promoter sequence to drive expression, and in some cases, a reporter or marker gene such as green fluorescent protein (GFP) or β-galactosidase. The DNA must be in a highly purified, linear form to increase the chances of integration into the host genome.

After successful injection, the embryos are cultured briefly and then implanted into the oviducts of pseudopregnant female mice, which have been hormonally prepared to support embryo development. A percentage of the offspring born from this process will carry the transgene. These founder animals are then screened using polymerase chain reaction (PCR) or Southern blotting to confirm the presence and copy number of the transgene.

One of the major features of DNA microinjection is that the integration of the foreign DNA occurs randomly in the genome. This randomness can lead to variable expression levels depending on the site of integration, the number of copies inserted, and whether the gene has disrupted any important endogenous sequence. Additionally, transgene expression may be silenced over time due to epigenetic modifications at the insertion site. Despite this variability, transgenic animals produced via microinjection have proven highly valuable in studies of gene overexpression, promoter activity, oncogene function, and biopharmaceutical protein production.

In pharmacological research, transgenic animals produced by DNA microinjection have been used to study drug metabolism, receptor activity, transporter function, and disease modeling. For example, mice engineered to overexpress human cytochrome P450 enzymes help in evaluating species-specific differences in drug metabolism. In toxicology, these models assist in assessing the response to xenobiotics, carcinogens, or endocrine disruptors in a genetically modified background.

However, DNA microinjection has some limitations. The process is technically demanding, has a low success rate, and often requires the injection of hundreds of embryos to obtain a few transgenic founders. Since the integration is random, there is a risk of insertional mutagenesis, where the transgene disrupts essential host genes. Furthermore, this method does not support precise gene editing or targeted gene knock-in or knock-out.

Despite the advent of modern tools like CRISPR-Cas9, DNA microinjection remains an important technique in certain contexts, especially when creating simple transgenic models for gene overexpression or when more advanced genome editing tools are not feasible. It laid the foundation for the field of molecular genetics and continues to contribute to the understanding of gene function and regulation in pharmacological and toxicological research.

Gene Editing Using CRISPR-Cas9

CRISPR-Cas9 gene editing is a groundbreaking and highly precise technology used to modify the genome of laboratory animals by adding, deleting, or altering specific DNA sequences. CRISPR, short for Clustered Regularly Interspaced Short Palindromic Repeats, functions as part of a natural bacterial defense system, and when combined with the Cas9 enzyme, it can be directed to create double-stranded breaks at desired genomic locations. This technology has revolutionized the production of genetically modified animals due to its simplicity, high efficiency, and cost-effectiveness, and has rapidly replaced traditional gene modification techniques such as embryonic stem cell manipulation and DNA microinjection in many laboratories.

The gene editing process begins with the design of a guide RNA (gRNA) that is complementary to the target DNA sequence. This gRNA forms a complex with the Cas9 protein, which acts as a molecular scissor to cut the DNA at the exact location specified by the guide. Once the DNA is cut, the cell attempts to repair the damage through one of two main mechanisms: non-homologous end joining (NHEJ) or homology-directed repair (HDR). NHEJ is error-prone and often introduces insertions or deletions that can disrupt gene function, leading to gene knock-outs. In contrast, HDR can be used to precisely insert or replace a DNA sequence, enabling the creation of knock-in models or correction of genetic mutations when a donor DNA template is provided.

CRISPR-Cas9 editing is usually performed by injecting the Cas9 mRNA or protein, along with the gRNA and optional donor DNA, directly into the fertilized zygote of animals such as mice, rats, rabbits, or pigs. The edited embryos are then implanted into pseudopregnant surrogate mothers. This approach allows for the generation of genetically modified animals within a single generation, drastically reducing the time required compared to conventional techniques.

The precision of CRISPR-Cas9 allows researchers to target specific exons, regulatory sequences, or non-coding regions of the genome. It also supports multiplex editing, where multiple genes can be edited simultaneously, which is useful for studying polygenic diseases or complex biological pathways. Moreover, CRISPR has been adapted for conditional editing, using systems such as CRISPRi or CRISPRa for gene silencing or activation without permanent DNA modification.

In pharmacological research, CRISPR-engineered animals are used to model human diseases more accurately, study drug targets, evaluate gene-drug interactions, and test the efficacy and safety of new therapies. For instance, CRISPR has been used to develop mouse models of cystic fibrosis, cancer, Alzheimer's disease, and sickle cell anemia by introducing the same mutations found in human patients. In toxicology, gene-edited models help determine the role of specific enzymes, receptors, or transporters in the metabolism and toxicity of xenobiotics.

While CRISPR-Cas9 offers many advantages, there are certain limitations. Off-target effects, where unintended parts of the genome are edited, can occur if the gRNA is not highly specific. These risks can be minimized by optimizing gRNA design, using high-fidelity Cas9 variants, and validating the genome of edited animals through sequencing. Another concern is mosaicism, where not all cells of the edited animal carry the intended genetic change, especially if editing occurs after the first cell division. Careful screening and breeding are required to establish stable and uniform genetic lines.

Ethical considerations also apply, particularly for editing in large animals or non-human primates. All CRISPR-based animal experiments must comply with institutional and national guidelines, including proper justification, risk assessment, and approval from animal ethics committees.

Despite these considerations, CRISPR-Cas9 has transformed the landscape of genetic research, offering unmatched speed, precision, and flexibility. It continues to be a central tool in creating disease models, understanding gene function, and developing targeted therapies in both pharmacological and toxicological research.

1.3.3 Maintenance and Welfare of Transgenic Animals

Special Housing and Breeding Needs

Transgenic animals, due to their altered genetic makeup, often have unique physiological, immunological, and behavioral characteristics, requiring specialized care to ensure their survival, welfare, and the validity of research data. The maintenance and breeding of transgenic colonies must be meticulously planned and carried out under controlled conditions, with strict attention to biosecurity, environmental parameters, and ethical guidelines. These animals are particularly sensitive to environmental stressors and infections, making it essential to provide them with housing and husbandry tailored to their genetic background.

Transgenic and genetically modified animals are usually maintained in barrier facilities or specific pathogen-free (SPF) animal houses. These facilities are designed to minimize exposure to infectious agents and environmental contaminants. Individually ventilated cages (IVCs) are commonly used for housing transgenic rodents. These cages are equipped with HEPA filters to supply filtered air and prevent cross-contamination between animals. IVCs also allow precise control of temperature, humidity, and ventilation, which is essential for animals with compromised immune systems, such as knock-out models for immune-related genes.

Some transgenic lines may exhibit reduced fertility, poor maternal behavior, or altered developmental patterns, necessitating assisted breeding strategies. For example, heterozygous breeding may be preferred over homozygous pairings in cases where homozygosity leads to embryonic lethality or severe health complications. Breeding schemes must be carefully designed and monitored to ensure the maintenance of genetic integrity and to avoid genetic drift. Genotyping of pups is routinely carried out using tail snips or ear punches followed by PCR to confirm the presence or absence of the transgene.

In many cases, specialized diets may be required, especially for models that mimic human metabolic or gastrointestinal diseases. For example, mice with lipid metabolism disorders may need low-fat diets, while others may require vitamin-enriched or sterile pelleted diets. The availability of fresh, clean drinking water is critical, and acidified or autoclaved water may be provided in SPF colonies to reduce microbial contamination.

Animal welfare in transgenic colonies requires continuous monitoring of health status, behavior, and physiological functions. Some transgenic animals may have increased susceptibility to stress, neurological disorders, or impaired mobility. Therefore, their cages must be equipped with appropriate environmental enrichment, such as nesting materials, shelters, chewable objects, or running wheels to support mental stimulation and natural behaviors. For larger species, such as rabbits or pigs, enrichment may also include visual and tactile elements, and opportunities for movement and social interaction.

Veterinary care should be readily available, and animal care staff must be trained to recognize early signs of distress or disease. Any unexpected phenotype, such as weight loss, aggression, abnormal posture, or unresponsiveness, must be documented and investigated promptly. Standard Operating Procedures (SOPs) should include guidelines for humane endpoints, analgesic administration, and euthanasia if required.

Regulatory bodies such as CPCSEA in India, and international organizations like AAALAC and FELASA, provide clear recommendations for the ethical care and use of genetically modified animals. These guidelines emphasize the 3Rs principle—Replacement, Reduction, and Refinement—to minimize the number of animals used and enhance welfare wherever possible.

Ethical and Regulatory Aspects

The use of transgenic and genetically modified animals in scientific research raises several ethical and regulatory considerations that must be carefully addressed to ensure humane treatment and scientific integrity. Because genetic modification may alter not only the physical characteristics but also the behavioral and physiological functions of animals, there is a moral responsibility to justify their use, minimize suffering, and follow established legal and institutional frameworks. Ethical oversight is especially important for transgenic models that experience pain, distress, or impaired functioning as a result of the introduced genetic alteration.

In India, the ethical use of animals in research—including transgenic animals—is governed by the Committee for the Purpose of Control and Supervision of Experiments on Animals (CPCSEA). According to CPCSEA guidelines, any research involving genetically modified animals must be reviewed and approved by an Institutional Animal Ethics Committee (IAEC). Proposals must include scientific justification for the use of transgenic models, details of the genetic modification, breeding plans, animal numbers, potential welfare concerns, and proposed mitigation strategies. Experiments involving higher-order animals or procedures that may cause severe pain or distress may require additional approval from CPCSEA's national-level review body.

One of the central ethical principles applied is the 3Rs principle—Replacement, Reduction, and Refinement. Researchers are encouraged to replace animals with alternative methods whenever possible, reduce the number of animals used without compromising scientific validity, and refine procedures to minimize pain and improve welfare. When using transgenic animals, refinement includes selecting models that show minimal distress, using humane endpoints, and providing supportive care throughout the study.

Another important regulatory requirement is the registration of facilities that produce or house transgenic animals. These facilities must meet high standards of biosecurity, housing, veterinary care, and staff training. The breeding and maintenance of transgenic animals must be done under Specific Pathogen-Free (SPF) or barrier conditions to avoid contamination and ensure the integrity of the genetic line. Routine health monitoring, genotyping, and phenotypic characterization must be documented and made available for inspection during audits.

In addition to national regulations, international guidelines such as those provided by the International Council for Laboratory Animal Science (ICLAS), Association for Assessment and Accreditation of Laboratory Animal Care International (AAALAC), and OECD standards must be followed when research is intended for global regulatory submission. These guidelines ensure that ethical standards are harmonized across countries and that the generated data is acceptable to regulatory agencies such as the FDA, EMA, or PMDA.

Special ethical attention is required when creating transgenic models that mimic severe human diseases, especially those involving cancer, neurodegeneration, or immune suppression. These models may exhibit chronic suffering or significant disability. Ethical review boards must assess the scientific merit against the potential harm to the animal and ensure that monitoring, analgesia, and endpoints are clearly defined and strictly followed.

Transparency and accountability are also essential. All procedures, welfare assessments, and interventions must be recorded accurately in animal records. Any adverse outcomes or unexpected phenotypes must be reported to the IAEC, and corrective actions should be taken immediately. Personnel involved in handling and caring for transgenic animals must undergo regular training in genetics, animal welfare, and legal compliance.

Health Surveillance and Monitoring

Health surveillance and monitoring of transgenic animals are essential practices in laboratory animal management to ensure animal welfare, maintain colony integrity, and generate scientifically valid and reproducible data. Transgenic animals, especially those with compromised immune systems or those modeling disease conditions, may be more susceptible to infections, physiological imbalances, and stress-related illnesses. Regular and systematic health monitoring helps in early detection of such problems, allowing timely intervention, prevention of disease spread, and reduction of confounding variables in experimental outcomes.

A comprehensive health surveillance program includes routine physical examination, behavioral observation, microbial monitoring, serological testing, parasitological screening, and necropsy evaluations. These assessments are performed at both individual and colony levels, depending on the species, genetic background, and type of genetic modification.

For rodent colonies, sentinel animals are often used as part of colony-wide health monitoring. These sentinels are placed in cages where they are exposed to soiled bedding from multiple cages, allowing indirect exposure to potential pathogens. Blood samples, fecal pellets, and nasal or oropharyngeal swabs from these sentinels are tested for common pathogens using serological assays (such as ELISA) and PCR-based techniques. Pathogens screened typically include mouse hepatitis virus (MHV), Sendai virus, parvoviruses, pinworms, mites, and Mycoplasma pulmonis. Positive findings may necessitate colony quarantine, treatment, or rederivation via embryo transfer or cesarean section.

In transgenic lines, especially those that model metabolic, cardiovascular, or neurodegenerative diseases, regular clinical observations are needed to monitor specific phenotypes such as weight loss, tremors, gait abnormalities, or changes in feeding and drinking behavior. Body weight, temperature, respiration rate, coat condition, and posture are observed and recorded on scheduled intervals. Any deviation from baseline values must be carefully interpreted, as they could be indicative of disease progression or underlying infections.

Veterinary oversight is vital in the health monitoring program. A trained laboratory animal veterinarian should oversee the surveillance plan, evaluate clinical cases, and recommend diagnostic tests or humane endpoints. Diagnostic tools such as hematological and biochemical profiling, radiographic imaging, and histopathological examination are used in advanced facilities to confirm health conditions or causes of death. In high-containment or immunocompromised colonies, necropsy-based monitoring is conducted regularly to detect subclinical infections or abnormalities.

Environmental monitoring is also part of overall health surveillance. Parameters such as ammonia concentration, microbial load in the air, water quality, and cage sanitation levels are routinely assessed. Deviations in environmental conditions can lead to respiratory distress, gastrointestinal disorders, or immunosuppression, especially in genetically sensitive strains.

Proper record keeping is mandatory. All health incidents, diagnostic findings, treatments administered, mortalities, and necropsy reports must be logged and maintained in institutional records. These records are reviewed by regulatory authorities such as CPCSEA and are essential for GLP compliance and accreditation audits.

1.3.4 Applications in Drug Discovery

Modeling of Human Diseases (e.g., Cancer, Diabetes, Alzheimer's)

Transgenic and genetically modified animals play a pivotal role in the modeling of human diseases, allowing researchers to recreate genetic, molecular, and physiological aspects of complex disorders in a controlled experimental setting. These models are crucial in drug discovery and development, as they enable scientists to study disease mechanisms, validate therapeutic targets, test drug efficacy, and monitor disease progression in real time. Among the many diseases modeled using genetically engineered animals, cancer, diabetes, and Alzheimer's disease represent some of the most thoroughly investigated areas due to their high global burden and complex pathophysiology.

In cancer research, transgenic models are used to study tumor initiation, growth, metastasis, and resistance to therapy. For example, oncogene knock-in models, such as those carrying mutant forms of *K-Ras*, *Myc*, or *TP53*, mimic spontaneous tumor development observed in human cancers. The MMTV-PyMT mouse is a well-known breast cancer model that develops aggressive, hormone-responsive tumors similar to human ductal carcinoma. Similarly, the APC^Min/+ mouse, which carries a mutation in the adenomatous polyposis coli gene, is widely used in studies of colorectal cancer. These models help identify early biomarkers, evaluate chemopreventive agents, and test targeted therapies such as tyrosine kinase inhibitors and monoclonal antibodies under physiologically relevant conditions.

For diabetes research, genetically modified models are essential for replicating the pathogenesis of both Type 1 and Type 2 diabetes. The NOD (Non-Obese Diabetic) mouse is an autoimmune model that spontaneously develops Type 1 diabetes due to destruction of pancreatic β-cells, mirroring the human disease. The db/db mouse, which carries a mutation in the leptin receptor gene, and the ob/ob mouse, which lacks the leptin hormone, are used to study obesity-induced insulin resistance and Type 2 diabetes. These models provide insight into glucose homeostasis, pancreatic function, insulin signaling, and diabetic complications such as nephropathy and neuropathy. They are also used to test hypoglycemic agents, insulin analogs, and newer classes of drugs such as SGLT2 inhibitors and GLP-1 receptor agonists.

In the field of neurodegenerative diseases, genetically modified animals have been instrumental in elucidating the molecular basis of disorders like Alzheimer's disease (AD). Transgenic mice expressing human genes associated with familial forms of Alzheimer's, such as mutated *APP* (Amyloid Precursor Protein), *PSEN1* (Presenilin 1), and *Tau*, develop hallmark features of the disease, including amyloid plaques, neurofibrillary tangles, cognitive decline, and synaptic dysfunction. The 5xFAD mouse, which carries five human mutations, is commonly used in preclinical studies for screening anti-amyloid drugs, β-secretase inhibitors, and neuroprotective agents. These models help assess not only pharmacodynamic efficacy but also behavioral endpoints like memory, learning, and motor coordination using tests such as the Morris water maze and Y-maze.

Importantly, transgenic disease models allow longitudinal studies, where disease progression can be tracked over time under treatment or control conditions. They also support biomarker validation by correlating tissue or serum markers with disease states and treatment outcomes. In many cases, these models also serve as platforms for non-invasive imaging techniques, such as PET or MRI, to monitor biological changes in vivo.

Despite their advantages, it is essential to acknowledge that no animal model perfectly replicates all aspects of human disease. Variability in gene expression, immune responses, and drug metabolism between species must be considered while interpreting results. Hence, findings from transgenic models are often complemented with human cell-based assays and clinical data to strengthen translational relevance.

Overall, the use of genetically modified animals for disease modeling has become a cornerstone of modern drug discovery. These models bridge the gap between in vitro studies and human clinical trials, offering a robust and biologically relevant framework for identifying and validating novel therapeutic strategies.

Target Validation and Gene Function Studies

Target validation and gene function studies are essential applications of transgenic and genetically modified animals in the process of drug discovery. These studies help determine whether a specific gene, protein, or molecular pathway is directly involved in the development or progression of a disease. Validating a target means establishing a cause-and-effect relationship between that target and the disease state. Only after this validation can a therapeutic intervention be designed to modulate the target and achieve the desired therapeutic outcome. Genetically modified animal models, especially knock-out, knock-in, and conditional gene models, play a central role in these investigations because they allow researchers to manipulate specific genes in a living organism and observe the resulting biological effects in a controlled and reproducible manner.

When a gene is knocked out in a transgenic animal and the animal shows a specific phenotype or disease-like condition, it indicates that the gene plays a critical functional role in that physiological process. For example, knock-out mice lacking the gene encoding the insulin receptor exhibit features of insulin resistance and hyperglycemia, confirming the importance of that gene in glucose homeostasis. Similarly, deletion of the low-density lipoprotein receptor gene in mice leads to hypercholesterolemia and atherosclerosis, supporting its role in lipid metabolism and cardiovascular disease. Such observations confirm the gene as a valid target for therapeutic intervention.

In some cases, gene function is studied not by knocking the gene out, but by overexpressing or introducing mutations through knock-in models. These help to understand gain-of-function effects or the consequences of specific point mutations found in human diseases. For instance, the insertion of a mutant human amyloid precursor protein gene into mice allows scientists to study the deposition of amyloid plaques and neuronal loss, which are key features of Alzheimer's disease. This helps establish that the amyloid pathway is not just associated with the disease but is actively driving its pathology, thereby validating it as a drug target.

Conditional knock-out models are used when global gene deletion causes embryonic lethality or widespread systemic effects. These models allow researchers to study gene function in a tissue-specific or time-specific manner using promoter-driven recombinase systems like Cre-loxP. For example, conditional deletion of the PPAR-γ gene in adipose tissue helps to reveal its role in fat metabolism without affecting other organs, offering more precise insight into its therapeutic potential for obesity and diabetes.

Transgenic animals are also used to study compensatory mechanisms and off-target effects. In many cases, deletion of one gene may lead to upregulation of another related gene that compensates for its loss. This helps researchers understand redundancy in biological pathways and may point to the need for multi-target or combination therapy approaches. Moreover, pharmacological agents can be tested in these models to observe whether inhibiting or activating the target gene leads to the desired therapeutic outcome without adverse effects, which is crucial before advancing to clinical trials.

Advanced techniques such as reporter gene assays, real-time imaging, and tissue-specific transcriptomic analysis are integrated into these studies to monitor gene activity and downstream effects. These tools provide dynamic data on how gene manipulation affects cellular pathways, protein expression, and physiological function in real-time. The results guide researchers in selecting the most promising targets for further drug development and in understanding the exact mechanism by which drugs interact with their intended targets.

Pharmacodynamic and Pharmacokinetic Profiling

Pharmacodynamic (PD) and pharmacokinetic (PK) profiling are integral steps in the preclinical evaluation of new drug candidates. These studies are necessary to understand how a drug behaves in a living organism—how it is absorbed, distributed, metabolized, and excreted (pharmacokinetics), and how it exerts its biological effect at the target site (pharmacodynamics). Genetically modified animals, including knock-out, knock-in, and humanized models, are particularly useful for studying the PD/PK profile of drugs in a mechanistically defined and disease-relevant background, thereby improving the accuracy and predictability of preclinical data.

Pharmacokinetic profiling typically involves administering the drug via different routes—such as oral, intravenous, subcutaneous, or intraperitoneal—and collecting biological samples like blood, urine, feces, or tissue at various time points. These samples are analyzed using validated bioanalytical methods like high-performance liquid chromatography (HPLC), mass spectrometry, or ELISA to determine drug concentrations over time. From these data, key PK parameters such as maximum concentration (Cmax), time to reach Cmax (Tmax), area under the curve (AUC), half-life (t½), volume of distribution (Vd), and clearance (Cl) are calculated using compartmental or non-compartmental analysis models.

Transgenic animals are particularly useful when studying drugs targeting human-specific proteins. For instance, humanized mouse models that express human versions of cytochrome P450 enzymes (such as CYP3A4 or CYP2D6) are used to investigate metabolism and potential drug-drug interactions in a way that mimics human liver enzyme activity. These models help in identifying active or toxic metabolites that may not be produced in wild-type rodents. Knock-out models, on the other hand, are used to assess the contribution of specific metabolic pathways or transporters. For example, a P-glycoprotein knock-out mouse can be used to study the role of this efflux transporter in limiting drug penetration across the blood-brain barrier.

Pharmacodynamic profiling focuses on measuring the drug's effect on the biological system over time. PD endpoints may include biochemical changes, physiological responses, behavioral alterations, or disease biomarkers. These are assessed using functional assays, imaging techniques, histopathology, or molecular methods such as quantitative PCR and Western blotting. In disease models, pharmacodynamic responses may be measured as improvement or delay in symptom progression, suppression of disease markers, or changes in gene expression profiles.

A classic example is the evaluation of anti-inflammatory drugs in knock-out mice lacking the COX-2 gene. The absence of this enzyme allows researchers to isolate the contribution of COX-1 to inflammatory pathways and study selective inhibition effects. Similarly, knock-in models with mutations in insulin signaling pathways are used to evaluate the glucose-lowering effects of anti-diabetic drugs and to understand dose-response relationships.

Integration of PK and PD data leads to PK/PD modeling, which helps establish the optimal dose and dosing frequency required to achieve desired therapeutic effects while minimizing toxicity. These models are crucial in dose selection for first-in-human studies and for identifying therapeutic windows. They also support regulatory submissions by providing evidence of a drug's safety margin and effectiveness under controlled experimental conditions.

Transgenic animals enhance the translational value of PD/PK studies by offering a biologically relevant system where both drug exposure and response can be studied in the context of human-like genetics or disease states. However, careful experimental design, including proper controls and ethical considerations, is essential to ensure that the results are meaningful and applicable for further development.

In essence, pharmacokinetic and pharmacodynamic profiling in genetically modified animals bridges the gap between molecular pharmacology and clinical drug development, providing vital data for making informed decisions about drug safety, efficacy, and dosing strategies in the early stages of the drug discovery pipeline.

1.4 Anaesthesia and Euthanasia of Experimental Animals

1.4.1 Types of Anaesthetics and Routes of Administration

Inhalational Agents (e.g., Isoflurane)

Inhalational anaesthetics are widely used in laboratory animal studies due to their rapid onset, easy control over anaesthetic depth, and fast recovery times. Among these, isoflurane is the most commonly used agent across various species, including rodents, rabbits, and small non-human primates. Isoflurane is a halogenated ether that produces general anaesthesia by depressing the central nervous system in a dose-dependent manner. It is delivered through a vaporizer connected to an anaesthetic machine, often mixed with oxygen or air.

Isoflurane is chosen for its low blood–gas partition coefficient, which allows for quick induction and emergence from anaesthesia. It provides smooth, consistent anaesthesia with minimal cardiovascular and respiratory depression when properly used. Its onset usually occurs within 30 seconds to 1 minute in mice and rats, and recovery is typically observed within 5 to 10 minutes after cessation. It is excreted largely through the lungs, with minimal metabolism by the liver, which reduces the risk of hepatic toxicity, making it suitable for repeat or long procedures.

Inhalational anaesthesia with isoflurane is administered using specially designed induction chambers and nose cones or masks that fit the animal species being used. The typical concentration for induction is 3% to 5% isoflurane, followed by maintenance at 1% to 3% depending on the procedure and species. Adequate scavenging systems must be in place to prevent occupational exposure in laboratory personnel, as prolonged exposure to isoflurane vapors can cause health risks.

For small animals like mice and rats, anaesthesia is usually induced in a sealed acrylic chamber, after which the animal is transferred to a nose cone for maintenance. In rabbits or larger animals, a face mask or intubation may be used for controlled ventilation, especially in surgical procedures requiring longer durations. Monitoring of respiration rate, heart rate, mucous membrane color, and reflexes is essential during anaesthesia to ensure the depth remains within the surgical plane and to avoid overdose.

Isoflurane has minimal analgesic properties, so it is often used in combination with analgesics such as buprenorphine or meloxicam, particularly in procedures involving pain or tissue damage. Recovery cages with controlled temperature and oxygenation support post-anaesthesia care and reduce the risk of hypothermia and respiratory depression.

While isoflurane is safe and effective, it must be used with proper training and safety measures. Equipment such as calibrated vaporizers, oxygen flow meters, and waste gas scavenging systems must be routinely maintained and validated. Animals must be observed during recovery for signs of delayed awakening, hypothermia, or respiratory distress, and supportive care should be administered when necessary.

Injectable Agents (e.g., Ketamine, Xylazine)

Injectable anaesthetics are widely used in laboratory animal research due to their ease of administration, portability, and effectiveness in producing general anaesthesia or sedation without the need for elaborate anaesthesia machines. Among these, ketamine and xylazine are two of the most commonly used agents, often administered in combination to achieve a balanced anaesthetic effect. This combination is extensively used in rodents, rabbits, and small laboratory animals for procedures ranging from simple restraint to surgical interventions.

Ketamine is a dissociative anaesthetic that acts by blocking N-methyl-D-aspartate (NMDA) receptors in the central nervous system. It produces a trance-like state characterized by immobility, amnesia, and profound analgesia while maintaining respiratory function and reflexes. However, ketamine alone does not provide adequate muscle relaxation, and its use as a sole agent may result in hypertonia or poor surgical conditions.

To overcome this, xylazine, an α2-adrenergic agonist, is co-administered. Xylazine provides muscle relaxation, sedation, and additional analgesia, complementing the effects of ketamine and producing a more stable and deeper plane of anaesthesia. The combination also reduces the dose requirement of ketamine, minimizing its cardiovascular side effects.

The standard intraperitoneal dose for mice is typically around ketamine 80–100 mg/kg and xylazine 5–10 mg/kg, while in rats, ketamine 50–75 mg/kg and xylazine 5–10 mg/kg is commonly used. Administration can be done via intramuscular (IM) or intraperitoneal (IP) routes, depending on the species and protocol. Onset of anaesthesia occurs within 5 to 10 minutes, and the duration of surgical anaesthesia lasts approximately 30 to 45 minutes, which may vary based on the dose, route, and animal condition.

During ketamine–xylazine anaesthesia, animals typically show decreased heart rate, respiratory rate, and body temperature. Continuous monitoring is essential to prevent hypothermia, bradycardia, or respiratory depression. Recovery begins within 60 to 90 minutes and can be prolonged in aged or compromised animals. Supportive measures such as warming pads, fluid replacement, and oxygen supply may be required in such cases.

Reversal of xylazine-induced sedation can be achieved using atipamezole, an α2-antagonist, especially in procedures requiring rapid recovery. Analgesic supplementation with agents like meloxicam or buprenorphine is recommended if the procedure involves significant tissue damage, as the ketamine–xylazine combination may not provide sufficient post-operative pain control.

Compared to inhalational anaesthetics, injectable agents offer the advantage of portability and simplicity, especially in field studies or situations where access to anaesthesia machines is limited. However, once administered, the depth and duration of anaesthesia cannot be easily adjusted, making precise control more challenging. Additionally, variability in absorption and metabolism among individual animals can affect the predictability of response.

Proper training in dosing, injection techniques, and monitoring is essential to minimize risks and ensure effective anaesthesia. All procedures involving injectable anaesthetics must be documented in the experimental protocol and approved by the Institutional Animal Ethics Committee, in compliance with CPCSEA or international guidelines.

Injectable anaesthesia using ketamine and xylazine remains a reliable and widely accepted method in experimental animal studies, offering a practical balance between depth of anaesthesia, analgesia, and muscle relaxation when administered with appropriate care and oversight.

Routes: Intraperitoneal, Intramuscular, Intravenous

The route of administration for anaesthetic agents plays a critical role in determining the onset, depth, duration, and safety of anaesthesia in experimental animals. Selection of the route depends on several factors, including the species, size of the animal, type of anaesthetic, duration of the procedure, and technical expertise available. The three most commonly used routes in laboratory settings are intraperitoneal (IP), intramuscular (IM), and intravenous (IV). Each route has distinct advantages, limitations, and procedural requirements.

Intraperitoneal (IP) route is widely used in small laboratory animals like mice and rats. It involves injecting the anaesthetic into the peritoneal cavity, located in the lower right quadrant of the abdomen to avoid puncturing vital organs such as the bladder, liver, or cecum. This route is relatively easy to perform and requires minimal restraint or equipment. Drugs administered intraperitoneally are absorbed into the bloodstream via the rich capillary network lining the peritoneum, leading to a moderately fast onset of action—typically 5 to 10 minutes. Common anaesthetic combinations such as ketamine–xylazine are frequently administered through this route. However, variability in absorption and occasional risks of peritonitis or injury to internal organs must be considered.

Intramuscular (IM) route is another frequently used method, particularly in rabbits, guinea pigs, and dogs. The anaesthetic is injected directly into a large muscle group, such as the thigh (quadriceps or hamstrings), lumbar, or gluteal muscles. The IM route offers a faster and more predictable absorption than IP, with onset usually observed within 3 to 5 minutes. The injected volume should be carefully limited—generally not exceeding 0.1 mL in mice, 0.3–0.5 mL in rats, or 2–5 mL in rabbits and dogs per site—to avoid muscle damage or necrosis. The IM route is preferred for agents requiring more precise onset, such as xylazine, medetomidine, or tiletamine-zolazepam. Repeated injections should be avoided in the same site to prevent tissue trauma.

Intravenous (IV) route provides the fastest and most accurate control over anaesthesia, making it ideal for short procedures, rapid inductions, or where fine-tuning of anaesthetic depth is needed. This route delivers the drug directly into the bloodstream, resulting in almost immediate onset—usually within 10 to 30 seconds. It is commonly used in larger animals such as rabbits, dogs, and non-human primates, and occasionally in rats or mice trained for restraint or with surgically implanted catheters. Veins commonly used include the lateral tail vein in rodents, marginal ear vein in rabbits, and cephalic or saphenous veins in dogs. IV anaesthesia requires precise dosing, proper vein identification, sterile technique, and monitoring for signs of extravasation or phlebitis. Drugs like thiopental, propofol, and ketamine are often administered intravenously for rapid induction or short-duration procedures.

Each route has its merits and limitations. IP is convenient but less precise, IM offers quicker absorption with moderate control, and IV provides the highest precision but requires technical expertise. Regardless of the route, it is essential to ensure proper dose calculation based on body weight, sterile technique, gentle handling, and close monitoring of anaesthetic depth, reflexes, respiration rate, and temperature. The selected route must be clearly justified in the experimental protocol and conform to ethical and regulatory standards for animal welfare.

Proper understanding and skilled execution of anaesthetic administration routes not only improve animal well-being but also contribute significantly to the reliability, reproducibility, and ethical integrity of pharmacological and toxicological research.

1.4.2.1 Physical Methods: Cervical Dislocation, Decapitation

Physical methods of euthanasia are approved techniques used to terminate experimental animals swiftly and humanely when performed correctly by trained personnel. These methods are particularly applicable in small laboratory animals like mice, rats, and birds, where they offer a rapid and effective means of ensuring death without the use of chemical agents that may interfere with tissue analysis. The two most commonly used physical methods are cervical dislocation and decapitation. Both are considered acceptable under institutional and national guidelines, such as those outlined by CPCSEA, when carried out with proper justification and training.

Cervical dislocation involves the dislocation of the cervical vertebrae from the skull, thereby causing rapid loss of consciousness through severe damage to the spinal cord and brainstem. It is typically performed in small animals weighing less than 200 grams, such as adult mice or young rats. The procedure requires manual skill: the handler firmly holds the animal at the base of the skull with one hand and applies a swift pulling and twisting motion on the tail or hind limbs with the other hand to dislocate the cervical spine. This results in immediate unconsciousness followed by death due to cessation of brainstem function and respiratory failure. Proper restraint and quick, decisive motion are critical to ensure a humane outcome. This method is not recommended for large or conscious animals without sedation, as the risk of improper execution and animal suffering increases.

Decapitation involves the severing of the head from the body using a sharp, guillotine-type instrument. It is a rapid and reliable method used primarily in neurophysiological, biochemical, or pharmacokinetic studies where anaesthetic agents may alter the results of tissue samples, especially brain or blood chemistry. The animal must be handled gently and securely restrained before decapitation to minimize stress. In some institutions, decapitation without prior sedation or anaesthesia requires special ethical approval. The instrument used must be well-maintained, clean, and sharp to ensure a swift, single-motion cut that causes instant death. After the procedure, confirmation of death is mandatory and is generally based on the absence of reflexes, respiration, and heartbeat.

Both cervical dislocation and decapitation are categorized as physical and non-pharmacological methods, and their use must be scientifically justified in the experimental protocol. Personnel must receive documented training and perform these procedures only when fully competent, as improperly done euthanasia can result in severe pain, distress, and ethical violations.

Furthermore, these methods must be carried out in a designated euthanasia area, separate from other experimental or housing areas, to prevent distress to other animals. Proper disposal of carcasses, cleaning of equipment, and recording of the euthanasia event are part of standard protocol requirements.

1.4.2.2 Chemical Methods: CO_2 Inhalation, Overdose of Anesthetics

Chemical methods of euthanasia are widely accepted in laboratory animal research due to their potential for painless, non-invasive, and stress-minimizing induction of death, especially when performed under controlled conditions by trained personnel. These methods are particularly suitable for small to medium-sized animals and are often preferred for their compatibility with tissue preservation and compliance with ethical guidelines. Among chemical methods, carbon dioxide (CO_2) inhalation and overdose of anesthetics are the most commonly used techniques, approved under national and international regulations, including CPCSEA guidelines in India.

CO_2 inhalation is frequently used for euthanizing rodents such as mice, rats, and guinea pigs. This method involves exposing the animal to a gradually rising concentration of carbon dioxide gas within a closed chamber. CO_2 causes central nervous system depression, leading to unconsciousness, respiratory arrest, and eventual death. To ensure minimal distress, the flow rate of CO_2 should be adjusted to displace 20% to 30% of the chamber volume per minute. Rapid flooding or pre-filled chambers are strictly discouraged as they can cause distress, dyspnea, and pain due to mucosal irritation and hypercapnia.

Animals must be continuously monitored during CO_2 exposure. Unconsciousness generally occurs within 1 to 2 minutes, and death follows shortly thereafter. However, due to the possibility of incomplete euthanasia, physical confirmation such as cessation of heartbeat, absence of corneal reflex, or secondary methods like cervical dislocation may be required to ensure irreversible death. The CO_2 used must be pharmaceutical or medical-grade, and the euthanasia chamber should be transparent, well-ventilated post-use, and cleaned thoroughly between procedures.

Overdose of anesthetics is another highly effective chemical method, particularly suitable when the animal is already under anaesthesia for a surgical or invasive procedure. Commonly used agents include pentobarbital, isoflurane, sevoflurane, or injectable combinations like ketamine-xylazine at overdose levels. Intravenous or intraperitoneal administration of pentobarbital sodium (200–400 mg/kg) results in deep anaesthesia followed by respiratory and cardiac arrest. For animals under gas anaesthesia, continuing isoflurane at high concentrations (e.g., 5% for rodents) leads to a painless transition to death.

Chemical overdose ensures minimal movement, vocalization, or distress, making it suitable for both terminal surgical procedures and studies requiring high-quality tissue samples. However, barbiturates are controlled substances and require proper storage, documentation, and disposal as per institutional and regulatory guidelines. Residues of these agents may also interfere with downstream molecular or biochemical assays, so their use must be carefully justified in protocols requiring tissue analysis.

The choice between CO_2 inhalation and anesthetic overdose depends on the species, purpose of euthanasia, equipment availability, and study requirements. Regardless of the method used, euthanasia must be performed in a designated area, and all personnel involved must be trained in both the technical execution and animal welfare assessment. Clear documentation, humane handling, and compliance with institutional standard operating procedures are mandatory.

Chemical methods, when performed appropriately, offer a highly humane and efficient means of euthanizing laboratory animals, preserving ethical standards and supporting the refinement principle of the 3Rs in experimental research.

1.4.3 Regulatory and Ethical Considerations

CPCSEA Recommendations

In India, the use of experimental animals for scientific and educational purposes is governed by the Committee for the Purpose of Control and Supervision of Experiments on Animals (CPCSEA), functioning under the Ministry of Fisheries, Animal Husbandry and Dairying, Department of Animal Husbandry and Dairying, Government of India. CPCSEA is the apex regulatory authority that ensures animals used in laboratories are treated with compassion, care, and under ethical norms. All experiments involving animals must strictly adhere to CPCSEA's guidelines, which are legally binding under the Prevention of Cruelty to Animals Act, 1960.

CPCSEA lays down clear recommendations and procedural requirements for the anaesthesia, euthanasia, housing, handling, and overall welfare of laboratory animals. For anaesthesia, the guidelines specify that the agent and route should be selected based on the species, type of experiment, duration of the procedure, and the expected pain or discomfort. It mandates that all surgical or painful procedures must be performed under appropriate anaesthesia, and analgesics must be used post-operatively to minimize suffering. Only trained personnel or veterinarians are allowed to administer anaesthesia, and the depth of anaesthesia must be monitored continuously using clinical signs and reflex testing.

In terms of euthanasia, CPCSEA recommends humane, scientifically validated, and ethically accepted methods that result in rapid, painless, and distress-free death. The guidelines endorse physical methods like cervical dislocation and decapitation only in small laboratory animals and under defined conditions. These procedures must be performed only by skilled personnel, and appropriate scientific justification is required in the experimental protocol. Chemical methods such as CO_2 inhalation or overdose of anaesthetics are recommended for most other cases, especially when tissue integrity must be preserved or when large numbers of animals are involved. All euthanasia events must be followed by confirmation of death and proper carcass disposal as per biohazard guidelines.

CPCSEA mandates the establishment of an Institutional Animal Ethics Committee (IAEC) in every registered animal facility. All experimental protocols involving animals must be submitted to the IAEC for review and approval. The IAEC is responsible for verifying that the proposed study adheres to ethical standards, ensures animal welfare, and justifies the use of animals based on the 3Rs—Replacement, Reduction, and Refinement. No animal experiment can commence without prior written approval from the IAEC.

The guidelines also require facilities to maintain comprehensive records of animal usage, breeding, health monitoring, anaesthesia logs, and euthanasia reports. These records are subject to audit by CPCSEA inspectors, and any deviation from approved practices can result in legal consequences, including suspension of the facility's registration.

CPCSEA further promotes training and education in laboratory animal science. It mandates that all scientific and technical staff involved in animal experimentation undergo certified training programs covering animal ethics, anaesthesia, euthanasia, housing, and handling procedures. Refresher training is also encouraged to ensure compliance with evolving ethical standards and scientific practices.

Minimizing Animal Pain and Distress

Minimizing pain and distress in laboratory animals is a fundamental ethical and scientific obligation in preclinical research. Pain and stress not only compromise animal welfare but also lead to significant physiological and behavioral changes that can introduce variability in experimental outcomes. Therefore, all efforts must be made to recognize, prevent, and manage pain and distress at every stage of the experimental procedure, in accordance with institutional and regulatory guidelines such as those set by CPCSEA.

Pain in animals can be caused by various factors, including surgical procedures, injections, disease models, or improper handling. It may present as behavioral changes like reduced activity, abnormal posture, vocalization, aggression, self-mutilation, or changes in grooming habits. Physiological indicators such as increased heart rate, respiratory rate, and stress hormone levels are also common. Researchers and animal care staff must be trained to identify such signs accurately and respond promptly.

The first step in minimizing pain and distress is adequate planning and experimental design. This includes selecting the least invasive procedures, using the minimum number of animals necessary, and choosing alternative methods whenever scientifically justified. Ethical review by the Institutional Animal Ethics Committee ensures that the study has a strong scientific rationale and that all humane considerations have been integrated into the protocol.

Proper anaesthesia and analgesia form the cornerstone of pain management. Animals undergoing any surgical or potentially painful procedure must receive suitable anaesthesia to render them fully unconscious and insensible to pain during the procedure. Post-operative pain must be managed using analgesics like buprenorphine, meloxicam, or carprofen, administered at correct doses and intervals based on the species and nature of the surgery. Analgesics should be continued for an appropriate duration even after the animal appears to recover, to ensure full pain control.

Refinement of techniques is another important strategy. Using fine-gauge needles for injections, minimizing the number of handling events, and applying local anaesthetics where possible help reduce procedural discomfort. For example, the use of topical lidocaine-prilocaine cream before tail vein injections in rodents can significantly reduce pain. Similarly, using warming pads and moistening of the eye during anaesthesia helps in preventing secondary complications like hypothermia or corneal ulcers.

Environmental enrichment and proper housing also play a vital role in reducing stress. Providing nesting material, hiding spaces, chewable items, or social housing, depending on the species, helps animals express natural behavior and feel secure. Stress associated with transport, noise, and frequent handling can be minimized through habituation and by following a consistent, gentle handling routine.

Humane endpoints must be clearly defined in every study protocol. These are specific clinical signs indicating that the animal's pain or condition has reached a point where it is no longer ethically justifiable to continue the experiment. Common endpoints include persistent weight loss, self-injury, tumor burden beyond defined limits, or unresponsiveness. When these criteria are met, the animal must be euthanized promptly using an approved humane method.

Post-procedural monitoring is essential for identifying delayed onset of pain or distress. Animals should be observed at regular intervals for clinical signs, food and water intake, mobility, and overall behavior. Detailed records must be maintained, and any abnormalities should be addressed by the attending veterinarian.

In addition to animal-level interventions, staff training and awareness are critical. Everyone involved in handling, caring, or experimenting on animals must be trained in recognizing pain, using analgesics, following humane practices, and complying with institutional SOPs. Routine refresher training and audits help reinforce ethical standards and scientific best practices.

By minimizing animal pain and distress, researchers uphold the ethical integrity of their work, ensure compliance with national and international regulations, and improve the reliability and reproducibility of experimental data. This commitment reflects the responsible use of animals in science and aligns with the broader principles of humane research and global scientific credibility.

Documentation and Justification for Euthanasia

Proper documentation and ethical justification for euthanasia are critical components of responsible animal research. Euthanasia, though a necessary part of many preclinical studies, must be scientifically justified and carried out in accordance with national and institutional guidelines to ensure the humane treatment of animals and uphold the integrity of scientific data. Regulatory authorities such as the CPCSEA in India, as well as international organizations like AAALAC and ICLAS, mandate transparent and detailed records whenever euthanasia is performed in a research setting.

The justification for euthanasia must be clearly stated in the experimental protocol submitted to the Institutional Animal Ethics Committee (IAEC) before the commencement of the study. Euthanasia may be planned as a part of study endpoints, such as tissue collection, blood sampling, organ harvesting, or completion of a disease model. It may also be required as an unplanned humane intervention in cases of unexpected suffering, deterioration in health status, or moribund condition, where continuation of life would cause undue distress to the animal. In both situations, the rationale must be based on scientific necessity and humane grounds.

All euthanasia procedures must be documented meticulously. This includes the date, time, method used (e.g., CO_2 inhalation, anaesthetic overdose, cervical dislocation), name of the person performing the procedure, and the identity of the animal (species, sex, age, ID number). If the animal was euthanized due to unforeseen complications or reached a humane endpoint earlier than anticipated, the exact reason should be recorded along with clinical observations leading up to the decision. These records must be maintained in bound laboratory notebooks, digital logs, or institutional forms that are subject to audit and inspection.

In studies requiring the collection of tissues for molecular, histological, or pharmacokinetic analyses, euthanasia must be justified not only ethically but also scientifically. For example, certain chemical methods may be chosen specifically to avoid contamination of tissues with anaesthetic residues, while others may be preferred to maintain tissue integrity. The method selected must align with study objectives and be approved by the IAEC in advance.

The euthanasia logbook is a mandatory part of institutional animal facility records. It should be updated regularly and retained for the period prescribed by the regulatory authority. These records are reviewed during IAEC meetings, CPCSEA inspections, and external quality assurance audits. Any deviation from approved euthanasia methods or procedural lapses must be investigated and addressed promptly through corrective actions and training.

Additionally, the person performing euthanasia must be trained and certified in the selected method. Institutions are responsible for providing such training and for evaluating competence before authorizing personnel to carry out euthanasia independently. Refresher training and performance reviews are recommended to maintain consistency and quality.

By maintaining thorough documentation and ensuring strong ethical justification, institutions demonstrate compliance with legal frameworks and reaffirm their commitment to humane and scientifically valid animal research. This practice not only supports animal welfare but also strengthens the credibility, reproducibility, and acceptability of the research in both national and international forums.

1.5 Maintenance and Breeding of Laboratory Animals

1.5.1 Breeding Strategies

1.5.1.1 Inbred Strains – Genetically Identical Lines

Inbred strains are laboratory animal lines that are genetically homogeneous, produced by mating closely related individuals—specifically, brother and sister—for at least 20 consecutive generations. This intensive inbreeding leads to genetic uniformity, meaning that all individuals in an inbred strain are almost genetically identical and homozygous at nearly all loci. The genetic similarity between two animals of the same inbred strain is typically more than 98%, making them ideal for controlled experimental studies where minimal genetic variability is crucial.

The primary goal of developing inbred strains is to reduce biological variability in experimental data. In pharmacological and toxicological studies, this uniformity allows for the detection of subtle drug effects, accurate comparison between treatment groups, and high reproducibility of results across different laboratories and time points. Inbred strains also provide a stable genetic background for creating genetically modified models, including knock-out and knock-in lines, ensuring consistency in phenotype expression.

Some of the most commonly used inbred strains in laboratory research include BALB/c, C57BL/6, DBA/2, and 129Sv mice, each having distinct behavioral, immunological, and physiological traits. For example, C57BL/6 mice are widely used in immunology and neuroscience due to their robust immune response and high susceptibility to diet-induced obesity, while BALB/c mice are known for their use in cancer and allergy models because of their sensitivity to tumor induction and IgE-mediated responses.

Inbred strains must be maintained under strictly controlled conditions to prevent genetic drift, spontaneous mutations, or accidental outcrossing. Breeding records must be meticulously maintained, and sibling mating must be continued to preserve the genetic integrity of the line. If the breeding performance declines or fertility issues arise due to inbreeding depression, embryo cryopreservation and rederivation may be employed to rejuvenate the colony while preserving the original genetic traits.

While inbred strains are valuable for eliminating background genetic noise, they also have certain limitations. Due to their homozygosity, these animals may exhibit increased sensitivity to environmental stressors, infections, or toxic agents and may not fully represent the genetic diversity of the general population. This narrow genetic base can limit the generalizability of research findings to broader clinical populations.

To ensure quality, inbred colonies are often maintained as part of a defined genetic resource by national repositories or commercial vendors, which supply verified and health-monitored breeding pairs or embryos. In animal research facilities, these strains are housed under specific pathogen-free (SPF) conditions to avoid infections that may alter phenotypic expression or compromise experimental outcomes.

1.5.1.2 Outbred Strains – Genetically Diverse Population

Outbred strains refer to populations of laboratory animals that are bred in a manner designed to maintain maximum genetic diversity, typically by avoiding mating between close relatives. These animals are not genetically identical but are selected to maintain heterozygosity, preserving natural variation similar to that found in wild or human populations. Outbred strains are widely used in preclinical studies where the goal is to evaluate variability, predict population-wide drug responses, or mimic real-world clinical scenarios where individuals differ in genetic makeup.

Unlike inbred strains, outbred animals are not bred through sibling matings. Instead, they are maintained through planned breeding systems such as rotational or random mating schemes. These strategies are carefully monitored to ensure that genetic diversity does not decline over generations. Mating pairs are selected from non-related individuals, and pedigree tracking is often maintained to prevent inadvertent inbreeding. This approach maintains a high degree of heterozygosity across the population.

Some of the commonly used outbred strains include Swiss albino mice, CD-1 mice, Wistar rats, Sprague Dawley rats, and Hartley guinea pigs. These strains are known for their robust breeding performance, larger litter sizes, rapid growth rates, and resistance to certain diseases. For example, Sprague Dawley rats are widely used in pharmacokinetics, toxicology, and behavioral research due to their docile temperament and well-characterized physiological responses.

One of the main advantages of outbred strains is that they better represent genetic variability in human populations, making them valuable in toxicological studies, safety pharmacology, vaccine development, and formulation screening. Since each individual in an outbred group is genetically unique, researchers can evaluate inter-individual differences in drug absorption, metabolism, efficacy, and side effects. This approach helps in identifying variability that might be encountered in human clinical trials, improving the external validity and predictive power of preclinical data.

However, the genetic diversity of outbred strains can also be a source of experimental variability, requiring larger sample sizes to achieve statistical significance. Unlike inbred animals, it is not possible to reproduce genetically identical test groups, which can complicate replication of studies across different laboratories. Furthermore, outbred strains may exhibit less uniformity in phenotypic traits, which may require more detailed baseline characterizations before experimental use.

Maintaining outbred colonies requires careful population management. Breeding should avoid selection pressures that might unintentionally narrow genetic variation over time. It is also important to periodically introduce new genetic stock from certified sources to refresh the gene pool and maintain colony vigor. All breeding and experimental records must be documented, and health surveillance protocols should be rigorously followed to ensure the reliability of the data obtained.

1.5.1.3 Specific Pathogen-Free (SPF) Animals

Specific Pathogen-Free (SPF) animals are laboratory animals that are free from a defined list of harmful pathogens, including bacteria, viruses, parasites, and fungi, which are known to interfere with animal physiology, immune response, and experimental outcomes. These animals are not germ-free but are maintained under controlled conditions that prevent the introduction and spread of particular infectious agents. SPF status is essential in pharmacological and toxicological research to ensure consistency, reliability, and reproducibility of experimental data by eliminating variables introduced by subclinical infections.

The list of pathogens excluded in SPF colonies is defined by each facility or supplier based on the species being housed and the nature of the research. For example, in SPF mice and rats, common excluded pathogens include mouse hepatitis virus (MHV), Sendai virus, Mycoplasma pulmonis, mouse parvovirus, pinworms, and ectoparasites. These organisms, even if not overtly symptomatic, can cause immunosuppression, altered metabolism, inflammation, or respiratory compromise, all of which may significantly confound pharmacological responses.

SPF animals are bred and housed under barrier conditions in specialized animal facilities equipped with HEPA-filtered air supply, airlocks, restricted personnel access, sterilized food and bedding, and individually ventilated cages (IVCs). Strict biosecurity protocols are enforced to prevent contamination, including the use of personal protective equipment (PPE), shower-in/out practices, sterilization of materials entering the facility, and designated work zones.

To maintain SPF status, routine health surveillance is conducted using sentinel animals, serological assays, polymerase chain reaction (PCR), and microbiological cultures. Sentinels are exposed to soiled bedding from other cages and are monitored for signs of infection. If a pathogen is detected, the colony may be quarantined, rederived via embryo transfer or hysterectomy, or subjected to eradication protocols to eliminate the infection and restore SPF conditions.

The use of SPF animals is particularly important in immunological studies, cancer research, and vaccine trials, where hidden infections can skew immune parameters and compromise results. In toxicology studies, infections can alter hepatic enzyme activity, immune markers, or body weight, leading to misleading safety or efficacy interpretations. SPF conditions also reduce mortality, improve breeding performance, and minimize variability in long-term studies such as chronic toxicity or lifespan evaluations.

Despite their advantages, SPF colonies are expensive to maintain and require highly trained personnel, rigorous documentation, and continuous facility monitoring. Breaches in biosecurity can lead to rapid spread of pathogens and necessitate costly decontamination procedures. Therefore, facilities must adopt standard operating procedures (SOPs) for animal handling, cage changing, waste disposal, and emergency response.

1.5.2 Nutrition, Disease Control, and Health Monitoring

Balanced Diet Requirements

A nutritionally balanced diet is a critical component in the care and maintenance of laboratory animals, directly impacting their growth, reproduction, immune function, response to drugs, and overall well-being. In research settings, animals must be provided with standardized and quality-controlled feed that meets their species-specific physiological and metabolic needs. Inadequate or imbalanced nutrition can result in altered experimental outcomes, increased morbidity, and compromised animal welfare, making diet formulation a vital part of laboratory animal science.

The basic dietary components for most laboratory animals—such as mice, rats, rabbits, guinea pigs, and dogs—include appropriate proportions of carbohydrates, proteins, fats, vitamins, minerals, and fiber. Commercially prepared pelleted diets are commonly used and are designed to provide complete nutrition with minimal batch-to-batch variability. These are often sterilized by irradiation or autoclaving to maintain hygienic standards, especially in SPF or barrier-maintained colonies.

In rodents, the typical diet contains 18–22% protein, 4–6% fat, 3–5% fiber, and the remaining fraction comprises digestible carbohydrates and essential micronutrients. Protein is sourced from casein or plant-based proteins and supports tissue repair, enzyme function, and immune responses. Fats, often from vegetable oils or fish oil, are essential for energy metabolism and fat-soluble vitamin absorption. Fiber helps maintain gut motility and microbiota balance, while vitamins like A, D, E, K, B-complex, and minerals such as calcium, phosphorus, zinc, iron, and magnesium are included to support enzymatic and structural functions.

Species-specific requirements must also be considered. Guinea pigs, for example, lack the enzyme to synthesize vitamin C and require its supplementation in the diet (usually around 10 mg/kg/day for adults). Rabbits need higher fiber content to prevent gastrointestinal stasis, and carnivorous species like ferrets require higher protein and fat content than rodents. In pregnancy and lactation, animals may need increased calories and nutrient density to support fetal development and milk production.

Proper storage and handling of feed are also crucial. Feed should be kept in sealed containers in a cool, dry, and pest-free environment to prevent degradation of nutrients, especially sensitive ones like vitamins A and C. Feed should be used before the manufacturer's expiry date, and any signs of mold, foul odor, or discoloration should lead to immediate disposal.

Water is another essential component of animal nutrition. Clean, fresh, and uncontaminated water should be available ad libitum, delivered through bottles, automated systems, or sipper tubes. Water may be acidified, chlorinated, or autoclaved in high-level biosecure colonies to prevent microbial growth. Water quality parameters like pH, hardness, microbial load, and contaminants should be monitored regularly as per institutional standards.

In studies involving metabolic, endocrine, or nutritional interventions, customized diets are used to test specific hypotheses. These may include high-fat diets, low-protein diets, cholesterol-rich feeds, or diets deficient in particular vitamins or minerals. All such modifications must be approved by the Institutional Animal Ethics Committee (IAEC), and animals must be closely monitored for any adverse effects.

Preventive Health Care: Vaccination, Deworming

Preventive health care in laboratory animals is essential for maintaining disease-free colonies, supporting animal welfare, and ensuring the reliability of experimental data. It includes a proactive approach to controlling infections and parasitic infestations that may compromise physiological stability or interfere with pharmacological and toxicological responses. Two key components of preventive health programs in laboratory settings are vaccination and deworming, though their application varies depending on the species, facility biosecurity level, and intended research use.

In small laboratory animals such as mice, rats, and guinea pigs, vaccination is generally not practiced as a routine measure in Specific Pathogen-Free (SPF) or barrier-maintained colonies. These animals are housed in highly controlled environments with stringent biosecurity, filtered air systems, sterilized bedding and food, and regular health surveillance, which minimizes exposure to infectious agents. However, for larger animals such as rabbits, dogs, pigs, and non-human primates, vaccination becomes more relevant and is applied based on institutional protocols and species-specific disease risks.

For example, non-human primates may be vaccinated against tetanus, measles, rabies, and tuberculosis, especially when they are involved in long-term studies or are housed in outdoor or semi-conventional facilities. Dogs may receive vaccines against canine distemper, parvovirus, adenovirus, and leptospirosis, while rabbits in certain regions may be vaccinated against rabbit hemorrhagic disease virus (RHDV). The vaccination schedule is developed in consultation with a laboratory animal veterinarian, and all vaccinations are documented in individual animal health records, including batch number, date of administration, dose, route, and site.

Deworming is a routine preventive measure in all animal colonies, especially those maintained in conventional or semi-barrier facilities. Parasitic infections—whether gastrointestinal or systemic—can adversely affect growth rate, immune response, organ function, and metabolism, potentially leading to variability in experimental results. Common parasites in laboratory animals include pinworms (Syphacia spp., Aspiculuris spp.), tapeworms, roundworms, and protozoa such as Giardia and Eimeria.

Deworming is typically done using broad-spectrum antiparasitic drugs such as albendazole, fenbendazole, ivermectin, or praziquantel, administered orally via feed, water, or direct gavage. For rodents, fenbendazole at 150 ppm in the feed for 5 to 7 days is a common regimen for pinworm control. In larger animals, drugs are dosed individually based on body weight and repeated at defined intervals (e.g., every 3 to 6 months) or as indicated by fecal examination results. Deworming is often paired with fecal flotation or PCR-based diagnostics to monitor parasitic load and effectiveness of treatment.

All preventive health care measures must be part of a written health management protocol approved by the Institutional Animal Ethics Committee (IAEC). Veterinary oversight is essential to adjust treatment plans based on emerging disease trends, animal response, and environmental conditions. Preventive measures should be coupled with good husbandry practices, including cage sanitation, proper waste disposal, pest control, and personal hygiene of caretakers, to ensure long-term health stability in the colony.

Routine Screening and Quarantine

Routine screening and quarantine are foundational elements of preventive health management in laboratory animal facilities. These procedures are critical for ensuring that only healthy animals, free from unwanted pathogens, are introduced into the research environment. By identifying infections at an early stage and preventing their spread, routine health screening and quarantine contribute directly to the integrity of experimental data, animal welfare, and biosafety compliance.

Routine screening involves periodic health monitoring of animals already housed within the facility. It includes clinical observation, microbiological testing, parasitological examination, and serological assays to detect bacterial, viral, fungal, and parasitic infections. Depending on the facility's biosafety level and the species involved, tests are performed on either a representative sample of animals or on sentinel animals. These sentinels are placed in strategic cage positions and are exposed to soiled bedding from the rest of the colony to detect subclinical infections. Common pathogens screened in rodent colonies include mouse hepatitis virus (MHV), Sendai virus, Mycoplasma pulmonis, mouse norovirus, parvoviruses, and pinworms.

Diagnostic techniques used in routine screening include polymerase chain reaction (PCR) for pathogen DNA, enzyme-linked immunosorbent assay (ELISA) for antibody detection, and culture-based methods for bacterial and fungal identification. Fecal samples are examined microscopically for helminth eggs and protozoan cysts. Testing is done at regular intervals—often quarterly or semi-annually—and any positive finding prompts immediate veterinary evaluation and may lead to treatment, isolation, or culling of affected animals.

Quarantine is the process of isolating newly arrived animals for a defined period, typically 2 to 4 weeks, before introducing them into the main animal colony. This time allows for acclimatization, health status assessment, and detection of any latent infections that might compromise the health of the existing colony. Quarantine is mandatory for animals sourced from other institutions, vendors, or non-SPF environments. During this period, animals are housed in separate rooms or units with independent airflow systems, and caretakers follow dedicated entry procedures to avoid cross-contamination.

Veterinary staff monitor quarantined animals for signs of illness, perform baseline health screenings (including fecal tests and serology), and evaluate any abnormalities in behavior, feeding, or appearance. If the animals are found healthy and free of pathogens, they are certified for entry into the main colony. If infection is detected, the animals may be treated, rederived (using embryo transfer), or excluded, depending on the facility's policies and scientific necessity.

A well-documented quarantine logbook must be maintained, recording the date of entry, source, species, purpose, test results, treatments (if any), and clearance date. Quarantine protocols must be reviewed and approved by the Institutional Animal Ethics Committee (IAEC), and the process must comply with CPCSEA or international standards.

In SPF and high-containment facilities, quarantine and routine screening are non-negotiable for maintaining pathogen-free status. These procedures not only protect animal colonies but also safeguard human handlers and researchers from zoonotic infections.

1.5.3 Record Keeping and Animal Facility Roles

Breeding Logs and Animal Census

Accurate and systematic record keeping is the backbone of effective animal facility management. Two of the most essential documents maintained in any research animal house are the breeding logs and the animal census. These records are not only vital for ensuring animal welfare and scientific consistency but also serve as compliance tools during audits by regulatory bodies like the CPCSEA, as well as during internal reviews and quality assurance checks.

Breeding logs are detailed records that track all breeding activities within the facility. They include information on parental identity, strain, genotype, date of mating, litter size, date of birth, number of pups born alive or dead, sex distribution, weaning date, and genotyping results. Each mating pair is assigned a unique identification number or cage number, and their performance over time is monitored for reproductive efficiency, frequency of successful litters, and health of offspring. This helps in identifying underperforming breeders, planning future matings, and maintaining the genetic integrity of inbred or transgenic lines.

For genetically modified animals, breeding logs must also record genotype outcomes, PCR or sequencing results, and whether the offspring meet the required genetic profile for experimental use. This level of detail is especially critical in maintaining colonies with conditional alleles, humanized genes, or knock-in/knock-out models, where precise genetic tracking is essential. Breeding data is usually maintained in digital software systems, though physical registers are also kept for redundancy and regulatory review.

Animal census is a dynamic and regularly updated record that reflects the total number of animals in the facility, categorized by species, strain, sex, age group, and housing location. The census helps in tracking animal utilization, projecting future space and resource needs, and complying with ethical approvals. The monthly or quarterly census reports submitted to the IAEC and CPCSEA include details of animals born, procured, used, euthanized, and remaining in stock, along with reasons for any unusual changes in numbers.

Each animal or group must be tagged or labeled clearly using ear tags, microchips, cage cards, or tattooing, depending on the species and facility standards. Cage cards serve as quick-access information tools, displaying animal strain, sex, birth date, genotype, project code, and the name of the principal investigator. These tags must be regularly cross-verified with log entries to avoid discrepancies.

Both breeding logs and census data are essential during protocol review processes, especially when the number of animals proposed for a study is being compared with actual usage. Discrepancies may lead to ethical concerns or suspicions of unauthorized use, hence regular and transparent documentation is essential. The data also helps in implementing the 3Rs principle by allowing efficient planning of breeding to avoid surplus or wastage.

In addition to regulatory purposes, accurate record keeping supports disease outbreak investigations, pedigree analysis, colony performance reviews, and grant audits. Institutions are encouraged to adopt centralized digital management systems to integrate breeding, census, health records, and usage logs in one platform, improving traceability, accountability, and operational efficiency.

Use of Software and Electronic Records

The adoption of software-based systems and electronic record-keeping in laboratory animal facilities has significantly enhanced the accuracy, efficiency, and transparency of animal management. As research environments become increasingly data-driven, digital tools provide a robust framework for maintaining essential records such as breeding logs, animal census, health surveillance, experimental tracking, protocol approvals, and inventory management, all while ensuring regulatory compliance and data integrity.

Modern Laboratory Animal Management Software (LAMS) platforms allow centralized and real-time tracking of all animal-related activities. These systems can record and retrieve detailed information about individual animals or entire colonies, including strain, sex, age, genotype, health status, breeding performance, and experimental use history.

Commonly used software solutions include LabTracks, Mosaic Vivarium, PyRat, Tick@Lab, eSirius, and Caliber Animal Facility Management System. Institutions may also develop custom in-house software tailored to their specific workflows and regulatory requirements.

One of the core features of these systems is the automated generation of breeding logs and genotype records. After each mating, the system can predict expected litter genotypes based on parental genetic makeup, issue alerts for upcoming weaning dates, and track animal performance across generations. For transgenic colonies, PCR results and gel images can be uploaded and linked to each animal's profile for easy reference and audit purposes.

Electronic animal census tools simplify the routine task of maintaining and updating population counts. These tools can auto-calculate births, deaths, euthanasia, and transfers across rooms or facilities. Scheduled reminders and alerts for events such as cage changes, health checks, and vaccinations help streamline animal care activities and reduce errors. The system also enables direct comparison of planned vs. actual animal usage, supporting both ethical accountability and resource planning.

Protocol management modules within these systems integrate with the Institutional Animal Ethics Committee (IAEC) workflow, allowing researchers to submit new protocols, request amendments, and report animal usage against approved limits. This minimizes paperwork, ensures regulatory timelines are met, and facilitates traceable, time-stamped documentation for compliance with CPCSEA and other global standards.

Health records, including quarantine details, medical treatments, anesthesia logs, euthanasia reports, and diagnostic results, are easily recorded and retrieved through searchable databases. Veterinarians and facility managers can use dashboards to monitor colony health, generate reports for audits, and make evidence-based decisions regarding treatment or colony culling.

A key advantage of electronic systems is the security and backup of data. Most platforms offer role-based access control, data encryption, cloud backups, and audit trails to ensure that records are tamper-proof and accessible only to authorized personnel. These features are essential for maintaining data integrity during regulatory inspections, funding audits, or GLP-compliant studies.

Integration of software systems with barcode scanners, RFID tagging, electronic cage cards, and environmental monitoring devices further enhances automation and accuracy. RFID-enabled systems, for instance, allow automatic tracking of animal movements and cage-level details without manual data entry.

Training in the use of electronic record systems is essential for all animal facility personnel, including animal caretakers, researchers, and administrative staff. Institutions should implement standard operating procedures (SOPs) to define workflows, ensure consistency in data entry, and establish responsibilities for updating and reviewing electronic records.

Responsibilities of Animal House Facility In-Charge

The Animal House Facility In-Charge holds a central role in overseeing all operational, ethical, and scientific aspects of the animal facility. This position is responsible for ensuring that all animal care and use activities are conducted in accordance with institutional guidelines, national regulatory standards such as those issued by CPCSEA, and international best practices. The In-Charge acts as a key liaison between investigators, technical staff, veterinary personnel, and the Institutional Animal Ethics Committee, ensuring seamless communication and proper implementation of animal care protocols.

The primary responsibility involves maintaining the overall functioning of the animal facility. This includes supervision of day-to-day activities such as animal husbandry, cage sanitation, feeding schedules, breeding management, and environmental monitoring. The In-Charge must ensure that housing conditions—such as temperature, humidity, ventilation, light-dark cycles, noise levels, and cleanliness—remain within the recommended parameters for each species. Regular checks must be conducted to verify that environmental parameters are being monitored and recorded properly through either manual or automated systems.

Another major duty is the coordination of animal procurement and quarantine procedures. The In-Charge must review all animal procurement requests, verify vendor certifications, check transport conditions, and ensure quarantine protocols are enforced before animals are introduced into the main colony. During the quarantine period, animals are monitored for clinical symptoms, and health screening tests are carried out. Only animals that meet specific pathogen-free standards or health clearance criteria may be admitted to the colony.

Breeding program oversight is an essential task, especially when maintaining transgenic or inbred lines. The In-Charge must develop breeding plans based on project requirements, colony performance, and genotype needs. Responsibilities include assigning breeding pairs, managing weaning schedules, ensuring proper genotyping, and avoiding inbreeding depression or genetic drift. All breeding records must be reviewed periodically for accuracy and trends in productivity.

Maintaining comprehensive records is another critical responsibility. The In-Charge must ensure the integrity of breeding logs, animal census, euthanasia registers, health records, treatment logs, and IAEC-approved protocol documentation. These records are necessary for internal reviews and must be readily available during CPCSEA inspections, GLP audits, or funding agency evaluations. In facilities using electronic software, the In-Charge is accountable for access control, data backup, and staff training in system usage.

Veterinary care coordination is also under the purview of the In-Charge. This includes reporting animal illness or distress to the attending veterinarian, assisting in health evaluations, implementing treatment plans, and managing isolation of infected animals. Preventive care programs, including vaccination, deworming, and routine health surveillance, are carried out under the supervision of the In-Charge. If unexpected morbidity or mortality occurs, the In-Charge must initiate post-mortem analysis, document the findings, and report the outcome to the relevant authorities.

The In-Charge plays a vital role in facilitating research by assisting investigators in planning experimental animal use. This includes advising on animal models, anaesthesia protocols, surgical techniques, and humane endpoints. All protocols submitted to the IAEC are reviewed by the In-Charge for logistical feasibility, resource availability, and ethical alignment before they are forwarded for committee review. During the study, the In-Charge monitors animal usage to ensure it does not exceed the approved numbers and that the animals are treated according to ethical standards.

Personnel training and supervision is another key area. The In-Charge is responsible for the initial and ongoing training of animal caretakers, researchers, and technical staff in areas such as species-specific handling, restraint techniques, anaesthesia, euthanasia, and record keeping. Refresher training on ethical guidelines, biosafety, and emergency protocols must also be arranged at regular intervals.

Facility maintenance and biosecurity management fall directly under the In-Charge's duties. This includes ensuring that all equipment such as biosafety cabinets, ventilated racks, sterilizers, and air handling systems are regularly calibrated and functional. Any breakdown or hazard must be reported and addressed without delay. Waste disposal, pest control, and cleaning schedules must be implemented consistently to prevent disease outbreaks or contamination.

The In-Charge is also involved in preparing the facility for external reviews and regulatory inspections. This includes organizing records, arranging site tours, answering technical questions, and implementing corrective actions as recommended by auditors. The In-Charge must submit monthly or quarterly reports to the IAEC and keep management informed about inventory status, animal usage trends, and any deviations from approved protocols.

In all aspects, the Animal House Facility In-Charge is expected to uphold the principles of replacement, reduction, and refinement. The position requires not only technical expertise but also ethical sensitivity, organizational skills, and the ability to coordinate multidisciplinary teams to ensure that animal research is conducted responsibly, efficiently, and in full compliance with legal and scientific expectations.

1.6.1 Composition and Functions of IAEC and CPCSEA

Institutional Animal Ethics Committee: Roles and Structure

The Institutional Animal Ethics Committee (IAEC) is the primary regulatory body within an institution that is responsible for overseeing and approving all activities involving the use of laboratory animals for research, teaching, or testing purposes. As mandated by the Committee for the Purpose of Control and Supervision of Experiments on Animals (CPCSEA), every registered establishment that uses animals for experimental purposes must constitute an IAEC. This committee ensures that all animal experiments comply with national ethical standards, legal requirements, and scientific validity.

The structure of the IAEC is defined by CPCSEA guidelines and comprises a multidisciplinary team to maintain transparency, scientific integrity, and ethical oversight. A typical IAEC includes the following members:

Chairperson: Appointed by the institution, preferably not directly involved in animal experimentation, to provide an impartial viewpoint and guide policy decisions.

Member Secretary: Usually the veterinarian or senior scientist who coordinates IAEC meetings and maintains records, correspondence, and reporting.

Biological Scientist: A subject expert in the biological sciences who evaluates the scientific merit of research proposals.

Scientist from a Different Discipline: A researcher from outside the field of biological sciences to provide cross-disciplinary insights.

Veterinarian: A registered veterinary professional responsible for evaluating animal welfare, assessing anaesthesia and euthanasia protocols, and providing input on species-appropriate care.

Non-Scientific Socially Aware Member: A layperson, such as a representative from a non-governmental organization (NGO) or a community leader, who ensures societal concerns and ethical issues are addressed.

CPCSEA Nominee: A representative appointed by CPCSEA who acts as an external observer and enforces compliance with national guidelines.

Scientist-in-Charge of the Animal Facility (optional): May be included to represent operational feasibility, housing, and health management concerns.

The role of the IAEC is multi-dimensional and extends across ethical review, procedural supervision, and compliance enforcement. Its core function is to review and approve all research proposals involving animals before any work begins. During the review process, the IAEC evaluates:

Scientific rationale and justification for using animals

Number of animals requested and statistical validity of the sample size

Species and strain selection and their appropriateness to the study

Experimental procedures, including surgery, dosing, sampling, and endpoints

Pain and distress assessment, anaesthesia, analgesia, and euthanasia plans

Alternatives to animal use, as per the 3Rs principle—Replacement, Reduction, and Refinement

Facility preparedness in terms of housing, equipment, and trained staff

The IAEC meets at regular intervals, generally once every two to three months, or more frequently if needed, to review new proposals, renewals, amendments, and to monitor ongoing projects. Each approved protocol is assigned a unique IAEC approval number and is valid for a fixed period, typically one year, after which renewal must be requested if the work continues.

In addition to protocol review, the IAEC is also responsible for conducting periodic inspections of the animal facility to verify that housing conditions, record-keeping, animal handling, and care standards meet regulatory norms. The committee also investigates protocol violations, unauthorized animal usage, and deviations from approved procedures. Recommendations made by the IAEC must be implemented promptly, and non-compliance can lead to suspension or revocation of animal research privileges.

The IAEC maintains comprehensive records of all meetings, approvals, adverse events, facility inspections, and correspondence with CPCSEA. These records are subject to periodic audits by CPCSEA inspectors and must be retained for official review. Annual progress reports summarizing all animal usage, protocol approvals, and training programs must be submitted to CPCSEA as part of regulatory compliance.

CPCSEA: Central Regulatory Body and Its Mandate

The Committee for the Purpose of Control and Supervision of Experiments on Animals (CPCSEA) is the central statutory body in India responsible for overseeing, regulating, and ensuring the ethical use of animals in scientific research, education, and testing. It functions under the Department of Animal Husbandry and Dairying, Ministry of Fisheries, Animal Husbandry and Dairying, Government of India. The CPCSEA derives its authority from the Prevention of Cruelty to Animals Act, 1960, which empowers it to establish rules, inspect facilities, and enforce compliance with animal welfare standards in institutions involved in animal experimentation across the country.

The primary mandate of CPCSEA is to ensure that animals used for experimentation are not subjected to unnecessary pain or suffering and that their use is scientifically justified, humane, and ethically responsible. To fulfill this mandate, the committee has laid down a comprehensive set of rules and guidelines applicable to all registered institutions. These guidelines cover every aspect of laboratory animal management, including procurement, transportation, housing, feeding, health care, breeding, experimentation, and euthanasia.

One of the major responsibilities of CPCSEA is the registration of establishments that intend to use animals for research or education. Institutions are required to submit detailed applications with information about their animal facilities, personnel qualifications, proposed research areas, and ethical protocols. Once approved, institutions receive a CPCSEA registration number, which is mandatory for conducting any form of animal experimentation legally in India.

CPCSEA also mandates the constitution of Institutional Animal Ethics Committees (IAECs) in all registered establishments. These committees function as internal regulatory bodies that review and approve protocols before any experiment involving animals can commence. The CPCSEA appoints a nominee member to each IAEC to ensure impartial monitoring and compliance with national guidelines. No animal experiment can proceed without the formal approval of IAEC, and every protocol must strictly follow the 3Rs principle—Replacement, Reduction, and Refinement.

The CPCSEA conducts regular inspections of animal houses to verify that animal care practices conform to prescribed standards. These inspections evaluate the physical infrastructure, housing conditions, animal health records, breeding practices, feed quality, staff training, and adherence to approved experimental procedures. Institutions are required to maintain meticulous documentation, which is reviewed during inspections. Non-compliance with CPCSEA norms can lead to suspension of registration, prohibition of animal usage, or legal action under the Prevention of Cruelty to Animals Act.

Training and awareness are another important focus area of CPCSEA. It conducts workshops, refresher courses, and certification programs for scientists, veterinarians, technicians, and animal caretakers to ensure that everyone involved in animal research is aware of their ethical responsibilities. These programs emphasize humane handling, anaesthesia and analgesia, euthanasia techniques, and alternatives to animal use wherever possible.

CPCSEA has also introduced guidelines for the classification of experiments based on the level of pain and distress caused to animals. Categories range from procedures that cause no pain or discomfort to those that cause severe distress. Each category has specific ethical requirements, and experiments in higher severity categories are subject to more rigorous scrutiny and justification.

In addition, the CPCSEA periodically updates its policies to reflect advancements in science and global ethical standards. It encourages the use of alternatives to animal experimentation such as in vitro models, computer simulations, and organ-on-chip technologies whenever feasible. It collaborates with international regulatory bodies and aligns its policies with global frameworks like those of the OECD, AAALAC, and ICLAS.

In essence, CPCSEA acts as the national guardian of laboratory animal welfare in India. Its mandate extends beyond mere compliance enforcement to fostering a culture of responsible science where the dignity and well-being of animals are respected, and scientific progress is achieved through ethically sound practices. Every institution, investigator, and caretaker working with laboratory animals is accountable to CPCSEA's rules, which are designed to balance the needs of science with the imperative of compassion.

1.6.2 Ethical and Legal Framework

Categories of Experiments (A to D)

The ethical and legal framework governing animal experimentation in India is structured under the Prevention of Cruelty to Animals (PCA) Act, 1960, as enforced by the CPCSEA. One of the core components of this framework is the categorization of experiments based on the level of pain and distress anticipated in animals during scientific procedures. These categories, labelled from A to D, are used by Institutional Animal Ethics Committees (IAECs) to evaluate and approve protocols appropriately. This classification system ensures that ethical oversight is aligned with the severity of the intervention, and that adequate safeguards, including pain management and humane endpoints, are applied.

Category A includes experiments that are virtually painless and non-invasive, causing no distress or discomfort to the animal. These may involve activities such as observational studies, routine behavioral analysis, collection of excreta (urine, feces) without any handling stress, or environmental enrichment studies. Animals used in this category remain fully conscious, unharmed, and are not subjected to any form of surgical or chemical intervention. Such studies are typically approved with minimal ethical concern, though proper housing and handling must still be ensured.

Category B involves procedures that cause mild pain or stress of short duration. Examples include mild restraint, non-invasive imaging, blood sampling from peripheral veins, injection of non-irritating substances, or oral gavage of test compounds at non-toxic doses. While these procedures may result in transient discomfort, they are generally reversible and do not impair the animal's health or welfare significantly. Investigators are required to monitor animals for behavioral changes and ensure recovery within a short timeframe. Analgesics are typically not needed in this category, but their availability is recommended in case of individual sensitivity.

Category C includes studies that are likely to cause moderate to severe pain or distress, which may be temporary or prolonged. This category covers surgical interventions, inoculation with pathogens, induction of chronic disease models, toxicological testing at high doses, or procedures requiring anesthesia or prolonged restraint. Protocols under this category must include detailed plans for anaesthesia, analgesia, post-operative care, and humane endpoints. Investigators must justify the necessity of such procedures and explain why alternatives (such as non-animal models or lower categories) cannot be used. These protocols undergo rigorous review by the IAEC and CPCSEA nominee and require strict adherence to the 3Rs principle.

Category D encompasses experiments that cause severe pain, suffering, or distress that cannot be relieved. These include procedures where animals may experience unrelieved pain due to scientific constraints, such as terminal disease models, lethal dose determinations (LD50), or organ harvest under minimal anaesthesia. Experiments in this category are considered only under exceptional circumstances, and the scientific justification must be very strong. CPCSEA mandates that the number of animals used be minimized, and that investigators explore every possible refinement to reduce suffering. Detailed monitoring plans, veterinary oversight, and reporting protocols are mandatory for such experiments. Often, these proposals are subject to additional scrutiny and may require direct CPCSEA approval, beyond institutional clearance.

Each experiment submitted to the IAEC must clearly state the proposed category and provide scientific and ethical justification for the same. This categorization allows IAECs to assess protocols more objectively and helps ensure that appropriate ethical safeguards are built into the study design. It also promotes accountability and transparency in the use of laboratory animals and ensures that procedures causing higher degrees of distress are minimized, justified, and carefully monitored.

This framework is also essential during inspections by CPCSEA and external agencies. All categorized experiments must be properly documented, and post-approval monitoring must be carried out to ensure that the actual severity matches the proposed severity. Any deviation must be reported, and corrective measures should be implemented immediately.

By classifying experiments based on their ethical severity, the CPCSEA ensures a tiered review system that balances scientific necessity with humane responsibility, thus reinforcing ethical standards across all institutions conducting animal-based research in India.

Proposals Requiring CPCSEA vs IAEC Approval

All research proposals involving animals must undergo a defined approval process before the commencement of any experimental procedure. This process is guided by the regulatory framework established under the Prevention of Cruelty to Animals Act, 1960, and enforced by the Committee for the Purpose of Control and Supervision of Experiments on Animals. Depending on the type of experiment, the species used, and the severity of procedures involved, the responsibility of approval lies either with the Institutional Animal Ethics Committee or directly with the CPCSEA.

Proposals involving common laboratory species such as mice, rats, guinea pigs, rabbits, and hamsters for academic research and routine pharmacological or toxicological studies are generally reviewed and approved at the institutional level by the IAEC. These include protocols falling under categories A, B, or C where procedures involve minimal to moderate pain or distress, provided that anaesthesia and humane endpoints are included. Such proposals must be scientifically justified and ethically compliant with the CPCSEA's standard guidelines. The IAEC has the authority to evaluate, approve, monitor, and suggest modifications to these protocols. Approval letters are issued at the institutional level and must be retained for record and inspection.

However, proposals involving higher-order species such as dogs, cats, pigs, non-human primates, or any large animals used for experimentation require direct CPCSEA approval. These animals are considered more sentient and ethically sensitive, and their use is restricted to only essential biomedical research with strong scientific justification. The IAEC can only perform the preliminary review and forward such proposals to the CPCSEA for final approval. The central committee evaluates the purpose, sample size, methodology, welfare measures, and available alternatives before granting permission. Experiments involving category D procedures—those that cause severe pain or unrelieved distress—also require CPCSEA clearance regardless of the species involved. This ensures that the highest ethical oversight is applied to the most invasive or potentially harmful procedures.

In addition, protocols involving regulatory toxicity testing such as repeated dose toxicity, reproductive toxicity, carcinogenicity studies, or any long-term safety evaluations required by national or international regulatory bodies must be forwarded to CPCSEA. These studies often involve large sample sizes, prolonged observation, and irreversible endpoints, hence central level evaluation is essential.

Educational institutions intending to use animals for teaching demonstrations are also required to submit proposals to CPCSEA through the IAEC. Demonstrations involving vertebrate dissection, pharmacological effects, or biological assays must receive specific approval for each academic year, and institutions are encouraged to use alternatives such as computer simulations or models wherever possible.

Amendments to approved protocols, deviations from approved procedures, or extension of study duration beyond the sanctioned period must also be reviewed either by the IAEC or referred to CPCSEA depending on the severity of the proposed changes. Institutions are required to maintain a clear register of all proposals, their category classification, approval status, and correspondence with CPCSEA for transparency and audit readiness.

This tiered system of approval allows for efficient management of animal use in research, where commonly practiced, low-risk procedures are expedited at the institutional level while ethically complex or high-risk experiments are scrutinized at the national level by CPCSEA. This ensures balance between scientific advancement and ethical responsibility in all animal research conducted across the country.

1.6.3 Approval Process and Documentation

Protocol Submission Format

Before initiating any scientific experiment involving animals, researchers must submit a well-defined protocol to the Institutional Animal Ethics Committee in the prescribed format approved by the Committee for the Purpose of Control and Supervision of Experiments on Animals. This format ensures that all necessary ethical, scientific, and logistical aspects of the proposed work are reviewed systematically and in compliance with national regulatory standards. The protocol submission format is standardized across institutions to maintain uniformity in ethical review and documentation.

The protocol submission begins with basic administrative details including the title of the project, name of the principal investigator, departmental affiliation, contact information, duration of the study, and whether the proposal is new or a continuation. It also asks whether the work is part of an academic thesis, a government-funded project, industrial testing, or a regulatory requirement.

A detailed scientific rationale is required next, explaining the objective of the study, the hypothesis being tested, and the expected outcome. This section should also include references to past research and a justification for why animal experimentation is necessary. Investigators must clearly state whether any alternatives such as in vitro systems, computer modelling, or human tissue-based methods were considered and why they were not applicable.

The format requires a complete description of the animals to be used, including species, strain, sex, age, weight range, source of procurement, and the number of animals needed for each group. A justification for the total number of animals is essential and should be based on statistical analysis such as power calculation, where applicable. The housing and husbandry conditions proposed for the animals should also be specified, including cage type, bedding, environmental conditions, diet, and water source.

A comprehensive methodology section is expected, detailing the procedures the animals will undergo, including dosing schedules, surgical interventions, behavioural testing, sample collection, and the use of instruments or devices. This section must describe the route of administration, frequency, volume, and any substances being administered. For surgical or painful procedures, details of anaesthesia, analgesia, post-operative care, and monitoring schedules must be provided. Investigators are required to list the category of the experiment (A to D) based on the anticipated level of pain or distress, and to define humane endpoints where applicable.

The euthanasia method must be described in accordance with CPCSEA guidelines. The method selected should be appropriate for the species, and confirmation of death must be specified. The fate of animals after the experiment—whether euthanized, re-used, or rehomed—must be recorded.

Investigators must declare the personnel involved in animal handling, surgical procedures, or data collection. Their qualifications, experience with the species involved, and training in laboratory animal techniques must be indicated. The format also includes a declaration by the principal investigator affirming that the protocol adheres to the 3Rs principle and that no procedure will begin without prior approval.

The IAEC reviews the protocol using this format, often along with annexures such as grant approvals, previous IAEC clearances, or study designs. If higher species or category D procedures are involved, the protocol is forwarded to CPCSEA for central approval. Once approved, a protocol number and approval validity period are issued, and a copy of the approved form must be retained in the laboratory and made available for inspection during audits.

This structured format ensures that every ethical and scientific consideration is addressed before animals are involved, promoting responsible research and compliance with national regulatory expectations.

Monitoring and Reporting During and After Experiments

Monitoring and reporting are essential components of ethical animal experimentation. They ensure that animal welfare is protected throughout the course of the study and that any deviation from approved protocols is immediately addressed. The Institutional Animal Ethics Committee, under the guidance of CPCSEA, mandates regular and documented oversight during and after the conduct of experiments to uphold scientific credibility and humane standards.

Once an animal study is initiated, continuous monitoring must be carried out by the research team and the animal facility staff. This includes daily observation of all animals for signs of pain, distress, illness, abnormal behaviour, surgical complications, or unexpected mortality. Parameters such as body weight, food and water intake, posture, mobility, grooming habits, and clinical signs like laboured breathing or discharge from eyes or nose must be closely observed. These observations are recorded systematically in laboratory animal monitoring sheets, which become part of the permanent project file.

If animals undergo surgical or invasive procedures, additional post-operative monitoring is mandatory. This includes assessing the surgical site for infection, monitoring recovery from anaesthesia, and documenting administration of analgesics or antibiotics. Pain scoring systems may be used to quantify discomfort and determine whether additional intervention is required. For studies with long durations or progressive disease models, animals should be monitored at predefined intervals and humane endpoints should be clearly followed to avoid unnecessary suffering.

Any adverse events or unanticipated findings—such as early deaths, abnormal reactions to test substances, or unexpected distress—must be reported immediately to the Institutional Animal Ethics Committee through an adverse event reporting format. The IAEC may then recommend modifications to the protocol, additional veterinary oversight, or even early termination of the study if deemed necessary.

At the conclusion of the study, the principal investigator must submit a completion report to the IAEC. This report includes the actual number of animals used, the number of animals that were euthanized, died naturally, or were excluded from the study, and whether the objectives of the study were met as planned. Any deviations from the approved protocol, including changes in dosing, sample collection, or surgical approach, must be clearly documented and justified. If euthanasia was performed, the method used and confirmation of death should be mentioned in detail.

Records of monitoring and reporting must be maintained for inspection by CPCSEA, IAEC reviewers, and institutional auditors. These records serve not only as a tool for animal welfare assurance but also as critical documentation supporting the transparency, reproducibility, and ethical conduct of the research.

Regular review and monitoring by the IAEC also include random facility visits, interviews with personnel, and evaluation of experimental logs. In long-term or high-risk studies, the IAEC may assign specific members or veterinarians to carry out focused post-approval monitoring. Findings from such reviews are documented and may be submitted to CPCSEA in the form of annual progress reports or during registration renewal.

Overall, effective monitoring and transparent reporting ensure that the research stays aligned with approved objectives, animal welfare is consistently prioritised, and institutions demonstrate full compliance with both scientific and ethical responsibilities.

1.6.4 Do's and Don'ts in Animal Research

Legal and Ethical Conduct of Research

Legal and ethical conduct forms the backbone of all animal research, ensuring that animals are treated humanely, experimental data remain scientifically valid, and the institution remains in compliance with national and international regulations. The CPCSEA mandates that all individuals involved in animal research—scientists, technicians, veterinarians, and caretakers—must strictly adhere to predefined rules, practices, and behavioural standards throughout the experimental process.

Before initiating any study, it is legally required that the researcher obtain prior approval from the Institutional Animal Ethics Committee. No animal experiment may be started, modified, or extended without written permission. This includes changes in sample size, route of administration, dosage, duration of exposure, or any procedure that could alter the approved protocol. Failure to comply with this requirement constitutes a legal violation and may result in suspension of research privileges or cancellation of project funding.

Ethically, researchers must uphold the principle of scientific necessity, meaning that the use of animals is justified only when no suitable alternative exists. Every effort must be made to replace, reduce, and refine the use of animals—commonly referred to as the 3Rs principle. This includes exploring non-animal methods, using the minimum number of animals needed for statistical significance, and employing procedures that cause the least pain and distress.

Animals must be handled gently and housed in clean, species-appropriate environments with adequate space, ventilation, food, water, and environmental enrichment. The use of anaesthesia and analgesia is legally required during painful procedures, and post-operative care must be provided as per veterinary guidance. Any animal showing signs of suffering beyond the defined humane endpoints must be euthanized promptly and humanely, using a method approved by CPCSEA.

Under no circumstances should animals be used for repeated procedures involving pain or stress unless scientifically justified and explicitly approved. Researchers are prohibited from using untrained personnel for procedures like injections, surgery, or blood collection. All individuals involved in the project must undergo prior training in animal handling, restraint, dosing techniques, and humane endpoints.

Animals must never be procured from illegal or unapproved sources. Purchase records, health certificates, and quarantine clearance must be documented for every new batch of animals. The use of endangered species or higher mammals like non-human primates must be specifically authorised by CPCSEA and used only in cases of absolute necessity.

At all stages of the research, proper records must be maintained, including cage cards, animal census, treatment logs, surgical records, and euthanasia reports. Data fabrication, non-reporting of adverse events, or concealment of animal deaths are considered serious violations, both ethically and legally.

Upon completion of the study, investigators must submit a final report to the IAEC, detailing animal usage, protocol deviations (if any), and the method of disposal or reuse of animals. Leftover animals cannot be repurposed for other studies unless prior permission is obtained.

The ethical tone of a laboratory is reflected in how it treats its animals—not merely by regulatory compliance but by embracing humane values in every aspect of animal care. Institutions are therefore expected to conduct regular training, internal audits, and awareness programs to ensure that all staff are informed and sensitized to the responsibilities entrusted to them when working with live animals. The legal and ethical framework is not just a set of rules, but a shared commitment to conduct research with integrity, compassion, and scientific excellence.

Prohibited Practices

In animal research, certain practices are strictly prohibited by regulatory authorities such as the Committee for the Purpose of Control and Supervision of Experiments on Animals. These practices are considered unethical, scientifically unjustifiable, or inhumane and must be completely avoided by all researchers, technical staff, and animal facility personnel. Violation of these prohibitions can lead to cancellation of project approvals, suspension of institutional registration, legal penalties, and loss of funding.

One of the foremost prohibited practices is the initiation of any animal experiment without prior written approval from the Institutional Animal Ethics Committee. Even minor changes to an approved protocol, such as dosage alteration, species substitution, or procedure extension, cannot be implemented without prior amendment approval. Conducting experiments without valid ethical clearance is a serious offence under national regulations.

Use of animals from unauthorised, unlicensed, or unregistered sources is also strictly banned. Animals must be procured only from CPCSEA-approved breeders or licensed suppliers. Bringing in animals from the wild, markets, or pet vendors for laboratory use violates ethical and legal standards and poses significant risks to animal health, research integrity, and biosecurity.

Performing surgical procedures or painful interventions without the use of appropriate anaesthesia and post-operative analgesia is prohibited. Similarly, reusing the same animal for multiple painful or stressful experiments without adequate recovery and separate approval is not allowed. Inducing death without a humane and CPCSEA-approved euthanasia method, such as by drowning, freezing, poisoning, or air embolism, is completely forbidden.

Housing animals in overcrowded, unhygienic, or poorly ventilated conditions that do not meet species-specific requirements is prohibited. Lack of access to clean food and water, inadequate environmental enrichment, and failure to provide rest or recovery periods also constitute unethical treatment.

Non-reporting or deliberate concealment of unexpected mortality, morbidity, or adverse effects observed during the experiment is strictly not permitted. Investigators are responsible for reporting all animal-related incidents truthfully to the IAEC. Data fabrication, falsifying animal numbers, or manipulating outcomes by neglecting animal care is not only unethical but also a punishable offence under research misconduct policies.

Use of endangered species or higher mammals such as non-human primates, dogs, or cats without explicit CPCSEA approval is prohibited, regardless of the nature of the experiment. Studies involving cosmetic testing on animals are also not permitted in India as per Ministry of Health and Family Welfare notifications.

Exporting or transferring laboratory animals to unregistered facilities or for non-scientific purposes such as entertainment, exhibition, or unapproved breeding is not allowed. Researchers are also not allowed to keep experimental animals at home, in unofficial labs, or outside institutional boundaries.

Finally, employing untrained or unqualified personnel for tasks like injections, surgical procedures, euthanasia, or animal restraint is strictly prohibited. All individuals involved in animal experiments must undergo training and certification as per institutional guidelines.

These prohibitions are enforced not only to prevent animal cruelty but also to maintain the scientific validity, reproducibility, and credibility of research. Institutions are required to ensure awareness, implement strict internal monitoring, and report violations promptly to regulatory bodies.

Importance of Humane Endpoints

Humane endpoints are pre-established criteria that define the earliest point at which an animal should be withdrawn from an experimental procedure or euthanized to prevent or minimize pain, distress, or suffering. These endpoints are critical in ensuring ethical and compassionate treatment of animals used in research, while still allowing the collection of valid scientific data. Their implementation reflects the fundamental principle of refinement in animal research and is a mandatory requirement under national regulatory frameworks such as those laid down by the CPCSEA.

The primary importance of humane endpoints lies in the protection of animal welfare. By identifying specific clinical, behavioral, or physiological signs that indicate declining health or irreversible distress, researchers can prevent the animal from reaching a moribund or suffering state. Signs such as rapid weight loss, labored breathing, unresponsiveness, self-mutilation, persistent diarrhea, visible tumors beyond ethical size limits, or neurological impairment are commonly used indicators. Establishing these limits in advance allows for timely intervention, treatment, or euthanasia before the animal experiences prolonged suffering.

From a scientific perspective, humane endpoints improve data quality by reducing confounding effects introduced by stress or severe illness. Animals under extreme distress may show altered physiological parameters such as hormone levels, immune response, or metabolic function, which can significantly affect experimental results. By terminating the experiment at a humane endpoint, researchers ensure that the data collected reflect the true effects of the treatment or condition under investigation, not secondary effects caused by suffering.

Humane endpoints are also vital for regulatory compliance. Institutional Animal Ethics Committees require investigators to clearly define humane endpoints in their research protocols and demonstrate how these will be monitored. Approval of the study is contingent on the adequacy of these provisions. During CPCSEA inspections or audits, failure to implement humane endpoints is considered a serious ethical and procedural lapse, and may lead to penalties, withdrawal of approvals, or revocation of institutional registration.

Practically, humane endpoints also support the efficient use of animals and resources. Animals that reach ethical limits can be removed from the study or humanely euthanized without unnecessary prolongation, allowing researchers to reallocate resources, avoid public concern, and maintain institutional credibility. This aligns with the broader scientific and societal expectation that animal use in research must be both necessary and humane.

To implement humane endpoints effectively, researchers and animal care staff must be trained to observe and recognize early signs of distress. Monitoring protocols must be clearly defined, with observation schedules adjusted to the nature and severity of the procedure. Decisions regarding endpoint criteria should be based on scientific evidence, veterinary input, and past experience with similar models.

In summary, humane endpoints are a cornerstone of responsible animal research. They reflect a commitment to reducing animal suffering, enhancing scientific validity, and upholding ethical standards in accordance with national and international expectations. Their use is not only a regulatory requirement but a moral obligation that reinforces trust in the research community.

1.7.1 Principles and Objectives of GLP

Reliability, Reproducibility, Traceability

Good Laboratory Practices (GLP) form the foundational framework for ensuring that non-clinical safety studies involving laboratory animals are conducted in a structured, transparent, and scientifically valid manner. In animal studies, the primary principles of GLP focus on reliability, reproducibility, and traceability, which are critical to generating high-quality data that can be used in regulatory submissions and further stages of drug development.

Reliability in GLP refers to the generation of consistent and scientifically sound results that accurately reflect the biological response of the animals under the specific experimental conditions. It ensures that the data obtained is free from bias, handled with integrity, and truly represents the impact of the test substance or intervention. This is achieved by adhering strictly to pre-approved protocols, defined procedures, and ethical guidelines throughout the study period.

Reproducibility is the ability of a study to be repeated under similar conditions by the same or different team and yield comparable results. This is particularly important in animal research, where biological variability can impact outcomes. GLP facilitates reproducibility by mandating comprehensive documentation of experimental design, animal selection, housing conditions, feeding regimens, treatment details, observation schedules, and endpoints. Standard Operating Procedures (SOPs) play a major role in minimizing variation and ensuring consistency across studies and institutions.

Traceability is the documented trail that allows every step of the study—from animal procurement to data analysis—to be tracked and verified. Each action taken during the study, whether it is weighing an animal, administering a dose, or recording an observation, must be logged in real time with the date, time, initials of the person, and any deviations noted. All records must be maintained in a manner that allows reconstruction of the full sequence of events at any point in time. This is vital during audits, inspections, or regulatory reviews and adds credibility to the study's outcomes.

Traceability also extends to the handling of test articles, reagents, instruments, and biological samples. Batch numbers, expiry dates, storage conditions, calibration records, and sample transfer logs are maintained to ensure complete transparency. Any correction in data entry or record must be done as per GLP standards, with a reason, date, and signature, ensuring that nothing is overwritten or lost.

By focusing on these principles, GLP protects the scientific integrity of animal studies and builds confidence among regulators, sponsors, and the public in the safety data generated for drugs, chemicals, vaccines, or medical devices.

Quality Assurance and Quality Control

Quality assurance (QA) and quality control (QC) are central components of GLP that serve to ensure that every aspect of the animal study meets predefined standards and is verifiable at all times. Both QA and QC operate to minimize errors, detect deviations, and uphold consistency in scientific practices.

Quality assurance is an independent monitoring system, usually conducted by a designated QA unit within the institution. This unit operates separately from the study team and is responsible for auditing the entire study process. It includes verifying protocol adherence, reviewing records, inspecting animal housing, monitoring staff compliance with SOPs, and ensuring that all observations are being recorded accurately and in a timely manner. QA audits are conducted at various stages: before the study begins (pre-study audit), during the study (in-process audit), and after the study is completed (final report audit). The QA unit also inspects data archival and document retention practices.

Any findings of non-compliance are reported in the form of audit observations and are shared with the study director for corrective and preventive actions. The QA unit also submits audit reports to management, ensuring institutional accountability and readiness for external regulatory inspections.

Quality control, on the other hand, refers to the procedures performed by the study team during the day-to-day execution of the study. This includes verifying instrument calibration before use, cross-checking dosing volumes, maintaining animal identification accuracy, confirming environmental parameters, and checking calculations in data entry sheets. QC ensures that any error or deviation is corrected at the earliest point before it affects the outcome of the study.

Together, QA and QC create a robust internal control system where problems are detected early, corrections are timely, and the study progresses with confidence in its scientific and ethical foundation. These functions also help prepare the facility for inspections by agencies such as the Drugs Controller General of India (DCGI), OECD GLP Monitoring Authority, or international regulators.

The principles and objectives of GLP not only improve the quality of data generated in animal studies but also promote a culture of discipline, transparency, and continuous improvement within the institution. They provide a framework for achieving both ethical excellence and regulatory readiness in all phases of non-clinical research.

1.7.2 Standard Operating Procedures (SOPs)

Definition and Format of SOPs

Standard Operating Procedures, commonly referred to as SOPs, are written documents that outline detailed, step-by-step instructions for performing specific operations consistently and correctly within a laboratory or animal facility. In the context of animal studies, SOPs are mandatory under Good Laboratory Practices and play a critical role in ensuring procedural uniformity, scientific reliability, animal welfare, and regulatory compliance. These documents eliminate variability caused by differences in individual technique or interpretation and help ensure that every task is performed according to scientifically validated methods and ethical guidelines.

An SOP typically follows a structured format to ensure clarity, completeness, and traceability. The general layout includes a title, SOP number, version number, effective date, and approval signatures from the responsible personnel or QA unit. The objective or purpose of the SOP is briefly stated to define its scope. This is followed by a list of responsibilities—who will perform and supervise the procedure—and the materials and equipment required, including specifications and calibration requirements.

The procedure section forms the core of the SOP, describing each step in a logical sequence, often accompanied by illustrations, tables, or flowcharts if necessary. The language must be precise, unambiguous, and action-oriented to avoid misinterpretation. Any safety precautions, ethical considerations, and humane handling practices should be clearly stated within the steps. Additional sections such as troubleshooting, documentation requirements, and references (e.g., CPCSEA guidelines, OECD principles) are added to support best practices.

Each SOP must be assigned a revision history to track changes over time. When revised, the new version must supersede the old, with proper archival of the outdated copies. SOPs must be reviewed periodically—usually once every one or two years—or when procedural changes occur, new equipment is introduced, or updated regulatory guidance is received.

All staff involved in animal care or experimentation must be trained in the relevant SOPs before they are allowed to perform those procedures independently. Training logs must be maintained as part of GLP compliance and reviewed during internal and external audits.

Examples: Dosing, Sample Collection, Animal Handling

Several essential SOPs are implemented in animal research facilities to standardize operations and ensure quality assurance across studies.

An SOP for oral dosing in rats might include steps such as verifying the animal ID, weighing the animal, calculating the dose based on body weight, preparing the test compound in the correct vehicle, and administering the dose using a calibrated gavage needle. The SOP would specify the restraint technique to be used, the maximum safe volume per administration, the need for observation post-dosing, and documentation in the dosing record sheet.

A sample collection SOP for blood sampling via the tail vein in mice would describe the animal's identification and health check, warming the tail to dilate vessels, cleaning the site with antiseptic, performing the puncture with a specific gauge needle, collecting the blood in labeled tubes, and applying pressure to the site post-collection. It would include the maximum volume allowed per collection and per day to prevent distress or hypovolemia, with details on alternate sites like retro-orbital sinus, saphenous vein, or cardiac puncture in terminal procedures.

An SOP on animal handling would detail species-specific restraint techniques. For mice, it may describe grasping the tail base, securing the scruff with a forefinger and thumb, and supporting the body while minimizing stress. For rabbits, it would involve proper lifting by supporting the hindquarters and shoulders simultaneously, avoiding ear handling, and placing animals on a non-slip surface. This SOP would also include behavioral signs of stress and steps to be taken to reduce it, such as using enrichment materials and maintaining low noise levels.

Each of these SOPs would include clear instructions on record-keeping, such as documenting the operator name, time of procedure, animal identification number, and any observations made during or after the procedure. Adherence to these SOPs ensures not only the scientific quality of data but also demonstrates institutional commitment to ethical standards and best practices in animal research.

1.7.3 Data Recording, Archiving, and Reporting

Raw Data vs Final Report

In animal research governed by Good Laboratory Practices (GLP), the distinction between raw data and the final report is fundamental to ensuring transparency, traceability, and scientific integrity. Raw data refers to the original observations, measurements, and recordings made during the conduct of the study, captured exactly as they occur. This includes handwritten entries in lab notebooks, instrument-generated printouts or digital files, cage-side observations, weight charts, dose calculation sheets, and environmental monitoring logs. Raw data must be recorded in real time, in a permanent and legible manner, using ink (if paper-based), with no overwriting or correction without proper justification, signature, and date. Any correction made must preserve the original entry.

Each data point is expected to be attributable, contemporaneous, original, and accurate. This principle—commonly known as ALCOA (Attributable, Legible, Contemporaneous, Original, and Accurate)—is critical in GLP-compliant animal research. The raw data must be traceable to the person who generated it and the time it was recorded. It forms the legal and scientific foundation of the study.

The final report is a comprehensive, structured document that compiles and interprets all the findings of the study based on the raw data. It includes the study title, objectives, background information, experimental design, materials and methods, results, statistical analysis, discussion, and conclusion. Importantly, every figure, graph, or table presented in the final report must be verifiable against the corresponding raw data. No inference or observation should appear in the final report unless it is directly supported by documented evidence from the raw dataset.

The final report must be signed by the study director and include a statement that the report represents an accurate account of the work performed. The Quality Assurance Unit reviews the report to ensure consistency with the raw data and records the audit status. Once finalized, no changes can be made without issuing an official amendment that is dated, justified, and signed.

Audit Trails and Compliance

An audit trail refers to the chronological documentation that allows tracing of every action, modification, or entry related to a study from beginning to end. In GLP animal studies, audit trails serve as the backbone of accountability and compliance. For paper-based systems, this includes logbooks, checklists, and signature sheets that trace each activity. In digital systems, audit trails include metadata—such as user ID, time stamps, data origin, software versions, and any modifications made to original entries.

Audit trails are essential for tracking the flow of data through all stages of the experiment—planning, execution, analysis, reporting, and archiving. For instance, a dosing record must indicate the date of dosing, the compound used, the animal ID, dose volume, the person who administered the dose, and any immediate reaction observed. If a correction is made to the dose volume after entry, the software or manual system must retain the original data and indicate who made the correction, when it was made, and why. This allows reviewers and inspectors to verify that the data have not been manipulated.

Regulatory bodies such as CPCSEA, OECD GLP Monitoring Authorities, and the Drugs Controller General of India (DCGI) emphasize that the absence of a clear audit trail is a red flag. During audits or inspections, institutions must demonstrate not only that the experiment was conducted properly but also that every aspect of the study was monitored, traceable, and conducted in compliance with approved SOPs and protocols.

Facilities must therefore adopt both procedural controls (e.g., logbooks, registers) and technological controls (e.g., password protection, access logs, auto time-stamping) to ensure secure and verifiable audit trails. These are reviewed regularly by Quality Assurance Units as part of internal audits and submitted for review during external inspections.

Importance of Integrity and Transparency

Integrity and transparency in data management are not only regulatory requirements but also the ethical pillars of credible scientific research. Data integrity means that the data are complete, consistent, and accurate throughout their lifecycle, from generation to reporting and archiving. Any compromise in integrity—such as backdated entries, concealed adverse effects, selective reporting, or undocumented changes—can invalidate the study, harm public trust, and lead to regulatory sanctions or withdrawal of funding.

Transparency ensures that the methodology, data, and decision-making processes are open for review, reproducible, and verifiable by third parties. In animal research, this is particularly important because the data often serve as the foundation for safety evaluations of drugs, chemicals, or biological products that will be administered to humans. Therefore, transparency in data not only protects the credibility of the research team but also safeguards public health and animal welfare.

To maintain both integrity and transparency, institutions must implement structured training, regular internal audits, SOP-based workflows, and an open culture of accountability. All deviations must be reported and justified, and all observations, whether positive, negative, or unexpected, must be recorded without bias. Each record, whether digital or physical, must be stored securely, backed up regularly, and protected from unauthorized access or alteration.

1.8.1 Definition and Significance of Bioassay

Concept of Biological Standardization

A bioassay, or biological assay, is a quantitative or qualitative method used to determine the concentration or potency of a substance—such as a drug, hormone, or toxin—by measuring its biological effect on a living system. Unlike purely chemical assays that rely on analytical instrumentation and chemical reactions, bioassays depend on observing physiological or biochemical responses in animals, tissues, organs, or cells in response to a test substance. These responses are then compared to those produced by a standard preparation of known activity, allowing the potency of the test sample to be calculated.

The central idea behind bioassay is the principle of biological standardization, which is essential when the exact chemical nature or structural information of a substance is unknown, or when a chemical assay does not accurately reflect the biological activity of a compound. For many biologically active substances—like insulin, digitalis, oxytocin, thyroxine, and certain vaccines—the pharmacological action is more clinically relevant than the mere chemical concentration. In such cases, bioassay serves as the definitive method for potency determination.

Biological standardization involves comparing the test substance against a reference standard that has been biologically characterized and assigned a defined unit of activity. These standards are provided by pharmacopoeias (like Indian Pharmacopoeia, British Pharmacopoeia, or WHO) and ensure uniformity in therapeutic efficacy and safety across different batches and manufacturers. For example, one unit of insulin is defined based on its hypoglycaemic effect in a fasting rabbit or mouse, not on its molecular weight.

In standardization, the test and standard preparations are administered under identical conditions—same species, route, dose, time, and observation parameters—to minimize biological variation. The biological response, such as muscle contraction, blood pressure change, enzyme activity, or survival rate, is recorded and plotted against the dose. Using statistical methods like interpolation, parallel line assay, or three-point assay, the relative potency of the unknown sample is calculated in comparison to the standard.

The significance of bioassays lies in their application during drug development, quality control, batch release, and regulatory compliance, particularly for biological products where variability cannot be captured by chemical analysis alone. For instance, in the case of vaccines, bioassays are critical to assess immunogenicity and efficacy before human use. Similarly, in herbal extracts or natural toxins, where the active compound may be a complex mixture, bioassays provide a measure of biological activity that chemical assays may not accurately capture.

Despite advancements in analytical technologies, bioassays remain indispensable in many areas of pharmacology, toxicology, and biotechnology. Their design, however, must follow rigorous ethical standards, statistical principles, and standardization protocols to ensure reliability and reproducibility. As the field advances, efforts are ongoing to develop in vitro and cell-based assays to reduce reliance on live animals, aligning bioassay methodologies with the broader goal of ethical and scientifically robust drug evaluation.

When Bioassays Are Preferred Over Chemical Methods

Bioassays are preferred over chemical methods in specific situations where measuring the biological activity of a substance is more meaningful or necessary than simply determining its chemical composition or concentration. While chemical assays are useful for quantifying known compounds with precise structures, they may not accurately reflect how a substance behaves in a biological system. In such cases, bioassays become essential, especially in pharmacology, toxicology, biotechnology, and regulatory sciences.

One of the primary circumstances where bioassays are preferred is when the active principle of a compound is unknown or chemically unstable. Many natural extracts, toxins, hormones, and biological drugs have complex mixtures or unstable components that degrade during chemical processing. A chemical assay may detect the presence of such components but cannot determine whether they are still biologically active. Bioassays, on the other hand, directly assess the pharmacological or physiological effects, providing a more functional measure of potency.

Bioassays are also the preferred choice when evaluating substances with biological variability in potency, such as insulin, adrenocorticotropic hormone (ACTH), gonadotropins, vaccines, digitalis, or certain antibiotics. Even when the molecular weight and structure are known, different batches may vary in activity due to changes in source material, formulation, or manufacturing process. In these cases, the therapeutic effect cannot be guaranteed by chemical assay alone. Bioassays help standardize the potency by comparing biological responses to an established standard.

When a drug exerts its effect through complex interactions in living systems, such as receptor binding, second messenger activation, enzyme modulation, or immune stimulation, a bioassay is necessary to capture these integrated outcomes. For example, interferons, monoclonal antibodies, and cytokines are better evaluated using cell-based or in vivo models rather than analytical quantification because their function depends on complex biological mechanisms.

Bioassays are also vital in toxicity testing, where the LD_{50} (lethal dose in 50% of animals) or IC_{50} (inhibitory concentration for 50% of the biological activity) is determined. These values cannot be measured chemically; they require biological endpoints such as mortality, behavioural changes, or organ damage. Similarly, anti-venom testing and neurotoxic evaluations rely heavily on biological endpoints that reflect real-time effects.

In cases where the substance acts on a biological target that lacks a chemical marker or assay method, such as muscle contraction in bioassay of oxytocin using uterine strip preparations, or smooth muscle relaxation for bronchodilators, bioassays are the only viable method. Here, the magnitude of biological effect is measured and compared to a standard preparation to assign potency to the unknown sample.

Lastly, in regulatory approval and quality control of biological products, especially those mentioned in pharmacopoeial monographs, bioassays are mandatory. Authorities such as the WHO, US FDA, EMA, and Indian Pharmacopoeia Commission recommend bioassays for biologics to ensure consistency in efficacy and safety, even when chemical assay data are available.

1.8.2 Types of Bioassays

1.8.2.1 Quantal Assays – All-or-None Response

Quantal bioassays are a type of biological assay in which the response to a drug or test substance is recorded in a binary or all-or-none fashion. This means that each experimental unit, such as an animal or tissue sample, either exhibits the defined biological effect or does not—there is no partial or graded response recorded. The term "quantal" refers to the discrete, yes-or-no nature of the outcome.

In these assays, the end-point is the occurrence or non-occurrence of a specific event, such as death, convulsion, muscle contraction, fall in body temperature beyond a certain threshold, or onset of sleep. The magnitude of the response is not measured; only its presence or absence is considered relevant for determining the potency of the substance being tested.

Quantal assays are particularly useful when testing substances that have threshold effects, where a specific dose either causes the desired biological outcome or has no visible effect. They are most commonly employed in toxicity testing, biological standardization of potent drugs, and determination of lethal doses (LD_{50}) or effective doses (ED_{50})—the dose at which 50% of the test population exhibits the defined effect.

A classic example of a quantal bioassay is the LD_{50} test for toxins, where groups of animals (e.g., mice or rats) are administered increasing doses of a test substance. The number of animals dying in each group is recorded, and the dose causing death in 50% of the subjects is statistically calculated. Another example is the sleeping time assay for barbiturates, where the response is defined as the induction of sleep (yes or no) after administration.

To carry out a quantal assay, test animals are divided into groups and treated with increasing doses of the standard and the test preparation under controlled conditions. The number of animals showing the positive response in each group is recorded, and the data are used to generate a dose-response curve. The results are analyzed using probit analysis or log-dose response transformation, from which the median effective dose or median lethal dose is derived.

While quantal assays are relatively simple to perform and require minimal instrumentation, they typically need a large number of test animals to achieve statistically meaningful results due to the binary nature of the data. Biological variability, ethical concerns related to high mortality in toxicity studies, and difficulty in standardizing the exact definition of a "positive" response are common limitations of this type of assay.

Nonetheless, quantal bioassays remain important tools in regulatory toxicology, vaccine potency testing, and pharmacological screening, especially when the therapeutic window is narrow and understanding the minimum effective or maximum tolerated dose is essential. They provide essential safety and efficacy information that cannot be obtained through chemical analysis alone.

1.8.2.2 Graded Response Assays – Continuous Response Scale

Graded response assays are a class of bioassays where the biological effect of a test substance is measured on a continuous or progressive scale, rather than as an all-or-none outcome. In these assays, the magnitude of the response increases proportionally or sigmoidally with the dose of the drug or compound being tested. Each experimental unit, such as an organ tissue, cell line, or whole animal, produces a measurable response intensity—for example, a rise in blood pressure, contraction of muscle tissue, fall in temperature, or enzyme activity level—depending on the dose administered.

Unlike quantal assays that only record the presence or absence of an effect, graded assays allow quantitative comparisons between the effects of various doses. These assays are particularly useful when there is a dose-dependent biological response, and the relationship between dose and response can be plotted as a dose–response curve. The more precise the measurements, the more accurate and reproducible the assay results will be.

Graded bioassays are commonly applied in pharmacological studies to determine the relative potency of a test substance compared to a standard drug. For example, the isolated guinea pig ileum preparation may be used to evaluate the potency of acetylcholine, histamine, or serotonin by measuring the amplitude of muscle contractions in response to increasing concentrations. Similarly, the frog rectus abdominis or rat phrenic nerve–diaphragm preparation is used to test neuromuscular blockers by recording twitch responses.

The experimental design involves exposing the test tissue or animal model to a range of concentrations of both the standard preparation (of known potency) and the test preparation (of unknown potency) under identical conditions. The biological response—such as contraction in millimeters or change in blood pressure in mmHg—is recorded for each dose. The data are then plotted on a log dose vs response curve, which typically results in a sigmoid-shaped graph.

From the graph, the effective dose (ED_{50})—the dose that produces 50% of the maximal response—can be calculated for both the standard and the test. The relative potency of the test sample is then determined by comparing the ED_{50} values or by the interpolation method, matching method, or three-point and four-point assays, depending on the nature of the study and required precision.

Graded assays have several advantages. They are highly sensitive, provide precise and reproducible data, and often require fewer animals or preparations than quantal assays. They also allow the assessment of partial agonists, antagonists, and synergistic effects, making them versatile tools in pharmacological evaluation. However, they require specialized equipment (such as kymographs, force transducers, or digital recorders), trained personnel, and careful standardization of environmental and procedural variables.

1.8.3.1 End-Point Method

The end-point method of bioassay is one of the most classical and straightforward approaches used to determine the biological activity or potency of a substance by observing a clearly defined biological end-point. In this method, the response is recorded when a specific and identifiable biological event occurs, such as the onset of convulsion, death, loss of muscle tone, induction of sleep, or blood clotting. The defining characteristic of the end-point method is that only the final observable effect is measured, without quantifying the magnitude or progression of the response.

This method is widely used in quantal assays, where the effect is binary (present or absent), and the biological system under observation is exposed to increasing doses of a standard preparation and a test preparation under identical conditions. The dose required to produce the desired end-point is recorded, and the potency of the test substance is calculated by comparing it to that of the standard.

A classical example of the end-point method is the minimum lethal dose (MLD) determination of a toxin in mice. In this case, increasing doses of the test sample are administered until the minimum dose that causes death in the animal is identified. Another well-known application is in the bioassay of digitalis, where the end-point is cardiac arrest in cats or frogs. Similarly, in the sleeping time assay of barbiturates, the end-point is the induction of sleep in the test animal.

In a typical procedure using this method, a group of animals is administered various doses of the standard and test substances. The dose at which the first or minimum observable effect (such as sleep or death) occurs is noted. The potency is calculated using ratios of doses between the standard and test, assuming the response at the end-point is biologically equivalent in both cases.

The advantages of the end-point method include its simplicity, minimal requirement of equipment, and ease of interpretation. It is particularly useful in toxicology, vaccine testing, and studies involving narrow therapeutic windows, where it is critical to identify the dose that causes a defined effect with precision.

However, the method has limitations. It provides no information about intermediate responses or the dose–response relationship. Since only the final event is considered, variations in individual sensitivity may affect reproducibility. It often requires a large number of animals, especially when responses are not consistent across the group. Also, ethical concerns arise when severe end-points such as death are used.

Despite its limitations, the end-point method remains an important tool in bioassay, particularly when graded responses cannot be reliably measured, or when regulatory agencies specify end-point-based testing for potency or safety evaluation of certain biological products. The method must be applied carefully, with attention to humane endpoints, ethical oversight, and strict adherence to standard protocols and CPCSEA regulations to ensure scientific validity and animal welfare.

1.8.3.2 Matching Method

The matching method is a type of bioassay in which the potency of an unknown test substance is determined by adjusting its dose until it produces a biological response that exactly matches the response produced by a known standard preparation. In this method, the observer matches the effect of the test sample with that of the standard, using a common measurable response such as muscle contraction, blood pressure change, or enzyme activity. This method is most often applied in graded response assays, where the response is quantifiable and can be visually or instrumentally compared between samples.

The matching method is relatively simple and practical, especially for quick comparisons when elaborate statistical procedures are not required. It is based on the assumption that the biological response is directly related to the concentration of the active principle, and that both the test and the standard act via the same mechanism and have a comparable dose–response relationship.

In a typical matching method, a standard solution of known concentration is applied to a biological system (e.g., isolated frog rectus abdominis muscle or guinea pig ileum), and the response is recorded, such as the height of contraction in millimeters. Next, different doses of the test solution are applied, and the dose that produces the same magnitude of response as the standard is identified. This dose is considered to be equivalent in potency to the known dose of the standard. The potency of the test is then calculated by comparing the doses using a simple ratio:

Potency of test = Dose of standard / Dose of test (for equal response)

For example, if 0.2 mL of a standard drug produces a contraction of 5 mm, and it takes 0.4 mL of the test preparation to produce the same 5 mm contraction, the test is half as potent as the standard.

This method is especially useful in teaching pharmacology laboratories and preliminary screening where rapid estimation is needed without complex calculations. It is also used when dealing with preparations that exhibit reproducible, linear responses at a particular range of doses.

However, the matching method has some limitations. It does not utilize multiple doses and thus provides no information about the overall dose–response curve. Because the entire conclusion is drawn from a single matched response, minor observational errors can lead to incorrect potency estimation. It is also less accurate and less statistically reliable than interpolation, bracketing, or parallel line assays, especially for regulatory or clinical applications.

Despite these limitations, the matching method is still used in certain classical pharmacological experiments and bioassays where simplicity, visual observation, and direct comparison are sufficient for approximate potency estimation. For improved precision, this method is often used in combination with repetition and averaging to minimize variability and observational bias.

1.8.3.3 Interpolation Method

The interpolation method is a commonly used quantitative technique in graded bioassays, where the potency of a test substance is estimated by interpolating its response on a standard dose–response curve. This method is based on the assumption that the biological effect of a substance increases in a predictable, dose-dependent manner, and that the relationship between log dose and response follows a sigmoid curve, typically becoming linear in the mid-range.

In this method, the standard preparation of known potency is administered in at least three different doses to a suitable biological system (e.g., isolated tissue, organ bath setup, or live animal), and the corresponding responses (such as muscle contraction, blood pressure rise, or inhibition of movement) are recorded. A dose–response curve is plotted using the log of each standard dose on the X-axis and the biological response on the Y-axis.

After constructing the curve using the standard, the test substance is then administered at a dose that falls within the linear portion of the standard curve, and the magnitude of its biological response is measured. The response value of the test is then traced horizontally across the graph to intersect the standard curve, and the corresponding log dose on the X-axis is identified. This interpolated log dose is then used to calculate the equivalent dose of the test sample and, ultimately, its potency relative to the standard.

For example, if the standard doses of a vasoconstrictor drug produce blood pressure increases of 10 mmHg, 20 mmHg, and 30 mmHg at doses of 1, 3, and 9 µg respectively, and the test sample at an unknown concentration produces a 20 mmHg rise, interpolation will identify what dose of the standard corresponds to this response. If the test dose required is double that of the standard to achieve the same effect, its potency is considered to be half.

This method is more accurate than the matching method because it uses a dose–response relationship rather than a single matched response. It can also accommodate intermediate responses, which are not covered by quantal methods. The interpolation method allows for graphical interpretation, making it a useful teaching tool in academic settings and a practical option in routine pharmacological screening.

However, it has limitations. The method is less statistically robust than more advanced techniques like the three-point or four-point bioassay, as it generally lacks replicate data and does not account for experimental variability. The precision of the method depends heavily on the accuracy of plotting, reading from the graph, and maintaining linear response conditions. Additionally, if the test response falls outside the linear portion of the curve, interpolation becomes unreliable.

1.8.3.4 Bracketing and Multiple Point Assays

Bracketing and multiple point assays are among the most precise and statistically reliable bioassay methods used to determine the relative potency of a test substance by comparing its effects to those of a standard preparation. These methods are built on the principle of graded responses and are particularly suited for assays where accuracy, reproducibility, and regulatory acceptance are essential—such as in the standardization of hormones, antibiotics, and vaccines.

The bracketing method involves selecting two doses of a standard that produce responses just below and just above the response produced by a single dose of the test sample. These doses effectively "bracket" the response of the test sample. The dose of the standard that would produce the same response as the test is then calculated by interpolation between the two bracketing doses. This method assumes that the dose-response relationship is linear between these two standard doses.

For example, if a test drug produces a muscle contraction of 30 mm, and the standard drug produces 25 mm at 2 µg and 35 mm at 4 µg, then the equivalent dose of the test can be estimated to lie between 2 µg and 4 µg of the standard. Using simple linear interpolation, the exact equivalent dose can be calculated mathematically. The relative potency is then expressed as:

Relative Potency = Equivalent Dose of Standard / Dose of Test

The multiple point assay (such as the three-point and four-point assays) builds on this principle but uses multiple doses of both the standard and the test, ensuring greater statistical validity and accuracy.

In the three-point bioassay, one test dose is compared against two standard doses. The standard doses are selected such that they lie on the linear portion of the standard dose–response curve, and the test dose ideally produces a response that falls between the two. The responses are then analyzed using a mathematical formula to estimate the relative potency of the test sample.

The four-point bioassay is a more advanced method where two doses of the standard and two doses of the test are used. This approach is designed to reduce biological variability and enhance precision. Each dose is repeated (often in triplicate), and the average response is taken to ensure reliability. The assumption is that the dose–response curve is linear and parallel between the test and standard preparations. The statistical analysis of the results provides not just the relative potency but also the confidence limits, making this method acceptable for regulatory submissions and quality control.

The advantages of bracketing and multiple point assays include high accuracy, precision, and the ability to detect small differences in potency. These methods are suitable for pharmacopoeial applications, product batch testing, and validation of biological drug formulations. They are especially important when small deviations in potency could significantly impact clinical efficacy or safety.

However, the limitations include the requirement of more complex calculations, trained personnel, and strict experimental controls. These methods are also more time-consuming and resource-intensive compared to simpler methods like matching or interpolation.

Despite the technical demands, bracketing and multiple point assays represent the gold standard for bioassay methodology, ensuring consistency and scientific rigor in evaluating the potency of biologically active substances.

Biological Variability

One of the most significant limitations in bioassays is biological variability, which refers to the natural differences in responses among living organisms or biological preparations when exposed to the same substance under identical experimental conditions. This variability can arise due to genetic, physiological, environmental, or handling-related factors, and it poses challenges to the consistency, accuracy, and reproducibility of bioassay results.

In animal-based assays, variability is often observed due to differences in species, strain, age, sex, nutritional status, circadian rhythms, disease status, and previous exposure to drugs or stress. For instance, even genetically similar animals housed in the same environment can show differences in immune response, receptor sensitivity, or metabolism, leading to variation in observed outcomes such as muscle contraction, sedation, or blood pressure changes. In isolated tissue preparations, variability can be introduced by tissue sensitivity, degradation, response fatigue, or differences in smooth muscle tone, affecting the uniformity of graded responses.

Biological variability can significantly impact dose–response relationships, making it difficult to obtain precise potency estimations. A test sample might appear less potent than the standard in one experiment and more potent in another, simply due to unpredictable variation in the biological model rather than actual differences in drug activity. This necessitates the use of multiple replicates, larger sample sizes, and statistical tools to average out fluctuations and ensure the reliability of the final result.

To manage biological variability, standardization is essential at every level of a bioassay—from animal selection and housing conditions to experimental design and endpoint definition. Randomization, blinding of observers, and repeated trials are key strategies used to minimize experimental bias and control for inter-subject differences. The use of inbred animal strains, cell lines, and computerized data acquisition systems can further reduce variability and improve consistency in bioassay results.

Despite its challenges, biological variability reflects the complex and dynamic nature of living systems and must be acknowledged rather than eliminated. Regulatory bodies such as CPCSEA, WHO, USFDA, EMA, and Indian Pharmacopoeia Commission accept a certain level of biological variability in bioassay data, provided the study is well-controlled, statistically analyzed, and the confidence limits are within acceptable ranges.

Therefore, while biological variability remains an inherent limitation in bioassays, its impact can be mitigated by robust experimental design, strict adherence to Good Laboratory Practices (GLP), and rigorous data analysis, ensuring that bioassays remain scientifically valid and regulatory compliant for potency estimation, product release, and quality control of

Ethical Issues in Using Animals for Standardization

The use of animals in bioassays, particularly for the purpose of drug standardization, raises several ethical concerns that must be addressed with care, responsibility, and regulatory compliance. While bioassays remain crucial in assessing the biological potency and safety of drugs, vaccines, and other therapeutic agents—especially when no alternative exists—the ethical implications of subjecting animals to experimental procedures have become a central focus in pharmacological research and drug development.

One of the primary ethical concerns is the pain, distress, and potential death that animals may experience during standardization procedures. Many classical bioassays involve procedures such as lethal dose determination (LD_{50}), induction of seizures, blood pressure manipulation, or invasive sampling. These can cause significant suffering if not properly controlled or if humane endpoints are ignored. Such practices, when conducted without adequate anaesthesia, analgesia, or post-procedural care, are considered inhumane and ethically unacceptable.

Another major issue is the use of large numbers of animals, especially in quantal assays where statistically significant results require testing on multiple animals across various dose levels. This can lead to overuse and wastage if the study design is not well justified or if alternatives are not considered. There is also growing criticism regarding the repetition of standardization protocols for every new drug batch or formulation, which may not always be necessary with modern analytical tools.

The practice of using animals for standardization also faces ethical scrutiny due to the availability of non-animal alternatives, such as in vitro cell-based assays, recombinant protein systems, organ-on-chip technologies, and computational models. Continued reliance on animal bioassays in cases where validated alternatives exist is considered ethically regressive and scientifically outdated. Regulatory agencies now emphasize the 3Rs principle—Replacement, Reduction, and Refinement—to address this issue. Institutions and researchers are expected to replace animal models wherever possible, reduce the number of animals used, and refine procedures to minimize suffering.

There is also the ethical obligation to ensure that all personnel involved in bioassays are adequately trained in humane handling, proper restraint, anaesthesia, and euthanasia techniques, and that all experimental procedures are reviewed and approved by the Institutional Animal Ethics Committee (IAEC) in accordance with CPCSEA guidelines. Any breach in ethical conduct, such as conducting experiments without approval, failure to report animal suffering, or deviation from approved protocols, is a serious violation and can lead to legal consequences, revocation of project funding, or institutional sanctions.

Furthermore, public sensitivity toward animal rights has increased the demand for transparency and accountability in research practices. Institutions are now expected to justify the scientific necessity for using animals in standardization, provide evidence of consideration of alternatives, and demonstrate compliance with all ethical and regulatory requirements through well-maintained documentation and regular audits.

Regulatory Acceptance and Trends Toward Alternatives

Regulatory agencies across the world have historically accepted animal-based bioassays as the gold standard for determining the potency, efficacy, and safety of various pharmaceutical and biological products. However, there has been a significant shift in regulatory perspective in recent decades due to growing ethical concerns, scientific advancements, and the development of reliable non-animal testing strategies. Today, while animal bioassays remain accepted and, in some cases, mandatory, there is a strong movement toward the replacement, reduction, and refinement (3Rs) of animal use in line with global regulatory and ethical expectations.

In India, regulatory oversight is provided by authorities such as the Central Drugs Standard Control Organization (CDSCO), Indian Pharmacopoeia Commission (IPC), and Committee for the Purpose of Control and Supervision of Experiments on Animals (CPCSEA). These bodies recognize the continued need for certain animal assays, particularly in the biological standardization of vaccines, hormones, toxins, and antitoxins, but also actively promote the integration of validated in vitro and ex vivo methods where applicable. The Indian Pharmacopoeia has already adopted several cell-based and chemical assay methods to replace older animal-based procedures.

Internationally, major regulatory authorities such as the U.S. Food and Drug Administration (FDA), European Medicines Agency (EMA), and World Health Organization (WHO) have issued guidelines supporting the use of alternatives to animal testing. The Organisation for Economic Co-operation and Development (OECD), through its Test Guidelines Programme, has validated and published numerous non-animal methods for toxicity testing, pharmacological screening, and drug evaluation, which are now accepted by over 40 member countries including India.

Examples of such alternatives include:

ELISA and other immunoassays for vaccine potency testing

Cell-based receptor-binding assays for hormonal bioactivity

Tissue-based organ bath alternatives using synthetic muscle strips

Computer simulations (in silico models) for dose prediction and toxicokinetics

Human-derived cell lines and 3D organoid cultures for pharmacodynamic profiling

As part of regulatory acceptance, these alternative methods must undergo a rigorous process of scientific validation, showing that they are predictive, reproducible, and reliable. Once validated, they are listed in international guidelines and accepted by agencies for regulatory submissions in place of animal tests. For example, the replacement of the rabbit pyrogen test with the Monocyte Activation Test (MAT) is now widely recognized and implemented.

Globally, there is also increasing collaboration between regulatory agencies and scientific organizations to accelerate the validation of alternatives. Initiatives like ICCVAM (Interagency Coordinating Committee on the Validation of Alternative Methods, USA) and EURL-ECVAM (European Union Reference Laboratory for Alternatives to Animal Testing) are at the forefront of promoting non-animal technologies.

The growing trend is also reflected in policy and legislation. For instance, cosmetic testing on animals has been banned in the European Union, India, and several other countries. Pharmaceutical industries are also increasingly shifting toward integrated testing strategies, which combine in vitro, in silico, and limited in vivo methods, to reduce the ethical and financial burden of animal studies.

Table 1: Common Laboratory Animals and Their Research Applications

Species	Scientific Name	Common Uses
Rat	Rattus norvegicus	Toxicology, pharmacokinetics, hypertension models
Mouse	Mus musculus	Genetic studies, oncology, neuropharmacology
Guinea Pig	Cavia porcellus	Anaphylaxis, auditory research, vitamin C metabolism
Rabbit	Oryctolagus cuniculus	Ocular studies, pyrogen testing, skin irritation tests
Dog	Canis lupus familiaris	Cardiovascular studies, gastrointestinal studies
Monkey	Macaca mulatta	Neuroscience, vaccine development, infectious disease models

Table 2: Comparison of Inbred vs Outbred Strains

Criteria	Inbred Strains	Outbred Strains
Genetic Variability	Low	High
Reproducibility	High	Moderate
Cost	Moderate to High	Low
Examples	BALB/c, C57BL/6	Swiss albino, Wistar

Table 3: Common Anaesthetics Used in Laboratory Animals

Agent	Type	Common Species	Comments
Isoflurane	Inhalational	Rodents	Rapid induction, good recovery
Ketamine	Injectable	Rodents	Often combined with xylazine

Xylazine	Injectable	Rodents	Used in combination for sedation
Pentobarbital	Injectable	Rodents	Narrow safety margin
CO_2	Euthanasia Agent	Rodents	Used for euthanasia under guidelines

Table 4: Key CPCSEA Guidelines for Animal Experiments

Guideline Aspect	Summary
Housing	Species-specific space, temperature and enrichment
Feeding	Nutritious, contamination-free diet and water
Ethical Clearance	All experiments must be IAEC approved
Record Keeping	Maintain breeding logs, health records
Training	Personnel must be trained and competent

Table 5: Types of Bioassays and Their Features

Bioassay Type	Description
Quantal	All-or-none response (e.g., death, survival)
Graded	Continuous range of responses (e.g., BP change)
End-Point	Defined response threshold measured
Interpolation	Dose-response plotted for test vs standard
Bracketing	Test dose bracketed between known standard doses

2. Preclinical Screening of Drugs Acting on the Central Nervous System (CNS)

2.1 General Principles of Preclinical Drug Screening

Preclinical drug screening plays a pivotal role in the drug development process. It involves testing new pharmaceutical compounds on living organisms or in vitro models before they are considered for human clinical trials. This phase is crucial for evaluating the safety, efficacy, and pharmacokinetics of potential drug candidates. Preclinical screening helps identify promising compounds and discard those that may pose risks or show little therapeutic potential.

Overview of Preclinical Drug Screening
Preclinical drug screening typically begins after a drug candidate has been identified through initial discovery processes such as high-throughput screening or rational drug design. The aim is to assess the compound's biological activity, toxicity, pharmacokinetics (absorption, distribution, metabolism, and excretion), and its potential therapeutic effects. This phase involves in vitro (test tube or petri dish) and in vivo (living organisms, usually animals) studies.

Preclinical studies are essential for determining whether a drug has the desired therapeutic effects and whether it can be administered safely. These evaluations serve as the foundation for making informed decisions about whether a compound should proceed to clinical trials in humans.

Key Objectives of Preclinical Screening

The core objective of preclinical drug screening is to gather comprehensive data on a drug candidate's safety and effectiveness. The following are the primary goals:

1. Safety Assessment:
   The potential toxicity of a drug must be assessed in preclinical studies. Toxicity can manifest in various forms, such as acute toxicity, chronic toxicity, genotoxicity, and carcinogenicity. These assessments help identify adverse effects that could endanger patients or impair drug efficacy.
2. Pharmacokinetics Evaluation:
   Understanding how a drug is absorbed, distributed, metabolized, and excreted in the body is vital. Pharmacokinetic studies allow researchers to determine the optimal dosage, frequency, and delivery method for the drug. These studies also provide insight into potential drug interactions and the drug's half-life.
3. Efficacy Testing:
   Preclinical studies test the therapeutic potential of the drug. This is typically done through animal models that simulate human diseases or conditions. Efficacy testing helps determine the drug's mechanism of action, optimal dose, and its effects on the disease process.
4. **Identification of Suitable Animal Models**:

One of the critical aspects of preclinical screening is the choice of animal models. The animal model should closely resemble the human disease being targeted to ensure the reliability of the results. Common models include rodents (mice, rats) for systemic drug testing, while larger animals (dogs, primates) may be used for more complex evaluations.

Phases of Preclinical Drug Screening

Preclinical drug screening follows a structured approach, divided into several stages:

1. InVitroScreening:
   In vitro studies are conducted to evaluate the drug's biological activity in controlled environments outside living organisms. This can involve cell cultures or tissue samples to assess the drug's mechanism of action, its interaction with receptors, and its potential therapeutic effects. In vitro tests often include assays for cytotoxicity, enzyme inhibition, receptor binding, and cell viability.
2. In Vivo Testing:Once the compound has demonstrated promising results in vitro, it progresses to in vivo testing in animals. This phase evaluates the pharmacokinetics, bioavailability, and therapeutic efficacy of the drug. Animal models are chosen based on their relevance to the human condition being studied. In vivo testing is also critical for evaluating potential side effects, adverse reactions, and the drug's impact on vital organs.
3. ToxicologyStudies:
   Safety is paramount in preclinical testing. Toxicology studies are designed to identify the potential harmful effects of the drug on various organs, tissues, and systems in the body. These studies are typically done in multiple stages, including acute, subacute, and chronic toxicity tests. In these studies, the drug is administered to animals in varying doses to determine its safety margin and the no-observed-adverse-effect level (NOAEL).

Regulatory Requirements and Ethical Considerations Preclinical studies must adhere to regulatory guidelines and ethical standards. Regulatory bodies like the FDA, EMA, and WHO provide detailed protocols for conducting preclinical testing. These guidelines ensure that preclinical trials are carried out with scientific rigor and patient safety in mind.

Additionally, ethical considerations in animal testing are critically important. Researchers must minimize animal suffering, follow the principles of the 3Rs (Replacement, Reduction, and Refinement), and obtain approval from ethics committees (e.g., Institutional Animal Care and Use Committees, or IACUCs).

2.1.1 Objectives of CNS Drug Screening

Central Nervous System (CNS) drug screening plays an essential role in identifying compounds that can be used to treat a range of neurological and psychiatric disorders. The aim of CNS drug screening is to assess the pharmacological activity, safety, and efficacy of a drug candidate before it is tested in humans. CNS disorders such as depression, schizophrenia, Alzheimer's disease, and epilepsy represent significant challenges in healthcare, and drug discovery in this area requires careful consideration due to the complexity of the brain and nervous system.

Objective 1: Identification of Drug Candidates with Desired Pharmacological Effects

One of the primary objectives of CNS drug screening is to identify compounds that demonstrate pharmacological activity relevant to a particular neurological condition. This involves evaluating the ability of a compound to affect specific pathways or receptors in the CNS, such as neurotransmitter systems (e.g., dopamine, serotonin, glutamate). By testing compounds for their effects on these pathways, researchers can determine whether the compound has potential as a therapeutic agent. Additionally, the mechanism of action of the compound should be well understood to ensure that it targets the disease appropriately.

Objective 2: Safety Assessment and Toxicity Evaluation

CNS drugs must be thoroughly assessed for safety before

proceeding to clinical trials. Preclinical drug screening for CNS drugs includes evaluating the toxicity of a drug candidate, particularly in the brain and nervous system. Adverse effects in the CNS can have serious consequences, including neurotoxicity, cognitive impairment, or mood disturbances. Preclinical testing includes acute, subacute, and chronic toxicity studies that focus on evaluating the drug's impact on neural structures and functions. The goal is to identify any potential toxic effects early in the development process and to determine safe dosage levels.

Objective3: Evaluation of Pharmacokinetic Properties

Understanding the pharmacokinetics (PK) of CNS drugs is crucial for assessing how the drug will behave in the body. The primary pharmacokinetic parameters for CNS drugs include absorption, distribution, metabolism, and excretion (ADME). A key challenge in CNS drug development is ensuring that the drug crosses the blood-brain barrier (BBB), which is a selective barrier that protects the brain from many harmful substances. The permeability of the drug through the BBB is assessed during preclinical screening, as well as its bioavailability, half-life, and metabolic stability. Ideally, the drug should have adequate brain penetration while avoiding rapid metabolism or clearance from the body.

Objective 4: Testing for Efficacy in Animal Models

Animal models are critical in CNS drug screening to evaluate the drug's therapeutic potential. These models simulate various CNS disorders, such as Parkinson's disease, Alzheimer's disease, epilepsy, and depression, allowing researchers to test the effects of drug candidates in a controlled environment. Animal models are used to assess behavioral changes, cognitive function, and motor skills in response to drug administration. Behavioral assays such as the forced swim test for antidepressants or the rotarod test for motor function are commonly used to evaluate the therapeutic efficacy of

CNS drugs. These preclinical studies help to predict how the drug might perform in human clinical trials.

Objective 5: Determining the Drug's Potential for Abuse or Dependence

For CNS drugs, especially those targeting conditions like pain or anxiety, it is essential to assess the potential for abuse or dependence. Drugs that act on neurotransmitter systems in the brain can potentially lead to addiction or other undesirable behaviors. Preclinical screening includes conducting assays to evaluate a drug's potential to produce rewarding effects, which might lead to abuse. The goal is to identify compounds that may be misused or cause dependence before they progress to human clinical trials.

Objective 6: Screening for Selectivity and Off-Target Effects
CNS drug candidates need to be screened for selectivity to ensure they affect only the desired receptors or pathways. Drugs that interact with multiple targets may lead to unwanted side effects, which can be detrimental to the drug's therapeutic profile. Preclinical screening involves assessing the selectivity of a compound for specific targets and evaluating whether it has any off-target effects, particularly in other organs or systems outside the CNS. The goal is to identify compounds that provide therapeutic effects without triggering side effects that may limit their safety and efficacy.

2.1.2 Stages of Preclinical Screening

The preclinical screening of drug candidates involves several critical stages that ensure the safety, efficacy, and potential success of a compound before human clinical trials. These stages are designed to systematically evaluate the drug's pharmacological, toxicological, and pharmacokinetic properties in order to identify any risks or challenges. The stages include:

1. Initial Screening and Compound Identification

The first stage of preclinical screening involves the identification of lead compounds that may have therapeutic potential. This is typically done through high-throughput screening (HTS) of large compound libraries to identify candidates that exhibit activity against a specific disease target, such as a receptor or enzyme. In this phase, researchers evaluate the compound's efficacy, potency, and selectivity for the target. Hits that show promise are then advanced to more detailed testing.

2. In Vitro Studies

In vitro studies are conducted in a laboratory setting using cell cultures to examine the effects of a drug candidate on cellular processes. These studies help assess the compound's activity, mechanism of action, and selectivity for the target. The main goal of this stage is to gather preliminary data on the compound's ability to interact with biological molecules in a controlled environment. Common assays used in in vitro studies include enzyme inhibition, receptor binding, and cellular viability assays.

3. In Vivo Studies

Following successful in vitro studies, the next stage involves in vivo studies, where drug candidates are tested in living organisms, typically in animal models. This stage assesses the drug's pharmacokinetics (e.g., absorption, distribution, metabolism, and excretion) and pharmacodynamics (e.g., its effects on the body). In vivo testing also helps to evaluate the compound's safety profile, including its potential for toxicity or adverse side effects. These studies provide data on the drug's efficacy in living systems and its ability to produce the desired therapeutic effects.

4. Toxicology and Safety Studies

Toxicological studies are an essential part of preclinical screening, as they help identify potential safety concerns associated with a drug candidate. These studies involve administering the drug to animals over a range of doses to observe potential acute, subacute, and chronic toxic effects. The goal is to determine the compound's safety margin, identify potential organ toxicity, and assess whether any undesirable effects are likely to occur in humans. These studies typically follow regulatory guidelines and are crucial in determining the maximum tolerated dose (MTD) and no-observed-adverse-effect level (NOAEL).

5. Pharmacokinetics and ADME Studies

Pharmacokinetics (PK) and ADME (Absorption, Distribution, Metabolism, Excretion) studies are performed to understand how the drug behaves in the body. This stage evaluates how efficiently the drug is absorbed, how it is distributed in tissues, how it is metabolized by enzymes, and how it is excreted. Understanding the pharmacokinetic profile helps optimize the drug's dosing regimen, bioavailability, and overall therapeutic potential. This phase also investigates whether the drug can cross biological barriers, such as the blood-brain barrier, which is crucial for CNS drug development.

6. Final Selection for Clinical Trials

The last stage of preclinical screening involves selecting the most promising drug candidates for human clinical trials. At this point, all data from in vitro, in vivo, toxicological, and pharmacokinetic studies are compiled to determine whether the drug has met the safety and efficacy thresholds required for clinical testing. If the drug passes this stage, it is then advanced to Phase I clinical trials in human volunteers.

2.1.3 In Vitro, In Vivo, Ex Vivo, and Alternative Models

Drug discovery and development involve testing compounds in various biological systems to assess their safety, efficacy, and pharmacological properties. In vitro, in vivo, ex vivo, and alternative models are used at different stages of preclinical drug screening. These models each provide distinct advantages and have specific roles in understanding how a drug will perform in living organisms.

1. In Vitro Models

In vitro models involve testing drug candidates in laboratory environments, using isolated cells, tissues, or cellular components. These models are the first step in the screening process and are valuable for assessing the basic pharmacological properties of a drug. In vitro testing allows researchers to perform high-throughput screenings and obtain preliminary data on the drug's interactions with biological targets, such as receptors or enzymes. For example, cell cultures are often used to evaluate the cytotoxicity of a drug or its ability to bind to specific receptors. While in vitro models are cost-effective and offer rapid results, they lack the complexity of a whole organism and may not fully replicate human physiology.

2. In Vivo Models

In vivo studies involve testing drugs in whole organisms, typically in animal models. These studies are essential for understanding how a drug behaves in a living system. In vivo testing provides comprehensive data on pharmacokinetics, pharmacodynamics, safety, and efficacy. Animal models are used to evaluate the drug's ability to reach the target tissue, the appropriate dosage for therapeutic effects, and potential toxicities. Common species used in in vivo testing include rodents, rabbits, and non-human primates. In vivo studies are indispensable in drug development, as they simulate real biological conditions, but they are expensive, time-consuming, and often subject to ethical concerns.

3. Ex Vivo Models

Ex vivo models involve testing drug candidates on tissues or organs removed from a living organism. These models allow for more direct observation of the effects of a drug on specific tissues or organs. Ex vivo testing is often used to evaluate drug absorption, distribution, and metabolism in isolated organs, such as the liver, heart, or lungs, while maintaining their biological integrity. These models offer more control over experimental conditions compared to in vivo models, and they allow researchers to study the drug's effects on specific tissue types. However, they do not provide the full complexity of an intact organism.

4. Alternative Models

Alternative models are non-traditional methods used in drug screening and testing, and they aim to reduce the reliance on animal testing. Some examples include organ-on-a-chip, 3D cell cultures, and computer-based modeling. These systems attempt to replicate the complex biological interactions that occur in the human body. Organ-on-a-chip technology uses microfluidic systems to culture human cells, simulating the functions of entire organs, such as the heart, liver, or brain. 3D cell cultures also provide a more realistic model for drug testing than 2D cell cultures. While alternative models offer exciting prospects for reducing animal testing and improving the predictive power of preclinical studies, they are still in the developmental phase and have limitations in terms of replicating full human physiology.

2.2 Behavioral and Muscle Coordination Studies

Behavioral and muscle coordination studies are essential in preclinical drug screening, particularly when investigating the central nervous system (CNS) effects of potential drug candidates. These studies help assess how a drug affects the motor functions and behavior of an organism, providing insights into its therapeutic potential or toxicity. One widely used method for evaluating motor function and behavior in animal models is the Open Field Test.

2.2.1 Open Field Test

The Open Field Test is a widely used assay for evaluating the effects of drugs on general activity, exploratory behavior, and anxiety levels in animals, particularly rodents. This test involves placing an animal, typically a mouse or rat, into a large, open, and often unmarked arena. The animal is free to move around the arena, which is equipped with a tracking system to monitor its movements. The test assesses several key behavioral parameters, including locomotor activity, exploration, and anxiety-like behavior.

The Open Field Test is valuable because it can provide a comprehensive profile of how a drug affects motor activity, emotional behavior, and even cognition. It is also one of the simplest and most cost-effective methods for screening drugs for CNS effects, particularly in the early phases of preclinical research.

Key aspects of the Open Field Test include:

1. Locomotor Activity: This is measured by tracking the distance the animal travels within the open field. Increased locomotion may indicate hyperactivity, while reduced movement may suggest sedation, motor impairment, or anxiety. These data are particularly useful for assessing stimulant or sedative effects of drugs.
2. Exploratory Behavior: The animal's tendency to explore the open field is another critical measurement. Increased exploration can indicate reduced anxiety or enhanced curiosity, while decreased exploration can be a sign of anxiety or a lack of motivation. In drug testing, this helps to

differentiate between central nervous system effects that alter the animal's mood or cognitive functions.
3. Anxiety-Like Behavior: In some versions of the Open Field Test, the arena may be divided into a center and peripheral zones. The animal's tendency to stay in the more enclosed areas (the periphery) versus the open areas (the center) is used as an indicator of anxiety levels. A drug that increases anxiety may result in the animal spending more time near the walls, while anxiolytic (anti-anxiety) drugs typically lead to more central exploration.
4. Muscle Coordination: The Open Field Test can also be used to assess the muscle coordination of an animal. By tracking movements such as rearing (standing on hind legs), grooming, or other motor behaviors, the test can help identify drugs that impact motor control, muscle coordination, or overall physical activity. For example, some drugs, such as those with sedative effects or neuromuscular blockers, may reduce an animal's ability to perform normal exploratory movements.

Applications of the Open Field Test:

- Screening for CNS activity: The Open Field Test is widely used for screening drugs that may affect the central nervous system, especially in the context of anxiety, sedation, and motor function.
- Assessing side effects of drugs: Many drugs, including those used for pain, anxiety, or depression, can have side effects on behavior and motor coordination. The Open Field Test allows researchers to identify these side effects early in the development process.
- Evaluating neurodegenerative diseases: The test is useful for assessing drug effects in models of diseases like Parkinson's disease or Alzheimer's, as these conditions typically involve changes in motor activity and exploratory behavior.
- Screening for potential therapeutic agents: In addition to assessing toxicity, the test can be used to screen drugs that may have therapeutic potential for improving motor

function, reducing anxiety, or enhancing cognitive performance.

The Open Field Test provides valuable behavioral insights in a relatively simple and controlled experimental design. However, it is important to note that it is often used in combination with other tests to provide a more comprehensive evaluation of a drug's effects on behavior and motor coordination. When interpreted alongside other behavioral assays, the Open Field Test can help build a detailed profile of a drug candidate's pharmacological effects, aiding in the decision-making process for drug development and clinical trials.

2.2.2 Hole Board Test

The Hole Board Test is a widely used behavioral assay designed to evaluate exploratory behavior, anxiety, and cognitive function in animals. It is particularly useful in preclinical drug screening, as it assesses both the motivation of an animal to explore and its response to environmental stimuli. The test provides important data about how a drug affects general activity, exploration, and anxiety levels, all of which are crucial for understanding a drug's central nervous system (CNS) effects.

The Hole Board Test typically involves placing an animal, often a rodent like a rat or mouse, in a specially designed apparatus with a flat surface containing several holes. The number of times the animal approaches, investigates, or interacts with these holes is recorded. The test measures various behaviors, including exploratory behavior, anxiety, and locomotor activity, making it a valuable tool for assessing CNS-active compounds.

Key elements of the Hole Board Test include:

1. Exploratory Behavior: In this test, the primary behavior being measured is the animal's motivation to explore the holes. Animals that exhibit higher exploration tendencies are likely showing curiosity and are less anxious, while reduced interaction with the holes could indicate anxiety or a lack of interest. Drugs that reduce anxiety typically result in higher exploration activity.
2. Locomotor Activity: The total number of approaches or entries into the holes is recorded, providing insight into the general motor activity of the animal. An increase in activity might indicate stimulation, while a decrease may suggest sedation or impairment due to drug action. This can also be an indicator of motor function or cognitive changes induced by drugs.
3. Anxiety-Like Behavior: Much like the Open Field Test, the Hole Board Test can be used to assess anxiety. The behavior of the animal can be indicative of stress or anxiety. If the animal spends less time exploring the holes or remains in a more central location, it can signal an increase in anxiety-like behavior. Anxiolytic drugs (those that reduce anxiety) are expected to increase exploration of the holes.
4. Cognitive and Memory Assessment: The Hole Board Test can also be adapted to evaluate memory and learning. For example, by introducing a novel object or changing the position of the holes, researchers can test the animal's ability to adapt to new environments or stimuli, which is especially useful when screening drugs with potential cognitive-enhancing effects.

Applications of the Hole Board Test:

- Screening for CNS-active drugs: This test is frequently used to screen compounds that may affect the central nervous system. It helps evaluate whether a drug increases or decreases exploratory behavior, and how it influences anxiety and motivation, which are key factors in many CNS disorders.
- Assessing anxiolytic and anxiogenic drugs: The Hole Board Test is often employed in the development of anxiolytic

(anti-anxiety) and anxiogenic (anxiety-producing) drugs. Anxiolytic drugs generally increase exploratory behavior, while anxiogenic drugs reduce it.
- Studying the effects of neurodegenerative diseases: The test is also valuable for understanding the impact of diseases such as Alzheimer's or Parkinson's on behavior and cognition. These diseases typically cause a reduction in exploratory behavior and cognitive dysfunction, which can be tracked using the Hole Board Test.
- Evaluating the effects of neuropharmacological agents: Drugs that impact cognition, learning, or emotional responses (such as antidepressants or cognitive enhancers) can be studied using this test. Changes in the animal's exploration patterns or interactions with the holes may reflect the drug's effects on cognitive function or emotional state.

The Hole Board Test is a relatively simple and efficient tool to assess various behavioral dimensions, including anxiety, exploration, and memory. However, it is often used in conjunction with other tests to obtain a comprehensive profile of a drug's effects on behavior. Together with tests such as the Open Field Test or Elevated Plus Maze, the Hole Board Test provides valuable data on the behavioral and cognitive impact of potential drug candidates, which is crucial for drug development and clinical application.

2.2.3 Rotarod Performance Test

The Rotarod Performance Test is a widely used method to assess motor coordination, balance, and overall motor function in animals. It is particularly valuable in preclinical drug screening for evaluating the neurotoxic effects of drugs and understanding their impact on motor control. The test is especially important when testing compounds that may affect the central nervous system (CNS), such as those intended for neurological disorders, Parkinson's disease, or drugs that may have sedative or stimulating effects.

The test involves an animal, typically a rodent, being placed on a rotating rod, which gradually accelerates. The main goal is to evaluate how long the animal can stay on the rod without falling off. The test measures the animal's ability to maintain balance and motor coordination under gradually increasing speed. This performance is an indication of the integrity of the animal's motor control systems, particularly the cerebellum, which is responsible for balance and coordination.

The Rotarod Test can be adapted to assess a variety of motor functions. One of the key parameters measured is latency to fall, which refers to the time an animal can stay on the rotating rod before losing balance and falling off. A longer latency to fall suggests better motor coordination and balance, while a shorter latency may indicate motor impairment or a lack of coordination. In drug testing, this measure is essential for evaluating the potential side effects of CNS-active drugs, such as sedatives, antidepressants, or neurotoxic compounds.

Additionally, the Rotarod Test can assess the speed of rotation and how quickly an animal adapts to increased speeds. This adaptation ability can provide insights into the effects of a drug on motor performance over time. For example, drugs that impair motor coordination, such as sedatives or tranquilizers, may result in a decreased ability to stay on the rod as the speed increases. Conversely, drugs with potential therapeutic benefits for motor disorders may improve performance by enhancing coordination and balance.

This test is highly valuable for studying a wide range of neurological conditions. For instance, Parkinson's disease is characterized by tremors, rigidity, and bradykinesia, all of which affect motor coordination. The Rotarod Test can be used to track the progression of these symptoms in animal models and evaluate the effectiveness of therapeutic agents aimed at improving motor function. Similarly, the test is used in preclinical studies of drugs targeting Alzheimer's disease, multiple sclerosis, and stroke to evaluate motor impairments.

The Rotarod Performance Test is also important in assessing neurotoxic effects of drugs. Certain drugs can cause balance issues, uncoordinated movements, or even paralysis. By evaluating the time an animal can stay on the rotating rod before falling, researchers can gauge the impact of a drug on the animal's motor control systems. In such cases, a decrease in latency to fall can be a clear indicator of motor impairment caused by the drug.

In addition to the latency to fall, rotational speed and distance traveled can also be measured, providing more detailed data on the animal's performance. Drugs that affect muscle strength, coordination, or both will show clear effects on these parameters.

The Rotarod Performance Test has several advantages, such as being relatively simple to set up and execute while providing reliable, quantitative data on motor performance. However, there are limitations as well. The test requires careful monitoring to ensure the animals are not harmed during the trial, and it may not be suitable for evaluating all types of neurological disorders, as it mainly focuses on coordination and balance.

2.2.4 Grip Strength Test

The Grip Strength Test is a widely used method to assess muscle strength and motor function, particularly in preclinical drug screening. It provides a simple and reliable measure of an animal's ability to hold onto a specific object, usually a metal grid or bar, and indicates muscle function and neuromuscular health. This test is essential in evaluating the effects of drugs on muscle strength and coordination, especially for drugs intended for the treatment of muscular disorders, neuromuscular diseases, or those that might impact muscle function as a side effect.

In the Grip Strength Test, the animal is placed on a specialized apparatus that requires it to grip a metal bar or mesh. The force applied by the animal's paws is measured through a sensitive gauge or strain gauge attached to the apparatus. The animal is gently pulled away from the bar, and the peak force exerted by the animal during the grip is recorded. This force is then used as an indicator of the animal's muscle strength and neuromuscular function. The test can be performed for both forelimbs and hindlimbs, depending on the goals of the experiment.

The Grip Strength Test is often used to assess neuromuscular impairments, which are common in diseases like amyotrophic lateral sclerosis (ALS), muscular dystrophy, and multiple sclerosis. It is also used to evaluate the impact of drugs on muscle strength and motor function. For example, neurotoxic drugs, such as certain chemotherapeutic agents, may lead to muscle weakness, and the grip strength test can quantify this reduction in strength. In contrast, therapeutic drugs that aim to improve muscle strength or neuromuscular function can show improvements in grip strength over time.

One of the significant advantages of the Grip Strength Test is its simplicity. The test is easy to set up and can be performed quickly, providing valuable quantitative data. It also requires minimal training and equipment, making it suitable for routine drug screening in preclinical research.

Additionally, the Grip Strength Test is non-invasive, which means that the animal is not subjected to surgery or invasive techniques during the assessment. This allows researchers to monitor muscle function repeatedly over the course of the study without causing harm to the animal. This feature is especially beneficial when assessing the effects of long-term treatments or monitoring the progression of a disease model.

However, like all behavioral tests, the Grip Strength Test does have limitations. The performance of the animal can be influenced by various factors, such as fatigue, motivation, and stress levels, which could lead to variability in results. It is also primarily a measure of muscle strength, and may not capture other aspects of motor function, such as coordination or balance, which are equally important for assessing the overall motor health of the animal.

In preclinical drug testing, the Grip Strength Test is often used in conjunction with other behavioral and coordination tests, such as the Rotarod Performance Test or the Open Field Test, to obtain a more comprehensive evaluation of the drug's impact on the animal's motor function. For example, a decrease in grip strength could be correlated with other signs of motor impairment, such as reduced balance or coordination.

The Grip Strength Test is especially valuable when studying drugs that target neuromuscular diseases or muscle-related disorders. It is also useful for identifying muscle-related side effects in drugs used to treat neurological disorders, cancer, or pain. By monitoring changes in grip strength over time, researchers can determine the effectiveness of a drug in improving or maintaining muscle strength in animals, providing valuable insight into its potential therapeutic benefits.

2.2.5 Interpretation and Applications in Motor Coordination

Motor coordination is a fundamental aspect of animal behavior that reflects the ability to integrate and control muscle movements. Evaluating motor coordination in preclinical drug screening is essential for understanding how certain compounds affect the central nervous system (CNS) and neuromuscular functions. A range of tests, including the Grip Strength Test, Rotarod Performance Test, and Open Field Test, offer insight into motor coordination by assessing strength, balance, and movement patterns. However, interpreting these tests requires careful consideration of various factors that influence motor performance.

When interpreting motor coordination tests, it is important to consider both neurological and muscular factors. Neurological factors refer to the brain's ability to control muscle movements, which involves the motor cortex, cerebellum, and spinal cord. Muscular factors involve the muscle's capacity to respond to neural signals and generate movement. Therefore, deficits in motor coordination can be attributed to neurological conditions, muscle weakness, or motor neuron dysfunction.

In preclinical drug studies, the evaluation of motor coordination is often used to determine the side effects or therapeutic potential of drugs, particularly those aimed at treating neurological disorders, muscle diseases, and pain. For example, drugs used to treat Parkinson's disease, multiple sclerosis, or amyotrophic lateral sclerosis (ALS) can lead to improvements or impairments in motor coordination, which can be detected through these tests.

For instance, motor impairments detected in tests like the Rotarod Performance Test or Grip Strength Test may suggest that a drug is having a negative impact on neuromuscular function, while improvements in performance can indicate therapeutic benefits. In the case of Parkinson's disease, drugs like dopamine agonists can be evaluated for their ability to restore motor coordination by improving the time an animal spends on a rotating rod in the Rotarod test.

On the other hand, drugs such as chemotherapy agents or certain neurotoxicants that affect motor function and coordination are also studied in preclinical trials to evaluate whether they induce impairments. For example, cisplatin, a chemotherapeutic drug, has been shown to cause motor coordination deficits in animal models, which can be measured using tests like the Rotarod Performance Test and Grip Strength Test. These deficits may result from neurotoxicity or muscle weakness, highlighting the importance of assessing both aspects in preclinical studies.

Motor coordination tests also have applications in the development of novel therapeutics aimed at improving neuromuscular diseases. For example, drugs aimed at improving motor coordination in patients with muscular dystrophy or spinal cord injury can be tested using preclinical models. Gene therapy or cell-based therapies are becoming increasingly common in these disease models. Preclinical evaluation through motor coordination tests helps determine the success of such therapies in improving movement and function.

Additionally, motor coordination testing plays a critical role in the screening of novel CNS drugs that aim to enhance cognitive and motor functions, especially in diseases such as Alzheimer's disease and stroke recovery. In these cases, the ability of a drug to improve balance, gait, and motor skills is essential. Preclinical motor coordination studies can help identify drugs that show promise in improving both cognitive function and physical ability, providing a more comprehensive approach to CNS therapy.

However, interpreting the results from motor coordination tests is complex and should be done in conjunction with other behavioral assays to obtain a comprehensive understanding of drug effects. For example, while the Rotarod test measures balance and coordination, it is important to combine it with the Grip Strength Test to assess both muscle strength and coordination. Additionally, tests like the Open Field Test provide information about locomotion and exploratory behavior, which can offer further insights into how a drug

2.3 CNS Stimulants and Depressants

The central nervous system (CNS) plays a pivotal role in regulating various physiological processes in the human body, such as mood, attention, motor coordination, and cognitive functions. Drugs that interact with the CNS can either stimulate or depress its activity, leading to alterations in brain function. CNS stimulants and CNS depressants are two broad categories of drugs that have distinct effects on the nervous system, and their roles in preclinical drug screening are critical for understanding their potential therapeutic and side effects. In this section, we will explore the characteristics, mechanisms, and applications of CNS stimulants and depressants, as well as their importance in drug development.

CNS Stimulants

CNS stimulants are a class of drugs that increase the activity of the brain and spinal cord. These drugs enhance alertness, increase arousal, elevate mood, and can also improve cognitive and physical performance. The action of CNS stimulants is typically linked to the modulation of neurotransmitters in the brain, such as dopamine, norepinephrine, and serotonin. These chemicals are involved in transmitting signals between neurons, and stimulating their release or inhibiting their reuptake leads to increased neuronal activity.

The most commonly known CNS stimulants include amphetamine and methylphenidate, which are used to treat attention-deficit hyperactivity disorder (ADHD) and narcolepsy. Caffeine, another well-known stimulant, enhances alertness by antagonizing adenosine receptors. These stimulants can increase heart rate, blood pressure, and energy levels, making them effective in treating conditions like ADHD, narcolepsy, and obesity. However, the potential for misuse and addiction is a concern with CNS stimulants, as they can lead to euphoria, dependence, and psychological effects such as anxiety, aggression, and even seizures in extreme cases.

Mechanism of Action of CNS Stimulants

CNS stimulants function through various mechanisms to enhance neurotransmission. Some stimulants, like amphetamines, work by promoting the release of neurotransmitters from the presynaptic neurons, particularly dopamine and norepinephrine. This increased release of neurotransmitters results in heightened sympathetic activity, leading to enhanced alertness, improved focus, and increased energy levels.

Other stimulants, such as methylphenidate, work by blocking the reuptake of dopamine and norepinephrine, thereby increasing their concentration in the synaptic cleft and prolonging their action. Caffeine works differently by blocking adenosine receptors, which normally promote relaxation and sleep. By inhibiting these receptors, caffeine increases neuronal firing and the release of excitatory neurotransmitters, leading to increased alertness and wakefulness.

In preclinical studies, CNS stimulants are often assessed for their ability to enhance cognitive functions and physical performance, particularly in animal models of neurodegenerative diseases or attention disorders. They are also evaluated for their potential to induce dependence, tolerance, and neurotoxicity, which are important considerations in clinical trials.

CNS Depressants

On the other hand, CNS depressants reduce the activity of the central nervous system, leading to calming effects. These drugs can lower heart rate, blood pressure, and induce sedation, relaxation, and sleep. CNS depressants are commonly used to treat anxiety, insomnia, seizure disorders, and as anesthetic agents. They include benzodiazepines, barbiturates, alcohol, and opioids.

Benzodiazepines, such as diazepam and lorazepam, enhance the action of the neurotransmitter gamma-aminobutyric acid (GABA), which inhibits neuronal firing. This results in a calming effect, reducing anxiety, promoting sleep, and preventing seizures. Barbiturates, another class of CNS depressants, also act on GABA receptors but have a more pronounced sedative and hypnotic effect. While both benzodiazepines and barbiturates are effective in treating anxiety and sleep disorders, the potential for addiction, overdose, and respiratory depression with these drugs is significant.

Opioids, such as morphine, codeine, and fentanyl, are powerful CNS depressants used for pain relief. They bind to specific receptors in the brain and spinal cord, inhibiting the transmission of pain signals and inducing feelings of euphoria. However, opioid use comes with high risks of dependence, addiction, and respiratory depression, making their use a major concern in clinical settings.

Mechanism of Action of CNS Depressants

The main action of CNS depressants is the enhancement of inhibitory neurotransmission or the suppression of excitatory neurotransmission. For instance, benzodiazepines bind to the GABA-A receptor, facilitating the binding of GABA, which in turn opens chloride channels and hyperpolarizes neurons, making them less likely to fire. This leads to a reduction in neuronal activity, resulting in anxiolysis, sedation, and muscle relaxation.

Barbiturates also enhance GABA activity, but their mechanism is broader, as they directly activate GABA receptors at higher doses. Additionally, barbiturates suppress the glutamatergic system, which is responsible for excitatory neurotransmission. Opioids, on the other hand, bind to mu, delta, and kappa opioid receptors, inhibiting the release of neurotransmitters and dampening the perception of pain while inducing sedation and euphoria.

CNS depressants are often tested in preclinical studies for their sedative, anxiolytic, and analgesic effects. These drugs are also assessed for toxicity, dependence potential, and withdrawal symptoms, which are important safety considerations for human use.

Applications and Clinical Use

CNS stimulants and depressants are used to treat a wide range of clinical conditions, and their use is highly dependent on the specific therapeutic goals. For example, CNS stimulants like methylphenidate and amphetamine are used in treating ADHD and narcolepsy, while CNS depressants like benzodiazepines and opioids are used for anxiety, insomnia, and pain management.

In preclinical drug development, these drugs are tested for their ability to modulate CNS activity and improve therapeutic outcomes in conditions like depression, anxiety, schizophrenia, pain disorders, and neurodegenerative diseases. Animal models are often used to assess the potential therapeutic effects, side effects, and risks of abuse associated with these drugs.

Furthermore, CNS stimulants are sometimes used in cases of fatigue, depression, and cognitive impairment, whereas CNS depressants are used to manage conditions like seizures, insomnia, and muscle spasms. However, the use of CNS depressants, especially opioids, must be carefully monitored due to their potential for addiction and overdose.

2.3.1 Models for Amphetamine and CNS Stimulants

The study of CNS stimulants, especially amphetamine and its derivatives, plays a significant role in understanding their pharmacological effects, mechanisms of action, and therapeutic potential. These substances are commonly used to treat disorders like attention-deficit hyperactivity disorder (ADHD) and narcolepsy, but they also have the potential for abuse, dependence, and neurotoxicity. Therefore, preclinical drug screening using suitable animal models is crucial for evaluating the safety, efficacy, and potential risks of CNS stimulants. In this section, we will explore the models commonly used to study amphetamine and other CNS stimulants.

Animal Models for Evaluating CNS Stimulants

Several animal models are employed in the preclinical evaluation of amphetamine and other CNS stimulants to simulate the effects seen in humans. These models help to understand the stimulant's action on behavior, cognition, and neurochemical pathways, allowing researchers to evaluate their potential for therapeutic use as well as to assess abuse potential and the risk of neurotoxicity.

1. Locomotor Activity Models

One of the most commonly used tests to study the effects of amphetamine is the locomotor activity test. In this model, animals, typically rodents like rats or mice, are placed in an open arena or enclosed space, and their movement is tracked. Amphetamine is known to increase the activity levels of animals due to its stimulating effects on the brain, particularly in the dopaminergic system. Researchers observe and measure the number of movements, the distance traveled, and the activity patterns in response to amphetamine administration.

The locomotor test is particularly useful in assessing the rewarding effects of CNS stimulants and understanding their potential for abuse. Animals given amphetamine typically exhibit increased locomotor activity, reflecting the drug's stimulating effects. This model helps in determining the dose-response relationship, as well as examining the effects of amphetamine over different time intervals to assess its acute and chronic effects on activity.

2. Conditioned Place Preference (CPP)

Another important model used in the study of amphetamine and other stimulants is the conditioned place preference (CPP) test. This behavioral paradigm is used to measure the rewarding effects of a drug. Animals are exposed to two distinct environments, and amphetamine is administered in one of these environments, while a saline solution is given in the other. Over time, animals will develop a preference for the environment associated with the drug administration due to the rewarding effects of amphetamine.

The CPP model provides insights into the abuse potential of amphetamine. A stronger preference for the environment where amphetamine was administered suggests a higher potential for addiction and abuse. This model is critical for evaluating the reinforcing properties of CNS stimulants, providing valuable data for assessing their risk for misuse.

3. Cognitive Function Models

Amphetamine and other CNS stimulants can also affect cognitive function, such as attention, learning, and memory. Animal models such as the radial arm maze and the Morris water maze are used to assess cognitive functions that are often affected by amphetamine use. These models are designed to test learning and memory capabilities in rodents by requiring them to navigate a maze to receive rewards or avoid punishment.

In the radial arm maze, animals must remember which arms they have already visited, demonstrating their ability to remember past actions and avoid errors. Amphetamine administration can alter performance on these tasks, typically improving short-term memory and increasing motivation, but it may also impair cognitive function at higher doses or with chronic use. These models help to evaluate how amphetamine affects brain functions related to attention and learning.

4. Dopamine Release and Neurochemical Models

Since amphetamine primarily works by increasing the release of dopamine in the brain, studies often focus on the neurochemical effects of the drug. The microdialysis technique is commonly used to monitor the dopamine levels in specific brain regions, such as the striatum and prefrontal cortex, after administration of amphetamine. This model allows researchers to observe the dose-dependent increase in dopamine release and evaluate the role of dopamine in the behavioral effects of the stimulant.

Additionally, positron emission tomography (PET) and single-photon emission computed tomography (SPECT) imaging techniques are used to assess the dopamine transporter binding and dopamine release in vivo. These models help to provide insights into how amphetamine affects the brain at the neurotransmitter level, which is crucial for understanding both the therapeutic and addictive effects of the drug.

5. Withdrawal and Dependence Models

Long-term use of amphetamine can lead to dependence, and preclinical models are also used to study withdrawal symptoms and dependence. In these models, animals are exposed to repeated doses of amphetamine, and the withdrawal effects are assessed when the drug is discontinued. These effects may include behavioral changes such as anxiety, depression-like symptoms, and changes in food intake and body weight. By evaluating the neurochemical changes during withdrawal, researchers can assess the dependence potential and the underlying mechanisms that contribute to addiction.

The self-administration model is another key method for studying amphetamine dependence. In this test, animals are trained to administer the drug to themselves by pressing a lever or performing a task, simulating human drug-seeking behavior. Amphetamine and other CNS stimulants are often found to be self-administered by rodents, providing evidence of their reinforcing and addictive properties.

6. Neurotoxicity Models

Finally, studies also focus on the neurotoxic effects of amphetamine. In these models, animals are exposed to high doses of amphetamine over a period of time to assess damage to the dopaminergic system and other brain structures. The assessment is typically carried out using histological techniques and brain imaging to identify any changes in brain structure or function. Amphetamine-induced neurotoxicity is an important consideration, especially when evaluating the safety of the drug for long-term use.

2.3.2 Models for CNS Depressants: Barbiturates

CNS depressants, such as barbiturates, are a class of drugs that exert their effects by depressing the activity of the central nervous system. These drugs are commonly used for their sedative, hypnotic, and anxiolytic effects, making them useful in treating conditions like anxiety, insomnia, and seizures. However, barbiturates also have a high potential for abuse, dependence, and overdose. Preclinical animal models play a crucial role in studying the pharmacology, toxicology, and safety profiles of barbiturates before clinical application. In this section, we will explore the animal models used to evaluate the effects of barbiturates and other CNS depressants.

Animal Models for CNS Depressants

The primary focus of CNS depressant studies, particularly those involving barbiturates, is to assess their sedative and hypnotic effects, their potential for abuse, and the neurotoxic outcomes of prolonged or high-dose use. Animal models help to evaluate these aspects and determine safe dosages and administration methods. Various behavioral and physiological models are used to investigate these drugs' effects on motor coordination, sleep, anxiety, and neurotoxicity.

1. Sedative and Hypnotic Effects: Sleep-Induction Models

One of the most common methods for evaluating the sedative and hypnotic effects of barbiturates is the use of sleep-induction models. In these models, animals are given a dose of barbiturates, and their time to onset of sleep, the duration of sleep, and the sleep patterns are observed. The pentobarbital sleep test is widely used for this purpose, where pentobarbital, a commonly used barbiturate, is administered to rodents.

Animals are placed in a controlled environment, and their behavior is closely monitored. The primary outcome measure is the time it takes for the animal to fall asleep after the administration of pentobarbital. Additionally, the duration of sleep is recorded, and the dose-response relationship is assessed to determine the sedative potency of the drug. The sedative effects are quantified by monitoring the animal's motor activity, with a reduction in movement indicating the desired depressive effect.

This test helps to assess the onset and duration of the hypnotic effects of barbiturates and compare them with other CNS depressants, such as benzodiazepines and alcohol. Moreover, it helps evaluate the potential for dependence and the abuse potential of barbiturates based on how they alter sleep patterns and behavior.

2. Motor Coordination and Ataxia Models

Barbiturates and other CNS depressants also affect motor coordination and muscle strength. The rotarod test is a widely used model for assessing the effects of CNS depressants on motor coordination. In this test, animals are placed on a rotating rod, and the time they can maintain balance is measured. The rotarod test is particularly useful for evaluating barbiturates' effects on motor coordination and the potential sedative side effects, such as ataxia and drowsiness.

High doses of barbiturates can cause motor impairment, leading to a shorter time spent on the rotating rod. By measuring the time to fall off, researchers can determine the degree of impairment and the dose-response effect of barbiturates on motor skills. This model also provides valuable data on how these drugs impair the central nervous system and their neurotoxic effects when administered chronically or at high doses.

3. Anxiety and Behavior Models

In addition to their sedative effects, barbiturates also have anxiolytic properties. The elevated plus maze (EPM) test is commonly used to assess the anxiolytic effects of CNS depressants. The EPM test involves placing animals in a maze with open and closed arms and measuring the time they spend in each. The longer an animal spends in the open arms, the more anxious it is presumed to be. After administering barbiturates, animals typically show an increased time in the open arms, indicating a reduction in anxiety.

The open field test is another behavioral test used to assess the effects of barbiturates on anxiety and locomotor activity. After administration of the drug, animals are placed in an open field, and their locomotor activity is recorded. CNS depressants like barbiturates tend to reduce locomotor activity and induce a sedative-like effect, which is observed as a decrease in the animal's movement.

These models are particularly useful for understanding the anxiolytic properties of barbiturates and their ability to reduce anxiety in conditions like generalized anxiety disorder or insomnia. It also provides insight into the dose-response effects of barbiturates on behavioral patterns.

4. Dependence and Withdrawal Models

As barbiturates can be habit-forming and lead to dependence, animal models are also used to study the potential for dependence and withdrawal symptoms. The self-administration model is used to assess the reinforcing properties of barbiturates. In this model, animals are trained to administer the drug to themselves by performing a task, such as pressing a lever. The frequency of self-administration reflects the drug's reinforcing effects and potential for abuse.

Additionally, withdrawal models are used to study the effects of discontinuing barbiturate administration. After long-term exposure to barbiturates, animals exhibit withdrawal symptoms when the drug is removed. These symptoms may include tremors, seizures, and anxiety-like behaviors, which mimic human withdrawal effects. Understanding these symptoms helps researchers to determine the dependence potential of barbiturates and guide the development of drugs with fewer addictive properties.

5. Neurotoxicity and Neurochemical Models

Finally, barbiturates can cause neurotoxicity with long-term use or in high doses. In animal models, the neurotoxic effects of barbiturates are studied using microdialysis or histological examinations. These techniques allow researchers to monitor changes in brain neurochemistry (such as dopamine and serotonin levels) and to detect any structural changes in the brain after repeated exposure to barbiturates.

High doses of barbiturates may lead to neurodegenerative effects, particularly on dopaminergic and GABAergic systems. In such models, animals are exposed to barbiturates for extended periods, and their brain function is assessed post-mortem to examine the effects of the drug on brain structure and neurochemical balance.

2.3.3 Locomotor Activity Assays

Locomotor activity assays are widely used in preclinical research to evaluate the effects of CNS stimulants and depressants on motor function. These assays are particularly useful in understanding how drugs influence the central nervous system's ability to regulate movement, coordination, and overall activity levels. Since changes in motor activity can reflect the neuroactive properties of a drug, these tests are critical for assessing the therapeutic potential, toxicity, and side effects of new compounds.

Purpose and Importance

The locomotor activity assay provides valuable insights into the pharmacological effects of CNS-active drugs. Drugs that stimulate the central nervous system, such as amphetamines or caffeine, are expected to increase motor activity, whereas CNS depressants like barbiturates or benzodiazepines typically reduce it. Therefore, the test can differentiate between stimulatory and depressant drugs and give an early indication of their potential use in treating disorders such as ADHD, narcolepsy, or insomnia. These assays are also helpful in evaluating the dose-response relationship and the duration of action of drugs, which is crucial for determining the optimal dosing regimen for clinical use.

Design and Methodology

The locomotor activity assay involves placing animals, typically rodents, in an open arena or chamber where their movements are tracked using automated systems. These systems often include infrared sensors, motion detectors, or video tracking systems that can measure the distance traveled, speed, time spent moving, and the number of rearing events (vertical movements) of the animal. The basic setup involves monitoring the animal's activity in response to drug administration, and the collected data is analyzed to determine any changes in movement behavior.

In the simplest form, the animal is placed in an open field or an enclosed space for a fixed period, often 30 to 60 minutes. The level of motor activity is recorded, and the data is used to assess the stimulatory or depressant effects of a drug. The test can be modified by varying parameters such as the environmental conditions, the duration of exposure, and the time points at which measurements are taken.

Key Parameters Measured

1. Total Distance Traveled: The most common measurement used in locomotor activity assays is the total distance traveled by the animal. This parameter is a measure of activity level and can indicate whether the drug causes hyperactivity or hypoactivity. Increased distance traveled suggests a stimulant effect, while reduced distance indicates a depressant effect.
2. Speed: The speed of movement is another important measure. It helps assess the intensity of movement and can reveal whether the drug causes restlessness or sedation.
3. Rearing Behavior: Rearing, or vertical movement, is often recorded as an indicator of exploratory behavior. Changes in rearing frequency or duration may indicate a drug's impact on exploratory behavior or anxiety levels.
4. Time Spent in Activity vs. Resting States: In some assays, the time spent moving and time spent resting are separately analyzed to determine the balance between activity and sedation induced by the drug.

Applications of Locomotor Activity Assays

1. Assessing CNS Stimulants and Depressants: These assays are essential for distinguishing between stimulants and depressants. Stimulant drugs (e.g., amphetamine, methylphenidate) typically increase motor activity, while CNS depressants (e.g., benzodiazepines, barbiturates) decrease movement.
2. Drug Abuse Potential: Locomotor activity assays can also be used to evaluate the abuse potential of a drug. For example, drugs that produce hyperactivity or excessive stimulation may have a higher risk for abuse. By tracking the behavioral changes after drug administration, researchers can assess whether a drug has reinforcing properties.
3. Neurotoxicity Evaluation: In addition to evaluating stimulatory or sedative effects, locomotor activity assays can help identify neurotoxic effects. For example, long-term exposure to high doses of a drug may result in motor impairments or coordination issues, which are reflected in decreased movement or abnormal patterns of activity.

4. Assessing Drug Tolerance and Withdrawal: In chronic drug administration studies, tolerance to the drug's effects and withdrawal symptoms can be assessed by measuring changes in locomotor activity. Drugs that induce tolerance will show reduced changes in motor activity over time, while withdrawal may result in hyperactivity or anxiety-like behavior.

Interpretation of Results

Interpretation of the results from locomotor activity assays involves understanding the dose-response relationship and determining the therapeutic index of the drug. If a drug induces a large increase in motor activity, it may indicate a stimulant effect, whereas a reduction in activity might suggest sedative or depressant effects. Variability in the results can also occur depending on the drug administration route, animal strain, and experimental conditions.

For example, while stimulants may increase movement, excessive stimulation may lead to motor coordination issues, such as tremors or hyperactivity, which are undesirable in therapeutic treatments. On the other hand, CNS depressants like benzodiazepines may impair movement and coordination, reflecting their sedative properties.

Limitations of Locomotor Activity Assays

Despite their widespread use, locomotor activity assays have limitations. One limitation is that these assays primarily measure gross motor activity and may not capture subtle neurological effects, such as cognitive impairments or mood changes. Additionally, the results may vary between animal species and even between individual animals within the same species. Moreover, these assays focus on the effects of the drug on movement, but may not provide a comprehensive understanding of the underlying mechanisms affecting behavior and neurochemistry.

2.3.4 Pentobarbital-Induced Sleep Time Assay

The Pentobarbital-Induced Sleep Time Assay is an important behavioral test used to evaluate the sedative and hypnotic effects of various compounds on the central nervous system. It involves the administration of pentobarbital, a barbiturate known for its ability to induce sleep, and measuring the duration of sleep induced by the drug. This assay is useful in assessing the sedative properties of new drugs or drug candidates, particularly those intended to treat insomnia, anxiety, or other disorders requiring central nervous system depression.

Purpose and Importance

The Pentobarbital-Induced Sleep Time Assay is primarily used to evaluate how a drug modulates the CNS activity. By observing the duration and onset of sleep induced by pentobarbital, researchers can assess how substances interact with the central nervous system and their potential as sedatives or sleep aids. This test is widely used in preclinical studies to determine the hypnotic effects of new drug candidates, their potential for abuse, and their effectiveness in promoting sleep without causing excessive sedation or toxicity.

Methodology

The assay begins with the administration of pentobarbital to the experimental animals, typically rodents, via intraperitoneal (IP) or subcutaneous (SC) injection. Pentobarbital, once administered, induces sleep by enhancing the inhibitory effects of GABA (gamma-aminobutyric acid), a neurotransmitter that reduces neuronal excitability in the CNS. After administration, the onset of sleep and the total duration of sleep are recorded. Sleep is typically defined as a loss of the righting reflex, in which the animal is unable to right itself when placed on its back.

The test compound, or test drug, is administered before pentobarbital to observe whether it enhances or inhibits the sleep-inducing effects of pentobarbital. The sleep time is measured as the duration from the loss of the righting reflex to its recovery. In some cases, additional behavioral observations are made to assess motor coordination and potential adverse effects like excessive sedation or respiratory depression.

Key Parameters Measured

1. Latency to Sleep Onset: The latency to sleep onset refers to the amount of time it takes for the animal to fall asleep after pentobarbital administration. A shorter latency suggests that the test compound may have sedative effects and can facilitate sleep induction.
2. Sleep Duration: This is the primary measure in the Pentobarbital-Induced Sleep Time Assay. It refers to how long the animal remains asleep after the induction of sleep. The duration of sleep is typically measured in minutes. Drugs that prolong the sleep duration may be considered potent sedatives.
3. Recovery Time: Recovery time refers to the duration it takes for the animal to regain its ability to right itself after the loss of the righting reflex. This parameter can be useful in assessing the reversibility of drug-induced sedation and whether a compound causes excessive sedation.

Applications

1. Evaluation of Sedative and Hypnotic Properties: The Pentobarbital-Induced Sleep Time Assay is used to determine the sedative effects of drugs, particularly in the development of sleep aids and anxiolytics. For instance, benzodiazepines are often tested in this assay to determine their effectiveness in inducing sleep without causing excessive sedation or addiction.
2. Assessment of Drug Interactions: This assay can also be used to study the interactions between sedative drugs and other substances. For example, it can evaluate how a non-sedative drug might alter the sleep-inducing effects of pentobarbital or other CNS-active compounds.

3. **Study of CNS Depression:** The assay is important for screening drugs that may potentially cause CNS depression or respiratory depression, as drugs that prolong sleep duration or cause a prolonged lack of righting reflex can be indicators of dangerous sedative effects.
4. **Preclinical Screening for CNS Drug Development:** In early-stage drug development, the Pentobarbital-Induced Sleep Time Assay is used to screen new drug candidates for their potential hypnotic effects and CNS activity. This information can help guide the design of further preclinical studies and clinical trials.

Interpretation of Results

In interpreting the results of the assay, the focus is on the relationship between the test drug and pentobarbital. Drugs that enhance the sedative effects of pentobarbital may be classified as potential CNS depressants or sedatives. Conversely, drugs that reduce the sleep time or interfere with the induction of sleep may have CNS stimulant properties or may block the sleep-inducing effects of pentobarbital. The dose-response relationship is also crucial to identify the potency of the drug, as a higher dose of the drug may result in more pronounced effects on sleep duration or latency.

Limitations of the Assay

While the Pentobarbital-Induced Sleep Time Assay is a valuable tool in assessing CNS activity, it has some limitations. Barbiturates like pentobarbital are non-selective CNS depressants, which means that the assay does not give detailed insights into the mechanism of action of a drug. Additionally, the assay focuses solely on sleep and sedation, so it may not capture other important neurological effects such as anxiolysis, muscle relaxation, or cognitive impairment.

Furthermore, pentobarbital itself has some potential side effects, such as respiratory depression, which can complicate the interpretation of results, especially at higher doses. Additionally, species-specific differences in the effects of pentobarbital and other CNS-active drugs may result in variability in the assay outcomes.

2.4 Anxiolytics and Anti-Psychotics

2.4.1 Elevated Plus Maze

The Elevated Plus Maze (EPM) is one of the most widely used experimental models for the preclinical screening of anxiolytic and anxiogenic agents. It is based on the natural aversion of rodents to open, elevated, and brightly lit spaces, and their inherent preference for enclosed, protected areas. The test is designed to evaluate anxiety-related behaviour in rodents, especially mice and rats, by observing their movement between open and closed arms of a maze elevated above the floor.

The apparatus consists of a plus-shaped structure elevated about 40 to 50 cm from the floor, with four arms arranged at right angles. Two of these arms are open (without walls), and two are closed (surrounded by vertical walls). The arms are usually 50 cm long and 10 cm wide, and the central platform connecting the arms is also 10 cm². The entire structure is typically made of wood, metal, or plastic and is placed in a quiet, dimly lit testing room to minimize external stress.

In a standard EPM test, the rodent is placed at the centre of the maze facing one of the open arms. Its behaviour is recorded for a duration of 5 minutes using either manual observation or a video tracking system. The key parameters observed include:

- Number of entries into open and closed arms
- Time spent in open and closed arms
- Number of head dips over the edges of open arms
- Stretch-attend postures and grooming behaviour

A drug with anxiolytic activity typically increases the number of entries and the total time spent in the open arms, indicating a reduction in anxiety and increased exploratory behaviour. In contrast, anxiogenic compounds reduce these parameters, reflecting heightened anxiety. The closed arm entries are often used as a measure of general locomotor activity, allowing researchers to distinguish between anxiolytic effects and motor impairment.

The EPM model is highly sensitive to benzodiazepines (e.g., diazepam, alprazolam), which are standard reference anxiolytics. It is also useful for screening newer classes of anti-anxiety agents such as $5-HT_1A$ agonists, CRF antagonists, and GABAergic modulators. The test can be adapted by modifying the light intensity, duration of testing, or environmental enrichment to evaluate different aspects of anxiety and risk assessment.

However, the EPM has certain limitations. The model may show habituation upon repeated testing, which reduces sensitivity to drugs in chronic studies. Additionally, results may vary depending on animal strain, sex, prior handling, and maze dimensions, necessitating strict standardization of test conditions. Furthermore, substances that cause sedation or motor inhibition may falsely appear to have anxiogenic effects due to reduced open arm entries.

Despite these limitations, the Elevated Plus Maze remains a robust, validated, and reproducible method for assessing anxiolytic potential in preclinical research. It provides valuable insights into the behavioural pharmacology of anxiety and is often used in conjunction with other models such as the light-dark box, open field test, and social interaction test to provide a comprehensive evaluation of a compound's effects on anxiety-like behaviour in rodents.

2.4.2 Light–Dark Box Test

The Light–Dark Box Test is a well-established behavioural model used in preclinical pharmacology to evaluate the anxiolytic or anxiogenic potential of drugs in rodents, especially mice. This model is based on the natural conflict in rodents between their drive to explore new environments and their fear of brightly lit open spaces. The animal's avoidance of the light compartment and preference for the dark indicates a higher anxiety level, while an increase in exploration of the light area is suggestive of anxiolytic activity.

The test apparatus consists of a two-compartment box, usually measuring around 40 cm × 20 cm × 20 cm, equally divided into a light chamber and a dark chamber. The light chamber is illuminated with a bright light (usually 400–500 lux), whereas the dark chamber is enclosed and not illuminated. A small opening or tunnel connects the two compartments, allowing the animal to move freely between them. The floor and walls are typically constructed from plastic or wood, and the setup is placed in a noise-free environment during the experiment.

In a standard protocol, the animal is gently placed in the center of the light compartment at the start of the test, and its behaviour is recorded for a 5-minute session. The parameters commonly observed and quantified include:

- Latency to first entry into the dark compartment
- Time spent in each compartment
- Number of transitions between compartments
- Number of rearing behaviours or stretch-attend postures

Anxiolytic drugs such as benzodiazepines (e.g., diazepam) typically increase the time spent in the light compartment, reduce latency to enter it, and increase the number of transitions, indicating reduced anxiety. In contrast, anxiogenic compounds or stressful stimuli tend to enhance avoidance of the light chamber and reduce exploratory transitions.

The Light–Dark Box Test is particularly advantageous because it is non-invasive, does not require prior training, and provides rapid and reproducible results. It also allows differentiation between anxiolytic effects and sedative or locomotor impairments, especially when coupled with additional measures such as locomotion tracking.

However, like other behavioural models, it has some limitations. The outcome can be affected by animal strain, sex, handling, light intensity, and prior exposure to the apparatus. Mice are generally more responsive in this model than rats. Additionally, certain CNS depressants may produce false positives by increasing time in the light area due to reduced aversion rather than true anxiolysis.

Despite these constraints, the Light–Dark Box Test remains a widely accepted screening tool for early detection of anti-anxiety effects, especially for GABAergic, serotonergic, and novel compounds targeting central mechanisms involved in anxiety regulation. It is often used in combination with Elevated Plus Maze and Open Field Test to provide a multi-faceted behavioural profile of investigational CNS-active compounds.

2.4.3 Social Interaction Test

The social interaction test is a sensitive and reliable behavioural model used in preclinical research to evaluate the anxiolytic and anxiogenic effects of drug candidates based on the natural social behaviour of rodents. This test is grounded in the observation that under conditions of anxiety, animals reduce their normal exploratory and social tendencies. Therefore, any pharmacological intervention that restores or increases social engagement can be interpreted as having potential anxiolytic activity. It is commonly used in rats and sometimes in mice, with standardization of strain, age, and environmental factors playing a vital role in ensuring reproducibility of results.

The experimental setup typically involves a square or rectangular open field arena, usually measuring about $60 \times 60 \times 30$ centimetres, with smooth, opaque walls and a clean floor. Two animals of the same species, sex, age, and weight, which have been housed separately to avoid familiarity, are placed simultaneously into the test arena. The lighting in the room is often kept low to moderate, as bright lighting increases anxiety and may confound results. Animals are allowed to explore the environment and interact for a fixed observation period, generally between 5 to 10 minutes. Their behaviour is recorded either manually by an observer or through automated video tracking systems.

The primary behavioural parameters recorded include the total duration and frequency of direct social behaviours such as sniffing, grooming, following, climbing over or under, and crawling together. The number of avoidance behaviours, episodes of aggression, and non-social activities such as rearing or wall-climbing are also noted to differentiate between drug effects on anxiety and general locomotion. A reduction in avoidance and an increase in meaningful social interaction indicate anxiolytic potential of the test substance.

Social interaction behaviour is significantly suppressed under stressful conditions such as novel environments or high illumination. This makes the test particularly useful in detecting low-dose anxiolytic effects of drugs like benzodiazepines, selective serotonin reuptake inhibitors, or novel compounds targeting central neurotransmitter systems. For instance, diazepam at doses between 1 to 2 mg/kg intraperitoneally has been shown to increase social interaction time in rats by nearly 40 to 60 percent compared to control.

It is essential to control for possible motor effects of the test compound. A drug that sedates or stimulates the animal may alter the movement and activity pattern, leading to misinterpretation of results as anxiolytic or anxiogenic. Therefore, social interaction data are often analysed alongside open field locomotion scores to confirm that changes in social behaviour are not secondary to motor impairment.

The test is considered ethically favourable as it does not involve painful stimuli or aversive procedures. However, it requires careful pairing of animals and proper pre-screening to avoid confounding results from aggressive interactions or territorial behaviour, particularly in males. Cleanliness of the arena and absence of odour cues from previous trials are also critical for reducing experimental variability.

The social interaction test complements other behavioural assays such as the elevated plus maze and light–dark box, providing a broader and more ecologically relevant understanding of anxiolytic potential. It remains a valuable component of behavioural pharmacology, especially when used with appropriate controls and careful interpretation.

2.4.4 Models of Catalepsy and Stereotypy

Catalepsy and stereotypy are two specific behavioural phenomena observed in rodents that serve as important experimental models in the preclinical screening of antipsychotic drugs, particularly those affecting the dopaminergic system. These models help in understanding the neuromotor side effects and central dopaminergic modulation caused by neuroleptic agents. Catalepsy is defined as a condition in which an animal maintains an imposed posture for an abnormally prolonged time, reflecting motor rigidity and reduced spontaneous movement. Stereotypy refers to repetitive, purposeless behaviours such as sniffing, gnawing, or head bobbing, which are commonly induced by psychostimulants or dopamine agonists.

In rodent models, catalepsy is most commonly induced using typical antipsychotics like haloperidol or chlorpromazine, which block dopamine D_2 receptors in the striatum. The most widely used test for catalepsy is the bar test, where the animal's forepaws are gently placed on a horizontal bar (usually 3 to 4 cm above the bench surface), and the duration for which the animal maintains this abnormal posture without correcting it is recorded. A cut-off time of 180 to 300 seconds is generally used. The test is simple to conduct and provides a quantifiable measure of drug-induced motor rigidity.

The intensity and duration of catalepsy produced are dose-dependent and are influenced by several factors such as animal strain, age, and handling. Drugs that reduce dopamine activity or increase cholinergic tone tend to enhance cataleptic behaviour. Conversely, drugs that increase dopaminergic tone or possess anticholinergic activity can reduce it. Therefore, the model is useful for evaluating not only antipsychotics but also agents that may be useful in counteracting extrapyramidal symptoms.

Stereotypy is typically induced using dopaminergic agonists such as apomorphine or high doses of amphetamine. Behavioural observation is the main method of assessment, usually conducted in a transparent cage or an open field. The animal is monitored for the frequency and type of repetitive behaviours such as head bobbing, licking, gnawing, grooming, or sniffing. These behaviours are scored either manually on a fixed scale or using video tracking systems for greater accuracy. The intensity of stereotypy is often correlated with increased dopaminergic transmission in the nigrostriatal or mesolimbic pathways.

These models are particularly valuable in differentiating typical and atypical antipsychotics. While typical antipsychotics like haloperidol produce strong catalepsy and suppress stereotypy, atypical antipsychotics like clozapine and olanzapine show less catalepsy and minimal suppression of stereotypy, suggesting a lower risk of extrapyramidal side effects. This distinction is critical in drug development, as antipsychotic efficacy must be balanced with an acceptable side-effect profile.

Both catalepsy and stereotypy models are easy to perform, require minimal equipment, and yield highly reproducible results when standard protocols are followed. However, interpretation of data requires caution, especially in compounds with mixed central actions, such as sedatives, muscle relaxants, or CNS stimulants, which may interfere with behavioural expression. Moreover, repeated testing may lead to behavioural adaptation, so animals must be appropriately rested between trials.

Together, these models provide critical insight into the dopaminergic involvement in psychosis and help in predicting motor side effects of new CNS-active drugs. When used in combination with behavioural, cognitive, and neurochemical tests, they contribute significantly to the preclinical evaluation of antipsychotic efficacy and safety.

2.4.5 Apomorphine-Induced Behavioral Models

Apomorphine-induced behavioural models are widely used in preclinical pharmacology to study the central dopaminergic system, especially for the evaluation of dopamine receptor agonists, antagonists, and modulators. Apomorphine is a non-selective dopamine agonist that acts primarily on D1 and D2 receptors in the nigrostriatal and mesolimbic pathways. When administered to rodents, apomorphine produces characteristic behavioural changes such as stereotypy, yawning, and rotational behaviour, which can be quantitatively assessed and used to screen for antipsychotic drugs, Parkinson's disease treatments, and dopaminergic dysfunctions.

The specific behavioural response to apomorphine depends on the dose, route of administration, and experimental model. In normal rats, subcutaneous administration of apomorphine at doses between 0.1 to 1.0 mg/kg typically induces stereotyped behaviours including sniffing, licking, gnawing, and repetitive head movements. These effects are usually observed within 5 to 10 minutes of dosing and may last for 30 to 60 minutes. The intensity and pattern of these behaviours are used to evaluate the functional status of dopamine receptors. Drugs that antagonize dopamine receptors, such as typical antipsychotics, tend to suppress these behaviours, indicating their receptor-blocking potential.

In more specialized models, such as the unilateral 6-hydroxydopamine (6-OHDA) lesioned rat, apomorphine administration leads to a distinct rotational behaviour. In this model, the dopamine-producing neurons in one hemisphere of the brain are destroyed, resulting in dopamine receptor supersensitivity on the lesioned side. Upon administration of apomorphine (usually 0.5 mg/kg s.c.), the animal exhibits contralateral rotations—i.e., turning away from the lesioned side—at a rate that can be quantified as rotations per minute over a fixed period, typically 30 minutes. This behaviour reflects the degree of dopamine receptor imbalance and is used as a sensitive marker to evaluate dopamine agonists and neurorestorative therapies in Parkinsonism.

Another relevant behavioural response is apomorphine-induced yawning, observed particularly in male rats. At lower doses (0.05–0.1 mg/kg), apomorphine selectively stimulates D2 receptors in the hypothalamus, leading to repeated yawns. This specific response is often used to assess the selectivity and efficacy of D2 receptor modulators and can be influenced by hormonal status, stress, and concurrent drug treatment.

Apomorphine models are advantageous due to their predictive validity, ease of use, and quantifiable outcomes. The behaviours induced are directly related to dopamine receptor activation, making the models highly relevant for studying schizophrenia, Parkinson's disease, and dopaminergic toxicity. Additionally, they allow differentiation between pre- and postsynaptic effects, since apomorphine acts on both receptor types depending on the dose.

However, these models also require careful interpretation. Apomorphine produces non-specific behavioural effects at higher doses, and the animal's prior exposure to stress or drugs can influence the response. Repeated testing may lead to sensitization or tolerance, and the use of different strains or sexes may yield variable results. Sedatives and motor-impairing drugs can also confound the expression of apomorphine-induced behaviours, leading to false interpretations.

2.5 Anti-Epileptics and Nootropics

The evaluation of anti-epileptic and nootropic agents in preclinical studies involves carefully designed experimental models that mimic the pathophysiological features of epilepsy and cognitive impairment in humans. These models help in understanding the mechanism of action, efficacy, safety, and side-effect profile of potential drug candidates before they proceed to clinical trials. Anti-epileptic drug (AED) screening focuses on the ability of a compound to prevent, reduce, or suppress seizure activity in animals, while nootropic testing is aimed at assessing learning, memory, and cognitive enhancement.

Animal models of epilepsy are broadly classified into acute seizure models, such as the Maximal Electroshock Seizure (MES) test and Pentylenetetrazole (PTZ)-induced seizures, and chronic seizure models like the kindling model. These tests are sensitive to different classes of anti-epileptic drugs and are chosen based on the type of epilepsy being modelled (generalized tonic-clonic, absence, myoclonic, or partial seizures).

In the MES model, a strong current (usually 50 mA for 0.2 seconds) is passed through the cornea or ear electrodes to induce seizures in rodents. The endpoint is the observation of tonic hind limb extension, and drugs that suppress this response are considered effective in controlling generalized tonic-clonic seizures. The PTZ model involves subcutaneous or intraperitoneal injection of PTZ, a GABA-A receptor antagonist, which induces clonic seizures within minutes. Drugs that prevent or delay the onset of seizures are considered useful for absence or myoclonic seizures. The kindling model, induced by repeated low-intensity electrical stimulation or chemical administration, mimics partial or focal epilepsy and is useful for evaluating drugs with long-term protective effects.

For nootropic screening, several behavioural paradigms are employed to assess different aspects of learning and memory, such as acquisition, retention, and retrieval. The Morris Water Maze is a spatial learning test where the animal learns to locate a submerged platform in a circular pool using visual cues. The latency to find the platform and the time spent in the target quadrant are used to evaluate cognitive performance. Passive Avoidance involves a learning task where the animal avoids entering a compartment previously associated with an aversive stimulus (usually a mild foot shock). Retention time is taken as a measure of memory. The Radial Arm Maze, consisting of a central platform with multiple arms baited with food, is used to assess working and reference memory.

These models are sensitive to cholinergic agents, NMDA receptor modulators, GABA enhancers, and neuroprotective drugs. Agents like donepezil, rivastigmine, piracetam, and memantine are often used as standard references. Test substances are administered before or after training to evaluate their impact on learning and memory processes.

Both anti-epileptic and nootropic evaluations require strict control of experimental variables such as animal strain, age, environmental conditions, and timing of drug administration. Ethical considerations are also critical, especially in seizure models where animals are exposed to intense stimuli.

Together, these models provide a comprehensive platform for identifying and characterizing CNS-active drugs with therapeutic potential in epilepsy and neurodegenerative disorders such as Alzheimer's disease, traumatic brain injury, or age-related cognitive decline.

2.5.1 Maximal Electroshock (MES) Model

The Maximal Electroshock (MES) model is one of the most widely accepted and standardized experimental procedures for the preclinical evaluation of potential anti-epileptic drugs (AEDs). This model primarily mimics generalized tonic-clonic seizures in humans and is particularly useful for screening compounds effective against such seizure types. It remains the gold standard for identifying drugs that act by stabilizing neuronal membranes or inhibiting seizure spread.

In a typical MES experiment, laboratory animals—usually albino rats or Swiss mice weighing between 20 to 30 grams—are subjected to an electrical stimulus using corneal or auricular electrodes connected to a controlled electroconvulsive device. The current applied is generally 50–60 Hz with an intensity of 50–80 mA, and the duration of shock is around 0.2 seconds. Before applying corneal electrodes, the eyes are moistened with saline or a drop of lignocaine to reduce discomfort and enhance conductivity.

The electric shock induces a sequence of well-defined seizure phases: tonic limb flexion, tonic limb extension, clonic convulsions, stupor, and post-ictal depression. The tonic hind limb extension (THLE) phase—where the animal extends its hind limbs for at least

3 seconds—is considered the critical indicator of a full electroshock seizure. The primary endpoint in this model is whether the test compound prevents or reduces the duration of the tonic extension phase. Complete abolition of THLE is considered indicative of a protective anti-epileptic effect.

MES is highly predictive of efficacy for drugs such as phenytoin, carbamazepine, valproate, and lamotrigine, which are known to be effective in controlling generalized seizures. The test compound is typically administered intraperitoneally or orally, and seizure testing is performed 30 to 60 minutes later, depending on the pharmacokinetics of the drug. Control animals receive a vehicle solution, and the percentage of animals protected in each group is calculated. Doses are usually selected to construct a dose–response curve, allowing estimation of the ED_{50} (the effective dose at which 50% of animals are protected).

This model offers several advantages. It is simple, rapid, reproducible, and sensitive to a wide range of anti-convulsant agents. It also allows for the evaluation of both acute and chronic effects of a compound and is adaptable to test drug combinations or formulations. Importantly, it helps in identifying proconvulsant effects of certain CNS-active compounds during safety pharmacology testing.

However, MES also has limitations. It does not detect agents that are effective only against absence seizures or those acting on GABAergic mechanisms, such as ethosuximide. In addition, the intense nature of the seizure poses ethical concerns, requiring the use of minimum effective stimulus, careful monitoring, and strict adherence to CPCSEA guidelines. Proper animal handling, use of anaesthetic eye drops, and quick post-seizure recovery management are necessary to minimize animal suffering.

2.5.2 Pentylenetetrazole (PTZ)-Induced Seizures

The Pentylenetetrazole (PTZ)-induced seizure model is a classical experimental method used for the preclinical evaluation of anti-epileptic drugs (AEDs) that are effective against absence seizures and myoclonic jerks. PTZ, also known as metrazol, is a central nervous system stimulant that acts as a non-competitive antagonist of the $GABA_A$ receptor complex, thereby reducing inhibitory neurotransmission. This leads to neuronal hyperexcitability and induction of seizures in laboratory animals, especially mice and rats.

In a typical protocol, Swiss albino mice or Wistar rats are used, weighing between 20 to 30 grams (for mice) or 180 to 220 grams (for rats). PTZ is administered usually via the intraperitoneal route at a dose ranging from 60 to 90 mg/kg in mice and 30 to 50 mg/kg in rats. The precise dose depends on the sensitivity of the animal species and the seizure severity desired. After administration, the animal is placed in an observation chamber, and behaviour is monitored continuously for a period of 30 minutes.

The behavioural stages typically observed include myoclonic jerks, forelimb clonus, tonic convulsions, rearing, loss of righting reflex, and in severe cases, death. The latency to seizure onset, severity of convulsions, number of convulsions, and mortality are key parameters recorded. A test drug is considered effective if it delays the onset of seizures, reduces the severity of convulsive activity, or completely prevents seizures or death when compared to the control group.

The PTZ model is particularly useful in identifying AEDs that act by enhancing GABAergic neurotransmission or modulating ion channels involved in neuronal excitability. Standard reference drugs include diazepam, clonazepam, valproate, and ethosuximide, all of which exert protective effects against PTZ-induced seizures by increasing inhibitory tone or reducing calcium influx.

The timing of test drug administration before PTZ challenge is crucial. Most drugs are administered 30 to 60 minutes prior to PTZ injection, depending on their route and expected onset of action. ED_{50} values (the dose providing 50% protection) can be calculated using a dose-response curve, and protection percentages are statistically compared using Chi-square or Fisher's exact test.

One of the key advantages of the PTZ model is its simplicity, sensitivity, and low cost, making it highly suitable for high-throughput screening of AEDs. It is also a good model to evaluate the threshold of seizure susceptibility, useful in mechanistic studies of epilepsy.

However, the model has some limitations. It is less predictive for drugs used in partial or focal epilepsy, and it does not detect AEDs that act exclusively on sodium channel inactivation, like phenytoin or carbamazepine. Moreover, variability in PTZ sensitivity due to strain, sex, age, and environmental factors must be controlled to ensure consistent results. Ethical considerations are also important, as PTZ can induce generalized tonic-clonic seizures and fatal convulsions if not carefully dosed and monitored.

Despite these limitations, the PTZ-induced seizure model remains a robust and widely accepted tool for the early screening of anti-absence and anti-myoclonic agents, particularly those enhancing GABAergic activity. It is often used in combination with the Maximal Electroshock Seizure (MES) test to provide a comprehensive pharmacological profile of investigational anti-epileptic drugs.

2.5.3 Kindling Model

The kindling model is a well-established and widely used experimental paradigm in preclinical pharmacology for studying chronic epilepsy and the development of seizure susceptibility over time. Unlike acute seizure models such as MES or PTZ, which involve immediate convulsive responses, the kindling model mimics the progressive nature of epilepsy, where repeated subthreshold electrical or chemical stimulations lead to a permanent increase in the excitability of specific brain regions. It is particularly useful for evaluating drugs targeting partial (focal) seizures and secondary generalization, and for studying neuroplasticity and epileptogenesis.

In the most commonly used electrical kindling model, adult male Wistar rats or C57BL/6 mice are surgically implanted with a bipolar electrode in a target brain area such as the amygdala, hippocampus, or piriform cortex. After post-surgical recovery, animals are subjected to daily low-intensity electrical stimulations, typically 1 second trains of 50–60 Hz biphasic square wave pulses lasting 1 millisecond per pulse and applied at a current strength that does not cause a seizure on the first day (usually 50–150 µA in rats). Over days or weeks, these stimulations gradually result in increasing seizure severity, as measured by a standard Racine scale:

1. Mouth and facial movements
2. Head nodding
3. Forelimb clonus
4. Rearing
5. Rearing and falling with generalized tonic–clonic seizures

The number of stimulations required to reach a specific seizure stage is referred to as the kindling acquisition rate, and this is used as an indicator of the progression of epileptogenesis. Once animals consistently display stage 5 seizures, they are considered to be fully kindled, and are highly sensitive to seizure triggers.

The chemical kindling variant involves repeated administration of subconvulsive doses of chemoconvulsants such as pentylenetetrazole (PTZ) or pilocarpine every 48 to 72 hours. With each administration, the seizure response intensifies, eventually culminating in generalized seizures. This method avoids surgical implantation but is less site-specific.

The kindling model is especially sensitive to AEDs used for focal epilepsy, such as carbamazepine, lamotrigine, levetiracetam, and valproic acid. It allows for testing both prophylactic and therapeutic effects, including evaluation of drugs that may delay kindling development or reduce the severity of kindled seizures. In addition, kindling can be combined with EEG recordings to correlate behavioural seizures with electrophysiological changes.

One major strength of the kindling model is its high translational relevance. The gradual progression of seizure severity closely resembles human temporal lobe epilepsy. It is also a valuable model for studying molecular mechanisms of epileptogenesis, including synaptic plasticity, gene expression changes, neuroinflammation, and oxidative stress.

However, the model has several limitations. It is labour-intensive, requiring weeks of stimulation, careful post-surgical care, and standardized electrode placement. Inter-animal variability in seizure progression is common, and repeated handling or stimulation can lead to stress-related complications. In addition, while the model reflects partial epilepsy, it is less predictive for drugs aimed at absence or generalized seizures.

Despite these challenges, the kindling model remains one of the most powerful tools in experimental epilepsy research. It is particularly important for studying chronic seizure disorders, neurobiological changes in epilepsy progression, and long-term efficacy of investigational anti-epileptic and neuroprotective compounds.

2.5.4 Morris Water Maze Test

The Morris Water Maze (MWM) test is a widely accepted and extensively validated experimental model used to assess spatial learning and memory in rodents, particularly in the context of nootropic drug screening and neurodegenerative disease research. Developed by Richard Morris in the early 1980s, this test is based on the natural swimming ability of rodents and their tendency to escape from water by finding a hidden platform using external spatial cues. It is particularly sensitive to damage or pharmacological interventions involving the hippocampus, the brain region primarily responsible for memory consolidation and spatial navigation.

The MWM apparatus consists of a large circular pool, typically around 120 to 150 cm in diameter and 50 cm deep, filled with water made opaque by adding non-toxic white dye or milk powder. The water temperature is maintained at 25 ± 1°C to avoid inducing hypothermia or stress. A small transparent platform, about 10 cm in diameter, is submerged 1 to 2 cm below the surface of the water in one of the four quadrants of the pool. The walls of the testing room contain prominent visual cues such as geometric shapes, coloured posters, or objects that remain fixed throughout the experiment.

The test is conducted in two main phases: the acquisition or training phase, and the probe test or retention phase. During the training phase, the animal is placed into the water from different starting points and allowed to swim until it finds the hidden platform. Each trial has a maximum time limit, usually 60 to 120 seconds, after which the animal is guided to the platform if it fails to locate it. The animal is allowed to rest on the platform for 15 to 30 seconds. This training is repeated for four to six trials per day over several consecutive days, depending on the experimental design.

The primary measure of learning is the escape latency, or the time taken to reach the platform, which typically decreases over training sessions as the animal learns to use spatial cues. Other parameters include path length, swimming speed, and search strategy. For the probe test conducted after the training phase, the platform is removed, and the animal is placed in the pool to swim freely for 60 to 90 seconds. The percentage of time spent in the target quadrant, number of crossings over the platform location, and search pattern are recorded to assess memory retention.

The MWM is sensitive to cognitive deficits induced by aging, scopolamine, β-amyloid, or cerebral ischemia, and is frequently used to evaluate the effectiveness of nootropic agents such as piracetam, donepezil, rivastigmine, and memantine. Nootropic drugs are administered before or during the training phase, and improved performance in escape latency and probe test scores is interpreted as a positive cognitive effect.

The test offers several advantages. It is non-invasive, requires no food or electric shock as motivation, and provides quantitative data that can be recorded using automated video tracking software. The spatial memory it measures closely parallels certain aspects of human cognition, particularly those affected in Alzheimer's disease and vascular dementia.

However, several factors can influence the outcome, including animal strain, sex, stress levels, visual acuity, and swimming ability. Therefore, it is essential to match control and test groups appropriately and control environmental variables such as lighting and noise. Animals with motor deficits or impaired vision are not suitable for this test as they may fail to perform due to non-cognitive limitations.

Despite these considerations, the Morris Water Maze remains one of the most reliable and scientifically respected methods for assessing spatial learning and memory in rodents. It plays a central role in nootropic drug discovery, neuroprotective agent development, and mechanistic studies involving hippocampal function and cognitive neuropharmacology.

2.5.5 Passive Avoidance Test

The Passive Avoidance Test is a fundamental and widely used behavioural model for assessing learning and memory retention in rodents. It is particularly valuable in the screening of nootropic agents, as well as in the evaluation of memory deficits caused by pharmacological agents, aging, or neurodegenerative diseases. The test is based on the natural tendency of rodents to prefer dark, enclosed spaces over illuminated ones, combined with their ability to remember aversive stimuli associated with the dark compartment. The animal learns to avoid an environment where it previously received an unpleasant stimulus, thus demonstrating associative learning and memory retention.

The apparatus typically consists of two compartments: one brightly lit chamber and one dark chamber, separated by a guillotine-type door. The dimensions are generally about $25 \times 25 \times 25$ cm for each chamber. The floor of the dark compartment is equipped with electrifiable metal grids, while the light chamber has a smooth, nonconductive floor. The light intensity in the illuminated compartment is kept at 400 to 600 lux to create a clear preference gradient.

In the training session, each animal (usually a mouse or rat) is placed in the light chamber. After an acclimation period of about 30 seconds, the door separating the two chambers is opened. The animal, driven by its innate preference for darkness, enters the dark chamber. Once all four paws are inside the dark compartment, the door is closed, and a mild foot shock (generally 0.5 to 1 mA for 1–2 seconds) is delivered via the grid floor. The animal is then returned to its home cage.

After 24 hours, the retention or test session is conducted. The animal is again placed in the light chamber, and the time it takes to enter the dark chamber is recorded. This duration is known as the step-through latency. A longer latency time indicates better memory retention, while a shorter latency suggests memory impairment. The cut-off time is typically set at 300 seconds, beyond which the trial is stopped if the animal does not enter the dark compartment.

This test is highly sensitive to amnesic agents such as scopolamine, alcohol, and benzodiazepines, which reduce the latency period. Conversely, nootropic drugs like piracetam, donepezil, rivastigmine, and herbal extracts like Bacopa monnieri tend to prolong latency, demonstrating their cognitive enhancement potential.

Several advantages make the Passive Avoidance Test a preferred method in preclinical research. It requires no food or water deprivation, uses the animal's natural exploratory behaviour, and provides quantitative, easily reproducible data. It is also a low-stress procedure when conducted with proper care and standardization.

However, the test has limitations. It assesses only a single trial of memory, mainly aversive learning, and may not reflect more complex cognitive processes such as spatial navigation or working memory. The outcome can be influenced by stress sensitivity, motivation, and motor ability. Animals with impaired locomotion may show artificially high latencies not related to memory retention.

Nevertheless, the Passive Avoidance Test remains a robust and ethically manageable tool in behavioural pharmacology. It is particularly useful when used in combination with other models like the Morris Water Maze and Radial Arm Maze, offering a more complete understanding of the nootropic profile and memory-related mechanisms of investigational compounds.

2.5.6 Radial Arm Maze

The Radial Arm Maze (RAM) is a widely accepted experimental model used to evaluate spatial learning, working memory, and reference memory in rodents, particularly in the preclinical screening of nootropic agents and the assessment of cognitive impairments in conditions like Alzheimer's disease, aging, or chemically induced amnesia. This model is especially sensitive to the functions of the hippocampus and prefrontal cortex, which are critical regions involved in memory and decision-making.

The apparatus consists of a central circular platform, usually 20 to 30 cm in diameter, from which eight equally spaced arms extend radially, each about 40 to 50 cm in length and 10 cm in width. At the end of each arm, a small food cup is placed, which can be baited with food rewards. The maze is elevated from the floor and surrounded by prominent visual cues placed on the walls of the testing room to facilitate spatial navigation.

There are two main types of memory assessed in the Radial Arm Maze:

- Working memory: The ability of the animal to remember which arms it has already visited within a single session.
- Reference memory: The ability to remember which arms are never baited across sessions.

In a typical experiment, the rodent is food-deprived for 12 to 24 hours to ensure motivation. During training sessions, a fixed number of arms (usually four) are baited with food. The animal is placed in the center and allowed to explore and retrieve the food. Each entry into an arm is recorded. Re-entries into baited arms that have already been visited reflect working memory errors, while entries into unbaited arms indicate reference memory errors.

Over successive training sessions, normal rodents learn to remember which arms are baited and avoid previously visited arms, resulting in fewer errors and faster task completion. Nootropic drugs, such as piracetam, donepezil, or bacosides, tend to reduce the number of both working and reference memory errors, demonstrating memory-enhancing properties. Conversely, administration of scopolamine, β-amyloid peptides, or other amnesic agents increases errors and impairs task performance.

The RAM offers several advantages. It provides a quantitative, sensitive, and reliable measure of memory functions without inducing stress or discomfort. The task engages natural foraging behaviour, making it ecologically valid. Additionally, it allows longitudinal testing, meaning the same animal can be assessed repeatedly over weeks to monitor progression or improvement.

However, the model also has some limitations. It requires extensive pre-training, which may last several days, especially in naïve animals. The outcome is sensitive to motivation, visual ability, and locomotor function—thus, any drug that affects feeding behaviour or movement can confound the interpretation of memory performance. Furthermore, the testing environment must remain stable and consistent to prevent misinterpretation due to altered spatial cue perception.

Despite these challenges, the Radial Arm Maze remains a powerful tool in neuropsychopharmacology. When carefully controlled and interpreted alongside complementary behavioural tests like the Morris Water Maze or Passive Avoidance Test, it provides valuable insights into the cognitive profile of new pharmacological agents and helps to identify potential treatments for cognitive decline and neurodegenerative diseases.

2.6.1 Parkinsonism Models: 6-OHDA and MPTP

Preclinical models of Parkinson's disease (PD) are essential for understanding the pathophysiology of dopaminergic neuron degeneration and for the evaluation of potential neuroprotective and symptomatic treatments. Two of the most widely used and validated models in rodents and primates are the 6-hydroxydopamine (6-OHDA) model and the 1-methyl-4-phenyl-1,2,3,6-tetrahydropyridine (MPTP) model. Both models aim to replicate the cardinal features of Parkinsonism, particularly the loss of dopaminergic neurons in the substantia nigra pars compacta and the resulting motor impairments, such as bradykinesia, rigidity, and tremor.

6-Hydroxydopamine (6-OHDA) Model

The 6-OHDA model is most commonly employed in rats and is based on the selective destruction of catecholaminergic neurons. 6-OHDA is a neurotoxin structurally similar to dopamine, and it is selectively taken up by dopamine transporters (DAT). Once inside the neuron, it undergoes autooxidation, generating reactive oxygen species that cause mitochondrial dysfunction and cell death. Since 6-OHDA does not cross the blood–brain barrier, it must be stereotactically injected directly into target brain areas such as the medial forebrain bundle, striatum, or substantia nigra.

The most common procedure involves a unilateral injection into the medial forebrain bundle, leading to hemiparkinsonism—a state where one hemisphere of the brain is lesioned, allowing the contralateral side to serve as an internal control. This model is advantageous because it provides consistent and reproducible dopamine depletion, with over 90% loss of striatal dopamine levels within days. Animals exhibit motor asymmetry, including rotational behaviour when challenged with dopaminergic drugs such as apomorphine (contralateral turning) or amphetamine (ipsilateral turning), which serves as a quantifiable behavioural measure of lesion severity.

This model is ideal for evaluating drugs that act as dopamine agonists, MAO-B inhibitors, or neuroprotective agents, and for testing cell-based or gene therapies aimed at restoring dopaminergic function. However, it lacks the progressive and systemic nature of human Parkinson's disease and does not replicate non-motor symptoms such as cognitive decline or olfactory deficits.

MPTP Model

The MPTP model is primarily used in mice and non-human primates, including monkeys, and closely mimics many features of idiopathic Parkinson's disease in humans. MPTP is a lipophilic compound that crosses the blood–brain barrier and is metabolized by astrocytes to MPP+ (1-methyl-4-phenylpyridinium ion), the active toxic metabolite. MPP+ selectively enters dopaminergic neurons via the dopamine transporter and accumulates in mitochondria, where it inhibits complex I of the electron transport chain, leading to energy failure, oxidative stress, and cell death.

In mice, MPTP is typically administered intraperitoneally at doses ranging from 20 to 30 mg/kg, either as a single high dose or multiple injections over several days. The resulting dopaminergic neuron degeneration is rapid, producing substantial depletion of striatal dopamine, especially in the substantia nigra pars compacta, and leads to hypokinesia, akinesia, and rigidity. Behavioural assessment is done using pole tests, rotarod, and open field activity to evaluate motor deficits.

In primates, MPTP produces a chronic and progressive Parkinsonism more analogous to the human condition, including postural instability and tremor, and is therefore widely used for preclinical evaluation of advanced therapeutics such as deep brain stimulation, stem cell transplants, and gene therapies.

Although highly useful, the MPTP model has limitations. In rodents, the degeneration is typically non-progressive and lacks features like Lewy body formation, an important pathological hallmark of PD.

Also, MPTP is toxic and must be handled with extreme care, using safety protocols to prevent accidental exposure.

Both 6-OHDA and MPTP models have contributed significantly to our understanding of Parkinson's disease and the mechanistic screening of dopaminergic and neuroprotective agents. They remain central to experimental neuropharmacology and continue to evolve with the integration of genetic and environmental risk factors, helping bridge the gap between laboratory research and clinical application.

2.6.2 Alzheimer's Models: Scopolamine and Aβ Peptides

Alzheimer's disease (AD) is the most common cause of dementia and is characterized by progressive loss of memory, cognitive decline, and behavioural disturbances. The pathological hallmarks of AD include extracellular amyloid-β (Aβ) plaque deposition, intracellular neurofibrillary tangles composed of hyperphosphorylated tau protein, oxidative stress, synaptic loss, and cholinergic neuronal degeneration, particularly in the hippocampus and cortex. To replicate these features for drug discovery and mechanistic studies, several animal models have been developed. Among them, scopolamine-induced amnesia and Aβ peptide-infusion models are widely used and well-validated for preclinical screening of nootropic agents and anti-Alzheimer's drugs.

Scopolamine-Induced Amnesia Model

Scopolamine is a muscarinic acetylcholine receptor antagonist that temporarily blocks cholinergic neurotransmission in the brain, particularly in the hippocampus and cortex. Since cholinergic dysfunction is a key feature of Alzheimer's disease, scopolamine administration in animals produces transient and reversible cognitive deficits, making it a useful pharmacological model for screening cognitive enhancers and cholinergic drugs.

In a typical study, mice or rats are administered scopolamine intraperitoneally at doses ranging from 0.5 to 3 mg/kg, approximately 30 minutes before behavioural testing. The resulting memory impairment is then assessed using various behavioural paradigms, such as:

- Morris Water Maze (spatial memory)
- Passive Avoidance Test (associative memory)
- Y-Maze (working memory)
- Novel Object Recognition Test (recognition memory)

Animals treated with scopolamine show increased latency in water maze, reduced time in target quadrant, shortened step-through latency in passive avoidance, and fewer spontaneous alternations in Y-maze, all indicating impaired memory. Co-administration of standard nootropics like donepezil, rivastigmine, or piracetam reverses these deficits, validating the model for cholinergic modulation screening.

Advantages of this model include simplicity, reproducibility, cost-effectiveness, and rapid induction of cognitive impairment. However, it only mimics functional cholinergic blockade and not the full neuropathology of Alzheimer's disease. It is best suited for symptomatic drug screening rather than disease-modifying therapies.

Amyloid-β (Aβ) Peptide-Induced Model

The Aβ peptide-induced model is used to reproduce the amyloidogenic pathology of Alzheimer's disease by introducing aggregated forms of Aβ peptides directly into the cerebral ventricles or hippocampus. Synthetic $A\beta_{1-42}$ is the most commonly used isoform, as it is highly prone to aggregation and neurotoxic.

The peptide is usually prepared in a fibrillated form and injected via intracerebroventricular (ICV) or intra-hippocampal microinjection in adult mice or rats under stereotaxic guidance. A dose of 2–5 µg in 3–5 µL is typically infused unilaterally or bilaterally. The animal is allowed to recover for several days before behavioural testing.

Aβ-injected animals exhibit significant memory impairment, oxidative stress, neuroinflammation, and cholinergic neuron loss, which closely resemble early AD pathology. They perform poorly in the Morris Water Maze, Radial Arm Maze, and Object Recognition Tests, showing deficits in spatial learning, retention, and recognition memory. The model also allows measurement of biochemical markers, including acetylcholine levels, lipid peroxidation, pro-inflammatory cytokines, and AChE activity.

This model is especially suitable for evaluating anti-amyloid, antioxidant, anti-inflammatory, and neuroprotective therapies, and for understanding molecular mechanisms of Aβ-induced neurotoxicity. However, limitations include surgical expertise, variability in Aβ aggregation state, and the non-progressive nature of the lesion compared to human AD.

Both scopolamine and Aβ models play complementary roles in Alzheimer's research. The scopolamine model is ideal for testing cholinergic enhancers, while the Aβ model helps evaluate disease-modifying approaches. When used in combination, they provide a comprehensive platform for the preclinical development of anti-Alzheimer's drugs, ensuring both symptomatic and neuroprotective effects are addressed.

2.6.3 Multiple Sclerosis: EAE Model

Multiple sclerosis (MS) is a chronic, inflammatory, and demyelinating disorder of the central nervous system that affects the brain and spinal cord. It is characterised by autoimmune-mediated destruction of myelin sheaths, axonal damage, and neurodegeneration, leading to motor, sensory, and cognitive impairments. To understand the pathophysiology of MS and to screen immunomodulatory and neuroprotective therapies, the most widely used and validated experimental model is Experimental Autoimmune Encephalomyelitis (EAE). The EAE model replicates several key clinical and pathological features of MS and is used extensively in both rodents and non-human primates.

The EAE model is typically induced in inbred strains of mice or rats by active immunization with myelin-derived peptides such as myelin oligodendrocyte glycoprotein (MOG$_{35-55}$), myelin basic protein (MBP), or proteolipid protein (PLP). These peptides are emulsified in complete Freund's adjuvant (CFA), which contains inactivated *Mycobacterium tuberculosis* to enhance the immune response. The emulsion is injected subcutaneously at multiple sites on the animal's back. To increase disease severity and ensure breakdown of the blood–brain barrier, pertussis toxin is also administered intraperitoneally on the day of immunization and 48 hours later.

The onset of symptoms typically occurs 7 to 14 days post-immunization, depending on the animal strain and protocol. Animals begin to show tail limpness, followed by hind limb weakness, ataxia, and eventually complete hind limb paralysis in severe cases. Clinical symptoms are scored daily using a standard EAE clinical scale:

- 0 = No clinical signs
- 1 = Limp tail
- 2 = Hind limb weakness
- 3 = Partial hind limb paralysis
- 4 = Complete hind limb paralysis
- 5 = Moribund or dead

The severity and progression of disease can be monitored over time, making the EAE model suitable for testing both preventive and therapeutic interventions. Histological examination reveals perivascular inflammatory cell infiltration, demyelination, astrocytosis, and axonal degeneration, similar to human MS pathology.

Immunomodulatory drugs such as interferon-β, glatiramer acetate, fingolimod, and dimethyl fumarate have been validated in EAE models before clinical use. The model also allows the testing of monoclonal antibodies, T-cell vaccines, herbal extracts, and gene therapy strategies. Biomarkers such as TNF-α, IL-6, IL-17, IFN-γ, and myelin-specific antibody levels can be measured to understand the mechanism of action of test drugs.

The EAE model can be adapted into different variants:

- Acute monophasic EAE in C57BL/6 mice using MOG_{35-55}
- Chronic progressive EAE in SJL mice using $PLP_{139-151}$
- Relapsing–remitting EAE, which mimics the most common clinical form of MS

Despite its advantages, the EAE model has limitations. It does not fully replicate the human heterogeneity of MS, particularly in terms of cognitive deficits, remyelination dynamics, and B-cell involvement. There are also ethical considerations, especially in severe paralysis stages, requiring humane endpoints and careful animal monitoring.

Nevertheless, EAE remains the gold standard model for preclinical testing in MS research. Its predictive validity, reproducibility, and immunological relevance make it indispensable for advancing our understanding of multiple sclerosis and for identifying new drugs that modulate immune responses, protect neurons, and promote remyelination.

2.6.4 Parameters for Cognitive and Motor Impairment

In experimental models of neurodegenerative diseases such as Parkinson's disease, Alzheimer's disease, and multiple sclerosis, the assessment of cognitive and motor impairments plays a central role in evaluating the progression of disease and the efficacy of therapeutic agents. These parameters provide objective, quantifiable measures of neurological dysfunction, allowing researchers to determine whether a test compound can reverse, delay, or prevent the decline in behavioural performance.

Cognitive Parameters

Cognitive function in rodents is commonly assessed using behavioural tasks that evaluate learning, memory, attention, and decision-making. These include both spatial and non-spatial paradigms:

- Escape Latency in Morris Water Maze: Measures the time taken to locate a hidden platform; increased latency indicates impaired spatial learning and memory.
- Time Spent in Target Quadrant (Probe Test): Used to assess memory retention after training; decreased time suggests memory loss.
- Step-Through Latency in Passive Avoidance Test: Shortened latency during the retention trial reflects poor associative memory.
- Number of Working and Reference Memory Errors in Radial Arm Maze: Increased errors reflect deficits in short-term (working) and long-term (reference) memory.
- Recognition Index in Novel Object Recognition Test: A lower preference for novel objects indicates impaired recognition memory.
- Spontaneous Alternation in Y-Maze: Decreased alternation percentage suggests reduced working memory and exploratory behaviour.

These tasks are sensitive to hippocampal and cortical damage and are routinely used in models involving scopolamine, amyloid-β peptides, or oxidative stress, as well as in aging studies.

Motor Parameters

Motor function assessments are critical in models of Parkinsonism, multiple sclerosis, and cerebellar disorders. The parameters evaluated are focused on coordination, balance, strength, and locomotor activity:

- Rotarod Performance: The duration an animal remains on a rotating rod is used to evaluate balance, coordination, and

motor learning. Decreased latency to fall indicates motor dysfunction.
- Open Field Test (Locomotor Activity): Total distance moved, movement speed, and number of rearing behaviours reflect general activity and exploration. Reduced activity may suggest motor or motivational deficits.
- Pole Test: In Parkinson's models, the time taken to descend a vertical pole is used to assess bradykinesia; increased time reflects motor slowness.
- Grip Strength Test: Measures forelimb or hindlimb strength using a tension gauge; lower force indicates muscular weakness or neuromuscular impairment.
- Gait Analysis and Footprint Test: Changes in stride length, base width, and paw print spacing are used to assess abnormalities in gait seen in models of spinal cord injury or demyelinating diseases.
- Catalepsy Scoring (Bar Test): Duration of posture maintenance in an abnormal position is used to evaluate muscle rigidity in Parkinsonian models.

Combined Interpretations

In many neurodegenerative models, both motor and cognitive functions are affected simultaneously. For example, in MPTP-induced Parkinsonism, animals show both motor deficits on the rotarod and memory impairments in the Y-maze. Similarly, in EAE models of multiple sclerosis, animals develop paralysis along with attention and memory deficits. Therefore, comprehensive behavioural profiling is essential to differentiate between pure cognitive dysfunction, pure motor impairment, or overlapping features, and to ensure accurate interpretation of drug effects.

These behavioural endpoints are typically supported by histological, biochemical, and molecular assays, including brain tissue staining, neurotransmitter quantification, and inflammatory marker profiling, to correlate functional impairments with pathological changes.

2.7.1 Screening Methods for Sympathomimetics

Sympathomimetic drugs are agents that mimic the effects of endogenous catecholamines like adrenaline, noradrenaline, and dopamine by stimulating adrenergic receptors. These drugs act on the sympathetic division of the autonomic nervous system, leading to physiological responses such as increased heart rate, bronchodilation, mydriasis, and vasoconstriction. Preclinical screening of sympathomimetic agents involves evaluating their functional effects on specific organ systems and receptor selectivity, using both in vivo and in vitro models.

1. Cardiovascular Models

One of the classical methods for screening sympathomimetics involves measuring cardiovascular parameters such as blood pressure and heart rate in anesthetized or conscious animals like rats, rabbits, or dogs. In these models, the test compound is administered intravenously or subcutaneously, and parameters are recorded using pressure transducers and data acquisition systems.

- Increase in systolic and diastolic blood pressure indicates alpha-adrenergic receptor stimulation.
- Increase in heart rate (tachycardia) suggests $beta_1$-adrenoceptor stimulation.
- Pressor response tests are conducted in anesthetized rats, where the change in mean arterial pressure is measured following drug administration.

To evaluate receptor selectivity, specific antagonists such as propranolol (beta-blocker) or prazosin (alpha-blocker) are administered before the test compound to observe any attenuation of response, confirming the receptor subtype involved.

2. Mydriasis Test in Mice

This simple and direct test evaluates the ability of a sympathomimetic agent to induce pupil dilation (mydriasis), which is a result of $alpha_1$-adrenoceptor activation on the radial muscles of the iris. The test compound is instilled into the conjunctival sac of mice or rabbits, and the diameter of the pupil is measured at regular intervals using calipers or image analysis software.

Increased pupil size, peaking within 10 to 30 minutes, confirms sympathomimetic activity. This method is useful for evaluating topical ocular agents and their local adrenergic effects.

3. Isolated Organ Bath Studies

In vitro organ bath experiments using isolated tissues like the rat vas deferens, rabbit aorta, or guinea pig trachea provide direct evidence of sympathomimetic activity. These tissues are suspended in physiological solution at 37°C, aerated with a gas mixture, and connected to a force transducer to record contraction or relaxation responses.

- Contraction of vas deferens or aortic strip suggests alpha-adrenergic stimulation.
- Relaxation of tracheal smooth muscle indicates $beta_2$-adrenoceptor stimulation.

These models allow for cumulative dose–response curve generation, helping determine EC_{50} values, potency, and efficacy of the test compound.

4. Nictitating Membrane Test in Cats

Although less commonly used today, this classical in vivo model evaluates alpha-adrenergic activity by observing the contraction of the nictitating membrane (third eyelid) in cats. Intravenous administration of a sympathomimetic agent causes visible elevation of the membrane, which can be graded on a semi-quantitative scale. Pretreatment with alpha-blockers confirms receptor involvement.

5. Locomotor Activity Tests

Increased locomotor activity in rodents after administration of sympathomimetic drugs like amphetamine or ephedrine is another indirect indicator of CNS stimulation via dopaminergic and noradrenergic pathways. This is measured in open field chambers using automated video tracking or photo-beam interruption systems.

These tests provide insight into central sympathomimetic actions, complementing the data obtained from peripheral models.

2.7.2 Screening Methods for Parasympatholytics

Parasympatholytic agents, also known as anticholinergics, are drugs that inhibit the parasympathetic nervous system by blocking muscarinic acetylcholine receptors (mAChRs). These agents produce effects opposite to those of parasympathomimetics, including mydriasis, reduced secretions, decreased gastrointestinal motility, bronchodilation, and tachycardia. Preclinical screening of parasympatholytic compounds is carried out using a combination of in vivo and in vitro assays that evaluate their ability to antagonize muscarinic receptor-mediated responses.

1. Mydriasis Assay in Mice or Rabbits

Mydriasis, or pupil dilation, is one of the simplest and most direct indicators of parasympatholytic activity. In this test, the compound is topically instilled into the conjunctival sac of one eye in a mouse or rabbit. The contralateral eye may serve as a control. The pupil diameter is measured using a millimeter ruler, image capture system, or digital caliper at intervals (e.g., 15, 30, 60, and 120 minutes).

Agents like atropine and tropicamide produce significant pupil dilation due to blockade of muscarinic receptors on the circular muscles of the iris, thus inhibiting miosis. This model is ideal for testing local ocular effects of anticholinergic agents.

2. Inhibition of Acetylcholine-Induced Contraction in Isolated Tissue

This in vitro organ bath method uses smooth muscle tissues such as guinea pig ileum, rat urinary bladder, or frog rectus abdominis, which contract in response to acetylcholine. The tissue is mounted in a bath filled with Tyrode's or Krebs-Henseleit solution, maintained at 37°C, and aerated with carbogen (95% O_2 and 5% CO_2). Acetylcholine is added cumulatively to produce a standard dose–response curve.

The test compound is then introduced, and a rightward shift in the dose–response curve indicates competitive antagonism. The pA_2 value (negative log of the antagonist concentration required to double the agonist concentration to produce the same effect) is calculated to quantify potency. Atropine serves as the standard reference compound in this assay.

3. Reduction in Intestinal Motility (Charcoal Meal Test)

This in vivo assay evaluates the ability of parasympatholytics to reduce gastrointestinal motility, a classical muscarinic response. Mice or rats are fasted overnight and then orally administered a suspension containing activated charcoal or carmine dye along with the test compound. After a set period (usually 30–60 minutes), the animals are sacrificed, and the distance travelled by the marker along the intestine is measured.

A significant reduction in transit distance compared to control indicates inhibition of gut motility by parasympathetic blockade. This model is suitable for testing systemic anticholinergic activity.

4. Inhibition of Salivation

Since salivary secretion is under strong parasympathetic control, parasympatholytic agents reduce salivary flow. In this model, pilocarpine (a muscarinic agonist) is used to stimulate salivation in rats or mice. The test compound is administered prior to pilocarpine, and after a fixed interval, the animal's mouth is examined or the salivary glands are excised and weighed.

A dose-dependent reduction in pilocarpine-induced salivation reflects parasympatholytic activity. Quantification may also involve pre-weighed filter papers placed in the oral cavity to absorb secretions, which are then weighed again to measure the volume of saliva.

5. Bronchodilation Model in Guinea Pigs

Bronchoconstriction in guinea pigs can be induced by acetylcholine aerosol or histamine, and the degree of airway resistance is measured using plethysmography. Test compounds with parasympatholytic activity, when administered by inhalation or injection, reduce airway resistance and delay the onset of bronchospasm.

This model is particularly useful for evaluating drugs intended for respiratory disorders like asthma and COPD, where antimuscarinic bronchodilators such as ipratropium and tiotropium are commonly used.

6. Heart Rate Response in Anesthetized Animals

The heart receives parasympathetic innervation through the vagus nerve, which slows the heart rate via muscarinic M_2 receptors. In anesthetized rats or dogs, vagal stimulation or exogenous acetylcholine can be used to induce bradycardia. The test compound is administered intravenously, and the reversal of bradycardia is measured using an ECG or pressure transducer system.

An increase in heart rate following vagal stimulation confirms the parasympatholytic effect on cardiac muscarinic receptors. This is a sensitive method for detecting systemic autonomic modulation.

2.7.3 Mydriasis and Pupil Dilation Assay

The Mydriasis and Pupil Dilation Assay is a classical and reliable in vivo method used in preclinical pharmacology to evaluate the autonomic effects of drugs acting on the iris musculature, particularly those with sympathomimetic or parasympatholytic properties. This assay provides a direct and quantifiable readout of adrenergic and muscarinic receptor activity and is widely employed in the screening of topical ocular drugs, as well as for assessing systemic autonomic influence on the pupil.

The test is typically performed on rabbits, mice, or rats, with New Zealand white rabbits being the preferred species due to the large and easily measurable pupils. In rodents, measurement can also be made with appropriate magnification or photographic systems.

Experimental Setup

Animals are lightly restrained, and test solutions are instilled into the conjunctival sac of one eye, while the other eye often serves as a vehicle-treated or untreated control. The volume used is typically 20 to 30 µL for rabbits and 5 to 10 µL for mice. The drugs used may include:

- Sympathomimetics (e.g., phenylephrine, ephedrine): Stimulate alpha-1 adrenergic receptors on the radial muscle, causing pupil dilation.
- Parasympatholytics (e.g., atropine, tropicamide): Block muscarinic receptors on the circular sphincter muscle, leading to dilation.

Pupil size is measured before administration (baseline) and at regular intervals post-instillation (e.g., 10, 20, 30, 60, and 120 minutes). Measurement is done using digital calipers, photographic image analysis, or infrared pupillometry, depending on species and available equipment.

Parameters Assessed

- Pupil diameter (in mm): The key quantitative endpoint.
- Time to peak dilation: Reflects the onset of action.
- Duration of mydriasis: Reflects the drug's pharmacodynamic profile.
- Reversibility: Important in evaluating recovery time and potential side effects.

Mydriasis induced by sympathomimetics is generally rapid in onset and short in duration, while parasympatholytics often produce longer-lasting dilation, sometimes lasting up to 24–72 hours depending on the drug. For example, tropicamide produces dilation for 4–6 hours, while atropine may last for several days.

Applications in Pharmacological Screening

- Identification of autonomic receptor activity: Helps in distinguishing alpha-adrenergic agonists from muscarinic antagonists.
- Dose–response studies: Quantitative comparison of different drug concentrations for potency and efficacy.
- Formulation testing: Evaluation of topical ocular drug formulations for delivery, absorption, and local tolerance.
- Systemic effect detection: Observation of pupil size in systemic drug administration to assess central and peripheral autonomic effects.

Advantages

- Non-invasive and simple to perform
- Rapid and reproducible results
- Applicable for both topical and systemic drug assessment
- Useful in both screening and mechanistic studies

Limitations

- Results may be affected by ambient light intensity, animal strain or pigmentation, and stress levels.
- Requires standardization of environmental conditions, including controlled light–dark cycles and room temperature.
- In small rodents, accurate pupil measurement may require specialized imaging equipment.

The Mydriasis and Pupil Dilation Assay remains a fundamental tool in autonomic pharmacology for assessing sympathetic and parasympathetic influence on ocular physiology. It is especially important in the development of ophthalmic preparations, autonomic modulators, and in understanding drug interactions at the receptor level in both central and peripheral nervous systems.

2.7.4 Intestinal Motility Models

Intestinal motility models are essential in preclinical pharmacology for evaluating drugs that affect the autonomic control of gastrointestinal (GI) function, particularly those that alter parasympathetic activity. These models are widely used to assess the prokinetic, antispasmodic, antidiarrheal, or laxative effects of investigational compounds. The parasympathetic nervous system, through acetylcholine acting on muscarinic receptors, plays a vital role in promoting smooth muscle contraction and peristalsis in the GI tract. Thus, changes in motility can be reliably used as a pharmacodynamic marker for parasympathomimetic and parasympatholytic drug activity.

Various in vivo and ex vivo methods are used to assess intestinal motility in animal models, each with its specific utility depending on the site of action, mechanism, and duration of effect.

1. Charcoal Meal Test (Gastrointestinal Transit Test)

This is one of the most widely used in vivo assays to evaluate the influence of drugs on small intestinal motility. It is commonly performed in mice or rats, which are fasted overnight but allowed free access to water.

A charcoal meal (a suspension of activated charcoal in gum acacia or carboxymethylcellulose) is administered orally, either alone or along with the test compound. After a fixed interval (usually 30 to 60 minutes), the animals are sacrificed, and the small intestine is dissected from the pylorus to the caecum.

The distance travelled by the charcoal from the pyloric sphincter is measured and expressed as:

Percentage GI transit = (Distance travelled by charcoal / Total length of small intestine) × 100

- Increased transit indicates prokinetic or parasympathomimetic activity.
- Decreased transit indicates antispasmodic or parasympatholytic activity.

This model is particularly sensitive to drugs such as neostigmine (a cholinesterase inhibitor) and atropine (a muscarinic antagonist).

2. Loperamide-Induced Constipation Model

This model is used to test laxative or prokinetic agents by first inducing constipation with loperamide, a peripherally acting μ-opioid receptor agonist that inhibits intestinal motility. The animals (usually rats or mice) are treated with loperamide for 2 to 3 days, followed by administration of the test drug.

Parameters assessed include:

- Frequency and weight of stools
- Time to first defecation
- Water content in faeces

An increase in faecal output or water content indicates a reversal of constipation and thus enhanced motility.

3. Isolated Guinea Pig Ileum Preparation

This ex vivo model uses strips of guinea pig ileum suspended in an organ bath containing Tyrode's solution, maintained at 37°C and aerated with 95% O_2 and 5% CO_2. Contractions are recorded using an isometric force transducer.

Acetylcholine is added in increasing concentrations to generate a concentration–response curve, and the test compound is then added to assess:

- Potentiation of contraction (parasympathomimetic effect)
- Inhibition of contraction (parasympatholytic or antispasmodic effect)

This model is particularly useful for mechanistic studies and for determining the receptor subtype selectivity of the compound (e.g., M_2 vs M_3 muscarinic receptors).

4. Faecal Pellet Output Test

This simple in vivo assay quantifies the number and weight of faecal pellets excreted by rodents over a fixed period, typically 4–6 hours. Animals are placed individually in clean cages with mesh floors, and excreted pellets are collected.

- Increased output may indicate diarrheal or laxative activity.
- Decreased output suggests antidiarrheal or motility-inhibiting effect.

This method is especially useful when evaluating chronic effects of GI drugs and their influence on colonic transit.

5. Spontaneous Intestinal Contractions in Isolated Tissue

Intestinal segments from rabbit jejunum, guinea pig ileum, or rat colon exhibit spontaneous rhythmic contractions when maintained in physiological saline. These contractions can be recorded continuously in an organ bath to assess the direct effects of drugs on myogenic motility.

Test substances may:

- Increase amplitude or frequency of contraction (stimulatory)
- Decrease or abolish contractions (inhibitory)

This model helps distinguish between neurogenic and myogenic mechanisms of action.

2.7.5 Cardiovascular Response Assays (Heart Rate and Blood Pressure)

Cardiovascular response assays are fundamental in preclinical pharmacology for evaluating the effects of autonomic drugs on heart rate, blood pressure, and vascular tone. These assays provide direct insight into the activity of sympathomimetic, sympatholytic, parasympatholytic, and parasympathomimetic agents on the cardiovascular system. Heart rate is primarily controlled by beta-1 adrenergic and muscarinic M2 receptors, while blood pressure is regulated by a complex interaction of cardiac output, vascular resistance, and neurohumoral modulation.

Both in vivo and ex vivo models are used to measure these parameters. The choice depends on the nature of the drug (central or peripheral action), its route of administration, and the level of precision required.

1. In Vivo Blood Pressure and Heart Rate Measurement in Anesthetized Animals

In this widely used model, rats or rabbits are anesthetized using agents like urethane (1.2–1.5 g/kg, i.p.), and a cannula is inserted into the carotid artery to measure arterial blood pressure. A second cannula may be inserted into the femoral vein or tail vein for drug administration. The pressure transducer is connected to a data acquisition system for real-time monitoring.

- Systolic, diastolic, and mean arterial pressures (MAP) are recorded in mmHg.
- Heart rate is derived from the pulsatile pressure wave.
- Acute changes following drug administration help identify pressor (increased BP) or depressor (decreased BP) responses.

This method is ideal for assessing adrenergic agonists and antagonists. For example:

- Phenylephrine increases BP and reflexively slows HR (α_1 agonist).
- Isoproterenol reduces BP and increases HR (β agonist).
- Atropine increases HR by blocking vagal tone (muscarinic antagonist).

2. Non-Invasive Blood Pressure Measurement (Tail-Cuff Method)

This technique is suitable for conscious, restrained rats or mice. A pneumatic tail cuff is wrapped around the tail, and the pulse is measured before and after occlusion using photoelectric sensors.

- Measures systolic blood pressure and heart rate.
- Requires training and acclimatization to reduce stress-induced variability.
- Useful in long-term studies involving chronic drug treatment or disease models like hypertension.

Though less accurate than direct measurement, it is non-invasive, simple, and can be repeated over multiple days.

3. Isolated Perfused Heart (Langendorff Preparation)

This ex vivo assay involves removing the heart from a rat or guinea pig and perfusing it retrogradely via the aorta with oxygenated Krebs-Henseleit buffer at a constant pressure or flow rate.

Parameters measured include:

- Heart rate
- Left ventricular developed pressure
- Coronary flow rate

This model allows precise evaluation of direct cardiac effects of test compounds without interference from systemic circulation or neural inputs. It is ideal for studying drugs with inotropic, chronotropic, or vasodilatory effects, such as dobutamine, propranolol, or verapamil.

4. Central and Reflex Cardiovascular Models

To evaluate central autonomic regulation, compounds are injected intracerebroventricularly (ICV) in anesthetized animals, and cardiovascular changes are recorded. Reflex tests, such as:

- Baroreflex sensitivity tests using phenylephrine or sodium nitroprusside,
- Vagal stimulation to assess muscarinic influence on heart rate, are used to understand parasympathetic contributions to cardiovascular control.

5. ECG Monitoring in Conscious Animals

Electrocardiography provides detailed information about cardiac rhythm, conduction, and rate. In telemetry-based studies, small transmitters are surgically implanted in rats or dogs, allowing continuous ECG and BP recording in freely moving animals. This is essential for assessing arrhythmogenic potential and cardiac safety of new drugs.

Table 6: Common Behavioral Tests for CNS Activity

Test Name	Purpose	Species Used	Measured Parameters
Open Field Test	Assess locomotor activity and anxiety	Mice, Rats	Movement count, rearing, center time
Elevated Plus Maze	Evaluate anxiolytic behavior	Mice, Rats	Time in open vs closed arms
Rotarod Test	Assess motor coordination and balance	Mice, Rats	Latency to fall, endurance
Tail Flick Test	Evaluate spinal reflex and analgesia	Rats	Reaction time to heat stimulus
Morris Water Maze	Test spatial learning and memory	Rats	Latency to locate hidden platform

Table 7: CNS Stimulants and Depressants Screening Models

Drug Class	Examples	Key Models	Parameters Measured
CNS Stimulants	Amphetamine, Methylphenidate	Open field test, locomotor activity	Increased activity, alertness
CNS Depressants	Pentobarbital, Diazepam	Pentobarbital-induced sleep, rotarod	Sleep onset, duration, coordination loss

Table 8: Models for Epilepsy Screening

Model	Induction Method	Measured Outcome	Usefulness

Maximal Electroshock (MES)	Electric shock via corneal/auricular electrodes	Tonic hindlimb extension	Detects tonic seizure suppressors
Pentylenetetrazole (PTZ)	PTZ injection	Clonic seizures	Screens for absence seizure drugs
Kindling Model	Repeated sub-threshold stimuli	Seizure threshold, chronic changes	Models chronic epilepsy & plasticity

Table 9: Models for Neurodegenerative Diseases

Disease	Model	Key Features	Evaluation
Parkinson's Disease	MPTP, 6-OHDA Lesions	Dopaminergic neuron loss, rigidity	Rotarod, apomorphine-induced rotation
Alzheimer's Disease	Scopolamine, Aβ peptide	Memory loss, amyloid aggregation	Maze tests, biochemical markers
Multiple Sclerosis	EAE (Experimental Autoimmune Encephalomyelitis)	Demyelination, limb paralysis	Clinical scoring, histology

Table 10: CNS Drug Categories and Common Animal Tests

Drug Category	Example Models	Measured Effects
Anxiolytics	Elevated plus maze, light-dark box	Increased open arm entry
Antipsychotics	Catalepsy, apomorphine-induced rotation	Reduction in stereotypy/catalepsy
Antiepileptics	MES, PTZ test	Suppression of seizures
Nootropics	Morris water maze, radial arm maze	Improved memory and learning
Neuroprotectives	MPTP model, oxidative stress assays	Neuron survival, reduced inflammation

3. Preclinical Screening of Drugs for Respiratory, Reproductive, and Gastrointestinal Systems

3.1 Respiratory Pharmacology Models

3.1.1 Anti-Asthmatic Drug Screening

3.1.1.1 Histamine-Induced Bronchospasm in Guinea Pigs

The histamine-induced bronchospasm model in guinea pigs is a well-established and reliable preclinical method for evaluating the anti-asthmatic potential of drugs, particularly those that function as histamine H_1 receptor antagonists, bronchodilators, or mast cell stabilizers. This model mimics the acute bronchoconstrictive phase of asthma, which is mediated largely by histamine release during allergic reactions. Guinea pigs are chosen due to their high sensitivity to histamine and the similarity of their airway responses to those of humans.

Principle of Bronchoconstriction by Histamine

Histamine is one of the key mediators released from mast cells during allergic responses. When administered through the respiratory tract, histamine binds to H_1 receptors on bronchial smooth muscle, leading to smooth muscle contraction, airway narrowing, and difficulty in breathing (dyspnea). In guinea pigs, this results in a characteristic sequence of events: rapid breathing (tachypnea), wheezing, asphyxia, and in untreated animals, often death due to respiratory arrest.

The basic idea of the assay is to pre-treat animals with a test compound, followed by histamine challenge, and then measure protection time or latency to onset of dyspnea or death. A compound is considered effective if it can delay or prevent the effects of histamine-induced bronchospasm compared to control animals.

Experimental Procedure

- Animals: Healthy male guinea pigs (weighing 250–400 g), housed under standard conditions, fasted overnight but given free access to water.
- Histamine solution: Typically prepared in normal saline at a concentration of 0.2% to 0.5% (freshly made).
- Exposure method: The animal is placed in an airtight chamber connected to a nebulizer. Histamine is nebulized into the chamber using compressed air or oxygen at a controlled flow rate.
- Observation: The animal's behaviour is monitored after exposure. The time from start of exposure to onset of dyspnea (laboured breathing, gasping) is recorded as the preconvulsive dyspnea time (PCD time).
- Treatment groups: Animals are divided into groups receiving different doses of the test drug, a positive control (e.g., salbutamol or chlorpheniramine), and a vehicle control.
- **Protection index: This is calculated using the formula:**

   % Protection = ((PCD in treated − PCD in control) / PCD in control) × 100

This model allows comparison of dose-response relationships, and calculation of ED_{50} values (the dose that offers 50% protection against histamine effects). The test can also be used to compare onset and duration of action for inhaled and systemic drug formulations.

Interpretation of Results

- An increase in preconvulsive time or complete prevention of dyspnea indicates strong anti-histaminic or bronchodilatory activity.
- Drugs that block H_1 receptors or induce smooth muscle relaxation (e.g., beta-2 agonists) are expected to show significant protection.

Advantages

- High sensitivity and reproducibility
- Easy to quantify onset and severity of bronchospasm
- Closely mimics acute allergic asthma symptoms

Limitations

- It models only the immediate bronchoconstrictive phase, not the late-phase inflammatory component of asthma.
- Requires careful monitoring due to ethical concerns over animal distress.
- Guinea pigs are costlier and more sensitive than mice or rats, requiring skilled handling.

This model remains an important part of preclinical respiratory pharmacology, especially in the early-phase screening of anti-asthmatic drugs targeting histaminergic pathways or aiming to provide symptomatic bronchodilation.

Pre-treatment and Protection Index Calculation

In the histamine-induced bronchospasm model in guinea pigs, the protective effect of a test compound is evaluated by administering it before histamine exposure (pre-treatment), and then comparing the response with untreated control animals. This approach helps determine whether the drug delays or prevents the onset of respiratory distress (dyspnea) caused by histamine-induced bronchoconstriction.

Pre-treatment Protocol

The test compound can be administered through various routes depending on its formulation:

- Oral (p.o.): Common for antihistamines or mast cell stabilizers (e.g., ketotifen).

- Subcutaneous (s.c.) or intraperitoneal (i.p.): Useful for systemic bronchodilators (e.g., aminophylline).
- Inhalational: Appropriate for beta-2 agonists or steroids (e.g., salbutamol, budesonide).

Pre-treatment is usually given 30 minutes to 1 hour prior to histamine challenge, ensuring sufficient systemic absorption and onset of pharmacological action. Control groups receive vehicle only, while standard groups are treated with a known anti-asthmatic for comparison.

Protection Index Calculation

After histamine exposure, animals are observed, and the preconvulsive dyspnea (PCD) time is recorded. This is the time (in seconds) from the beginning of histamine exposure to the onset of laboured breathing or gasping.

To calculate the Protection Index (PI):

**% Protection =
((PCD time in treated group − PCD time in control group) /
PCD time in control group) × 100**

This value quantifies the efficacy of the test compound in preventing or delaying bronchospasm. A higher percentage indicates greater protective action.

Parameters: Latency to Dyspnea and Survival Time

Two important parameters are used to assess drug efficacy in this model:

1. Latency to Dyspnea (Preconvulsive Time)

- Defined as the interval between the onset of histamine exposure and the appearance of severe respiratory distress (gasping, loss of coordination).
- It is a direct measure of bronchial reactivity.
- A longer latency period suggests that the drug is effectively antagonizing bronchoconstriction.

This is the primary parameter used to compare across groups and calculate the protection index.

2. Survival Time

- In the absence of effective protection, guinea pigs may succumb to respiratory failure due to histamine-induced bronchospasm.
- Total survival time is recorded from the beginning of exposure until death.
- In treated animals, increased survival time or complete survival indicates potent bronchodilatory or antihistaminic effects.

This parameter is especially useful when testing drugs with life-saving potential in severe asthma or anaphylactic models.

These parameters—when evaluated together—help in characterizing the pharmacological profile of novel anti-asthmatic agents, establishing dose-response curves, and selecting lead compounds for further development.

3.1.1.2 Acetylcholine-Induced Bronchospasm

Use of Acetylcholine Aerosol Challenge

The acetylcholine-induced bronchospasm model is a widely used preclinical method for evaluating drugs that exert anticholinergic or bronchodilatory effects on the airways. Acetylcholine plays a significant role in bronchoconstriction through the stimulation of muscarinic receptors present on bronchial smooth muscles. This model is particularly useful for assessing the activity of parasympatholytic agents such as ipratropium bromide, tiotropium, or atropine. Guinea pigs are commonly employed in this assay due to their heightened responsiveness to cholinergic agents, which closely resembles the human airway response in obstructive lung diseases.

The experimental setup involves the use of an aerosol chamber or a whole-body plethysmograph connected to an ultrasonic or jet nebulizer. The test animals are usually male guinea pigs weighing between 250 to 400 grams and are housed under standard laboratory conditions. The animals are fasted for 12 hours before the experiment but allowed free access to water. Acetylcholine is freshly prepared in normal saline at concentrations typically ranging between 0.5 to 2 percent, depending on the desired intensity of bronchospasm. The aerosol is generated by the nebulizer and delivered into the chamber at a flow rate of 6 to 10 litres per minute for a period of 60 to 90 seconds.

Following exposure to the acetylcholine aerosol, guinea pigs exhibit signs of bronchoconstriction such as rapid breathing, gasping, and laboured movement. The key parameter recorded in this model is the latency to the onset of preconvulsive dyspnea, which refers to the time from the beginning of exposure to the point where the animal shows clear signs of respiratory distress. This time interval is inversely proportional to the bronchoconstrictive effect of acetylcholine. A compound with effective bronchodilatory or antimuscarinic activity is expected to delay this onset, thus indicating protection against acetylcholine-induced bronchospasm.

Test compounds are administered to the animals thirty to sixty minutes before the aerosol challenge. They may be given orally, subcutaneously, intraperitoneally, or by inhalation, depending on their formulation and route of action. The study usually includes multiple groups such as untreated controls, positive controls receiving a standard anticholinergic drug, and treatment groups receiving varying doses of the test drug. The percentage of protection provided by the drug is calculated using the following formula:

Percentage protection = ((Treated group latency − Control group latency) / Control group latency) × 100

This formula helps in quantifying the protective effect of the test compound and determining the dose-response relationship. Additionally, the survival time may be recorded in cases where severe bronchospasm leads to respiratory arrest, although ethical endpoints generally require animals to be removed from the study before death occurs.

This model provides a robust and reproducible method for evaluating agents that act on muscarinic receptors in the airways. It is particularly relevant for the screening of drugs used in chronic obstructive pulmonary disease and asthma, where bronchial smooth muscle tone is a critical therapeutic target. The results obtained from this assay can be correlated with those from histamine-induced bronchospasm models to differentiate between antihistaminic and anticholinergic mechanisms of action. Proper standardisation of environmental conditions, including temperature, humidity, and airflow, is essential to maintain the reliability and consistency of the assay.

Assessment of Cholinergic Bronchoconstriction

The assessment of cholinergic bronchoconstriction in the acetylcholine aerosol challenge model is based on the ability of acetylcholine to induce acute and dose-dependent narrowing of the bronchial airways through the stimulation of muscarinic receptors located on the smooth muscle of the respiratory tract. Specifically, the M_3 subtype of muscarinic receptors, which is abundantly expressed in the airway smooth muscle, mediates the contractile response when activated by endogenous acetylcholine or exogenously administered cholinergic agents. In guinea pigs, this results in pronounced bronchospasm that mimics certain aspects of asthma and chronic obstructive pulmonary disease in humans.

Following exposure to acetylcholine aerosol, guinea pigs demonstrate characteristic symptoms of bronchoconstriction such as reduced exploratory behaviour, rapid and laboured respiration, wheezing, and in severe cases, convulsive dyspnea. The key observable parameter is the latency to onset of dyspnea, which represents the time taken for the animal to shift from normal breathing to visible signs of respiratory distress. This time is carefully monitored using a stopwatch, beginning at the start of acetylcholine nebulization and ending at the appearance of defined respiratory symptoms such as gasping or loss of motor coordination. A shorter latency period reflects stronger bronchoconstrictive action, whereas delayed onset suggests a reduced response.

In addition to behavioural observation, some experimental setups allow the use of non-invasive respiratory monitoring systems like whole-body plethysmography, which can measure parameters such as tidal volume, respiratory rate, and enhanced pause (Penh). These physiological readouts provide a more objective and quantifiable measure of bronchoconstriction. However, due to cost constraints and accessibility, manual observation of latency time remains the most commonly used endpoint in basic pharmacology laboratories.

Comparison with Anticholinergic Bronchodilators

The efficacy of test drugs with potential anticholinergic activity is evaluated by their ability to protect the animals against acetylcholine-induced bronchospasm. Compounds such as atropine, ipratropium bromide, or tiotropium, which are known muscarinic antagonists, serve as positive controls. These drugs act by competitively inhibiting the binding of acetylcholine to muscarinic receptors, thereby preventing smooth muscle contraction and maintaining airway patency.

Animals pre-treated with anticholinergic agents before acetylcholine exposure show a prolonged latency to dyspnea, indicating effective protection. In some cases, these drugs may completely prevent the onset of respiratory distress during the observation period, especially at higher doses. The protection offered by the test compound is quantitatively compared to the standard anticholinergic by calculating the percentage protection using the same latency-based formula.

This comparative approach helps in establishing the relative potency and efficacy of new bronchodilator agents. A test compound producing similar or superior protection compared to a standard drug may be considered a promising candidate for further development. Moreover, the specificity of action can be confirmed by conducting antagonist reversal studies, where a selective muscarinic blocker is used to reverse the effect of the test compound, thereby confirming its mechanism of action.

This model thus provides a direct and meaningful assessment of cholinergic bronchoconstriction and the therapeutic potential of antimuscarinic drugs in respiratory pharmacology. Its simplicity, reliability, and ability to produce consistent results make it a valuable tool in the early screening phase of drug discovery for conditions like asthma and chronic obstructive pulmonary disease.

3.1.2.1 Cigarette Smoke-Induced COPD Model

Exposure Protocol and Duration

The cigarette smoke-induced model of chronic obstructive pulmonary disease (COPD) is a highly relevant in vivo method used in experimental pharmacology to mimic the chronic inflammatory and structural changes seen in human COPD. It replicates the long-term exposure to cigarette smoke that is a major etiological factor in human disease. The model is generally performed in mice, particularly strains like C57BL/6, which show a reproducible response to smoke exposure. Sometimes rats or guinea pigs are used depending on the study goals.

In a standard protocol, animals are exposed to mainstream and sidestream cigarette smoke using a whole-body or nose-only exposure chamber. Commercially available cigarettes, usually containing 11–12 mg of tar and 0.8–1 mg of nicotine, are used. The smoke from each cigarette is drawn using a peristaltic pump into the exposure chamber.

Exposure is carried out twice daily for 30–60 minutes per session, for a period ranging from 4 to 24 weeks, depending on whether the study aims to model early inflammation, progressive lung function decline, or emphysematous changes. During each session, animals inhale the smoke from 5–10 cigarettes, and airflow is maintained using charcoal filters to ensure smoke consistency. The total particulate matter and carbon monoxide levels in the chamber are monitored to ensure standardized exposure.

Throughout the exposure period, body weight, respiratory rate, and general health status are monitored. The animals are sacrificed at pre-decided time intervals for analysis of biochemical, histopathological, and functional parameters.

Inflammatory Marker Assessment in Bronchoalveolar Lavage Fluid

After the final exposure, the animals are anesthetized and the trachea is cannulated for bronchoalveolar lavage (BAL). This involves flushing the lungs with ice-cold phosphate-buffered saline (PBS) in aliquots (usually 1 mL × 3 times in mice) and gently aspirating the fluid back. The collected BAL fluid is centrifuged, and the supernatant is used for biochemical assays, while the cell pellet is used for cytological analysis.

The BAL fluid is analyzed for:

- Total leukocyte count and differential cell count (neutrophils, macrophages, lymphocytes)
- Pro-inflammatory cytokines such as TNF-α, IL-6, IL-1β
- Chemokines like MCP-1, MIP-2

- Matrix metalloproteinases (MMP-9, MMP-12), which are involved in alveolar destruction
- Reactive oxygen species (ROS) and oxidative stress markers

These markers help to assess the degree of inflammation, immune cell recruitment, and oxidative damage induced by cigarette smoke. Effective test compounds are expected to significantly reduce these values when compared to the control group.

Histopathology of Lung Tissue

For histological analysis, the lungs are perfused with saline, inflated with 10% neutral-buffered formalin, and then fixed overnight. Tissue sections are embedded in paraffin, sectioned, and stained using Hematoxylin and Eosin (H&E) for general morphology and Masson's Trichrome for collagen deposition.

Common histopathological findings include:

- Alveolar wall destruction leading to enlarged airspaces (emphysema)
- Bronchiolar inflammation
- Goblet cell hyperplasia and mucus gland hypertrophy
- Peribronchial inflammatory infiltrates
- Fibrosis and airway remodeling

Quantitative scoring systems are often employed to assess mean linear intercept (MLI) and destructive index (DI) to measure alveolar damage. Therapeutic agents such as steroids, PDE4 inhibitors, antioxidants, or novel anti-inflammatory molecules are tested in this model to determine their potential in preventing or reversing COPD pathology.

This model closely parallels human COPD in terms of pathophysiology, chronicity, and treatment resistance, making it a valuable tool for preclinical evaluation of drugs targeting airway inflammation, oxidative stress, and lung tissue remodeling.

3.1.2.2 Elastase-Induced Emphysema Model

Use of Porcine Pancreatic Elastase

The elastase-induced emphysema model is a widely used experimental model for studying emphysema, a component of chronic obstructive pulmonary disease (COPD), that is characterized by irreversible alveolar destruction and airspace enlargement. The model mimics the pathogenesis of emphysema caused by an imbalance between proteases and antiproteases in the lungs. Porcine pancreatic elastase (PPE) is the most commonly used enzyme in this model due to its strong ability to degrade elastin fibers in the lung extracellular matrix.

The procedure involves the intratracheal administration of PPE to rodents, typically mice or rats. Animals are anesthetized using a light dose of ketamine (100 mg/kg) and xylazine (10 mg/kg). A small incision is made in the neck to expose the trachea, and a single dose of 0.3–0.6 units of PPE in 50–100 µL of sterile saline is instilled directly into the trachea using a microsyringe. Alternatively, non-invasive oropharyngeal aspiration may be used. Following instillation, the animal is kept in a vertical position for one to two minutes to allow even distribution of the enzyme.

PPE digests elastin and other components of the alveolar wall, leading to alveolar rupture, loss of septal integrity, and enlargement of the airspaces. Within 14 to 28 days, the structural changes closely resemble human centrilobular emphysema, and the model becomes suitable for evaluating therapeutic agents that prevent or reverse tissue damage.

This model is simple, quick to induce, and reproducible, making it ideal for testing anti-protease agents, antioxidants, and drugs that promote tissue regeneration or remodeling.

Lung Compliance and Elastance Measurement

To evaluate functional changes in lung mechanics following elastase administration, lung compliance and elastance are measured using invasive pulmonary function testing systems such as FlexiVent or Buxco in anesthetized animals.

- Lung compliance refers to the ability of the lungs to expand and is calculated as the change in lung volume per unit change in transpulmonary pressure (mL/cm H_2O). In emphysema, lung compliance increases due to the loss of elastic recoil.
- Elastance is the inverse of compliance and reflects the stiffness of the lung tissue. A decrease in elastance is observed in elastase-treated animals due to reduced tissue integrity.

Animals are ventilated through a tracheal cannula, and pressure–volume loops are recorded. Parameters like static compliance (Cst), dynamic compliance (Cdyn), tissue resistance (G), and tissue elastance (H) provide detailed information about respiratory mechanics.

Improvement in these values after treatment indicates the therapeutic efficacy of test compounds in restoring lung function or halting progression of emphysema.

Morphometric Changes in Alveolar Spaces

To assess the structural damage and extent of emphysema, lung tissues are fixed under constant pressure, embedded in paraffin, and stained with hematoxylin and eosin (H&E) for morphometric analysis. Histological examination is focused on the alveolar architecture, and the following parameters are quantified:

- Mean Linear Intercept (MLI): Represents the average distance between alveolar walls. Increased MLI indicates enlarged airspaces due to alveolar destruction.

- Destructive Index (DI): Calculated as the percentage of alveoli showing structural destruction, such as wall thinning or rupture.
- Alveolar Septal Thickness: Measured to assess inflammatory thickening or fibrosis.

Digital image analysis software is used to evaluate high-resolution lung sections under a microscope. Increased MLI and DI values confirm emphysematous damage, and any significant reversal of these changes after drug treatment supports its potential as an anti-emphysematous agent.

The elastase-induced emphysema model is ideal for mechanistic studies and preclinical screening of therapeutic compounds targeting protease activity, inflammation, oxidative stress, or promoting alveolar regeneration. Its ability to provide both structural and functional endpoints makes it a powerful tool in respiratory drug research.

3.1.3.1 Passive Cutaneous Anaphylaxis (PCA)

The passive cutaneous anaphylaxis (PCA) model is a well-established in vivo technique used for screening anti-allergic agents, particularly those targeting mast cell degranulation, histamine release, and vascular permeability. This model mimics type I hypersensitivity reactions, which are IgE-mediated and involve mast cell activation, histamine release, and capillary leakage. PCA is commonly performed in rats or mice, with Wistar rats and BALB/c mice being the preferred strains due to their immune responsiveness and manageable size.

Immunization Procedure and Dye Extravasation

The PCA model begins with passive sensitization, where serum containing antigen-specific IgE antibodies is injected intradermally into the dorsal skin of recipient animals. Typically, the serum is collected from a donor animal previously immunized with an allergen such as ovalbumin, egg albumin, or bovine serum albumin (BSA) along with an adjuvant.

In mice, 50 µL of immune serum is injected intradermally at multiple dorsal skin sites. The animal is then left for 24 to 48 hours, allowing the IgE antibodies to bind to FcεRI receptors on mast cells within the skin. Following sensitization, the animals are challenged intravenously with a solution containing the specific antigen (e.g., ovalbumin) and Evans blue dye (usually 1% in saline, 1 mL/kg).

Upon antigen exposure, cross-linking of surface-bound IgE on mast cells leads to degranulation and histamine release, causing vasodilation and increased vascular permeability. As a result, the blue dye leaks out of the blood vessels and accumulates in the surrounding dermal tissues at the site of prior sensitization. The intensity and area of blue coloration directly reflect the severity of the allergic reaction.

Measurement of Vascular Permeability and Allergic Response

After 30 minutes of antigen challenge, the animals are euthanized, and the dorsal skin is carefully removed. The blue spots on the inner surface of the skin are visually inspected and quantified. The following parameters are assessed:

- Diameter of the blue spot (in mm): Measured using a millimeter scale or digital calliper.
- Optical density of dye extracted from skin: The dyed area is excised, weighed, and incubated in formamide at 55–60°C for 24 hours. The absorbance of the supernatant is then measured at 620 nm using a spectrophotometer.
- Dye content (µg/mg tissue) is calculated using a standard curve of Evans blue.

These values indicate the extent of histamine-induced vascular leakage, and hence the intensity of the allergic response. This model is sensitive, quantitative, and reproducible.

Inhibition by Antihistamines and Mast Cell Stabilizers

The test compound is administered before the antigen challenge, typically 30 minutes to 1 hour before intravenous injection of the antigen–dye mixture. Depending on the drug's formulation, it may be given orally, intraperitoneally, or subcutaneously.

Effective antihistamines (e.g., chlorpheniramine, cetirizine) inhibit the histamine-mediated capillary leakage, resulting in reduced dye extravasation. On the other hand, mast cell stabilizers (e.g., sodium cromoglycate, ketotifen) prevent mast cell degranulation itself, reducing not only histamine release but also the secretion of other inflammatory mediators like leukotrienes and prostaglandins.

The percentage inhibition of dye leakage by the test drug is calculated using the formula:

Percentage inhibition = ((Control dye content − Treated dye content) / Control dye content) × 100

This provides a direct quantitative estimate of the anti-allergic effect.

The PCA model is one of the most predictive in vivo models for evaluating anti-allergic drugs, especially in early-stage screening. It allows for the identification of compounds that act through histamine receptor antagonism or mast cell stabilization, and is a reliable method for mechanistic investigation of type I hypersensitivity.

3.2.1.1 Male Sexual Behavioural Models in Rodents

Mount Latency, Intromission Latency, Ejaculation Latency

Male sexual behavioural models in rodents are extensively used in preclinical pharmacology to assess the aphrodisiac activity of investigational compounds. These models provide direct and measurable endpoints reflecting various phases of sexual performance, including sexual motivation, penile erection, mounting, and ejaculation. The tests are generally conducted in male rats or mice that are sexually experienced and have shown prior mating responses. The evaluation is based on the quantification of specific behavioural parameters observed during a defined interaction period with a receptive female in oestrus.

Before initiating the experiment, the male animals are kept under standard laboratory conditions and are acclimatized to the experimental environment. Female animals are brought into oestrus using hormonal treatments such as estradiol benzoate (10 µg/rat, subcutaneous) administered 48 hours before the test, followed by progesterone (500 µg/rat, subcutaneous) four hours prior to mating. Receptivity is confirmed by the lordosis reflex.

The male animal is then placed in a mating arena, and a female in estrus is introduced. The following key parameters are recorded:

- Mount Latency (ML): This is defined as the time interval between the introduction of the female and the first mounting attempt by the male, with or without penile insertion. It reflects sexual motivation and libido. A reduction in mount latency following drug administration suggests an increase in sexual desire or enhanced arousal.
- Intromission Latency (IL): This is the time from the introduction of the female to the first vaginal penetration by the male, indicated by rhythmic pelvic thrusting and a momentary pause before dismount. Intromission latency provides insight into the initiation of sexual performance and erectile function. A shorter intromission latency indicates facilitated penile erection and enhanced sexual responsiveness.
- Ejaculation Latency (EL): This is measured from the first intromission to ejaculation, identified by a longer series of pelvic thrusts, followed by a sudden dismount and momentary immobility. Ejaculation latency represents the completion of the sexual performance. A moderate increase

in this parameter may indicate improved endurance, whereas a drastic prolongation may suggest delayed orgasm or ejaculatory dysfunction.

These behavioural parameters are typically observed during a 30-minute mating session and can be videotaped for accurate scoring. Along with these latencies, other parameters like number of mounts, intromission frequency, post-ejaculatory interval, and copulatory efficiency are also recorded to give a complete profile of male sexual activity.

Compounds that reduce mount and intromission latencies, while prolonging ejaculation latency in a balanced manner, are considered to possess aphrodisiac potential. Standard reference drugs include testosterone, sildenafil citrate, and yohimbine, which act via hormonal or neurogenic pathways. The test compound is typically administered 30 to 60 minutes before the mating test via oral or intraperitoneal route.

This model serves as a comprehensive screening tool for sexual function enhancers, and helps in evaluating drugs targeting androgenic, dopaminergic, nitrergic, or serotonergic mechanisms involved in sexual behaviour. It also provides valuable insights into side effects on sexual performance of other therapeutic drugs such as antidepressants, antihypertensives, or anxiolytics.

Intromission Frequency and Post-Ejaculatory Interval

In male sexual behavioural models in rodents, intromission frequency and post-ejaculatory interval are additional key indicators used to assess the intensity, endurance, and recovery aspect of sexual performance. These parameters provide deeper insights into how a test drug affects not just the initiation but also the sustained reproductive behaviour of the male rodent.

Intromission Frequency (IF) refers to the total number of vaginal penetrations made by the male before the first ejaculation. Each intromission is identified by rhythmic pelvic thrusts with a pause, distinguishing it from a simple mount. This parameter reflects the degree of sexual vigour, erectile function, and copulatory efficiency of the male.

An increase in intromission frequency typically indicates enhanced sexual stamina and repeated erectile competence, suggesting that the test compound may be promoting sexual endurance. Conversely, a reduction in this frequency may point towards erectile dysfunction or a diminished sexual drive. It also indirectly assesses penile sensitivity and neurological control over sexual performance.

Post-Ejaculatory Interval (PEI) is defined as the time elapsed between ejaculation and the next mount or intromission. In rodents, following ejaculation, males typically undergo a refractory period where sexual interest and activity are temporarily reduced. The duration of this interval reflects the recovery time needed to reinitiate sexual behaviour.

A shorter post-ejaculatory interval suggests rapid recovery and sustained libido, which may be attributed to central nervous system stimulatory effects or elevated testosterone levels. A prolonged PEI may be due to sedative effects, dopaminergic blockade, or age-related sexual fatigue.

Both intromission frequency and post-ejaculatory interval are observed during a fixed mating session, usually lasting 30 minutes, or until the male completes at least one full copulatory cycle. The recording of these endpoints, along with mount latency, intromission latency, and ejaculation latency, allows researchers to generate a complete sexual behaviour profile.

These measurements are highly useful in preclinical testing of aphrodisiac agents, erectogenic drugs, and in evaluating the sexual side effects of other pharmacological treatments. Substances like sildenafil citrate, apomorphine, and testosterone are often used as positive controls for enhancing performance and decreasing PEI. The data from this model help in understanding the central and peripheral mechanisms regulating sexual behaviour and guiding further development of reproductive pharmacotherapeutics.

Interpretation of Enhanced Sexual Performance

The interpretation of enhanced sexual performance in male sexual behavioural models relies on the combined analysis of various parameters that reflect different phases of the copulatory cycle in rodents. An investigational compound is considered to possess aphrodisiac or pro-sexual activity when it significantly improves multiple behavioural indices without causing undue stress, sedation, or motor impairment.

A decrease in mount latency is interpreted as an improvement in sexual motivation or libido, suggesting that the compound may stimulate the central nervous system pathways responsible for sexual arousal. This effect is often associated with increased dopaminergic tone or androgenic modulation, both of which are vital for initiating sexual behaviour.

A shortened intromission latency, along with an increased number of intromissions, indicates that the drug facilitates erectile function and penile penetration. This enhancement may be due to increased nitric oxide release, improved penile blood flow, or direct action on the spinal reflex arc responsible for erection. A high intromission frequency also points to sustained sexual vigour, allowing the animal to perform repeated penetrations before ejaculation.

Ejaculation latency, when moderately prolonged, may be interpreted as a sign of increased sexual endurance, allowing the male to maintain copulatory activity over a longer period. However, if it is excessively delayed, it might reflect orgasmic inhibition or impaired ejaculatory mechanisms, which is not desirable in all therapeutic contexts.

A shorter post-ejaculatory interval is considered favourable, as it indicates rapid recovery and sustained sexual interest. It suggests that the drug may reduce the refractory period, which is influenced by central neurotransmitters such as dopamine and serotonin.

Overall, a compound that reduces mount and intromission latencies, increases intromission frequency, moderately delays ejaculation, and shortens the post-ejaculatory interval is considered to exhibit a complete and balanced enhancement of sexual performance. This profile suggests potential utility in managing erectile dysfunction, premature ejaculation, or age-related decline in sexual function. Importantly, these interpretations must be made alongside proper control comparisons and observations for any non-specific behavioural effects to ensure that the enhancements are due to sexual stimulation rather than general arousal or hyperactivity.

3.2.1.2 Hormonal and Neurological Modulation Studies

Testosterone and Dopamine Involvement

Hormonal and neurological pathways play a crucial role in regulating male sexual behaviour, and preclinical studies often explore how investigational compounds influence these systems to enhance or impair performance. Among the various modulators, testosterone and dopamine are two key regulators of male sexual function in rodents and humans. Understanding their involvement helps in interpreting the mechanism behind a compound's aphrodisiac or sexual dysfunction-inducing effects.

Testosterone, the primary androgen hormone, is essential for maintaining libido, erection, and copulatory efficiency. In male rodents, testosterone levels are strongly correlated with sexual motivation and performance, particularly the initiation phase of mating behaviour. Orchiectomy (castration) in male rats leads to a sharp decline in sexual activity, including increased mount latency, reduced intromission frequency, and absence of ejaculation. These behaviours can be restored by administering exogenous testosterone, often given in the form of testosterone propionate at doses ranging from 0.5 to 2 mg/kg, subcutaneously, for 5 to 10 days.

Testosterone acts centrally on the preoptic area of the hypothalamus, which is the major integrative centre for male sexual behaviour, and peripherally on penile tissue and reproductive organs. It also enhances the expression of nitric oxide synthase, thereby improving penile erection. When a test compound elevates serum testosterone levels or mimics its effect on target tissues, enhanced sexual performance is observed in animal models.

Dopamine is a vital neurotransmitter in the mesolimbic and nigrostriatal pathways, with a well-documented role in sexual arousal, motivation, and reward processing. In male rats, dopamine levels rise in the nucleus accumbens and medial preoptic area during sexual activity. Dopamine agonists, such as apomorphine or bromocriptine, enhance mounting and intromission behaviours and reduce mount latency. These compounds act primarily on D_2 receptors, which are known to facilitate sexual motivation and erection.

Conversely, dopamine antagonists (e.g., haloperidol) significantly suppress sexual activity, indicating the importance of dopaminergic tone in normal reproductive function. When an investigational drug shows pro-sexual effects in male behavioural models, researchers often test whether the effect is attenuated by pre-treatment with dopamine antagonists to determine the involvement of dopaminergic pathways.

Therefore, drugs that increase endogenous testosterone, act as androgen receptor agonists, or modulate dopaminergic transmission may exhibit aphrodisiac activity. Preclinical studies often complement behavioural testing with serum hormone estimation, receptor binding assays, or brain dopamine level quantification using HPLC or immunohistochemistry to establish a clear mechanistic link.

These hormonal and neurological modulation studies provide a valuable framework for interpreting the pharmacological basis of observed changes in sexual behaviour and help in classifying compounds as hormone-dependent, neurogenic, or mixed-mechanism aphrodisiacs.

Use of L-DOPA and Apomorphine as Positive Controls

In male sexual behavioural studies, certain well-characterized pharmacological agents are employed as positive controls to validate the model and confirm its sensitivity in detecting pro-sexual activity. Two of the most widely used agents for this purpose are L-DOPA (levodopa) and apomorphine, both of which are known to enhance male sexual behaviour through central dopaminergic mechanisms.

L-DOPA is a metabolic precursor of dopamine that crosses the blood–brain barrier and is converted to dopamine by aromatic L-amino acid decarboxylase in the brain. It increases the dopaminergic tone in regions such as the medial preoptic area and nucleus accumbens, which are critically involved in regulating sexual motivation and performance. When administered systemically, typically at doses ranging from 50 to 100 mg/kg intraperitoneally in rats, L-DOPA significantly reduces mount latency and intromission latency, and enhances copulatory activity.

The action of L-DOPA is particularly effective in animals with reduced sexual motivation, such as aged or castrated males, or those treated with dopamine antagonists. Its inclusion in experimental protocols helps establish the dopaminergic dependence of the observed behavioural response and validates the model's responsiveness to neurogenic aphrodisiacs.

Apomorphine, a non-selective dopamine agonist that acts primarily on D_2-like receptors, is another potent pro-sexual agent used as a standard reference. It directly stimulates dopaminergic receptors in the hypothalamus and midbrain, thereby promoting sexual arousal and performance. In preclinical studies, apomorphine is usually administered subcutaneously at doses ranging from 0.05 to 0.5 mg/kg. Even at low doses, it can significantly reduce mount and intromission latencies and enhance erectile function, often without affecting general locomotor activity.

Unlike L-DOPA, apomorphine does not require metabolic conversion and has a rapid onset of action. It is particularly useful for distinguishing compounds that act through direct dopamine receptor stimulation from those that rely on increasing dopamine synthesis or release. However, at higher doses, apomorphine may cause side effects like stereotypy or sedation, so dose selection must be carefully optimized.

The use of L-DOPA and apomorphine as positive controls allows researchers to:

- Confirm the validity and sensitivity of the sexual behavioural model
- Compare the magnitude and onset of pro-sexual effects of new test compounds
- Elucidate the dopaminergic involvement in observed behavioural changes

Their predictable pharmacological profile and well-established efficacy make them essential tools in the mechanistic exploration and benchmarking of investigational aphrodisiac agents in male rodents.

3.2.2.1 Estrous Cycle Monitoring in Female Rats

Vaginal Smear Technique and Cytology Interpretation

Monitoring the estrous cycle in female rats is a fundamental method in reproductive pharmacology for evaluating the effects of antifertility agents, as well as for identifying the optimal reproductive phase for mating studies. The estrous cycle in rats typically lasts 4 to 5 days and comprises four distinct phases: proestrus, estrus, metestrus, and diestrus. These stages can be distinguished by examining the cytology of vaginal smears, which reflects the hormonal milieu regulating the female reproductive system.

The vaginal smear technique is a simple, non-invasive procedure that involves daily collection and microscopic examination of vaginal epithelial cells. This technique allows for the identification of changes in hormone levels, ovulatory status, and cycle regularity, which are crucial in determining whether a test compound affects ovarian function, ovulation, or the pituitary-gonadal axis.

Procedure for Vaginal Smear Collection:

1. Time of collection: Smears are typically collected at a fixed time each morning, preferably between 8:00 and 10:00 a.m., to maintain consistency, as hormone levels follow a circadian rhythm.
2. Sample collection: A small plastic pipette or dropper is filled with 10–20 µL of normal saline or sterile distilled water. The tip is gently inserted 5–10 mm into the vaginal opening of the rat (without causing discomfort or penetration into the cervix).
3. Irrigation and withdrawal: The fluid is gently flushed into the vaginal canal and then re-aspirated, collecting cells lining the vaginal wall. The collected fluid is placed onto a clean glass slide and spread evenly to form a thin smear.
4. Staining: The slide may be air-dried and stained using methylene blue, Giemsa, or hematoxylin-eosin stain to enhance cell visibility under a light microscope.
5. Microscopic examination: The stained slide is observed under 10× and 40× objectives, and the types of cells present are used to determine the estrous cycle phase.

Cytological Features of Each Estrous Phase:

- Proestrus:
    - Predominantly nucleated epithelial cells
    - Few leukocytes or cornified cells

- o Indicates rising estrogen levels and follicular development
- Estrus:
  - o Presence of anucleated cornified epithelial cells
  - o No leukocytes
  - o Corresponds to the period of ovulation and peak fertility
- Metestrus:
  - o Mixed population of cornified epithelial cells and leukocytes
  - o Indicates recent ovulation and luteal formation
- Diestrus:
  - o Dominated by leukocytes, few epithelial cells
  - o Indicates a non-receptive phase, with lower estrogen levels and corpus luteum activity

Interpretation and Relevance:

A normal cycling female rat will exhibit all four phases over 4 to 5 days in sequence. Disruption or alteration in the regularity, duration, or cytological profile of the cycle after administration of a test compound may indicate:

- Antifertility effect through suppression of ovulation
- Estrogenic or antiestrogenic activity
- Luteolytic or anti-progestational effects

For example, prolonged diestrus or absence of proestrus may suggest that the test drug interferes with the hypothalamic-pituitary-ovarian axis, suppressing gonadotropin secretion or ovarian responsiveness.

This method is essential for:

- Selecting the appropriate phase for mating in fertility studies
- Evaluating the mechanism of action of antifertility agents
- Monitoring reproductive toxicity or endocrine-disrupting potential

Due to its non-invasive nature, repeatability, and predictive value, vaginal smear cytology is a cornerstone technique in reproductive pharmacology and a valuable tool for preclinical screening of contraceptive agents.

Disruption Patterns Induced by Test Substances

Test substances with antifertility potential often alter the regular progression of the estrous cycle in female rats. These disruption patterns can be identified by abnormalities in the sequence, duration, or cytological composition of the estrous phases. A normal estrous cycle involves a predictable rotation through proestrus, estrus, metestrus, and diestrus within 4–5 days. Antifertility compounds may disrupt this rhythm through central hormonal interference, ovarian dysfunction, or uterine alterations.

The most common disruption patterns observed include:

- Prolonged diestrus: This suggests inhibition of follicular maturation and suppressed estrogen production, often associated with anti-gonadotropic or anti-estrogenic effects of the test drug.
- Extended estrus or pseudopregnancy-like state: Seen with compounds having estrogenic or luteotrophic activity, causing persistent vaginal cornification.
- Anovulatory cycles: Absence of the proestrus–estrus transition indicates failure of ovulation. This is usually due to suppression of luteinizing hormone (LH) surge by central acting drugs.
- Irregular or arrested cycles: Disorganized appearance of cell types over several days implies general hormonal imbalance or toxic damage to the hypothalamic–pituitary–gonadal axis.

These changes are observed by daily monitoring of vaginal smears and are confirmed over two or more complete cycles. Such disruptions, when consistently reproduced, confirm the antifertility potential of the compound being studied.

3.2.2.2 Anti-Implantation Studies

Mating and Implantation Detection

Anti-implantation studies are designed to evaluate whether a test substance can prevent implantation of a fertilized ovum in the uterine endometrium. These studies are crucial for identifying agents that may act as post-coital contraceptives by interfering with early pregnancy events, such as fertilization, zygote transport, or endometrial receptivity. The most commonly used species for such studies are albino rats and mice due to their well-characterized reproductive cycles and short gestation periods.

Mating Procedure:

- Adult, cyclic female rats are paired with proven fertile males in a 1:1 ratio, typically overnight.
- The following morning, vaginal smears are examined microscopically for the presence of spermatozoa. The day sperm is first observed is considered Day 1 of pregnancy.
- Alternatively, the presence of a vaginal plug is also taken as confirmation of mating.

Test Compound Administration:

- The suspected antifertility compound is administered during the pre-implantation window, usually Day 1 to Day 5 of pregnancy.
- It can be administered orally, subcutaneously, or intraperitoneally depending on the pharmacokinetics of the drug.

Implantation Detection:

- On Day 10 or 11 of gestation, animals are sacrificed and the uterus is examined for implantation sites.

- The uterus is removed, and the number of implantation sites is counted visually. These appear as well-defined swellings along the uterine horns.
- If implantation sites are not visible, uterine flushing or dye injection methods (such as intravenous injection of 1% Chicago Blue dye) can be used to reveal faint sites by highlighting increased vascular permeability.

Interpretation:

- A significant reduction in the number of implantation sites in the treated group compared to the control indicates anti-implantation activity.
- Complete absence of implants, despite confirmed mating, suggests that the compound interfered with ovum transport, endometrial preparation, or blastocyst viability.

This model helps differentiate drugs with anti-fertilization, anti-ovulatory, or embryotoxic mechanisms, and is particularly useful in developing emergency contraceptives or post-coital birth control methods. The model is sensitive, reliable, and provides early insight into a compound's potential as a fertility-regulating agent.

Evaluation of Pre- and Post-Coital Contraceptive Effects

In reproductive pharmacology, the evaluation of pre-coital and post-coital contraceptive effects of test substances is a critical step in identifying compounds that can prevent conception or implantation depending on the timing of administration. These two categories differ based on whether the drug is administered before or after mating and hence provide insights into the stage of the reproductive process being affected—either ovulation and fertilization (pre-coital) or embryo transport and implantation (post-coital).

Pre-coital contraceptive evaluation involves administration of the test compound before mating, usually during the estrous cycle or early in the fertile window (i.e., before ovulation). This approach is used to assess whether the drug:

- Inhibits ovulation by altering the LH surge or follicular maturation
- Affects oocyte quality or sperm receptivity
- Induces hostile cervical mucus or disrupts tubal motility

The experimental procedure typically includes:

- Selecting proestrus or estrus phase females
- Administering the compound 12 to 24 hours before pairing with a fertile male
- Confirming mating through vaginal smear or copulatory plug
- Allowing pregnancy to proceed up to day 10 to 12, then sacrificing the animal to examine the number of implantation sites

A reduction or complete absence of implantation sites suggests that the compound has pre-coital contraceptive action, likely through anti-ovulatory or anti-fertilization mechanisms.

Post-coital contraceptive evaluation, on the other hand, focuses on compounds administered after confirmed mating, typically within 24 to 72 hours. This is the period between fertilization and implantation. The compound may interfere with:

- Zygote transport through the oviduct
- Endometrial receptivity
- Blastocyst viability or uterine signalling

In this case, the procedure is:

- Confirming mating on Day 1 of pregnancy using sperm detection
- Administering the test compound on Day 1, 2, or 3 post-coitus
- Sacrificing animals on Day 10 or 11 and inspecting the uterus for implantation swellings

A significant decrease in implantation numbers compared to controls confirms post-coital antifertility action, which is particularly relevant for emergency contraceptive development.

The evaluation of both types allows the classification of test agents into prophylactic contraceptives (pre-coital) or emergency/post-coital contraceptives, helping determine their most suitable therapeutic application. In both models, care is taken to rule out embryotoxicity by ensuring that the compound does not simply induce resorption or abortion, which would require additional studies to assess abortifacient properties.

3.2.2.3 Abortifacient and Anti-ovulatory Tests

Dosing During Early Pregnancy

The evaluation of abortifacient and anti-ovulatory activity is a crucial component of antifertility drug screening. These studies help in identifying compounds that can terminate early pregnancy (abortifacients) or prevent ovulation (anti-ovulatory agents). The selection of proper dosing schedules during the reproductive cycle or early gestation is essential to distinguish between these two mechanisms.

In abortifacient studies, the primary goal is to test whether a compound can disrupt an established pregnancy shortly after implantation. In rodents like rats or mice, implantation occurs between Day 4 and Day 5 after mating. Therefore, the test drug is administered after Day 5, commonly between Day 6 to Day 9 of gestation, when the blastocyst has adhered to the uterine lining and placentation begins.

The experimental procedure includes:

- Confirming mating on Day 1 by presence of spermatozoa in a vaginal smear.
- Administering the test substance from Day 6 to Day 9, once daily, via oral or parenteral route.

- Sacrificing the animals on Day 10 or Day 12 of pregnancy.
- Carefully dissecting and examining the uterine horns for:
  - Number of implantation sites
  - Evidence of resorption (darkened or hemorrhagic swellings)
  - Live or dead fetuses

A test compound is considered to have abortifacient activity if there is a significant reduction in the number of viable fetuses, with increased resorption sites, compared to the control group. The uterine weight may also be recorded as a secondary parameter. It is important to differentiate abortifacient activity from general maternal toxicity, which is evaluated by monitoring maternal body weight, food intake, and behaviour during treatment.

In contrast, anti-ovulatory testing involves administering the test compound before ovulation, typically during proestrus or early estrus phases, or from Day 1 to Day 4 of gestation, when fertilization and early embryonic development take place. The test substance may interfere with:

- Follicular rupture
- LH surge inhibition
- Oocyte maturation
- Zygote transport

Following treatment, the female is sacrificed on Day 10 or 11, and the number of implantation sites is compared with the control. A total absence of implantation sites despite confirmed mating suggests that ovulation did not occur, or fertilization or embryo transport was impaired. This distinguishes it from abortifacient effects, which act after implantation.

Careful staging of the dosing period allows researchers to identify which reproductive event is affected, thereby classifying the compound as:

- Ovulation inhibitor

- Fertilization blocker
- Implantation disruptor
- Early pregnancy terminator

Together, these studies provide comprehensive data on the stage-specific antifertility action of a compound and are essential in the development of non-hormonal contraceptives, emergency contraceptive pills, or abortive agents with defined therapeutic windows.

Effects on Corpus Luteum and Ovulation Rates

In anti-ovulatory and abortifacient studies, it is essential to examine the effects of test compounds on the corpus luteum and ovulation rates, as these directly reflect interference with normal ovarian function. The corpus luteum (CL) is a temporary endocrine gland formed after ovulation from the ruptured follicle. It secretes progesterone, which is necessary for preparing the endometrium for implantation and maintaining early pregnancy. Any disruption to the development, function, or hormonal output of the corpus luteum can impair fertility.

Assessment of ovulation rates is commonly done by counting corpora lutea on the surface of the ovaries. This is performed after sacrificing the animal, usually on Day 10 of gestation. Each corpus luteum corresponds to one ovulated oocyte. In control females, the number of corpora lutea typically matches or slightly exceeds the number of implantation sites in the uterus.

If a test drug significantly reduces the number of corpora lutea, it suggests inhibition of ovulation, possibly through central suppression of gonadotropin-releasing hormone (GnRH) or luteinizing hormone (LH). Drugs acting on the hypothalamic–pituitary–gonadal axis may block the LH surge required for follicle rupture, resulting in failure of ovulation and, consequently, infertility.

The morphology of the corpus luteum is also examined histologically. In a healthy state, the corpus luteum appears yellowish, vascular, and plump, indicating active progesterone secretion. If a test substance causes regression or luteolysis, the CL appears pale, fibrotic, and shrunken, often accompanied by reduced serum progesterone levels, which can be confirmed biochemically.

A functional corpus luteum is essential not only for implantation but also for the maintenance of pregnancy until placental takeover, especially in rodents, where the luteal phase is the dominant source of progesterone in early gestation. If the corpus luteum is prematurely regressed, even after successful implantation, embryo resorption and early abortion may occur due to hormonal insufficiency.

In summary, a test compound showing:

- Decreased ovulation rates (fewer corpora lutea) indicates anti-ovulatory action
- Morphological regression of corpus luteum or progesterone deficiency suggests luteolytic or abortifacient activity

These findings, when correlated with implantation data, estrous cycle alterations, and pregnancy outcomes, provide a clear understanding of the mechanism of antifertility action and help in the classification of the compound for its intended contraceptive use.

3.3.1.1 Tail Flick Test

Application of Radiant Heat

The tail flick test is one of the most widely used preclinical models for evaluating the analgesic activity of test compounds, especially those that act via central (spinal) mechanisms. This method is based on the principle that application of a noxious thermal stimulus to the tail of a rodent evokes a spinal reflex, leading to a sudden flicking or withdrawal of the tail. Analgesic drugs elevate the pain threshold, thereby increasing the latency to tail flick. The model is highly sensitive to centrally acting agents such as opioids and is conducted in rats or mice.

A focused beam of radiant heat is applied to the middle or distal one-third of the tail using a tail flick apparatus. The animal is restrained gently in a cylindrical holder with its tail protruding. The apparatus contains an infrared light source or heated nichrome wire as the heat stimulus, with a sensor or manual trigger to start and stop the timer. When the tail is flicked or withdrawn, the operator stops the timer, and the latency time is recorded in seconds.

Measurement of Latency and Cut-off Time

The tail flick latency is defined as the time interval between the onset of heat application and the flicking response of the tail. It is a direct measure of the nociceptive threshold. A longer latency time in drug-treated animals compared to controls indicates analgesic action.

To prevent tissue damage or burns, a cut-off time is established, usually 10 to 12 seconds for rats and 6 to 8 seconds for mice. If the animal does not respond within this period, the heat source is automatically turned off, and the maximum value is recorded. This precaution ensures ethical compliance and animal welfare.

The percentage of analgesia or % Maximum Possible Effect (%MPE) can be calculated using the formula:

%MPE =((Test latency − Baseline latency) / (Cut-off time − Baseline latency)) × 100

This normalized value allows comparison between different doses and time points, and helps construct dose-response curves.

Analgesics like morphine, pentazocine, and tramadol significantly prolong tail flick latency, while NSAIDs may show less pronounced effects as they act peripherally rather than centrally.

Evaluation of Spinal Reflex Pathways

The tail flick response is mediated by simple spinal reflex arcs, involving nociceptors, dorsal horn neurons, and motor neurons, without requiring supraspinal (brain) involvement. Therefore, this model is ideal for detecting drugs that act at the spinal cord level, such as opioid receptor agonists, GABA modulators, or NMDA antagonists.

By using spinally transected animals, researchers have further validated that the tail flick reflex is independent of higher brain centers. Thus, the test helps distinguish between central and peripheral analgesics, making it a valuable tool in the early screening of compounds targeting pain pathways localized in the spinal cord.

This method is simple, fast, and reproducible, with high sensitivity for centrally acting analgesic agents. It is commonly used in parallel with hot plate test and writhing test to evaluate a compound's overall analgesic profile.

3.3.1.2 Hot Plate Test

Temperature-Controlled Surface Method

The hot plate test is a classic and highly reliable method for evaluating centrally acting analgesic agents in preclinical pharmacology. This method is based on the principle that thermal nociceptive stimuli, when applied to the paws of rodents, evoke characteristic responses such as paw licking, jumping, or rearing. Analgesic drugs increase the pain threshold, thereby delaying the animal's reaction to the heat. Unlike the tail flick test, which primarily assesses spinal reflexes, the hot plate test involves supraspinal integration, making it suitable for compounds that act on the brain and spinal cord.

In this model, animals such as mice or rats are placed on a temperature-controlled metal surface maintained at a constant temperature, typically 52 ± 0.5°C for mice and 55 ± 0.5°C for rats. The animal is confined within a cylindrical glass or acrylic enclosure to prevent escape, and the latency to a nociceptive response is measured. Commonly observed behavioural responses include paw licking, paw shaking, hind paw withdrawal, or jumping, which indicate discomfort caused by the heat.

Before the experiment, animals are habituated to the enclosure without heat to reduce anxiety-related movement. The baseline reaction time (latency in seconds before the first pain response) is recorded prior to drug administration. The test compound is then administered by the appropriate route (oral, subcutaneous, intraperitoneal), and the latency is re-evaluated at intervals such as 15, 30, 60, and 90 minutes post-dose to assess the onset and duration of analgesic effect.

To prevent thermal injury, a cut-off time is pre-set—usually 15 seconds in mice and 20 seconds in rats. If the animal fails to respond within this limit, it is removed immediately from the hot plate, and the cut-off value is recorded to avoid burns.

The analgesic effect can be quantified using the % Maximum Possible Effect (%MPE) formula:

%MPE =((Test latency − Baseline latency) / (Cut-off time − Baseline latency)) × 100

This index helps in standardizing results across groups and doses and allows comparative analysis with reference drugs like morphine, tramadol, or codeine, which typically show significant prolongation in latency.

The hot plate test is ideal for screening analgesic agents that act through opioid receptors, central neurotransmitter modulation, or supraspinal pathways involved in pain processing. It is also used to detect tolerance development upon repeated dosing and to study synergistic effects of drug combinations.

This test provides a high degree of reproducibility, sensitivity, and predictive value for central analgesics, making it a gold-standard model in pain research.

Measurement of Paw Licking or Jumping Response

In the hot plate test, measurement of specific behavioural responses such as paw licking and jumping is used to assess the level of thermal nociception and the effectiveness of a test drug in modulating pain perception. These responses are considered indicators of discomfort or pain arising from exposure to a moderately painful thermal stimulus.

Paw licking is one of the earliest and most consistent nociceptive responses. It involves the animal lifting and licking its forepaw or hind paw, indicating an attempt to soothe the discomfort caused by the hot surface. This action is initiated through supraspinal processing, meaning that the brain is actively involved in recognizing and reacting to the painful stimulus. Increased latency to paw licking after drug administration signifies a central analgesic effect.

Jumping response typically occurs slightly later than paw licking and is considered a more intense reaction to the heat. It reflects a stronger pain sensation or an effort to escape the thermal source. Animals may suddenly leap or rear up when the pain becomes intolerable. This behaviour also relies on higher-order sensory integration and is thus useful in detecting supraspinal modulation of nociceptive signals.

During the experiment, the latency period (in seconds) from the time the animal is placed on the hot plate to the first appearance of either paw licking or jumping is recorded using a stopwatch or electronic sensor. If both behaviours occur, the earliest response is used as the endpoint for latency measurement. Consistent use of the same response type across all test animals ensures uniformity in data collection.

After administering a test compound, repeated measurements are taken at predetermined intervals (e.g., 15, 30, 60, 90 minutes), allowing researchers to plot the time course of analgesic action. A significant increase in latency to paw licking or jumping, compared to the baseline and control groups, confirms the efficacy of the analgesic agent.

These behavioural responses are objective, quantifiable, and reproducible, making them valuable endpoints for studying the pharmacodynamics of centrally acting analgesic drugs and for differentiating drug classes based on their site of action in the central nervous system.

The hot plate test is one of the most reliable models for assessing central analgesic activity of drugs in rodents. This model specifically evaluates compounds that act on supraspinal and spinal pathways involved in pain perception, making it ideal for detecting drugs that modulate central nervous system mechanisms, particularly those acting through opioid, dopaminergic, serotonergic, or noradrenergic receptors.

When a compound exhibits increased latency to nociceptive responses such as paw licking or jumping in the hot plate test, it indicates that the pain threshold has been elevated, and this effect is mediated through central neural circuits. Unlike peripheral models (such as the acetic acid writhing test), which assess inhibition of inflammatory mediators at the site of pain, the hot plate test detects analgesic actions originating within the brain and spinal cord.

The analgesic efficacy is often quantified by calculating the percentage of maximum possible effect (%MPE) using the recorded latencies. This allows comparison across different doses and drugs. Compounds like morphine, tramadol, and codeine produce dose-dependent increases in latency and serve as positive controls in validating central activity.

In addition to confirming central analgesia, the test also helps in:

- Differentiating between central and peripheral mechanisms of action.
- Evaluating tolerance development through repeated dose studies.
- Exploring synergistic effects when drugs are combined with known central agents.

Overall, the hot plate test provides a direct, sensitive, and well-characterized method for assessing central analgesic potential, especially during the early stages of drug screening. When combined with other tests like the tail flick and writhing assays, it contributes to a comprehensive evaluation of a compound's analgesic profile.

3.3.1.3 Acetic Acid-Induced Writhing Test

Intraperitoneal Injection of Acetic Acid

The acetic acid-induced writhing test is one of the most commonly used models for evaluating the peripheral analgesic activity of compounds, especially non-steroidal anti-inflammatory drugs (NSAIDs). This method involves the administration of a diluted solution of acetic acid intraperitoneally into mice, which leads to the release of endogenous pain mediators such as prostaglandins, serotonin, and bradykinin in the peritoneal cavity. These mediators sensitize the nociceptive receptors, resulting in a characteristic abdominal response known as writhing or stretching behaviour.

Adult mice, usually weighing between 20 and 30 grams, are selected and maintained under controlled environmental conditions with access to standard food and water. The animals are grouped appropriately, typically consisting of one control group, one positive control group (receiving a standard NSAID like aspirin or diclofenac), and treatment groups receiving the test compound at different doses.

A 0.6% v/v solution of glacial acetic acid in distilled water is freshly prepared and injected into the peritoneal cavity at a dose of 10 mL/kg body weight using a 1 mL syringe with a 26-gauge needle.

The injection is given gently in the lower right quadrant of the abdomen to avoid injury to internal organs. After injection, the animals are placed individually in transparent observation cages and left undisturbed for 5 minutes, allowing the acetic acid to diffuse and induce nociceptive responses.

Counting of Abdominal Constrictions

The primary endpoint of this test is the number of writhes observed in a fixed period following the injection. A writhing response is defined as a constriction of the abdomen, characterized by stretching of the hind limbs, contraction of the abdominal wall, and elongation of the body. Occasionally, the mouse may show turning or twisting movements and arching of the back.

Writhing is counted manually by an observer blinded to the treatment groups, starting from 5 minutes to 20 minutes post-injection, giving a total observation period of 15 minutes. Each clear instance of abdominal constriction is counted as one writhe.

The total number of writhes in each group is averaged, and the percent inhibition of writhing is calculated using the following formula:

% Inhibition =((Mean writhes in control group – Mean writhes in treated group) / Mean writhes in control group) × 100

This value helps quantify the analgesic effect of the test drug compared to the untreated control. A higher percentage of inhibition indicates stronger peripheral analgesic activity. Standard NSAIDs like aspirin (100 mg/kg, oral) typically show around 60–80% inhibition, serving as reference benchmarks.

Sensitivity to NSAIDs and Peripheral Analgesics

The writhing test is particularly sensitive to peripherally acting analgesic agents, mainly those that inhibit cyclooxygenase (COX) enzymes and reduce prostaglandin synthesis. Therefore, NSAIDs like diclofenac, ibuprofen, indomethacin, and paracetamol exhibit a dose-dependent reduction in the number of abdominal writhes.

This model is useful not only for screening new anti-inflammatory or analgesic molecules but also for determining the minimal effective dose and onset of action. However, it is less effective for drugs that act centrally, such as opioids, which may show only partial inhibition unless administered at high doses.

Due to its simplicity, cost-effectiveness, reproducibility, and clear behavioural endpoint, the acetic acid-induced writhing test remains one of the most dependable methods for assessing non-narcotic pain relief in early-stage drug discovery. It also complements other models such as the tail flick and hot plate tests to provide a full profile of a compound's analgesic potential.

3.3.2.1 Carrageenan-Induced Paw Edema

Phases of Inflammation: Histamine, Serotonin, Prostaglandins

The carrageenan-induced paw edema model is one of the most widely accepted in vivo methods for screening anti-inflammatory activity of test compounds. It is a well-characterized model of acute inflammation and mimics the pathophysiological sequence seen in early phases of human inflammation. This model primarily evaluates the ability of drugs to inhibit localized swelling caused by the injection of carrageenan, a sulfated polysaccharide derived from red seaweed.

In this method, adult Wistar rats, generally weighing 150 to 200 grams, are used. The animals are fasted overnight and grouped into control, standard, and treatment groups (n = 5–6 per group). The right hind paw of each animal is marked at the ankle joint, and initial paw volume is measured using a plethysmometer, which calculates displacement volume by dipping the paw into a mercury or water column.

A freshly prepared suspension of 1% carrageenan in sterile saline (0.9%) is injected subplantarly (into the subcutaneous tissue) of the right hind paw in a volume of 0.1 mL using a fine needle. This injection induces acute inflammation, resulting in paw swelling, which is then measured at regular intervals—typically at 1, 2, 3, and 4 hours post-injection.

The inflammatory response to carrageenan is biphasic:

- The first phase (0–1.5 hours) is mediated primarily by histamine and serotonin released from mast cells. These mediators cause immediate vasodilation and increased vascular permeability, leading to initial fluid accumulation in the tissue.
- The second phase (1.5–5 hours) involves the release of bradykinin, leukotrienes, and prostaglandins, especially PGE_2, which amplify the inflammatory response. The late phase is predominantly prostaglandin-dependent and is more sensitive to NSAIDs, which block cyclooxygenase enzymes.

By administering the test compound 30–60 minutes before carrageenan injection, its ability to reduce the extent of paw edema is assessed. The paw volume at each time point is measured using the plethysmometer, and the increase in volume from baseline is calculated.

The percentage inhibition of edema is determined using the formula:

% Inhibition = $((V_c - V_t) / V_c) \times 100$
Where:
V_c = Mean paw volume of control group
V_t = Mean paw volume of treated group

A standard anti-inflammatory drug such as indomethacin (10 mg/kg, oral) or diclofenac sodium (10 mg/kg, oral) is used for comparison. These drugs typically show 40–70% inhibition of paw edema at 3 to 4 hours post-carrageenan administration.

The carrageenan-induced paw edema model is widely preferred because of its:

- High reproducibility
- Clear biphasic mediator profile
- Specificity for prostaglandin-mediated inflammation

This model is ideal for detecting non-steroidal anti-inflammatory activity and is often used as a first-line assay in the evaluation of potential anti-inflammatory therapeutics during drug discovery.

Paw Volume Measurement Using Plethysmometer

The plethysmometer is an essential tool in the carrageenan-induced paw edema model, used for accurate and quantitative measurement of paw swelling. It works on the principle of fluid displacement, where the volume of the paw is measured based on how much liquid (typically water or mercury) is displaced when the animal's paw is immersed in the measuring chamber. This method is sensitive, reproducible, and allows for non-invasive monitoring of inflammation over time.

Before starting the experiment, the plethysmometer is calibrated with distilled water and set to zero using a standard reference cylinder. Each rat's right hind paw is marked at a constant anatomical point (usually the lateral malleolus or 1 cm above the paw base) to ensure that the paw is dipped up to the same level at each time point.

The measurement process involves:

- Holding the animal gently and steadily.
- Slowly immersing the right hind paw vertically into the measuring chamber filled with the test fluid.
- Recording the initial paw volume (V_0) before carrageenan injection, which serves as the baseline.

- After carrageenan injection (0.1 mL of 1% solution into the subplantar region), paw volume is measured again at 1, 2, 3, and 4 hours post-injection.
- The volume difference at each time point ($V_t - V_0$) represents the extent of edema, indicating the degree of inflammation.

The volume is typically recorded in millilitres (mL) or cubic centimetres (cm^3). The edema inhibition percentage is calculated using the previously mentioned formula to compare the test group with the control group.

Use of the plethysmometer ensures minimal handling stress, consistency in measurement, and real-time monitoring of drug effectiveness. It allows researchers to track not just the peak anti-inflammatory effect, but also the onset and duration of action. Combined with proper statistical analysis, this data provides solid evidence of the anti-inflammatory efficacy of the tested compound.

Acute Inflammation Model

The carrageenan-induced paw edema test is considered a classical acute inflammation model, widely used in preclinical research to evaluate the anti-inflammatory potential of new drug candidates. It is specifically designed to mimic the early and transient inflammatory responses that occur in acute tissue injury, infection, or immune stimulation. This model is highly reproducible, easy to perform, and provides measurable endpoints, making it ideal for screening anti-inflammatory agents, especially non-steroidal anti-inflammatory drugs (NSAIDs).

Acute inflammation, by definition, is a rapid-onset protective response to harmful stimuli, which is characterized by redness, swelling, pain, heat, and loss of function. In this model, the injection of carrageenan into the subplantar region of the rat's hind paw initiates an acute inflammatory reaction that closely follows this pathophysiology.

The model progresses through a biphasic mediator response:

- The early phase (0 to 90 minutes) is dominated by histamine, serotonin, and to some extent bradykinin, which increase vascular permeability and cause plasma exudation.
- The late phase (1.5 to 5 hours) involves the induction of cyclooxygenase-2 (COX-2) and the synthesis of prostaglandins, especially PGE_2, which sustain edema and pain.

Because of this clear temporal mediator profile, the carrageenan model allows researchers to:

- Differentiate between drugs that block histamine/serotonin pathways (e.g., antihistamines)
- Evaluate NSAIDs that specifically inhibit prostaglandin synthesis during the later phase
- Study the dose–response relationship and duration of action of new compounds

The acute inflammation induced by carrageenan is self-limiting and typically resolves within 6 to 8 hours, eliminating the need for prolonged animal observation. This also ensures minimal long-term stress to the animals, aligning with ethical research practices.

Overall, the carrageenan-induced paw edema is an established acute inflammation model that offers both mechanistic insights and quantitative data, supporting its widespread use in anti-inflammatory drug development.

3.3.2.2 Cotton Pellet-Induced Granuloma

Chronic Inflammation Model

The cotton pellet-induced granuloma model is a classical in vivo method used for the evaluation of chronic anti-inflammatory activity of test compounds. Unlike acute inflammation models such as carrageenan-induced paw edema, which assess the early exudative phase, this model evaluates the proliferative phase of inflammation, which is characteristic of chronic tissue response. It is particularly useful for screening drugs that affect fibroblast proliferation, collagen formation, and granuloma tissue development, often influenced by steroidal anti-inflammatory drugs (SAIDs) and some long-acting NSAIDs.

This method is usually conducted in adult Wistar rats, weighing between 150–200 grams, maintained under standard environmental conditions. Prior to implantation, animals are anaesthetized using an appropriate light anaesthetic, such as ketamine and xylazine, to minimize pain and stress.

Procedure:

- Sterile cotton pellets weighing 10±1 mg are prepared by rolling surgical cotton into uniform sizes and sterilizing them in an autoclave.
- A small mid-dorsal skin incision is made in the lumbar region, and a subcutaneous tunnel is formed using blunt dissection or forceps.
- One sterile pellet is implanted subcutaneously into each rat, and the incision is closed with sterile sutures or clips.
- The test compound is administered once daily for seven consecutive days, either orally or intraperitoneally, depending on the formulation and pharmacokinetics.
- A standard drug such as dexamethasone (0.5–1 mg/kg) or indomethacin (10 mg/kg) is used as a positive control.

On the eighth day, the animals are sacrificed under anaesthesia. The pellets along with the surrounding granulomatous tissue are carefully removed, cleaned of extraneous tissue, and dried at 60°C for 24 hours to obtain a constant dry weight.

Granuloma formation is indicated by the increase in dry weight of the pellet, which represents the extent of cellular infiltration, fibroblast proliferation, and connective tissue growth around the foreign body. The anti-inflammatory effect of the test compound is calculated by comparing the mean granuloma weights of the test and control groups.

The percentage inhibition of granuloma formation is calculated using the formula:

% Inhibition $= ((W_c - W_t) / W_c) \times 100$
Where:
W_c = Mean dry weight of granuloma in control group
W_t = Mean dry weight of granuloma in treated group

This model is highly effective in detecting drugs that inhibit the chronic proliferative phase of inflammation, involving macrophages, fibroblasts, and collagen deposition. It mimics the granulation tissue development seen in conditions like rheumatoid arthritis, chronic wounds, and tuberculous granulomas.

Due to its reproducibility and sensitivity, the cotton pellet granuloma model is a standard chronic inflammation model in pharmacological research, and complements acute models to provide a full assessment of a drug's anti-inflammatory profile.

Pellet Weight Gain as Index of Granuloma Formation

In the cotton pellet-induced granuloma model, the increase in dry weight of the implanted pellet is the primary quantitative index used to evaluate the extent of granuloma formation, which reflects the chronic inflammatory response of the host tissue. After subcutaneous implantation, the sterile cotton pellet acts as a foreign body, triggering a localized tissue reaction characterized by the infiltration of macrophages, lymphocytes, fibroblasts, and subsequent collagen deposition.

Over a period of seven days, the surrounding tissue mounts a proliferative response, resulting in the development of granulation tissue that adheres tightly around the pellet. The test compound, administered daily during this period, may modulate this process by inhibiting fibroblast activity, collagen synthesis, or inflammatory cytokine release. The effect is assessed by comparing the dry weight of the granuloma tissue formed around the pellet in treated versus control animals.

At the end of the experiment (typically on Day 8), animals are sacrificed, and the pellets along with surrounding tissue are:

- Carefully excised without disturbing the capsule
- Blotted to remove blood or fluid
- Dried in an oven at 60°C for 18 to 24 hours until a constant dry weight is achieved
- Weighed on an analytical balance with precision up to 0.1 mg

The net weight gain of the pellet (i.e., final dry weight minus the initial weight of the sterile pellet) represents the amount of newly formed granulation tissue, and is directly proportional to the severity of chronic inflammation.

The anti-inflammatory effect of the test compound is expressed as percentage inhibition of granuloma formation, calculated by the formula:

% Inhibition = $((W_c - W_t) / W_c) \times 100$
Where:
W_c = Mean dry weight of granuloma in control group
W_t = Mean dry weight of granuloma in treated group

A higher percentage inhibition indicates stronger chronic anti-inflammatory activity. Standard anti-inflammatory drugs like dexamethasone or prednisolone typically produce 40–70% reduction in pellet weight gain.

This index provides a direct and quantifiable measure of tissue proliferation and fibrosis during chronic inflammation, making the cotton pellet model especially valuable for screening corticosteroids, immunosuppressants, and long-acting NSAIDs. It complements acute inflammation models and helps characterize a drug's long-term modulatory effect on inflammatory tissue remodelling.

Relevance to Steroidal Anti-Inflammatory Drugs

The cotton pellet-induced granuloma model holds particular importance in evaluating the efficacy of steroidal anti-inflammatory drugs (SAIDs), as this model specifically targets the chronic proliferative phase of inflammation. Steroids such as dexamethasone, prednisolone, and hydrocortisone exert potent anti-inflammatory effects primarily by suppressing immune cell proliferation, reducing fibroblast activity, and inhibiting the synthesis of pro-inflammatory cytokines and mediators that drive tissue granulation and fibrosis.

Unlike NSAIDs, which are more effective in acute models that involve inhibition of prostaglandin synthesis, SAIDs demonstrate marked inhibition of granuloma tissue development in the cotton pellet model. This is because their mechanism of action includes:

- Downregulation of inflammatory gene expression via nuclear glucocorticoid receptors
- Suppression of macrophage and lymphocyte recruitment
- Inhibition of collagen and extracellular matrix production by fibroblasts
- Reduced angiogenesis, which limits nutrient supply to proliferating inflammatory tissue

In this model, a standard SAID like dexamethasone at 0.5 to 1 mg/kg (oral or intraperitoneal) typically reduces granuloma formation by 50–80%, confirming its effectiveness in suppressing the long-term inflammatory cascade. This profound effect on chronic inflammation and tissue proliferation makes the model highly relevant in preclinical screening of drugs intended for conditions such as rheumatoid arthritis, autoimmune disorders, chronic dermatitis, and fibrotic diseases.

Thus, the cotton pellet granuloma assay serves as a discriminatory model to differentiate steroidal drugs from non-steroidal agents and is crucial in determining the long-term anti-proliferative and immunosuppressive potential of candidate compounds. It is also instrumental in studying the dose-response relationship, duration of action, and side effect profile of SAIDs in chronic inflammatory settings.

3.3.3.1 Brewer's Yeast-Induced Pyrexia in Rats

Induction of Fever by Subcutaneous Yeast Suspension

The Brewer's yeast-induced pyrexia model is a well-established and reliable method for evaluating the antipyretic activity of pharmaceutical compounds in rats. It mimics the pathophysiological basis of fever in humans, making it highly relevant in the screening of drugs that aim to reduce elevated body temperature caused by infection, inflammation, or immune responses.

In this model, fever is induced by the subcutaneous injection of a suspension of Brewer's yeast, which is a complex pyrogenic stimulus composed of dead yeast cells. The yeast contains β-glucans and mannans that stimulate the release of pro-inflammatory cytokines such as interleukin-1β (IL-1β), interleukin-6 (IL-6), and tumor necrosis factor-α (TNF-α). These cytokines act on the hypothalamus, increasing the synthesis of prostaglandin E_2 (PGE_2), which resets the thermoregulatory set-point, leading to a rise in body temperature.

Procedure:

- Healthy adult Wistar rats weighing 150–200 grams are selected and fasted overnight with free access to water.
- Baseline rectal temperature is measured using a lubricated digital or thermistor thermometer inserted 2–3 cm into the rectum. The temperature is recorded in degrees Celsius (°C).

- A freshly prepared 20% suspension of Brewer's yeast in 0.9% saline is injected subcutaneously in the nape of the neck at a dose of 10 mL/kg body weight.
- After injection, the animals are housed individually and left undisturbed for 18 hours to allow development of fever. During this period, the body temperature typically rises by 1.0 to 2.0°C.
- At the end of 18 hours, only animals showing a rise in temperature of at least 0.5°C above baseline are included in the study for further testing.

The test compound, standard drug (such as paracetamol 150 mg/kg oral), and vehicle control are administered at this point. Rectal temperatures are then measured at fixed intervals—commonly at 1, 2, 3, and 4 hours post-treatment.

The antipyretic effect is determined by the reduction in rectal temperature compared to the post-yeast injection baseline. The mean temperature drop is calculated and statistically compared between test and control groups.

This model is specifically suited to assess drugs that inhibit prostaglandin synthesis, since PGE_2 is the final mediator in the fever pathway. NSAIDs such as ibuprofen, aspirin, and indomethacin, as well as centrally acting antipyretics like paracetamol, show significant activity in this model.

The Brewer's yeast-induced pyrexia test is valued for its:

- High reproducibility and sensitivity to standard antipyretic agents
- Ability to mimic clinical fever, involving endogenous cytokine and prostaglandin release
- Simple and non-invasive nature, with direct measurement of core body temperature

Thus, it remains a gold standard model in preclinical screening of antipyretic drugs, providing essential information on the onset, magnitude, and duration of fever-reducing effects.

Rectal Temperature Measurement

Rectal temperature measurement is the most direct and reliable method for monitoring core body temperature in rodents during antipyretic studies such as the Brewer's yeast-induced pyrexia model. It provides a consistent and accurate reflection of the animal's thermoregulatory status, allowing researchers to quantify both the induction of fever and the temperature-lowering effect of test drugs.

To ensure accuracy and animal safety, the procedure follows standardized steps:

- A digital rectal thermometer or a thermistor probe specifically designed for small animals is used. The tip is lubricated with a non-irritating jelly (e.g., glycerin or paraffin) before insertion.
- The rat is gently restrained without causing stress, and the thermometer is inserted approximately 2 to 3 cm into the rectum, depending on the size and age of the animal.
- The thermometer is held in place steadily until it gives a stable reading, usually within 20 to 30 seconds.
- The temperature is recorded in degrees Celsius (°C) with precision up to one decimal point.

Baseline temperatures are recorded prior to yeast administration, typically ranging between 37.0°C to 38.0°C in healthy adult rats. After the subcutaneous injection of Brewer's yeast, rectal temperatures are measured again after 18 hours, and only animals showing a temperature rise of 0.5°C or more from baseline are selected for drug testing.

Following administration of the test or standard antipyretic drug, rectal temperature is recorded at regular intervals—commonly 1, 2,

3, and 4 hours—to determine the onset, peak effect, and duration of action. The average temperature drop in treated animals is then compared with the control group to assess statistical significance of antipyretic activity.

Using rectal temperature measurement allows for:

- Non-invasive, repeatable, and real-time data collection
- High sensitivity to centrally acting antipyretics
- Easy plotting of temperature-time profiles to assess drug kinetics

It is important that temperature recording be done at consistent times and environmental conditions, as stress, movement, or external temperature fluctuations may influence results. Proper animal handling and habituation before testing improve the accuracy and reliability of the measurements. This simple yet precise approach remains central to evaluating antipyretic potential in preclinical pharmacology.

Assessment of Antipyretic Action of Test Drugs

The antipyretic action of test drugs is assessed by evaluating their ability to lower elevated body temperature induced experimentally in animal models, most commonly using the Brewer's yeast-induced pyrexia test. This model is particularly effective for screening centrally acting antipyretics, especially those that inhibit prostaglandin E_2 synthesis in the hypothalamus, where thermal regulation is controlled.

Once the fever is induced by subcutaneous administration of 20% Brewer's yeast suspension, a waiting period of 18 hours is allowed for the fever to develop. Animals that show a minimum increase of 0.5°C in rectal temperature from baseline are considered febrile and included in the study. The selected animals are then divided into groups:

- Control group receives vehicle (e.g., 0.5% carboxymethyl cellulose),
- Standard group receives a known antipyretic (e.g., paracetamol at 150 mg/kg orally),
- Test groups receive the investigational compounds at different doses and routes.

After administration, rectal temperatures are recorded at 1, 2, 3, and 4 hours to monitor the temperature-lowering effect over time. The data is tabulated as mean ± standard error for each group at each time point.

The degree of antipyresis is assessed by calculating the reduction in rectal temperature from the elevated baseline and comparing it with the control group. A statistically significant temperature decrease in the test group, especially one comparable to or exceeding that of the standard drug, indicates a positive antipyretic effect.

The response can also be expressed as percentage reduction in temperature, using the formula:

% Reduction $=((T_0 - T_t) / T_0 - T_n) \times 100$
Where:
T_0 = Post-yeast temperature before drug
T_t = Temperature after test drug administration
T_n = Normal (pre-yeast) baseline temperature

This method provides a quantifiable and reproducible endpoint for the efficacy of a test compound. A dose-dependent reduction in fever with proper time-course correlation further strengthens the evidence for central antipyretic activity.

Through this approach, one can determine:

- Onset time of action (how quickly the drug starts working),
- Peak effect (maximum temperature reduction),
- Duration of effect (how long the fever is suppressed).

The Brewer's yeast-induced model, coupled with accurate rectal temperature monitoring, remains a gold standard technique for preclinical screening of fever-reducing drugs, offering insights into both efficacy and mechanism.

3.4.1.1 Pylorus Ligation (Shay Rat Model)

Procedure and Gastric Content Collection

The pylorus ligation model, also known as the Shay rat model, is one of the most established experimental methods for evaluating the anti-ulcer activity of test compounds. This model induces gastric ulceration by preventing gastric emptying through surgical ligation of the pyloric end of the stomach, leading to accumulation of gastric acid, pepsin, and mucus. The prolonged exposure of the gastric mucosa to these aggressive secretions results in ulcer formation, allowing for the assessment of both acid-inhibitory and mucosal-protective effects of anti-ulcer agents.

Animals and Preparation:

Healthy adult Wistar rats, typically weighing 150–200 grams, are selected. Animals are fasted for 18–24 hours before the procedure to ensure an empty stomach, while maintaining free access to water. This reduces variability in gastric secretion and helps in clear ulcer visualization.

Surgical Procedure:

- Animals are anaesthetized using a combination of ketamine (50 mg/kg) and xylazine (5–10 mg/kg) administered intraperitoneally to ensure a deep and painless surgical plane.
- A midline abdominal incision is made under aseptic conditions to expose the stomach.
- The pyloric end of the stomach (near the duodenum) is gently ligated using sterile non-absorbable silk suture,

ensuring the vasculature is not constricted, which could cause necrosis.
- After ligation, the stomach is repositioned, and the abdomen is closed in layers using absorbable sutures for muscle and non-absorbable sutures for the skin.

Postoperative Procedure:

- The animals are kept in individual cages without food or water for 4 hours post-ligation.
- After the observation period, animals are sacrificed humanely (e.g., with an overdose of anesthetic), and the stomach is excised carefully by cutting at the esophagus and duodenum.
- The gastric content is collected by opening the stomach along the greater curvature into a clean Petri dish.
- The content is transferred to a centrifuge tube and centrifuged at 2000–3000 rpm for 10 minutes to remove particulate matter.

The supernatant is then analyzed for:

- Volume (mL) of gastric juice
- pH using a digital pH meter
- Total acidity (in mEq/L) using titration with 0.01 N NaOH and phenolphthalein as an indicator
- Free acidity, by titrating only up to the first colour change

Ulcer Index Evaluation:

The stomach is rinsed gently with saline, pinned on a corkboard, and examined under a dissecting microscope or magnifying lens. The ulcer score is determined based on the number and severity of ulcers using a standard scoring system:

- 0 = No ulcer
- 1 = Superficial erosion

- 2 = Deep ulcers
- 3 = Perforated ulcers

The Ulcer Index (UI) is calculated using the formula:

$$UI = UN + US + UP \times 10^{-1}$$

Where:
UN = Average number of ulcers per animal
US = Average severity score
UP = Percentage of animals with ulcers

The percentage protection is calculated as:

% Protection = ((UI control − UI treated) / UI control) × 100

Significance:
This model is especially useful for detecting the activity of H_2 blockers, proton pump inhibitors, anticholinergics, cytoprotective agents, and antioxidants. It is sensitive to agents that reduce acid secretion or enhance mucosal defence.

The Shay rat model remains a cornerstone method in gastrointestinal pharmacology, offering reliable insights into mechanisms of ulcerogenesis and anti-ulcer drug actions.

Measurement of Volume, pH, and Ulcer Index

In the pylorus ligation (Shay rat) model, after the stomach is carefully removed and the gastric contents are collected, three primary parameters are quantitatively assessed to evaluate the anti-ulcer potential of test compounds: volume of gastric juice, pH of the secretion, and the ulcer index. These values collectively reflect both the secretory profile and the mucosal integrity of the stomach under the influence of the test substance.

1. Volume of Gastric Juice (in mL):

The collected gastric content is first centrifuged at 2000–3000 rpm for 10 minutes to remove solid debris. The clear supernatant is then transferred into a graduated measuring cylinder or volumetric tube, and the total volume is noted. Increased volume is generally associated with enhanced acid output and correlates with ulcer severity. A significant reduction in volume in the treated group indicates that the test compound has anti-secretory activity.

2. pH Measurement:

Using a calibrated digital pH meter, the pH of the gastric juice is determined by immersing the pH electrode into the supernatant. In pylorus-ligated control animals, the pH is typically very acidic, around 1.0 to 2.0, due to unchecked acid accumulation. A higher pH in the test group indicates a suppression of acid secretion or neutralization effect, suggesting antisecretory or buffering activity of the compound under investigation.

3. Ulcer Index (UI):

After collecting the gastric content, the stomach is opened along the greater curvature, rinsed gently with saline, and pinned on a flat surface. Using a dissecting microscope or magnifying glass, the gastric mucosa is examined for lesions, which may appear as:

- Hemorrhagic streaks
- Superficial erosions
- Deep penetrating ulcers
- Perforations

Each lesion is scored using a standard grading scale:

- 0 = Normal stomach
- 1 = Red coloration or spots
- 2 = Superficial ulceration
- 3 = Deep ulcers
- 4 = Perforation

The ulcer index is then calculated using the formula:

Ulcer Index (UI) = UN + US + UP × 10^{-1}
Where:
UN = Average number of ulcers per animal
US = Average severity score
UP = Percentage of animals with ulcers

To quantify the protective effect of the drug, the percentage inhibition or protection is calculated as:

% Protection = ((UI control − UI treated) / UI control) × 100

This measurement reflects how effectively the test compound prevented ulcer formation or reduced its severity.

By evaluating these three parameters together, researchers can distinguish between antisecretory effects (volume and pH) and cytoprotective effects (ulcer index), giving a clear picture of the mechanism and efficacy of the test compound in protecting the gastric mucosa. These data serve as crucial indicators during the preclinical development of anti-ulcer drugs.

Indicators of Acid Secretory Inhibition

In the pylorus ligation (Shay rat) model, several measurable indicators reflect the inhibition of gastric acid secretion, which is a primary goal of evaluating potential anti-ulcer agents, particularly those acting as proton pump inhibitors, H_2 receptor antagonists, or anticholinergics. These indicators are sensitive to changes in acid output, and their values help to determine the extent to which a test drug suppresses or modulates gastric secretory activity.

1. Decrease in Gastric Juice Volume:

A significant reduction in the volume of gastric juice collected from the pylorus-ligated stomach is a direct indicator of reduced gastric secretion. In control rats, the volume typically ranges between 3 to 6 mL after 4 hours of ligation. Drugs that block acid production pathways, such as omeprazole or ranitidine, markedly lower this volume, indicating suppression of gastric glandular activity.

2. Increase in pH of Gastric Secretion:

Another key indicator is the rise in pH value of the gastric contents. Control animals usually have a very low pH (1.0 to 2.0) due to active acid secretion. Test drugs that inhibit H^+,K^+-ATPase (proton pumps) or histamine-mediated acid release elevate the pH towards a less acidic range, often between 3.5 to 6.0, depending on the dose and duration. This increase confirms the neutralization or inhibition of hydrochloric acid production in the gastric mucosa.

3. Reduction in Total and Free Acidity:

Acidity is measured by titrating the gastric juice with 0.01 N NaOH using Topfer's reagent for free acidity (until red colour disappears) and phenolphthalein for total acidity (until pale pink persists). It is expressed in mEq/L. A significant drop in both total and free acidity post-treatment indicates that the test compound has inhibited acid secretion, either through parietal cell suppression or by blocking upstream mediators like gastrin, histamine, or acetylcholine.

4. Decrease in Ulcer Index:

Although the ulcer index is a broader parameter, a marked reduction in ulcer formation or severity often results from suppressed acid secretion, especially in models where ulcers are induced purely by acid accumulation. Therefore, a lower ulcer index alongside decreased acidity strongly supports antisecretory activity.

These indicators, when interpreted together, provide a robust evaluation of a drug's ability to modulate gastric secretory functions. They are essential in identifying acid-suppressing compounds and differentiating them from cytoprotective or mucosal-strengthening agents in the early stages of anti-ulcer drug development.

3.4.1.2 Ethanol-Induced Gastric Ulcer

Mucosal Erosion via Ethanol Administration

The ethanol-induced gastric ulcer model is a widely accepted method for assessing the cytoprotective potential of anti-ulcer agents, particularly those that work by strengthening the gastric mucosal barrier rather than by inhibiting acid secretion. Ethanol acts as a direct irritant to the gastric lining, causing acute mucosal damage through oxidative stress, lipid peroxidation, and disruption of the mucosal defense mechanisms, including the mucus-bicarbonate layer and epithelial integrity.

Animal Preparation and Fasting:

Adult Wistar rats, weighing between 150 and 200 grams, are used. The animals are fasted for 24 hours before the experiment, with water allowed up to 2 hours before dosing. This ensures an empty stomach and consistent results across animals.

Ethanol Administration Procedure:

- A test compound or standard drug (e.g., sucralfate 100 mg/kg or omeprazole 20 mg/kg) is administered orally to the animals, typically 30 to 60 minutes prior to ethanol challenge.

- Absolute ethanol (typically 95% or 100%) is administered orally at a dose of 1 mL per rat, directly using an oral gavage needle.
- Ethanol rapidly penetrates the gastric epithelium, dissolves lipids, and leads to vascular damage, hemorrhage, and necrosis, usually within 30 to 60 minutes.

Sacrifice and Stomach Examination: After the required time (usually 1 hour post ethanol administration), the animals are sacrificed under light anesthesia. The stomach is carefully removed, opened along the greater curvature, rinsed gently with normal saline, and pinned on a flat board for examination.

Ulcer Scoring and Index Calculation: The gastric mucosa is observed for visible hemorrhagic lesions, band-like erosions, and diffuse necrotic patches. These are scored based on length and severity:

- 0 = Normal stomach
- 1 = Red spots
- 2 = Hemorrhagic streaks
- 3 = Small ulcers (<1 mm)
- 4 = Large ulcers (>1 mm)
- 5 = Perforations

The ulcer index is calculated by:

Ulcer Index = (UN + US + UP × 10^{-1})
UN = Average number of ulcers
US = Average severity score
UP = Percentage of animals with ulcers

The percentage protection offered by the test drug is then calculated as:

% Protection = ((UI control − UI treated) / UI control) × 100

Interpretation and Significance:
This model is especially useful for screening compounds that enhance:

- Mucus secretion
- Prostaglandin synthesis
- Epithelial regeneration
- Antioxidant defenses

Drugs that reduce ulcer index significantly in this model are considered to possess cytoprotective activity rather than antisecretory action, and the model is therefore ideal for identifying prostaglandin analogs, flavonoids, antioxidants, mucosal protectants, and natural compounds used in gastric ulcer therapy.

The ethanol-induced gastric ulcer model remains a robust, reproducible, and ethically acceptable acute injury model, suitable for mechanistic studies and drug screening in gastrointestinal pharmacology.

Scoring of Ulceration Severity

In the ethanol-induced gastric ulcer model, the evaluation of ulcer severity is based on a well-defined scoring system that helps quantify the extent of gastric mucosal damage after ethanol administration. Since ethanol causes rapid and direct injury to the gastric epithelium, the resulting lesions are typically hemorrhagic, band-like, and necrotic, making them easily visible on gross examination of the stomach's inner surface.

After sacrificing the animal (usually 1 hour post ethanol administration), the stomach is dissected along the greater curvature, rinsed gently with normal saline, and pinned flat on a corkboard. The inner mucosal surface is then observed under adequate lighting or using a dissecting microscope to detect the location, length, and appearance of ulcerative lesions.

The severity of ulcers is scored using a standardized numeric scale. A commonly used scoring system includes:

- 0 = Normal stomach, no visible lesions
- 1 = Red coloration or pinpoint hemorrhagic spots
- 2 = Hemorrhagic streaks or thin bands
- 3 = Small ulcers (≤1 mm in diameter)
- 4 = Deep ulcers (>1 mm) with necrotic base
- 5 = Perforated ulcers

Each animal's stomach is examined systematically, and the total score per stomach is calculated by summing the scores of all visible lesions. This raw score can be averaged for all animals in the group to obtain a mean ulcer score, which reflects the average severity of ulceration in that group.

This ulcer score contributes to the calculation of the Ulcer Index (UI), which is given by:

Ulcer Index = UN + US + UP × 10^{-1}
Where:
UN = Average number of ulcers per animal
US = Average severity score per animal
UP = Percentage of animals with ulcers

The effectiveness of a test compound in reducing mucosal injury is then expressed as percentage protection:

% Protection = ((UI control − UI treated) / UI control) × 100

This scoring system allows researchers to:

- Standardize lesion severity comparisons across treatment groups
- Distinguish between mild and severe forms of injury
- Identify dose-dependent effects of test compounds

Accurate and consistent scoring of ulcer severity is essential for reproducibility, statistical analysis, and preclinical validation of gastroprotective agents, particularly those that act via cytoprotective mechanisms such as mucus enhancement, antioxidant activity, or epithelial regeneration.

Use of Cytoprotective Agents for Comparison

In the ethanol-induced gastric ulcer model, cytoprotective agents are used as positive controls to compare the effectiveness of test compounds in preventing or minimizing mucosal injury. Since ethanol causes direct damage to the gastric lining by disrupting the mucus-bicarbonate barrier, increasing oxidative stress, and inducing vascular necrosis, this model is ideal for identifying drugs that protect the stomach through non-antisecretory mechanisms.

Cytoprotective agents work by enhancing mucosal defense rather than suppressing acid secretion. These drugs promote:

- Mucus and bicarbonate secretion
- Epithelial cell regeneration
- Prostaglandin synthesis
- Blood flow to the gastric mucosa
- Antioxidant defense mechanisms

A standard drug often used in this model is sucralfate at a dose of 100–200 mg/kg orally, administered 30–60 minutes before ethanol exposure. Sucralfate forms a protective gel-like complex over the gastric mucosa, shielding it from irritants and allowing healing. Another common agent is misoprostol, a synthetic prostaglandin E1 analog that enhances mucus and bicarbonate production and preserves mucosal blood flow.

In studies, these agents typically result in a 50–80% reduction in ulcer index, showing significant protection against ethanol-induced lesions. The protective effect of test compounds is interpreted by comparing their ulcer scores and percentage protection against these reference agents.

Including a cytoprotective control group helps:

- Validate the experimental model
- Determine whether the test drug acts via mucosal protection rather than acid suppression
- Assess relative efficacy and safety

Thus, cytoprotective agents serve as essential benchmark standards in this model, offering a frame of reference for evaluating the gastric mucosal protective ability of new compounds during early-phase anti-ulcer drug development.

3.4.1.3 Cold Restraint Stress Model

Immobilization Under Cold Exposure

The cold restraint stress (CRS) model is a well-recognized method to study stress-induced gastric ulceration, particularly relevant to the evaluation of anti-ulcer agents with anti-stress or mucosal protective properties. In this model, the experimental ulceration is triggered by subjecting animals—usually rats—to physical restraint combined with cold temperature, which activates a series of physiological and neuroendocrine stress responses known to promote gastric mucosal injury.

Adult Wistar rats (150–200 g) are fasted for 24 hours before the experiment, with water allowed ad libitum. The animals are then placed in restraint devices, such as cylindrical plastic tubes or wooden boards with soft bindings, to immobilize the body and limbs gently but effectively. After immobilization, the restrained animals are kept in a cold environment (usually $4 \pm 1°C$) for a fixed period, typically 2 to 3 hours.

This dual exposure to cold and immobilization induces physiological stress involving:

- Hypersecretion of gastric acid
- Vasoconstriction of gastric mucosal blood vessels

- Activation of hypothalamic–pituitary–adrenal (HPA) axis
- Increased release of corticosterone, catecholamines, and oxidative radicals

Together, these responses compromise mucosal integrity and lead to the development of hemorrhagic erosions and ulcers, particularly in the fundic region of the stomach.

Stress-Induced Gastric Mucosal Injury

At the end of the stress exposure, animals are sacrificed under anesthesia, and the stomach is removed, opened along the greater curvature, rinsed with saline, and examined for lesions. The mucosa typically shows:

- Linear hemorrhagic streaks
- Punctate or confluent erosions
- Dark red ulcerated patches

The number, length, and severity of lesions are recorded to calculate the ulcer score or ulcer index, using a standard grading scale:

- 0 = No lesion
- 1 = Red coloration
- 2 = Small erosions (<1 mm)
- 3 = Linear ulcers (>1 mm)
- 4 = Extensive mucosal necrosis

The ulcer index is calculated and the % protection by test compounds is determined using:

% Protection = ((UI control − UI treated) / UI control) × 100

A reduction in ulcer index in test groups compared to control confirms the protective or anti-stress gastric activity of the compound.

Relevance to Stress-Related Ulceration

This model is highly relevant in simulating real-life clinical situations where psychological or physiological stress contributes to gastric ulcer development—such as in ICU patients, surgical stress, trauma, or chronic anxiety. Unlike chemically induced ulcers, stress ulcers result from neurohumoral disturbances, including:

- Reduced gastric mucosal blood flow
- Impaired mucus and bicarbonate secretion
- Oxidative stress and lipid peroxidation
- Increased acid secretion

Drugs evaluated in this model include centrally acting anti-ulcer agents, antioxidants, adaptogens, and prostaglandin analogs, which are capable of maintaining mucosal defenses during acute stress. Standard drugs include ranitidine (50 mg/kg) or omeprazole (20 mg/kg).

The cold restraint stress model is thus a critical tool in preclinical screening, especially for drugs intended to manage ulcers caused by physical or emotional stress, and helps in identifying compounds with broad-spectrum gastroprotective properties.

3.4.2.1 Cisplatin-Induced Emesis in Ferrets

Emesis Scoring Based on Retching and Vomiting Frequency

The cisplatin-induced emesis model in ferrets is a gold-standard preclinical model used for evaluating the anti-emetic potential of investigational drugs. Ferrets are among the few small laboratory animals capable of vomiting, making them highly suitable for studying nausea and vomiting mechanisms relevant to humans. Cisplatin, a platinum-based chemotherapeutic agent, is widely used to induce vomiting in this model due to its ability to stimulate central and peripheral emetic pathways.

In this model, cisplatin is administered intraperitoneally at a dose of 5–7 mg/kg, causing delayed and sustained emesis, typically starting within 30 minutes to 1 hour of injection. The animals are then observed in transparent enclosures, and emetic episodes are recorded over a 6–8 hour period, with occasional extension to 24 hours in delayed phase studies.

The scoring of emesis is done by manually counting the episodes of retching (dry heaves) and actual vomiting (expulsion of gastric contents):

- Retching: Rhythmic contractions of abdominal and thoracic muscles without expulsion
- Vomiting: Forceful expulsion of stomach contents through the mouth

Each instance is recorded separately, and the total number of emetic events (retching + vomiting) is calculated. Data is usually expressed as:

- Number of retches
- Number of vomits
- Total emetic events per animal

This quantification provides a sensitive and reproducible endpoint for assessing the efficacy of anti-emetic compounds.

Time of Onset and Duration

Cisplatin induces a biphasic emetic response:

- Acute phase: Occurs within 0 to 4 hours post-administration, largely due to peripheral stimulation of $5\text{-}HT_3$ receptors in the gastrointestinal tract.
- Delayed phase: Appears between 4 to 24 hours and is mediated through central mechanisms, including substance P release in the nucleus tractus solitarius (NTS) and area postrema of the brainstem.

Time-based analysis includes:

- Latency to first emetic event (onset time)
- Duration of emetic response (total time from first to last event)
- Frequency per time interval, such as number of episodes per hour

Recording these parameters helps identify the onset of drug action, duration of effectiveness, and whether the test compound is more effective in acute or delayed phases.

Use of 5-HT$_3$ Antagonists and Neurokinin Blockers

The cisplatin model is particularly useful in assessing standard and investigational anti-emetics targeting different receptor pathways:

- 5-HT$_3$ receptor antagonists (e.g., ondansetron, granisetron): These are effective in acute phase emesis and work by blocking serotonin receptors on vagal afferents in the GI tract and brainstem.
- Neurokinin-1 (NK$_1$) receptor antagonists (e.g., aprepitant, fosaprepitant): These are effective in both acute and delayed phases, as they inhibit the action of substance P in the brainstem.
- Dopamine D$_2$ antagonists (e.g., metoclopramide) and corticosteroids (e.g., dexamethasone) are also evaluated in combination therapies.

Control animals typically show 20–40 emetic events in the first 6 hours post-cisplatin. A significant reduction in frequency, delayed onset, or shorter duration in treated groups indicates effective anti-emetic activity.

This model offers high translational value for testing compounds intended for chemotherapy-induced nausea and vomiting (CINV), and is critical in the development of supportive care drugs in oncology.

3.4.3.1 Castor Oil-Induced Diarrhea in Mice

Mechanism via Ricinoleic Acid

The castor oil-induced diarrhea model in mice is a simple, rapid, and highly reproducible method for screening the antidiarrheal potential of pharmaceutical agents. Castor oil is metabolized in the small intestine to yield ricinoleic acid, which is the principal active agent responsible for initiating diarrheal activity. Ricinoleic acid stimulates the intestinal mucosa, leading to:

- Irritation and inflammation of the intestinal lining
- Stimulation of prostaglandin release
- Increased secretion of fluids and electrolytes
- Enhanced intestinal motility

These effects combine to produce diarrhea that is typically observed within 30 to 60 minutes after castor oil administration. The pathophysiology mimics that of secretory diarrhea, making this model suitable for evaluating drugs with anti-secretory, anti-motility, or anti-spasmodic properties.

Stool Frequency, Consistency, and Water Content

For the experiment, healthy adult mice (20–30 grams) are fasted for 12 to 18 hours prior to dosing, with water provided ad libitum. Animals are divided into control, standard, and treatment groups (usually 5–6 mice per group). Test compounds are administered orally, followed by castor oil (0.5–1.0 mL per animal orally) after 30 to 60 minutes.

The animals are then placed individually in cages lined with clean blotting paper or filter paper, which is changed periodically to prevent over-soiling and allow clear visualization of fecal output. Observation is continued for up to 4 hours.

Parameters recorded include:

- Time of onset of diarrhea after castor oil
- Total number of fecal outputs (both wet and dry)
- Number of wet or unformed stools
- Weight of total fecal output (optional)
- Stool water content, calculated by drying feces at 60°C and noting the difference between wet and dry weight

The antidiarrheal activity of the test compound is indicated by:

- Delay in onset of first loose stool
- Reduction in total stool frequency
- Lower number of wet stools
- Decrease in stool water content

These values are statistically compared with the control group to assess the significance of inhibition.

Inhibition by Antidiarrheal Agents (Loperamide, Atropine)

Loperamide, an opioid receptor agonist, is used as the standard drug in this model. It acts by:

- Inhibiting peristalsis
- Increasing intestinal transit time
- Enhancing fluid and electrolyte absorption

The typical dose of loperamide in mice is 2–5 mg/kg orally, which reduces both stool frequency and water content significantly.

Atropine, a muscarinic receptor antagonist, also exhibits antidiarrheal action by reducing gastrointestinal motility and secretions. It is particularly useful in identifying drugs with anticholinergic effects.

The percentage inhibition of diarrhea is calculated using:

% Inhibition = ((Nc − Nt) / Nc) × 100
Where:
Nc = Mean number of wet stools in control group
Nt = Mean number of wet stools in treated group

This model is especially useful for early screening of herbal extracts, natural products, or synthetic compounds, and offers insight into whether the effect is peripherally or centrally mediated. Its predictive value, ease of operation, and low cost make it a preferred method for initial antidiarrheal assessment in drug development programs.

3.4.3.2 Intestinal Transit Assay

Use of Charcoal Meal or Carmine Red

The intestinal transit assay is a well-established in vivo method used to evaluate the effect of test drugs on gastrointestinal motility, particularly useful for identifying compounds with antidiarrheal, antispasmodic, or motility-reducing properties. This model uses non-absorbable markers such as charcoal meal (10% activated charcoal in 5% gum acacia) or carmine red dye (3% in 0.5% methylcellulose) to visually trace the movement of intestinal contents over a defined period.

Adult mice, usually fasted for 12 to 18 hours, are used with water allowed ad libitum. Animals are divided into appropriate groups: vehicle control, standard (e.g., loperamide), and test drug groups. The test or standard compound is administered orally, and after 30–60 minutes, a single dose of the marker suspension (0.2 mL charcoal meal or carmine red) is given via oral gavage.

After 30 minutes of marker administration, the animals are euthanized humanely, and the entire small intestine—from the pyloric sphincter to the ileocecal junction—is quickly and carefully removed. The distance travelled by the marker from the pylorus is measured using a calibrated ruler, and the total length of the small intestine is also recorded.

The intestinal transit ratio or percentage propulsion is calculated using the formula:

% Transit = (Distance travelled by marker / Total length of small intestine) × 100

For example, if the marker travelled 25 cm out of a 50 cm small intestine, the transit would be:

(25/50) × 100 = 50%

This provides a quantitative measure of gastrointestinal motility. A significant reduction in the transit percentage compared to control indicates that the test drug has motility-suppressing properties, which may contribute to antidiarrheal or spasmolytic effects.

Evaluation of Motility-Reducing Agents

This model is highly sensitive to agents that affect smooth muscle tone, neural regulation, or fluid absorption in the gut. Some commonly evaluated drug classes include:

- Opioid agonists (e.g., loperamide): reduce intestinal peristalsis by acting on µ-opioid receptors in the myenteric plexus.
- Anticholinergics (e.g., atropine): inhibit acetylcholine-mediated contraction of intestinal smooth muscle.
- Calcium channel blockers: reduce smooth muscle contractility and slow intestinal propulsion.
- Herbal preparations with known antispasmodic action.

Loperamide at a dose of 2–5 mg/kg significantly reduces intestinal transit, often lowering it by 50–70% compared to the control group.

The intestinal transit assay complements other models like castor oil-induced diarrhea, providing a mechanistic understanding of whether a drug reduces diarrhea by inhibiting excessive motility. It is also useful in screening for constipation-causing effects in chronic use studies and aids in the characterization of drug-induced gastrointestinal side effects during safety pharmacology evaluations.

3.4.4.1 Faecal Output Test

Measurement of Stool Number, Weight, and Water Content

The faecal output test is a fundamental in vivo model used to evaluate the laxative activity of investigational compounds. This method provides simple and reliable endpoints to assess bowel motility, stool frequency, water retention, and the evacuation effect of test drugs. It is particularly useful in distinguishing between agents that exert osmotic, stimulant, or bulk-forming mechanisms of action.

Healthy adult mice or rats are used for this assay. Animals are typically fasted for 12 to 16 hours, with water allowed freely to avoid dehydration, which could influence bowel motility. The animals are then divided into groups: control (vehicle), standard laxative, and test compound groups. The test drug is administered orally at a suitable dose, usually in suspension form.

Each animal is then placed individually into a metabolic cage or a wire-bottom cage lined with pre-weighed clean filter paper to collect fecal matter. The observation period ranges from 4 to 8 hours, depending on the pharmacokinetic properties of the drug. During this period, the following parameters are recorded:

- Total number of faecal pellets excreted
- Wet weight of total fecal matter (measured immediately after collection)
- Dry weight (after drying the faeces at 60°C for 24 hours)
- Water content calculated as:

Water Content (%) = ((Wet Weight − Dry Weight) / Wet Weight) × 100

A significant increase in stool number and water content in the test group compared to the control indicates positive laxative activity. In contrast, a reduction would suggest constipating or motility-reducing properties.

This method is particularly sensitive for evaluating:

- Onset of action (how quickly the effect starts)
- Intensity of response (mild, moderate, or strong laxation)
- Dose-response relationship

Data are usually expressed as mean ± standard error, and results are statistically analyzed using ANOVA or t-test to determine significance between groups.

Identification of Stimulant vs Bulk-Forming Laxatives

The faecal output model helps distinguish between stimulant laxatives and bulk-forming agents, based on their pattern of effect:

- Stimulant laxatives (e.g., senna, bisacodyl, castor oil) work by irritating the colonic mucosa, leading to increased peristalsis and secretion of water and electrolytes into the bowel. These agents typically result in a rapid increase in stool number and high water content, often within 2 to 4 hours post-administration.
- Bulk-forming laxatives (e.g., psyllium husk, methylcellulose) are natural or synthetic fibers that absorb water, swell in the colon, and stimulate defecation by increasing stool bulk and moisture content. These agents show gradual onset, with a moderate increase in stool mass and water retention, often after 12–24 hours.

The faecal output test thus serves as a functional tool to:

- Confirm the laxative effect of a test compound
- Classify its mechanism of action based on time to onset, stool consistency, and water retention
- Compare efficacy with standard drugs in the same class

This model is widely used in the preclinical screening of gastrointestinal drugs, particularly for herbal formulations, dietary fibers, probiotics, and new chemical entities developed to treat constipation and bowel irregularities.

3.4.4.2 GI Transit Time Assay

Time Taken for Coloured Markers to Pass Through GI Tract

The Gastrointestinal (GI) transit time assay is a reliable in vivo method used to measure the rate at which contents pass through the entire GI tract, providing insight into the motility-enhancing or delaying effects of natural or synthetic compounds. This assay is particularly suitable for identifying laxative properties, as increased motility results in faster transit and reduced time for material to pass through the gut.

In this method, non-absorbable coloured markers such as carmine red dye (3% in 0.5% methylcellulose) or activated charcoal suspension (10% in 5% gum acacia) are used. These markers are visually traceable and do not interfere with digestive enzymes or absorption processes. The animals used are typically adult mice or rats, fasted overnight (12–18 hours) to standardize gut contents, with water provided freely.

After administering the test compound or standard laxative orally, the marker suspension is given after an appropriate time interval, depending on the drug's expected onset of action. Animals are then individually housed in cages and observed continuously or sacrificed at predefined time points (commonly at 30, 60, 90, or 120 minutes) to evaluate the extent of marker movement.

Upon sacrifice, the entire GI tract from the stomach to the anus is carefully excised and laid on a clean surface. The total length of the intestine is measured with a ruler, and the distance travelled by the marker (as indicated by the leading edge of the coloured content) is recorded.

The GI transit percentage is calculated as:

% Transit = (Distance travelled by marker / Total length of GI tract) × 100

This provides a quantitative measure of gastrointestinal propulsion. In control animals, GI transit may range from 40–60%, depending on species, fasting, and environmental conditions. A significant increase in % transit in the test group indicates enhanced motility, supporting laxative activity.

Application for Natural or Synthetic Laxative Evaluation

The GI transit time assay is particularly useful in evaluating:

- Stimulant laxatives: which act by increasing peristaltic activity through mucosal irritation or neurotransmitter release (e.g., castor oil, bisacodyl)
- Bulk-forming agents: which increase luminal content volume and enhance movement via mechanical stretch
- Natural products and herbal extracts: such as Aloe vera, senna, triphala, and others traditionally used in gastrointestinal cleansing
- Osmotic laxatives: like lactulose or magnesium hydroxide, which draw water into the lumen and facilitate stool passage

This assay also supports mechanistic studies for compounds that might have prokinetic effects on the small or large intestine. Comparison with standards like castor oil (1–2 mL/kg) or loperamide (to delay motility) helps to classify test substances based on their ability to accelerate or inhibit transit.

Thus, the GI transit time assay is a vital tool in the preclinical evaluation of laxatives, helping researchers quantify onset, speed, and extent of intestinal propulsion, and differentiate between mechanisms of action in both natural and synthetic drug candidates.

Table 11: Anti-Asthmatic Drug Screening Models

Model	Species	Measured Parameters	Application
Histamine-Induced Bronchospasm	Guinea pigs	Latency to dyspnea, survival time	Evaluate histamine antagonists
Acetylcholine-Induced Bronchospasm	Guinea pigs	Bronchospasm severity, protection index	Evaluate anticholinergic bronchodilators

Table 12: COPD Screening Models

Model	Key Inducer	Duration	Measured Outcomes
Cigarette Smoke-Induced	Cigarette smoke exposure	8–12 weeks	Inflammatory markers, lung histopathology
Elastase-Induced Emphysema	Porcine pancreatic elastase	Single or repeated doses	Lung compliance, alveolar changes

Table 13: Anti-Allergic Drug Models

Model	Species	Induction	Evaluation
Passive Cutaneous Anaphylaxis (PCA)	Rats, Mice	SRBC/IgE with dye extravasation	Inhibition of vascular permeability, allergic response

Table 14: Aphrodisiac Activity Assessment

Parameter	Interpretation
Mount Latency	Decreased latency = enhanced desire
Intromission Frequency	Increased frequency = increased potency
Ejaculation Latency	Longer time = delayed climax
Post-Ejaculatory Interval	Shorter interval = enhanced recovery

Table 15: Antifertility Screening Techniques

Model	Species	Outcome
Estrous Cycle Monitoring	Female rats	Cycle disruption
Anti-Implantation Test	Mice/Rats	Implantation inhibition
Abortifacient Test	Rats	Termination of pregnancy

Table 16: Analgesic Activity Tests

Test	Response Type	Measured Parameter	Analgesic Type
Tail Flick	Spinal reflex	Latency	Opiates
Hot Plate	Central pain processing	Reaction time	Opiates
Acetic Acid-Induced Writhing	Peripheral pain response	Writhing count	NSAIDs

Table 17: Anti-inflammatory Models

Model	Inflammation Type	Species	Measured Parameter
Carrageenan-Induced Paw Edema	Acute	Rats	Paw volume
Cotton Pellet-Induced Granuloma	Chronic	Rats	Dry weight of granuloma

Table 18: Antipyretic Activity Model

Model	Species	Fever Induction	Assessment
Brewer's Yeast-Induced Pyrexia	Rats	Subcutaneous yeast injection	Rectal temperature reduction

Table 19: Anti-Ulcer Screening Models

Model	Key Indicators	Usefulness
Pylorus Ligation	Ulcer index	Assess acid secretion blockers
Ethanol-Induced Ulcer	Mucosal erosion	Test cytoprotectives
Cold Restraint Stress	Stress-induced lesions	Test anti-stress drugs

Table 20: Anti-Diarrheal and Laxative Models

Test	Outcome	Drug Type
Castor Oil-Induced Diarrhea	Stool frequency and consistency	Antidiarrheals
Intestinal Transit Assay	Charcoal transit distance	Motility inhibitors
Fecal Output Test	Number and weight of stools	Laxatives

M. Yaso Deepika, P. Naveen, A. Divya, K. Manjeera

4. Preclinical Screening for Cardiovascular, Metabolic, and Oncology Drugs

4.1 Cardiovascular Pharmacology

4.1.1 Antihypertensive Drug Screening

4.1.1.1 DOCA-Salt Induced Hypertension Model

Mechanism and Pathophysiology

The DOCA-salt induced hypertension model is a well-established experimental method used for evaluating the efficacy of potential antihypertensive agents, particularly those acting on the renin–angiotensin system, mineralocorticoid receptors, and ion transport mechanisms. This model mimics a state of low-renin hypertension caused by sodium and fluid retention, which results from the combined administration of the mineralocorticoid deoxycorticosterone acetate (DOCA) and high dietary salt. The mineralocorticoid action of DOCA promotes sodium retention and potassium excretion in renal tubules, while high salt intake exacerbates fluid accumulation and vascular resistance. The resultant increase in extracellular fluid volume leads to persistent elevation of arterial blood pressure. This model exhibits features of volume-dependent hypertension, cardiac hypertrophy, renal alterations, and sympathetic nervous system involvement, making it suitable for the evaluation of centrally and peripherally acting antihypertensive compounds.

Dosing Regimen of DOCA and Salt

Adult male Wistar rats, weighing between 180 to 250 grams, are commonly selected for this model. Prior to DOCA administration, rats are uninephrectomized under general anesthesia using ketamine and xylazine to remove one kidney and enhance sensitivity to mineralocorticoid-induced salt retention. After a one-week recovery period, DOCA is administered subcutaneously at a dose of 20 to 30 mg/kg body weight, two to three times per week. DOCA is typically dissolved in a vehicle such as sesame oil to enhance its bioavailability. Along with DOCA, animals receive a 1% sodium chloride and 0.2% potassium chloride solution as drinking water ad libitum throughout the treatment period, which usually spans three to four weeks. This combination leads to a gradual but sustained rise in systolic and diastolic blood pressure, usually evident within 10 to 14 days of initiation.

The hypertensive state is maintained throughout the experimental period, during which test drugs are administered either orally or intraperitoneally, depending on their pharmacokinetic profile. Standard antihypertensive agents such as captopril, hydralazine, or losartan are used as reference drugs to validate the sensitivity and reliability of the model.

Blood Pressure Measurement (Tail-Cuff, Telemetry)

The effectiveness of the test compound is assessed by periodic monitoring of blood pressure using non-invasive or invasive methods. The non-invasive tail-cuff plethysmography technique is widely used due to its simplicity and cost-effectiveness. In this method, animals are pre-warmed to 32 to 34°C for 10 to 15 minutes to dilate tail arteries, and then placed in restrainers where a pneumatic cuff and sensor are placed around the base of the tail. Blood pressure is recorded using an automated tail-cuff apparatus, and the average of three to five consistent readings is taken for each animal. This technique provides values for systolic pressure and heart rate.

For more accurate and continuous blood pressure monitoring, telemetry is used in selected studies. This involves the surgical implantation of a pressure transducer catheter into the carotid artery or abdominal aorta under sterile conditions. The device is connected to a telemetric transmitter placed in the peritoneal cavity or subcutaneous space. Data are collected wirelessly using receiver plates and software, allowing real-time monitoring of systolic, diastolic, and mean arterial pressure, as well as heart rate variability and circadian rhythms over extended periods.

In this model, systolic blood pressure typically rises from a baseline of 110–120 mmHg to 160–200 mmHg over three weeks. A significant and dose-dependent reduction in blood pressure in treated animals compared to DOCA-only controls is considered indicative of antihypertensive activity. The model also allows for assessment of secondary parameters such as body weight, cardiac hypertrophy index, and serum electrolytes, which may provide additional insights into the mechanism of action and safety of the test compound.

4.1.1.2 Renal Artery Ligation Model

Surgical Procedure (2K-1C and 1K-1C Models)

The renal artery ligation model is a classical and highly specific method used to study renovascular hypertension, particularly useful for screening drugs that act on the renin–angiotensin–aldosterone system (RAAS). Two major variants are employed: the two-kidney, one-clip (2K-1C) model and the one-kidney, one-clip (1K-1C) model. In the 2K-1C method, both kidneys are retained, but a silver clip is placed on the renal artery of one kidney, partially restricting blood flow. In contrast, in the 1K-1C model, one kidney is surgically removed, and the remaining kidney's artery is clipped.

For the 2K-1C procedure, adult male Wistar rats (180–250 g) are anesthetized using ketamine (50 mg/kg) and xylazine (10 mg/kg), given intraperitoneally. A left subcostal incision is made to expose the renal artery. A U-shaped silver clip with an internal diameter of

0.2 mm is placed around the renal artery just proximal to the renal hilum. Care is taken not to occlude the vessel completely, but to induce partial stenosis. The abdomen is closed in two layers, and postoperative analgesics and antibiotics are administered.

In the 1K-1C model, one kidney (usually the right) is removed surgically, and a clip is applied to the renal artery of the remaining kidney in the same manner. This model causes more severe and sustained hypertension due to complete dependence on a single hypoperfused kidney, and it mimics malignant hypertension in humans.

Development of Renovascular Hypertension

In both models, hypertension develops due to renal ischemia, which triggers the juxtaglomerular apparatus to increase secretion of renin, initiating the RAAS cascade. Elevated renin converts angiotensinogen to angiotensin I, which is further converted by angiotensin-converting enzyme (ACE) to angiotensin II—a potent vasoconstrictor and stimulator of aldosterone secretion. Aldosterone promotes sodium and water retention, leading to volume expansion and peripheral resistance, which together elevate systolic and diastolic blood pressure.

In the 2K-1C model, blood pressure rises gradually, usually becoming significantly elevated within two weeks post-surgery, and stabilizes around 160–200 mmHg. The non-clipped kidney undergoes compensatory natriuresis, while the clipped kidney remains hypoperfused, sustaining the RAAS activation. In contrast, the 1K-1C model causes faster and more severe elevation in blood pressure, typically within 7–10 days, often exceeding 200 mmHg, due to the lack of a contralateral kidney for compensation.

Evaluation of Drug Efficacy

Test compounds are administered after confirming hypertension, either orally or intraperitoneally, for a period ranging from 7 to 21 days, depending on the design. Standard antihypertensive agents such as enalapril (10 mg/kg), losartan (30 mg/kg), or hydralazine (5 mg/kg) are included as positive controls. Blood pressure is measured using a non-invasive tail-cuff method or implantable telemetry system, with recordings taken at regular intervals to assess the time-course and intensity of antihypertensive effect.

In addition to blood pressure, other parameters such as heart rate, plasma renin activity, angiotensin II concentration, aldosterone levels, urinary sodium excretion, and renal function markers (creatinine, BUN) are measured to evaluate the mechanism of action and safety profile of the test drug.

A statistically significant reduction in blood pressure in the test group compared to the hypertensive control group, along with improvement in RAAS-related biomarkers, confirms the efficacy of the compound. This model is highly predictive of the therapeutic potential of ACE inhibitors, angiotensin receptor blockers, renin inhibitors, and aldosterone antagonists, and is widely accepted for regulatory pharmacology studies related to hypertension.

4.1.2 Antiarrhythmic Drug Screening

4.1.2.1 Induction of Arrhythmias

Chemical Inducers (Aconitine, $BaCl_2$)

Chemical induction of arrhythmias in preclinical models offers a reproducible and rapid approach to evaluate the antiarrhythmic potential of new drug candidates. Among the most widely used agents are aconitine and barium chloride ($BaCl_2$), both of which induce arrhythmias by altering electrophysiological properties of cardiac myocytes.

Aconitine-induced arrhythmia is a preferred model in rats or guinea pigs for testing drugs that act on voltage-gated sodium channels. Aconitine binds persistently to the sodium channel in its open state, preventing inactivation and leading to persistent inward sodium current, delayed repolarization, and generation of ectopic action potentials. This results in ventricular premature beats, tachycardia, and fibrillation. Aconitine is administered intravenously at a dose ranging from 10 to 20 µg/kg, slowly infused over 1–2 minutes until the appearance of the first arrhythmic event. The dose required to induce arrhythmias (ED_{50}) and the time to onset are recorded. Test drugs are administered prior to aconitine challenge, and their effectiveness is assessed by observing increased latency, reduced arrhythmia score, or complete suppression of arrhythmic episodes.

Barium chloride-induced arrhythmia is another robust model where $BaCl_2$ (typically 3 mg/kg IV) induces arrhythmia by blocking inward rectifier potassium channels, disrupting resting membrane potential, and enhancing myocardial excitability. This model produces ventricular extrasystoles, fibrillation, and sometimes cardiac arrest, which are particularly responsive to drugs that block potassium and calcium channels.

Both models allow quantification of arrhythmias using standardized arrhythmia scoring systems, such as:

- 0 = Normal ECG
- 1 = Occasional premature beats
- 2 = Bigeminy/trigeminy
- 3 = Ventricular tachycardia
- 4 = Ventricular fibrillation
- 5 = Death due to cardiac arrest

The reduction in score, increase in survival time, and delay in onset of arrhythmia in the treatment group as compared to control confirm the protective antiarrhythmic effect.

Electrical Stimulation Protocols

Electrical induction of arrhythmias involves applying controlled electrical stimuli to the myocardium to provoke abnormal rhythm patterns, particularly reentrant arrhythmias. These methods are often conducted in anesthetized dogs, pigs, or isolated Langendorff-perfused hearts of rats or guinea pigs, and are used to study reentrant circuits, conduction delay, and refractory periods.

Programmed electrical stimulation (PES) is performed using a stimulating electrode placed on the epicardial or endocardial surface of the heart, where basic pacing stimuli (S1) are followed by extrastimuli (S2, S3) to test ventricular and atrial vulnerability. The parameters recorded include:

- Inducibility of tachyarrhythmias
- Sustained vs non-sustained episodes
- Effective refractory period (ERP)
- Conduction time and dispersion

The ability of a test drug to prevent or terminate induced arrhythmias, increase ERP, or suppress afterdepolarizations is taken as an indication of antiarrhythmic efficacy. Drugs can be classified based on Vaughan Williams classification (Class I–IV) depending on their mechanism of action observed in these protocols.

Both chemical and electrical induction methods provide complementary insights and together form the core preclinical toolkit for assessing antiarrhythmic properties, establishing dose–response relationships, and predicting clinical relevance in therapeutic drug development.

4.1.2.2 ECG Monitoring and Analysis

Placement of Electrodes and Recording System

Electrocardiogram (ECG) monitoring is a critical component of preclinical antiarrhythmic drug evaluation, providing real-time data on cardiac electrical activity and allowing for detailed analysis of drug-induced changes in conduction patterns, rhythm, and repolarization. The ECG setup varies depending on the animal model and study design, but the fundamental principles of electrode placement and lead configuration remain consistent across species.

In rodent models such as rats or mice, ECG recording is typically performed under light anesthesia (e.g., ketamine 50 mg/kg with xylazine 10 mg/kg, intraperitoneally) to minimize motion artifacts without significantly altering cardiac function. Surface electrodes (needle or clip type) are placed subcutaneously in the limbs to simulate the standard lead II configuration, with the positive electrode on the left hind limb, negative on the right forelimb, and ground on the right hind limb. In larger animals like rabbits, dogs, or pigs, adhesive skin electrodes or implanted telemetry probes are used for prolonged monitoring.

The ECG signal is amplified and recorded using systems such as PowerLab (ADInstruments), BIOPAC, or DSI telemetry platforms, with data acquisition software calibrated to analyze heart rate, waveform intervals, and arrhythmias automatically. Sampling rates of 1–5 kHz are preferred to ensure high-resolution waveform capture.

Parameters: QT Interval, QRS Complex, Arrhythmia Scoring

Key ECG parameters monitored in antiarrhythmic screening include:

- P wave: Reflects atrial depolarization
- PR interval: Time from atrial to ventricular depolarization, indicating AV node conduction
- QRS complex: Represents ventricular depolarization; prolonged QRS indicates intraventricular conduction delay
- QT interval: Measures the total duration of ventricular depolarization and repolarization.
    - Corrected QT interval (QTc) is calculated to adjust for heart rate using formulas like Bazett's or Fridericia's correction:
        - $QTc = QT / \sqrt{RR}$ (Bazett's)
- RR interval: Time between successive R waves, used to determine heart rate

Arrhythmia scoring is applied when using chemically or electrically induced models. Events such as:

- Premature ventricular contractions (PVCs)

- Ventricular tachycardia (VT)
- Ventricular fibrillation (VF)
- Atrioventricular block are documented and graded based on frequency, duration, and severity. A standard arrhythmia scoring system (e.g., Lambeth conventions) may be used for consistency in reporting.

The QT prolongation is a critical parameter in regulatory toxicology as it is associated with the risk of torsades de pointes, a potentially fatal ventricular arrhythmia. Test compounds causing QTc prolongation over 10% from baseline, or values exceeding 500 ms in rats, warrant detailed cardiac safety evaluation.

Acute vs Chronic Arrhythmia Screening

ECG monitoring is used both in acute and chronic studies depending on the pharmacological profile and intended use of the test compound.

- Acute screening involves a single or short-term administration of the test compound followed by arrhythmia induction (chemical or electrical). ECG is recorded for 1 to 4 hours post-dose to observe immediate electrophysiological effects, arrhythmia suppression, and onset of drug action.
- Chronic screening evaluates the long-term effects of repeated or continuous drug administration. This is crucial for identifying cumulative toxicity, structural cardiomyopathy, or late-onset proarrhythmia. Chronic telemetry implants are used in large animals or conscious rodents for this purpose, enabling uninterrupted 24-hour monitoring across multiple days or weeks.

In both types, ECG analysis is essential not only to evaluate antiarrhythmic efficacy but also to detect proarrhythmic liability, making it a cornerstone in cardiovascular safety pharmacology. The data derived from ECG monitoring support decision-making in dose selection, therapeutic index estimation, and regulatory risk assessment of novel compounds targeting cardiac rhythm disorders.

4.1.3.1 Ischemia–Reperfusion Injury Model

Surgical Induction of Coronary Artery Occlusion

The ischemia–reperfusion (I/R) injury model is a well-validated preclinical method used to evaluate the cardioprotective and antianginal effects of investigational drugs. It mimics the pathophysiological events that occur during myocardial infarction and revascularization procedures such as thrombolysis or angioplasty in humans. The model enables the study of both ischemic injury due to lack of blood flow and reperfusion injury caused by sudden restoration of oxygen, both of which play a critical role in acute coronary syndromes.

This model is typically performed in anesthetized rats, rabbits, or dogs, with male Wistar rats (250–300 g) being a common choice due to ease of handling and predictable outcomes. The animals are anesthetized using a combination of ketamine (50 mg/kg) and xylazine (10 mg/kg) given intraperitoneally. After ensuring deep anesthesia and analgesia, the animal is secured in the supine position on a surgical platform.

A left thoracotomy is performed at the fourth or fifth intercostal space, and the pericardium is carefully opened to expose the beating heart. A 6-0 silk suture is then passed under the left anterior descending (LAD) coronary artery, approximately 2 mm below the left auricle, and tied over a small plastic or polyethylene tubing to create a reversible ligature. This occlusion results in regional ischemia, characterized by pallor of the myocardium, ST-segment elevation on ECG, and reduced ventricular contractility.

The duration of ischemia typically ranges from 30 to 45 minutes, followed by reperfusion achieved by removing or loosening the ligature. Reperfusion is confirmed visually by hyperemic response in the previously occluded area. ECG and hemodynamic parameters such as heart rate, blood pressure, and left ventricular function are continuously monitored using appropriate instruments.

Infarct Size Measurement and Histology

After a reperfusion period of 2 to 24 hours, depending on the experimental design, the animals are sacrificed under deep anesthesia. The heart is excised quickly and rinsed in cold saline to remove blood. The left ventricle is sliced into transverse sections of approximately 2 mm thickness, and infarct size is evaluated using triphenyl tetrazolium chloride (TTC) staining. TTC is a redox indicator that stains viable myocardium deep red, while infarcted (necrotic) tissue remains pale or white.

The slices are then scanned or photographed, and the area at risk (AAR) and infarct size (IS) are quantified using image analysis software. The infarct size is expressed as a percentage of the AAR or total left ventricle using the formula:

Infarct Size (%) = (Infarcted area / Total area at risk) × 100

Histological examination may also be performed. Sections are fixed in 10% formalin, embedded in paraffin, and stained using hematoxylin and eosin (H&E) or Masson's trichrome stain. Histological features assessed include:

- Myocyte necrosis
- Edema
- Leukocyte infiltration
- Fibrosis or scar formation

Test drugs are administered prior to ischemia (pre-treatment), during ischemia (co-treatment), or just before reperfusion (post-treatment) to evaluate their ability to reduce infarct size, prevent myocyte death, and preserve cardiac structure and function. Standard antianginal agents used for comparison include nitroglycerin, nicorandil, verapamil, and trimetazidine.

This model is particularly suitable for identifying compounds with anti-ischemic, anti-apoptotic, antioxidant, calcium channel blocking, or mitochondrial protective properties, and remains a cornerstone in the preclinical evaluation of antianginal drugs and cardioprotective agents.

4.1.3.2 Biochemical Markers of Cardiac Injury

CK-MB, LDH, Troponins

The assessment of biochemical markers of myocardial injury plays a central role in the preclinical evaluation of antianginal and cardioprotective drugs, especially in ischemia–reperfusion injury models. These markers provide objective, quantifiable evidence of myocyte membrane damage or necrosis, and help in correlating infarct size with the severity of biochemical leakage. Among the most commonly used cardiac biomarkers in experimental studies are creatine kinase-MB (CK-MB), lactate dehydrogenase (LDH), and cardiac troponins (cTnI and cTnT).

Creatine kinase-MB (CK-MB) is an isoenzyme of creatine kinase predominantly found in the myocardium. It plays a role in the energy shuttle mechanism of cardiac muscle and is released into the bloodstream when there is damage to the cardiac sarcolemma. In preclinical models, serum CK-MB levels are measured 2 to 6 hours after reperfusion, using spectrophotometric enzyme activity assays or ELISA kits. The normal CK-MB range in rats is around 100–300 IU/L, which can rise up to 500–1000 IU/L following myocardial infarction. A significant reduction in CK-MB levels in drug-treated animals compared to untreated I/R controls is indicative of membrane stabilization and reduced infarction.

Lactate dehydrogenase (LDH) is a cytoplasmic enzyme involved in anaerobic glycolysis, and while it is non-specific to the heart, it is widely used in conjunction with CK-MB as a supportive marker of tissue necrosis. Serum LDH activity is measured by monitoring the conversion of pyruvate to lactate at 340 nm using a standard kinetic assay. Elevated LDH levels in plasma, typically observed within 6–12 hours post-reperfusion, correlate with the extent of necrotic damage. In rodent models, basal LDH levels may range from 300–600 IU/L, and post-infarction values can exceed 1000 IU/L.

Cardiac troponins, particularly troponin I (cTnI) and troponin T (cTnT), are the most specific and sensitive indicators of cardiac muscle injury. They are structural proteins that regulate calcium-mediated contraction in myocardial fibers and are not normally found in circulating blood. Following myocardial cell death, these proteins are released into the bloodstream in proportion to the extent of irreversible myocardial damage. In rats, cTnI levels can rise above 2.0 ng/mL after a significant infarction. These are typically measured using high-sensitivity immunoassay kits, with values recorded at 2, 6, and 24 hours post-reperfusion for time-course analysis.

Together, these biochemical parameters offer strong support to histological and functional data in ischemia–reperfusion studies. They provide early, sensitive, and quantitative insight into drug-mediated protection against myocardial damage. A dose-dependent reduction in CK-MB, LDH, and troponin levels, coupled with improved cardiac histology and reduced infarct size, is strong evidence supporting the antianginal and cardioprotective effects of the test compound.

4.1.4.1 High-Fat Diet-Induced Atherosclerosis

Diet Composition and Duration

The high-fat diet (HFD)-induced atherosclerosis model is widely employed in preclinical studies to evaluate the antiatherosclerotic efficacy of novel compounds. It closely mimics the dietary and metabolic causes of atherosclerosis in humans and is useful for screening drugs that act on lipid metabolism, inflammation, endothelial function, and plaque formation. This model is generally used in rabbits, rats, and increasingly in apolipoprotein-deficient mice (e.g., ApoE$^{-/-}$ or LDLr$^{-/-}$ mice), which are genetically predisposed to hyperlipidemia and vascular lesions.

In rats or rabbits, a high-fat diet is formulated to elevate plasma lipid levels and promote arterial plaque formation. A typical HFD contains:

- Cholesterol: 0.5% to 2%
- Cholic acid: 0.1% to enhance cholesterol absorption
- Coconut oil or lard: 20% to 40% as saturated fat source
- Basal feed: standard rodent chow or wheat bran to balance nutrition

The diet is administered ad libitum for 8 to 12 weeks, during which the animals are monitored for weight gain, food intake, and general health. In genetically modified mouse models, the progression of atherosclerosis can be accelerated by combining the HFD with western-type diets containing 21% fat and 0.2% cholesterol.

After the dietary induction period, test compounds are administered either during the progression phase (therapeutic model) or from the beginning of the diet (preventive model). Standard antiatherosclerotic agents such as atorvastatin (10 mg/kg/day) or fenofibrate (50 mg/kg/day) are used as positive controls.

Serum Lipid Profile: Total Cholesterol, HDL, LDL, Triglycerides

The efficacy of the test drug is evaluated by analyzing the serum lipid profile, which reflects the compound's impact on lipid metabolism and cardiovascular risk markers. Blood samples are collected from the retro-orbital plexus or tail vein under mild anesthesia after a 12-hour fasting period. Serum is separated by centrifugation and analyzed using colorimetric enzymatic kits or automated biochemistry analyzers.

The key parameters assessed include:

- Total cholesterol (TC): Measures all circulating cholesterol. Values increase significantly in HFD-fed animals, often reaching 200–400 mg/dL in rats or 500–1000 mg/dL in rabbits.
- Low-density lipoprotein cholesterol (LDL-C): Major atherogenic fraction. A target of drug therapy is reducing

LDL-C levels, which may rise above 100–200 mg/dL in models with induced atherosclerosis.
- High-density lipoprotein cholesterol (HDL-C): Protective lipoprotein involved in reverse cholesterol transport. Test drugs are evaluated for their ability to maintain or elevate HDL levels, ideally above 40–50 mg/dL in rodents.
- Triglycerides (TG): Elevated in dyslipidemia and contribute to small dense LDL formation. Levels typically increase to 150–300 mg/dL, and normalization suggests improvement in lipid handling.

Ratios such as LDL/HDL, TC/HDL, and atherogenic index of plasma (AIP) are calculated to assess cardiovascular risk. AIP is given by:

AIP = log (TG/HDL-C)

A decrease in total cholesterol, LDL, triglycerides, and atherogenic indices along with an increase in HDL suggests potent antiatherosclerotic activity.

This model can be extended to include histological examination of aortic root and arch, oil red O staining of lipid plaques, and inflammatory markers such as CRP and IL-6, offering a complete assessment of plaque formation and regression under drug treatment.

4.1.4.2 Aortic Lesion Analysis

Histological Staining (Oil Red O, H&E)

Aortic lesion analysis is an essential endpoint in preclinical antiatherosclerotic drug screening, offering direct visualization and quantification of atherosclerotic plaques. Following high-fat diet induction, the aorta, particularly the aortic arch and thoracic region, develops lipid-rich lesions that resemble human atheromas in structure and progression. These lesions are best evaluated through histological techniques, primarily Oil Red O staining for lipid detection and hematoxylin and eosin (H&E) staining for tissue architecture and inflammation.

At the end of the treatment period, animals are euthanized humanely, and the entire aorta from the heart to the iliac bifurcation is carefully excised. The surrounding connective tissue and adipose fat are removed under a dissecting microscope to avoid damaging the intima. The aorta is either opened longitudinally for en face staining or sectioned transversely for cross-sectional analysis at standard anatomical locations (e.g., aortic root, ascending arch).

For Oil Red O staining, the aorta is fixed in 10% formalin, then rinsed and immersed in 60% isopropanol. It is stained with Oil Red O working solution (0.5% in isopropanol diluted with water) for 15–20 minutes, followed by brief destaining and counterstaining with hematoxylin. This method stains neutral lipids bright red, allowing clear demarcation of fatty streaks and lipid cores. The stained aorta is pinned flat on black wax for en face photography, and images are analyzed using software like ImageJ to calculate the percentage of lesion area relative to total surface area.

For H&E staining, aortic cross-sections are embedded in paraffin blocks, sectioned at 5 μm thickness, and stained using standard protocols. Hematoxylin stains nuclei blue, while eosin stains cytoplasm and extracellular matrix pink. This allows the assessment of:

- Intimal thickening
- Foam cell accumulation
- Fibrous cap development
- Media degeneration and calcification
- Inflammatory cell infiltration

Lesion Scoring and Morphometry

Lesion scoring provides a semi-quantitative method for classifying the severity of atherosclerotic changes. A common scoring system ranges from:

- Grade 0 – No visible lesion
- Grade 1 – Isolated foam cells
- Grade 2 – Small lipid core with minimal thickening
- Grade 3 – Well-developed plaques with fibrous cap
- Grade 4 – Advanced lesions with necrotic core and media disruption

Alternatively, morphometric analysis using image analysis software enables the quantification of plaque dimensions, such as:

- Intimal area (IA)
- Medial area (MA)
- Intima-to-media ratio (I/M)
- Lumen stenosis (%) = [(IA) / (IA + Lumen area)] × 100

In studies involving transgenic mice, especially ApoE$^{-/-}$ or LDLr$^{-/-}$ strains, atherosclerotic burden is evaluated across multiple aortic regions including sinus of Valsalva, arch, thoracic, and abdominal aorta, providing a comprehensive map of lesion distribution.

Drugs showing a statistically significant reduction in lesion area, plaque thickness, and inflammatory features, compared to high-fat diet controls, are considered promising antiatherosclerotic candidates. When combined with lipid profile data and inflammatory biomarkers, aortic lesion analysis provides a strong preclinical validation platform for cardiovascular drug development.

4.1.5.1 Saluretic and Natriuretic Tests

Measurement of Urinary Na^+, K^+, Cl^- Excretion

Saluretic and natriuretic activity screening is an essential pharmacological evaluation for drugs that enhance renal excretion of electrolytes and water. These tests help classify diuretics based on their action on different nephron segments and are fundamental to identifying loop diuretics, thiazides, and potassium-sparing agents. The terms saluretic and natriuretic refer to the excretion of salt (NaCl) and sodium ions, respectively, both of which contribute to fluid elimination and blood pressure reduction.

Healthy adult Wistar rats (150–250 g) or albino mice (25–30 g) are generally used for these studies. Animals are fasted overnight (water allowed ad libitum) to standardize hydration. They are divided into control, standard, and test drug groups (n = 6 per group). The animals are placed in individual metabolic cages that allow accurate collection of urine over a fixed duration, usually 5 to 6 hours post-dosing.

Test compounds are administered orally or intraperitoneally, depending on their solubility and intended clinical route. The standard volume of fluid load is often provided using 0.9% saline or isotonic sodium carboxymethylcellulose, administered at a dose of 25 mL/kg (in rats) to maintain hydration and renal perfusion.

Urine is collected and measured for volume and electrolyte content. The following ions are quantified using:

- Na^+ and K^+: Flame photometry or ion-selective electrodes
- Cl^-: Argentometric titration using silver nitrate, or using chloride assay kits

The data are typically expressed as:

- Total amount excreted per animal
- Electrolyte concentration (mEq/L)
- Ratios such as Na^+/K^+ to assess potassium-sparing vs potassium-wasting effects
- Saluretic index and natriuretic index

The saluretic effect is evaluated by the sum of Na^+ and Cl^- excretion, whereas natriuretic activity is based specifically on sodium elimination. Potassium loss is considered important for assessing hypokalemic side effects of certain diuretics.

A potent saluretic will significantly increase both sodium and chloride excretion without excessively raising potassium output. On the other hand, a potassium-sparing diuretic will increase sodium output but minimize or reduce potassium loss.

Standard Diuretics (Furosemide, Hydrochlorothiazide)

Standard drugs are included in the study to validate the sensitivity and specificity of the assay. Commonly used reference compounds include:

- Furosemide (10–20 mg/kg, orally or intraperitoneally): A loop diuretic acting on the thick ascending limb of the loop of Henle. It produces strong natriuresis and saluresis, with a high Na^+/K^+ excretion ratio. It causes significant potassium loss.
- Hydrochlorothiazide (10 mg/kg, orally): A thiazide diuretic that works on the distal convoluted tubule. It produces moderate natriuretic and saluretic effects but may cause hypokalemia with long-term use.
- Spironolactone or amiloride (not always used): Represent potassium-sparing diuretics acting on the collecting duct; used to distinguish the mechanism of test compounds.

In effective diuretic screening, an increase of at least 100–200% in sodium excretion over the control group is considered significant. Concurrent measurement of urine volume and electrolyte concentrations provides a complete profile of the diuretic class, potency, and electrolyte-sparing properties of the test drug.

These tests not only provide efficacy data but also guide formulation design and dose selection in later clinical development phases.

4.2.1.1 Streptozotocin (STZ)-Induced Diabetes

Dose and Route (Single vs Multiple Low Dose)

The streptozotocin (STZ)-induced diabetes model is widely used in experimental pharmacology for evaluating antidiabetic agents, especially those aimed at type 1 and type 2 diabetes mellitus. STZ is a naturally occurring nitrosourea compound that exhibits selective toxicity to the pancreatic beta cells through mechanisms involving DNA alkylation, oxidative stress, and activation of poly ADP-ribose polymerase (PARP). This leads to decreased insulin secretion and persistent hyperglycemia.

There are two common dosing regimens depending on the type of diabetes to be mimicked:

- Single high-dose protocol: A single intraperitoneal injection of STZ is administered at 50–65 mg/kg body weight in citrate buffer (pH 4.5). This rapidly induces type 1 diabetes-like condition by causing near-complete beta-cell necrosis within 2–3 days. Hyperglycemia develops within 48 to 72 hours and remains stable.
- Multiple low-dose protocol: To model type 2 diabetes or slowly progressive beta-cell dysfunction, multiple low doses of STZ (e.g., 25–35 mg/kg/day for 5 consecutive days) are administered intraperitoneally. This leads to partial beta-cell loss, moderate insulinopenia, and impaired glucose tolerance. This approach often requires a high-fat diet or nicotinamide co-treatment to better mimic insulin resistance.

The animals are fasted overnight prior to STZ administration to ensure uniform uptake by pancreatic cells. STZ is light-sensitive and unstable in aqueous solution, so it must be prepared fresh and used within 10–15 minutes of dissolution.

Blood Glucose Monitoring

Blood glucose levels are typically monitored at baseline, and then 72 hours post-STZ injection, followed by weekly intervals. Blood is collected from the tail vein or retro-orbital sinus under mild anesthesia. Glucometers calibrated for small animal use or glucose oxidase-peroxidase method (GOD-POD) is employed for accurate estimation.

- Fasting blood glucose (FBG) levels above 200 mg/dL in rats are considered diabetic.
- In type 2 models, an oral glucose tolerance test (OGTT) is performed after 2–3 weeks to assess glucose handling capacity and drug effect on glucose excursion.

OGTT involves administering 2 g/kg of glucose orally, followed by glucose measurements at 0, 30, 60, 90, and 120 minutes. The area under the curve (AUC) is calculated to quantify the glucose-lowering effect of test drugs.

Insulin Resistance and Beta-Cell Destruction

In STZ models, especially when combined with high-fat diet or nicotinamide, a significant feature is the presence of insulin resistance, a hallmark of type 2 diabetes. This is evaluated using:

- HOMA-IR (Homeostasis Model Assessment of Insulin Resistance):

    HOMA-IR = (Fasting insulin in µU/mL × Fasting glucose in mg/dL) / 405

- Serum insulin levels: Measured by ELISA kits, typically showing reduced values in type 1 models and variable levels in type 2 models, depending on disease progression and insulin sensitivity.
- Pancreatic histopathology: At the end of the study, the pancreas is excised and stained with hematoxylin-eosin or immunohistochemistry for insulin, to visualize islet cell morphology, inflammatory infiltration, and degree of beta-cell damage.

This model allows assessment of multiple drug classes including insulin sensitizers (e.g., metformin, pioglitazone), insulin secretagogues (e.g., glibenclamide), and herbal or novel agents that may modulate oxidative stress or beta-cell regeneration. STZ-induced diabetes remains one of the most reliable, cost-effective, and regulatory-accepted models in preclinical antidiabetic drug development.

4.2.1.2 Alloxan-Induced Diabetes

Mechanism: ROS-Mediated Pancreatic Toxicity

The alloxan-induced diabetes model is one of the classical methods used in experimental pharmacology to evaluate antidiabetic agents, especially for type 1 diabetes mellitus. Alloxan is a pyrimidine derivative that is selectively toxic to pancreatic beta cells, primarily due to its ability to generate reactive oxygen species (ROS) within these cells. The selective uptake of alloxan by beta cells occurs via GLUT2 glucose transporters, which are abundantly expressed on these insulin-secreting cells.

Upon entering the beta cells, alloxan undergoes redox cycling and produces superoxide radicals, hydrogen peroxide, and hydroxyl ions, all of which contribute to oxidative damage to cellular membranes and DNA. This leads to cell membrane disruption, mitochondrial dysfunction, and irreversible beta-cell necrosis, resulting in a marked reduction in insulin secretion and subsequent hyperglycemia.

Typically, adult Wistar rats (180–250 g) or Swiss albino mice are fasted overnight (12–16 hours), and alloxan is freshly prepared in cold sterile normal saline or citrate buffer (pH 4.5). It is administered as a single intraperitoneal or intravenous dose, commonly at:

- 150 mg/kg (IP) in rats
- 90–120 mg/kg (IP) in mice

Because alloxan initially causes a transient release of insulin from partially damaged beta cells, animals may experience hypoglycemia within 1–2 hours of dosing. To counter this and prevent mortality,

5% glucose solution is administered orally or intraperitoneally for the next 24 hours. Hyperglycemia typically stabilizes after 48–72 hours, and blood glucose levels are then checked using glucometer or enzymatic assays.

Rats with fasting blood glucose levels above 200 mg/dL (in some cases, thresholds are set at 250 mg/dL) are considered diabetic and suitable for further study. This model provides a simple and reproducible means of inducing insulin-deficient diabetes, suitable for testing agents that either mimic insulin, enhance insulin release, or protect beta cells.

Glucose Tolerance Test

The oral glucose tolerance test (OGTT) is commonly performed in alloxan-induced diabetic animals to evaluate the ability of test compounds to improve glucose handling and insulin responsiveness. This is especially important for screening herbal products, insulin mimetics, and insulin secretagogues.

The procedure involves fasting the animals for 12 hours, followed by oral administration of glucose at a dose of 2 g/kg body weight. Blood samples are collected from the tail vein at 0 (fasting), 30, 60, 90, and 120 minutes post-glucose administration. Plasma or serum glucose levels are measured using either glucometer or glucose oxidase-peroxidase (GOD-POD) method.

The area under the curve (AUC) for glucose concentration over time is calculated to quantify glucose tolerance:

$$AUC = \Sigma\ [(G_1 + G_2) \times (t_2 - t_1) / 2]$$

Where G_1 and G_2 are glucose levels at times t_1 and t_2, respectively. A lower AUC in the treatment group compared to the diabetic control indicates improved glucose clearance and is suggestive of antidiabetic activity.

This model is suitable for evaluating natural compounds, antioxidants, and traditional formulations that may possess beta-cell protective, insulinotropic, or free radical scavenging properties. When combined with pancreatic histopathology and insulin assays, the alloxan model offers a complete evaluation platform for insulin-dependent diabetes therapeutics.

4.2.1.3 Parameters for Anti-Diabetic Activity

Fasting Blood Glucose and Oral Glucose Tolerance Test (OGTT)

Fasting blood glucose (FBG) is the most fundamental parameter used to assess the diabetic state and the effect of antidiabetic agents. In preclinical models like STZ- or alloxan-induced diabetes, animals are fasted overnight for 12–16 hours, and blood is collected from the tail vein, retro-orbital plexus, or saphenous vein. Glucose levels are estimated using glucometers calibrated for small animals or through colorimetric enzymatic assays (glucose oxidase–peroxidase method).

In healthy rats, FBG values typically range from 80 to 120 mg/dL, while in diabetic animals, levels exceed 200 mg/dL. A statistically significant reduction in FBG levels after administration of the test drug for a specified duration (e.g., 7–28 days) indicates hypoglycemic or antihyperglycemic activity.

The Oral Glucose Tolerance Test (OGTT) evaluates the animal's ability to metabolize an oral glucose load. After fasting, animals receive 2 g/kg of glucose orally, and blood glucose levels are measured at 0, 30, 60, 90, and 120 minutes. The area under the curve (AUC) is calculated using the trapezoidal rule, and a reduction in AUC compared to diabetic controls suggests improved glucose tolerance and insulin action.

HbA1c (Glycated Hemoglobin)

Hemoglobin A1c (HbA1c) is a long-term marker that reflects the average blood glucose levels over the past 2–3 weeks in rodents. It is formed by non-enzymatic glycation of hemoglobin in circulating red blood cells. Since the lifespan of a rat RBC is about 45–60 days, changes in HbA1c can be observed over a few weeks in experimental studies.

Normal HbA1c values in rats range between 3% to 6%, while diabetic animals exhibit levels exceeding 8% to 10%, depending on the severity of hyperglycemia. Commercial ELISA kits or ion-exchange HPLC methods are used for estimation. A significant reduction in HbA1c in treated animals confirms sustained antihyperglycemic efficacy of the test compound.

Insulin Levels

Serum insulin levels provide insight into the secretory function of pancreatic beta cells and the mechanism of drug action—whether the compound is insulinotropic (stimulating insulin release) or acts independently of insulin. Blood samples are collected under fasting conditions, and insulin is measured using species-specific ELISA kits.

- In type 1 diabetic models, insulin levels are markedly reduced.
- In type 2 models, insulin may be normal or elevated, depending on insulin resistance.

Improvement in insulin levels following treatment with a test drug may suggest beta-cell protection, regeneration, or insulin secretagogue action.

HOMA Index (Homeostatic Model Assessment)

The HOMA-IR (insulin resistance) and HOMA-β (beta-cell function) indices are calculated using fasting glucose and insulin levels to estimate insulin sensitivity and beta-cell function.

HOMA-IR is calculated by the formula:

HOMA-IR = (Fasting insulin in µU/mL × Fasting glucose in mg/dL) / 405

Higher HOMA-IR values indicate greater insulin resistance. A reduction in HOMA-IR after treatment reflects improvement in insulin sensitivity.

In studies where insulin sensitizers like metformin or pioglitazone are tested, HOMA-IR is a sensitive parameter to confirm their mechanism of action.

Together, these parameters—FBG, OGTT, HbA1c, insulin levels, and HOMA index—offer a comprehensive assessment of the antidiabetic efficacy, duration of action, and possible mechanism of investigational compounds. They allow differentiation between insulin-dependent and insulin-independent agents and help correlate biochemical and pharmacodynamic outcomes in preclinical models.

4.2.2.1 Triton WR-1339-Induced Hyperlipidemia

Mechanism of Lipoprotein Lipase Inhibition

The Triton WR-1339-induced hyperlipidemia model is a well-established acute pharmacological tool for evaluating the lipid-lowering potential of investigational antidyslipidemic agents, especially those targeting cholesterol and triglyceride metabolism. Triton WR-1339, chemically known as Tyloxapol, is a nonionic surfactant that induces hyperlipidemia by inhibiting lipoprotein lipase (LPL)—the key enzyme responsible for hydrolysis and clearance of plasma triglyceride-rich lipoproteins.

Lipoprotein lipase is bound to the endothelial surface of capillaries in adipose tissue and muscle, and it normally facilitates the breakdown of very low-density lipoproteins (VLDL) and chylomicrons into free fatty acids and glycerol. Triton interferes with this enzymatic activity by physically blocking the binding of lipoproteins to the enzyme, resulting in accumulation of triglycerides and cholesterol in the blood within hours of administration.

This model allows observation of early hyperlipidemic effects without the need for long dietary interventions and is particularly useful for compounds that reduce lipid synthesis, enhance lipolysis, or increase LDL clearance.

Triton WR-1339 is administered as a single intraperitoneal injection at 300 mg/kg in rats, or intravenously at 200 mg/kg in mice, freshly prepared in normal saline and warmed to body temperature to ensure solubility. The test drug or standard antidyslipidemic agent is typically given 30 minutes before or immediately after Triton injection to evaluate its ability to prevent or reverse acute lipid rise.

Timeline and Lipid Profile Assessment

Following Triton administration, a time-dependent increase in plasma total cholesterol, triglycerides, LDL-C, and VLDL-C is observed, usually peaking within 18 to 24 hours. For this reason, blood samples are collected at baseline and 24 hours post-Triton administration, typically via retro-orbital or tail vein puncture, under mild anesthesia.

Blood is centrifuged at 3000 rpm for 10 minutes, and serum is analyzed for the following lipid parameters using enzymatic colorimetric kits:

- Total cholesterol (TC)
- Triglycerides (TG)
- High-density lipoprotein cholesterol (HDL-C)
- Low-density lipoprotein cholesterol (LDL-C) (calculated using Friedewald formula)
- Very low-density lipoprotein (VLDL-C) = TG/5 (approximation in mg/dL)

The lipid-lowering efficacy of the test drug is determined by comparing post-treatment levels with Triton-only controls. A significant reduction in serum cholesterol and triglycerides, along with restoration of HDL-C levels, indicates promising antidyslipidemic activity.

Additionally, ratios such as:

- TC/HDL-C
- LDL-C/HDL-C
- Atherogenic Index (log[TG/HDL-C])

are calculated to evaluate the cardioprotective potential of the compound.

A standard drug like simvastatin (10 mg/kg), atorvastatin (5–10 mg/kg), or fenofibrate (30–50 mg/kg) is used as a reference control to validate the model.

In conclusion, the Triton WR-1339 model provides a rapid and reproducible approach for screening antihyperlipidemic agents, particularly in the early stages of drug discovery, by producing transient yet significant dyslipidemia and allowing quantification of lipid-lowering effects within a short experimental timeline.

4.2.2.2 High Cholesterol Diet Model

Diet Formulation and Duration

The high cholesterol diet (HCD) model is a widely used preclinical tool to induce hyperlipidemia and simulate dyslipidemic conditions resembling human metabolic syndrome. It allows long-term evaluation of antidyslipidemic drugs, especially those targeting cholesterol biosynthesis, lipoprotein clearance, and hepatic lipid regulation. This model is particularly effective in rats, rabbits, or genetically modified mice that are prone to lipid accumulation and metabolic disturbances.

The diet is typically formulated by supplementing the standard laboratory feed with additional cholesterol and saturated fats. A commonly used HCD in rats contains 1–2% pure cholesterol, 10–20% coconut oil or lard, and sometimes 0.5% cholic acid to enhance intestinal absorption of lipids. In rabbits, diets may include 0.5–1% cholesterol and 3–5% peanut or corn oil. The total feeding period ranges from 4 to 12 weeks depending on the species and study objectives. During this time, animals are monitored weekly for weight, food intake, and signs of fatty liver or lethargy.

This prolonged dietary challenge leads to a progressive increase in serum cholesterol, low-density lipoproteins (LDL), triglycerides, and very low-density lipoproteins (VLDL), along with a decrease in protective high-density lipoproteins (HDL). The gradual lipid accumulation makes this model suitable for testing agents that act on lipid absorption, biosynthesis, hepatic processing, or reverse cholesterol transport.

Test compounds are administered orally or intraperitoneally along with the high cholesterol diet, either from the beginning (preventive protocol) or after dyslipidemia is established (therapeutic protocol). Standard reference drugs include atorvastatin, simvastatin, or ezetimibe.

Atherogenic Index and Hepatic Lipid Content

After the treatment period, blood samples are collected under fasting conditions via retro-orbital puncture or cardiac puncture. Serum is separated and analyzed for lipid profile parameters including total cholesterol, triglycerides, LDL, HDL, and VLDL. The atherogenic index, which predicts cardiovascular risk, is calculated using the following formulas:

Atherogenic index = log (triglycerides / HDL-C)

Alternatively, total cholesterol to HDL-C ratio or LDL-C to HDL-C ratio may also be calculated. An increase in these ratios indicates elevated risk of atherosclerosis, whereas a decrease following treatment reflects antidyslipidemic efficacy.

At necropsy, the liver is dissected, weighed, and preserved for biochemical analysis and histology. For hepatic lipid quantification, liver samples are homogenized in chloroform-methanol solution (2:1 v/v) and centrifuged. The organic phase is collected, evaporated, and the residue is dissolved in isopropanol for measurement of total cholesterol and triglycerides using colorimetric assay kits. Accumulation of hepatic cholesterol and triglycerides is a hallmark of diet-induced steatosis and reflects the systemic burden of dyslipidemia.

Histological analysis of liver sections stained with hematoxylin and eosin or Oil Red O helps in visualizing lipid droplets, hepatocyte ballooning, and early signs of fatty liver disease. Reduction in hepatic lipid content, normalization of atherogenic index, and improvement in serum lipid profile collectively establish the lipid-lowering potential of the test compound in this model.

4.2.2.3 Lipid Profile Analysis

Total Cholesterol, HDL, LDL, VLDL, Triglycerides

Lipid profile analysis is a critical component in evaluating the efficacy of antidyslipidemic agents in both acute and chronic preclinical models of hyperlipidemia. The profile includes quantitative estimation of serum total cholesterol, triglycerides, high-density lipoprotein (HDL), low-density lipoprotein (LDL), and very low-density lipoprotein (VLDL). These parameters provide comprehensive insight into lipid metabolism and the balance between atherogenic and protective lipoproteins.

Total cholesterol refers to the sum of cholesterol carried by all lipoproteins in circulation. HDL, often referred to as good cholesterol, promotes reverse cholesterol transport and is cardioprotective. LDL is the primary carrier of cholesterol to peripheral tissues and its elevation is a major risk factor for atherosclerosis. VLDL mainly carries triglycerides and contributes to the formation of small, dense LDL particles. Triglycerides are the main form of stored fat in the body and are elevated in various metabolic disorders.

In preclinical studies, blood samples are collected from fasted animals after treatment using retro-orbital, tail vein, or cardiac puncture methods. The blood is centrifuged to separate serum or plasma, and lipid parameters are measured using validated laboratory protocols.

Enzymatic Colorimetric Assays

Enzymatic colorimetric methods are the most widely used and reliable techniques for lipid estimation in preclinical pharmacology. These methods are based on specific enzyme reactions followed by color development, which is proportional to the concentration of the analyte. The assays are compatible with automated analyzers as well as manual spectrophotometry.

Total cholesterol is measured by enzymatic hydrolysis using cholesterol esterase, followed by oxidation using cholesterol oxidase. The resultant hydrogen peroxide reacts with a chromogen to produce a colored compound measured at 500–520 nm.

Triglycerides are quantified by lipase-mediated hydrolysis to glycerol, followed by a series of enzymatic reactions leading to a chromogenic endpoint. The final absorbance is read at 505–550 nm.

HDL cholesterol is measured after selective precipitation of LDL and VLDL using phosphotungstate and magnesium chloride. The supernatant is then analyzed by the cholesterol oxidase method. LDL and VLDL concentrations are often calculated using the Friedewald formula:

LDL-C = Total cholesterol − HDL-C − (Triglycerides / 5)

This equation is valid when triglyceride levels are below 400 mg/dL. For higher values, direct LDL measurement methods or ultracentrifugation may be used.

These biochemical values, when compared between control, hyperlipidemic, and treated groups, allow the calculation of therapeutic response. Parameters such as percent reduction in LDL, increase in HDL, and normalization of triglycerides provide evidence for the lipid-modifying action of the test compound. Regular monitoring of lipid profile, along with histological and inflammatory biomarkers, strengthens the pharmacodynamic assessment of antidyslipidemic agents.

4.3.1.1 Ehrlich Ascites Carcinoma (EAC)

Inoculation Route, Cell Count, and Ascitic Fluid Analysis

The Ehrlich Ascites Carcinoma (EAC) model is a widely employed in vivo system for evaluating the antitumor potential of experimental drug candidates. EAC is an undifferentiated carcinoma that can grow both in solid and ascitic forms, making it highly versatile for screening drugs with cytotoxic, antiproliferative, or apoptosis-inducing properties. This model is frequently used in Swiss albino mice, as they are immunocompetent and offer a predictable tumor growth pattern.

In the ascitic form, EAC cells are maintained by serial intraperitoneal (IP) transplantation in mice. Donor mice with established ascites (typically 8–10 days after tumor cell injection) are euthanized under mild anesthesia. The peritoneal cavity is opened, and the ascitic fluid containing viable tumor cells is aspirated under sterile conditions. The collected fluid is diluted with sterile isotonic saline or phosphate-buffered saline (PBS), and the viable cell count is determined using a hemocytometer with trypan blue dye exclusion to differentiate live from dead cells.

A standard inoculum of 1×10^6 to 2×10^6 viable EAC cells in 0.2 mL is injected intraperitoneally into each experimental mouse. The test drug is typically administered via IP, oral, or intravenous route starting from the second or third day post-inoculation and continued for 9–14 days, depending on the experimental design.

On the final day, animals are sacrificed under anesthesia, and the ascitic fluid is collected and measured. Key parameters evaluated include:

- Volume of ascitic fluid: Directly reflects tumor burden.
- Packed cell volume: Measured after centrifugation at 3000 rpm for 10 minutes.
- Viable and non-viable tumor cell counts: Assessed by trypan blue staining.
- Cell morphology: Examined under a light microscope to assess signs of apoptosis or cytoplasmic vacuolation.

Survival Time and Tumor Inhibition Rate

One of the most critical endpoints in EAC studies is mean survival time (MST), which provides an overall measure of therapeutic benefit. Animals are monitored daily for signs of ascites accumulation, distress, and survival, and the number of days each mouse survives is recorded. The MST is calculated using the formula:

MST = Σ (individual survival days) / total number of animals in group

The increase in lifespan (% ILS) is calculated by comparing treated animals with the tumor control group using the formula:

% ILS = [(MST of treated group − MST of control group) / MST of control group] × 100

A value greater than 25% is generally considered significant for antitumor activity.

Another critical parameter is the tumor growth inhibition rate, which is calculated based on reduction in ascitic fluid volume or viable cell count in treated animals compared to control:

Tumor Inhibition (%) = [(Control − Treated) / Control] × 100

These data help determine whether the compound has cytostatic (growth inhibition) or cytotoxic (cell-killing) effects. Additionally, some studies evaluate hematological parameters (WBC count, RBC count, hemoglobin) and liver/kidney function tests to assess drug-induced systemic toxicity.

The EAC model, due to its rapid growth kinetics, reproducibility, and responsiveness to a wide range of anticancer agents, remains a foundational screening tool for early-stage antitumor drug development.

4.3.1.2 Dalton's Lymphoma Ascites (DLA)

Evaluation of Body Weight and Abdominal Distension

Dalton's Lymphoma Ascites (DLA) is another extensively used transplantable murine tumor model for evaluating the antineoplastic activity of investigational compounds. It originates from a spontaneous lymphoid tumor in mice and proliferates rapidly when introduced intraperitoneally. The DLA model offers a practical and sensitive platform for testing cytotoxic agents, especially in the early phases of preclinical screening.

DLA cells are maintained in Swiss albino mice by serial intraperitoneal passages. For tumor induction, ascitic fluid containing viable DLA cells is harvested from donor mice, diluted in sterile saline or PBS, and the number of viable cells is counted using a hemocytometer. A standard inoculum of 1×10^6 to 2×10^6 viable cells in 0.1 to 0.2 mL is injected intraperitoneally into each mouse.

Within 6 to 8 days, the tumor-bearing animals begin to show abdominal swelling, increased body weight, and signs of fluid accumulation in the peritoneal cavity due to tumor growth. These are measured as key parameters of tumor progression. Body weight is recorded at baseline and at regular intervals (every 2–3 days), using a digital balance. Abdominal girth or circumference is measured using a flexible tape or caliper at the same intervals to quantify ascitic tumor growth.

A progressive increase in these parameters indicates uncontrolled tumor cell proliferation and ascites formation. Test drugs are usually administered starting from day 2 or 3 post-inoculation for a total duration of 10 to 14 days. A significant reduction in weight gain and abdominal distension in the treated group, compared to tumor control, reflects effective tumor inhibition.

Cell Viability (Trypan Blue Exclusion)

On the final day of the experiment or when animals are sacrificed, ascitic fluid is collected from the peritoneal cavity under mild anesthesia. The volume of fluid is measured, and the sample is centrifuged to separate tumor cells from the supernatant. The cell pellet is resuspended in PBS or saline for cell viability analysis.

Cell viability is assessed using the trypan blue exclusion method, which differentiates live (unstained) cells from dead (blue-stained) cells. A small aliquot of the cell suspension is mixed with 0.4% trypan blue dye in a 1:1 ratio and loaded into a hemocytometer. Under a light microscope, at least 200 cells are counted to determine the percentage of viable cells using the formula:

Cell Viability (%) = (Number of viable cells / Total number of cells) × 100

A decrease in the percentage of viable cells in the treated group indicates the cytotoxic effect of the test compound. In addition, the total viable cell count is calculated and compared to control to assess tumor suppression quantitatively.

The DLA model allows for rapid, cost-effective screening of potential antitumor agents. It is also frequently used to evaluate adjunct parameters such as hematological profiles, liver and kidney function, and oxidative stress markers, providing a comprehensive preclinical toxicity and efficacy profile for novel anticancer drugs.

4.3.2.1 Xenograft Models

Human Cancer Cell Lines in Immunodeficient Mice

Xenograft models involve the transplantation of human cancer cell lines into immunodeficient mice, making them an essential tool for evaluating the in vivo efficacy of anticancer drugs against human tumors. These models provide a more clinically relevant setting than murine tumor models, as they reflect human tumor histology, molecular pathways, and drug responsiveness. The immunodeficient status of the host animals, such as nude (athymic) mice or SCID (severe combined immunodeficient) mice, is critical to prevent rejection of the human tumor cells.

Human tumor cell lines from different tissue origins (e.g., MCF-7 for breast cancer, A549 for lung cancer, HT-29 for colon cancer, HeLa for cervical cancer) are cultured in vitro under sterile conditions using appropriate media like RPMI-1640 or DMEM supplemented with 10% fetal bovine serum. Once the cells reach logarithmic growth phase, they are harvested, counted, and resuspended in sterile PBS or Matrigel.

A suspension of 1×10^6 to 5×10^6 viable cells in 0.1–0.2 mL is injected subcutaneously into the flank or dorsal region of each mouse using a sterile 26G needle. The animals are monitored for tumor take, which typically occurs within 7 to 14 days, depending on the cell line. Once tumors become palpable (approximately 100 mm^3), treatment with test compounds is initiated, typically for 2 to 4 weeks, depending on the tumor growth rate and drug protocol.

The xenograft model allows evaluation of cytostatic effects, cytotoxicity, and anti-angiogenic activity of investigational agents. Moreover, since the tumors are of human origin, these models offer a bridge between rodent and human systems, often correlating better with clinical efficacy data.

Tumor Volume Measurement: $V = (W^2 \times L)/2$

Tumor volume is the primary endpoint in xenograft studies, reflecting the effectiveness of a test compound in suppressing tumor growth. Tumors are measured using digital Vernier calipers every 2–3 days. The two dimensions recorded are:

- W = Width of the tumor (smaller dimension)
- L = Length of the tumor (larger dimension)

The tumor volume (V) is calculated using the following empirical formula:

$V = (W^2 \times L) / 2$

This formula assumes an ellipsoid shape of the tumor and gives results in cubic millimeters (mm^3). Serial measurements allow plotting of tumor growth curves and calculation of tumor growth inhibition (TGI%), defined as:

TGI (%) = [(Mean tumor volume of control − Mean tumor volume of treated) / Mean tumor volume of control] × 100

At the end of the study, tumors are excised, weighed, and preserved for histopathological analysis to assess changes in cell density, mitotic index, necrosis, and angiogenesis markers. In addition, molecular assays such as TUNEL staining for apoptosis or Ki-67 immunostaining for proliferation may be performed.

The xenograft model, especially when combined with bioluminescent imaging or fluorescent-labeled cells, allows for real-time monitoring of tumor progression, making it a powerful tool in modern preclinical oncology research.

4.3.2.2 Syngeneic Tumor Models

Mouse-Derived Tumor Cells in Immunocompetent Hosts

Syngeneic tumor models are developed by implanting mouse-derived tumor cell lines into genetically identical or compatible immunocompetent mice. Unlike xenograft models, which require immunodeficient animals to prevent rejection of human cells, syngeneic models preserve a fully functional immune system, allowing the study of tumor–immune system interactions. This makes them particularly valuable for evaluating immunotherapies, immune checkpoint inhibitors, cancer vaccines, and anti-inflammatory agents.

Commonly used syngeneic tumor cell lines include:

- B16-F10 (melanoma) in C57BL/6 mice
- 4T1 (breast carcinoma) in BALB/c mice
- LLC1 (Lewis lung carcinoma) in C57BL/6 mice
- CT26 (colon carcinoma) in BALB/c mice

The selected cell line is cultured under sterile conditions, harvested at the logarithmic growth phase, and suspended in PBS or culture medium. A dose of 1×10^5 to 1×10^6 viable cells in 0.1–0.2 mL is injected subcutaneously, intradermally, or orthotopically (into the organ of origin) depending on the tumor type and experimental objective.

Tumor growth is monitored every 2–3 days using calipers, and tumor volume is calculated using the formula:

Tumor volume (mm³) = (W² × L) / 2

The growth kinetics in syngeneic models are generally faster than xenografts, and most tumors reach endpoint volumes (1000–2000 mm³) within 2–4 weeks. Mice are randomized into treatment groups once tumors are palpable, and test drugs or biological agents are administered via appropriate routes.

Immune Modulation Studies

A key advantage of syngeneic models is their ability to replicate intact host immune responses, including both innate and adaptive immune components. This allows comprehensive analysis of how the test compound influences:

- T cell infiltration ($CD4^+$, $CD8^+$ subsets)
- Regulatory T cells (Tregs)
- Myeloid-derived suppressor cells (MDSCs)
- Cytokine profiles (e.g., IFN-γ, IL-2, IL-10, TNF-α)
- Macrophage polarization (M1/M2 ratio)

Tumors and spleens are harvested at the end of the study for flow cytometry, ELISA, or qPCR-based analysis of immune markers. Histological and immunohistochemical techniques (e.g., CD3, PD-L1, FOXP3 staining) help visualize immune infiltration and tumor immune evasion mechanisms.

Syngeneic models also allow evaluation of tumor microenvironment modulation, angiogenesis inhibition, and metastasis, particularly in models like 4T1, which naturally metastasizes to the lungs.

Because they reflect both tumor biology and host immunity, syngeneic models are essential in the early stages of immuno-oncology research and are often used in combination with checkpoint inhibitors (e.g., anti-PD-1, anti-CTLA-4) to assess therapeutic synergy and resistance mechanisms.

4.3.3.1 Tumor Volume and Growth Inhibition

Caliper Measurements and Graphical Analysis

Tumor volume measurement is a fundamental parameter used to assess the cytotoxic and therapeutic efficacy of anticancer compounds in both xenograft and syngeneic tumor models. Regular monitoring of tumor size provides a non-invasive, quantitative method for evaluating the antiproliferative effect of test drugs and the overall progression of the disease.

After tumor induction, measurements are taken using a digital Vernier caliper at consistent intervals (usually every 2 or 3 days). Two perpendicular dimensions are recorded for each tumor:

- W (width): the shortest diameter
- L (length): the longest diameter

The tumor volume (V) is then calculated using the standard ellipsoidal formula:

$V = (W^2 \times L) / 2$

This formula assumes the tumor approximates an ellipsoid shape and is widely accepted for its simplicity and accuracy in preclinical oncology studies. Volumes are expressed in cubic millimeters (mm^3).

The data collected over time are plotted on a graph, with tumor volume on the Y-axis and time (in days) on the X-axis. Separate curves are generated for each group—control, standard treatment, and test drug groups. This allows visual comparison of tumor growth trends, rate of expansion, and degree of inhibition.

To quantify therapeutic impact, tumor growth inhibition (TGI) is calculated at the end of the study using the formula:

TGI (%) = [(Mean tumor volume of control group − Mean tumor volume of treated group) / Mean tumor volume of control group] × 100

In general, a TGI value of above 50% is considered pharmacologically significant, while values over 70% indicate strong cytotoxic or cytostatic activity. Some protocols also include tumor doubling time, relative tumor volume, and growth delay time as additional endpoints.

These measurements are often complemented by tumor weight at necropsy, histopathological evaluation, and molecular assays to confirm the mechanism of action and extent of tumor necrosis, proliferation, and apoptosis. Together, tumor volume analysis and graphical interpretation form the core of in vivo anticancer drug evaluation, helping researchers to distinguish between partially effective, ineffective, and highly potent compounds during drug development.

4.3.3.3 Hematological and Biochemical Markers

WBC, RBC, Hemoglobin, ALT, AST

Evaluation of hematological and biochemical markers is essential for understanding both the therapeutic efficacy and the systemic toxicity of anticancer agents in preclinical models. While tumor volume and survival are primary endpoints, these biomarkers offer additional insight into the physiological impact of treatment, especially on the bone marrow, liver, and immune system.

Hematological parameters such as white blood cell (WBC) count, red blood cell (RBC) count, and hemoglobin concentration are critical indicators of drug-induced myelosuppression or recovery. Blood samples are collected from treated and control animals, usually via retro-orbital or cardiac puncture under anesthesia. The following markers are typically measured using an automated hematology analyzer or manual counting methods:

- WBC count: A decrease may indicate myelosuppression, which is common with cytotoxic drugs. A significant drop below the physiological range suggests immunosuppression, while a marked increase may reflect inflammation or leukemic response.
- RBC count and hemoglobin: These values assess the oxygen-carrying capacity and erythropoietic function. A fall in RBC or hemoglobin may result from hemorrhage, hemolysis, or bone marrow suppression caused by aggressive chemotherapy.

In tumor-bearing animals, untreated controls often show disrupted hematological profiles due to tumor-related cachexia, immune exhaustion, or organ infiltration. An effective drug should ideally normalize these values without causing undue suppression.

Biochemical markers, especially liver enzymes such as alanine aminotransferase (ALT) and aspartate aminotransferase (AST), are routinely assessed to monitor hepatic function and toxicity. Elevated ALT and AST levels in serum indicate hepatocellular injury, which may be induced by the test compound or result from tumor-related metabolic burden.

The serum is separated from collected blood samples by centrifugation at 3000 rpm for 10 minutes and analyzed using commercial diagnostic kits based on colorimetric or kinetic methods. Normal ranges for rats and mice must be used for interpretation, as these values vary significantly from human references.

ALT and AST are particularly important in distinguishing between safe and hepatotoxic molecules, and they often accompany histopathological analysis of liver tissue for confirmation. Prolonged elevation of these enzymes, along with changes in total protein, albumin, or bilirubin, may warrant dose adjustment or drug reformulation.

Together, these hematological and biochemical markers serve as important secondary endpoints that complement tumor volume and survival data, providing a comprehensive safety and efficacy profile of investigational anticancer agents. They help in making informed decisions during dose selection and progression to clinical phases.

4.4.1.1 Carbon Tetrachloride (CCl_4)-Induced Liver Injury

Mechanism: Free Radical-Mediated Lipid Peroxidation

The carbon tetrachloride (CCl_4)-induced liver injury model is one of the most widely used experimental methods to study hepatoprotective effects of pharmacological agents. CCl_4 is a hepatotoxin that generates reactive free radicals, leading to oxidative stress, lipid peroxidation, and hepatic cellular damage, mimicking features of acute liver injury observed in humans.

Once administered, CCl_4 is metabolized by the cytochrome P450 enzyme system, particularly the CYP2E1 isoenzyme, in the hepatocytes. This metabolism produces trichloromethyl free radicals ($\bullet CCl_3$) and trichloromethyl peroxyl radicals ($\bullet OOCCl_3$). These radicals bind covalently to cellular macromolecules, triggering a chain reaction that damages membrane lipids, proteins, and nucleic acids. The result is hepatocellular necrosis, inflammation, and increased liver enzyme levels in the blood.

Histopathologically, CCl_4 causes centrilobular necrosis, ballooning degeneration, and fatty changes in liver tissues. Biochemically, it elevates serum levels of liver enzymes, disrupts antioxidant balance, and reduces hepatic glutathione levels.

Dose and Route (Usually 1 mL/kg IP in 1:1 Olive Oil)

To induce liver injury in rats or mice, CCl_4 is dissolved in olive oil in a 1:1 ratio to reduce its volatility and ease of handling. The standard dose for rats is 1 mL/kg body weight, administered intraperitoneally (IP). A single dose produces acute hepatotoxicity within 24 to 48 hours, whereas repeated dosing over 7 to 14 days may be used to induce sub-chronic liver damage.

Animals are usually fasted overnight before administration to enhance susceptibility to hepatotoxins. After CCl_4 exposure, the test compound (hepatoprotective agent) is administered either prophylactically (before or with CCl_4) or therapeutically (after liver injury is induced).

At the end of the experiment, animals are euthanized, and blood is collected for serum biochemical analysis, while liver tissue is harvested for histopathological examination and oxidative stress assays. Key indicators of hepatoprotection include:

- Reduction in ALT, AST, ALP, and bilirubin levels
- Restoration of hepatic antioxidant enzymes (e.g., SOD, catalase, glutathione)
- Preservation of liver architecture in histology

This model remains a gold standard for evaluating hepatoprotective activity of herbal extracts, natural compounds, and synthetic molecules, and is often used for comparison with standard drugs such as silymarin or N-acetylcysteine.

4.4.1.2 Paracetamol-Induced Hepatotoxicity

Overdose Model and Threshold Doses

Paracetamol-induced hepatotoxicity is a widely accepted and clinically relevant model used to evaluate the hepatoprotective potential of investigational drugs. Paracetamol, also known as acetaminophen, is a common over-the-counter analgesic and antipyretic. However, at high doses, it can cause acute liver damage due to the formation of a toxic metabolite called N-acetyl-p-benzoquinone imine (NAPQI).

In normal therapeutic doses, paracetamol is primarily metabolized by glucuronidation and sulfation, forming water-soluble, non-toxic metabolites that are excreted in urine. A small fraction is metabolized by cytochrome P450 enzymes, especially CYP2E1, into NAPQI. Under normal conditions, NAPQI is detoxified by conjugation with glutathione (GSH). However, during an overdose, glutathione reserves are depleted, and excess NAPQI binds to cellular proteins and lipids, resulting in oxidative stress, mitochondrial dysfunction, and cell death.

To induce hepatotoxicity in laboratory animals like Wistar rats or Swiss albino mice, a single oral or intraperitoneal dose of paracetamol is given, typically in the range of:

- 500 to 1000 mg/kg in rats
- 250 to 500 mg/kg in mice

Animals are usually fasted for 12–16 hours before dosing to enhance the toxic effect. Signs of liver damage become evident within 24 to 48 hours after administration, making this a rapid and efficient model for acute toxicity studies.

Hepatic Necrosis and Mitochondrial Damage

Following an overdose, NAPQI accumulation results in centrilobular hepatic necrosis, which can be confirmed histologically. The injury begins in the zone 3 region of the hepatic lobule, which is rich in CYP450 enzymes and relatively poor in oxygen supply, making it highly vulnerable to oxidative stress.

Histological examination of liver tissue typically reveals:

- Ballooning degeneration of hepatocytes
- Sinusoidal congestion
- Pyknotic nuclei
- Infiltration of inflammatory cells

Biochemically, hepatotoxicity is confirmed by elevated serum levels of:

- Alanine aminotransferase (ALT)
- Aspartate aminotransferase (AST)
- Alkaline phosphatase (ALP)
- Total and direct bilirubin

Mitochondrial dysfunction is evidenced by decreased ATP levels, reduced mitochondrial membrane potential, and increased lipid peroxidation in hepatic tissues. Assays for malondialdehyde (MDA), glutathione (GSH), and superoxide dismutase (SOD) are commonly used to evaluate oxidative stress status.

In hepatoprotective studies, the test compound is administered either before (preventive model) or after (curative model) paracetamol exposure. A successful hepatoprotective agent should restore normal liver enzyme levels, reduce histopathological damage, and improve antioxidant enzyme activity. Standard reference compounds include silymarin (100 mg/kg orally) or N-acetylcysteine, which act by replenishing glutathione stores and neutralizing NAPQI.

This model closely simulates human drug-induced liver injury and is extensively used to assess the mechanism and efficacy of liver-protecting agents in preclinical research.

4.4.2.1 Liver Enzymes

ALT, AST, ALP, GGT

Assessment of liver enzyme levels is fundamental in determining the extent of hepatocellular injury and evaluating the hepatoprotective potential of experimental drugs in preclinical models. These enzymes are located in the hepatocytes or biliary epithelium, and their leakage into the bloodstream occurs when liver cells are damaged by toxicants like carbon tetrachloride, paracetamol, or alcohol. Their quantification provides a reliable and non-invasive biochemical marker of liver function.

Alanine aminotransferase (ALT) is a cytosolic enzyme that plays a role in amino acid metabolism by converting alanine to pyruvate. It is considered the most specific marker for liver injury, as it is predominantly found in hepatocytes. When liver cells are damaged, ALT is released into circulation, and elevated levels in serum indicate hepatocellular necrosis or inflammation. In healthy rats, normal ALT levels usually range from 30 to 60 IU/L, while hepatotoxicity can raise it several fold depending on the extent of damage.

Aspartate aminotransferase (AST) is present in both the cytosol and mitochondria of liver cells but also exists in cardiac and skeletal muscle tissues. While it is less specific to the liver than ALT, it serves as a valuable marker in conjunction with ALT. The AST to ALT ratio is sometimes used to distinguish between different patterns of liver injury, although in rodents this ratio is not always consistent due to species variation.

Alkaline phosphatase (ALP) is a membrane-bound enzyme found in the bile canalicular surface of hepatocytes and in the epithelium of bile ducts. Elevated ALP levels suggest cholestasis, bile duct obstruction, or infiltrative liver disease, and it complements transaminase data when evaluating hepatobiliary function. In rats, normal ALP values are typically less than 150 IU/L, but may vary with age, sex, and strain.

Gamma-glutamyl transferase (GGT) is another enzyme associated with bile ducts and is considered a marker of biliary dysfunction and hepatobiliary obstruction. It is particularly useful in models that induce cholestasis or prolonged bile retention. GGT levels are usually low in normal rodents, and marked elevation is a strong indicator of biliary involvement.

These enzymes are estimated using commercially available colorimetric or kinetic assay kits that rely on specific substrate conversion producing a measurable color change. Blood samples are collected from fasted animals via tail vein or retro-orbital plexus, and serum is separated for analysis. Comparing the enzyme levels between treated and control groups helps determine the extent of hepatic protection or injury.

Together, ALT, AST, ALP, and GGT form the core biochemical parameters for liver function assessment in preclinical studies. A significant reduction in their levels in drug-treated animals, compared to toxin-treated controls, indicates a protective effect and supports the further development of the test compound as a potential hepatoprotective agent.

4.4.2.2 Bilirubin and Protein Estimations

Total and Direct Bilirubin, Albumin, Globulin

Estimation of bilirubin and serum proteins is essential for assessing hepatic synthetic and excretory function, particularly in preclinical studies involving hepatotoxicity and hepatoprotective screening. These parameters provide insight into the severity and type of liver injury, including hepatocellular damage, cholestasis, and impaired liver metabolism.

Bilirubin is a breakdown product of heme derived from senescent red blood cells. It exists in two major forms in the blood:

- Unconjugated (indirect) bilirubin, which is lipid-soluble and circulates bound to albumin.
- Conjugated (direct) bilirubin, which is water-soluble and excreted into bile after hepatic conjugation with glucuronic acid.

The total bilirubin level reflects the sum of both forms and is a key indicator of liver excretory capacity. Elevated total bilirubin, particularly with a higher proportion of direct bilirubin, typically indicates hepatic dysfunction or biliary obstruction. Increased indirect bilirubin may suggest hemolysis or impaired hepatic uptake and conjugation.

In healthy rats, total bilirubin levels are typically below 0.5 mg/dL, while experimental hepatotoxicity may raise levels to 1.5–3 mg/dL or more. Estimations are done by diazo-based colorimetric methods where bilirubin reacts with diazotized sulfanilic acid to form azobilirubin, measurable at 540 nm.

Albumin is a major plasma protein synthesized exclusively by hepatocytes. Its concentration reflects the synthetic function of the liver. A decrease in serum albumin levels suggests chronic liver disease, hepatocellular failure, or malnutrition. In rats, normal albumin levels range from 3.5 to 5.0 g/dL. Persistent hypoalbuminemia may contribute to ascites formation and altered drug binding in vivo.

Globulin includes a range of plasma proteins, such as immunoglobulins, clotting factors, and transport proteins. While not synthesized entirely by the liver, many of its components are liver-derived. The albumin-to-globulin (A/G) ratio is a useful index in liver injury models; a reversal of this ratio (A/G < 1) often reflects chronic inflammation or hepatic fibrosis.

Serum total protein, albumin, and globulin concentrations are measured using:

- Biuret method for total protein
- Bromocresol green dye-binding method for albumin
- Globulin is calculated by subtracting albumin from total protein

Assessment of these protein parameters, along with bilirubin, provides a comprehensive view of liver performance in terms of both excretory and biosynthetic activity. Their normalization in drug-treated groups compared to toxin-exposed controls is a strong indicator of hepatoprotective efficacy. These estimations, in conjunction with liver enzymes and histopathology, contribute to a robust interpretation of the test compound's protective potential.

4.4.2.3 Oxidative Stress Markers

MDA, SOD, GSH, CAT

Oxidative stress markers play a central role in evaluating liver damage and the protective effects of pharmacological agents in hepatotoxicity models. Many hepatotoxins, including carbon tetrachloride and paracetamol, exert their toxic effects through the generation of reactive oxygen species, which disturb the antioxidant defense system in hepatocytes. Therefore, measuring both pro-oxidant and antioxidant biomarkers provides critical insight into the extent of cellular damage and the antioxidant potential of test drugs.

Malondialdehyde (MDA) is a reactive aldehyde formed as a by-product of lipid peroxidation when free radicals attack the polyunsaturated fatty acids in cell membranes. Elevated MDA levels are a hallmark of oxidative stress and cellular injury in the liver. It is typically estimated using the thiobarbituric acid reactive substances (TBARS) assay, where MDA reacts with thiobarbituric acid to form a pink chromogen measurable at 532 nm. Increased MDA concentration in liver tissue or serum indicates a higher degree of oxidative lipid damage.

Superoxide dismutase (SOD) is an essential antioxidant enzyme that catalyzes the dismutation of superoxide radicals into hydrogen peroxide and oxygen, thus preventing further free radical propagation. Its activity is measured in liver homogenates using assays based on its ability to inhibit the autoxidation of epinephrine or reduction of nitro blue tetrazolium. A reduction in SOD activity in hepatotoxic models suggests compromised enzymatic defense, while restoration after treatment indicates antioxidant activity of the test compound.

Reduced glutathione (GSH) is a tripeptide present in high concentrations in hepatocytes and plays a major role in detoxification and neutralization of peroxides and free radicals. It also participates in conjugation reactions essential for drug metabolism. GSH levels decrease markedly in liver injury models due to excessive consumption. It is estimated spectrophotometrically using Ellman's reagent, which forms a yellow complex with sulfhydryl groups measurable at 412 nm. Elevated GSH levels after drug treatment reflect replenishment of intracellular antioxidant capacity.

Catalase (CAT) is another key antioxidant enzyme that decomposes hydrogen peroxide, a toxic by-product of SOD activity, into water and oxygen. It functions primarily in peroxisomes and is crucial for limiting oxidative stress. Catalase activity is measured by monitoring the rate of hydrogen peroxide decomposition at 240 nm. A decrease in CAT activity indicates accumulation of hydrogen peroxide and oxidative damage, while recovery of catalase activity shows protective action.

These oxidative stress markers are assessed using liver tissue homogenates prepared in cold phosphate buffer followed by centrifugation. The supernatants are used for biochemical assays. Together, MDA, SOD, GSH, and CAT provide a comprehensive overview of oxidative balance in hepatic tissues. In hepatoprotective studies, normalization of these markers compared to toxin-only controls supports the antioxidant efficacy of test agents and justifies further development for therapeutic application.

4.4.3.1 Tissue Fixation and Sectioning

Formalin Fixation and Microtome Slicing

Histological examination of liver tissue is a critical component of hepatoprotective drug evaluation, allowing direct visualization of cellular architecture, pathological lesions, and tissue-level changes that occur due to toxic insults. It provides confirmatory evidence to support biochemical findings and helps determine the extent and pattern of hepatic damage or recovery after treatment.

The process begins with tissue fixation, which is essential to preserve the structure of liver cells and prevent autolysis or decomposition. After sacrificing the animal, a small portion of liver (typically from the left lobe) is excised immediately, rinsed with ice-cold saline to remove blood, and immersed in 10% neutral buffered formalin. This fixative penetrates the tissue and cross-links proteins, stabilizing the tissue morphology.

The liver sample is kept in formalin for at least 24 to 48 hours to ensure complete fixation. Following this, the tissue is subjected to a standard dehydration process using increasing concentrations of ethanol (70%, 80%, 90%, and absolute alcohol), followed by clearing in xylene and embedding in molten paraffin wax. After embedding, the paraffin block is allowed to harden.

Using a rotary microtome, thin sections of liver tissue are cut at 4 to 6 micrometer thickness. These sections are carefully transferred onto glass microscope slides coated with an adhesive (like egg albumin or poly-L-lysine) to enhance adherence. The slides are then incubated on a warm plate to help the tissue settle flat and firmly.

Before staining, the paraffin is removed through a process of deparaffinization in xylene followed by rehydration through descending grades of alcohol and finally distilled water. These slides are then ready for routine or special staining procedures. Proper fixation and sectioning are crucial to maintain cell details and allow accurate interpretation of liver pathology under the microscope.

This histological preparation forms the foundation for subsequent staining and microscopic evaluation, helping to assess necrosis, inflammation, fatty change, fibrosis, or any regenerative activity in the liver tissue, which are vital indicators in hepatoprotective research.

4.4.3.2 Staining and Microscopic Analysis

H&E Staining for Necrosis, Inflammation, Fatty Changes

Following fixation, embedding, sectioning, and mounting of liver tissue, the most commonly employed staining technique for histopathological evaluation is hematoxylin and eosin (H&E) staining. This routine stain allows for detailed visualization of liver architecture and cellular morphology, enabling identification of pathological features such as necrosis, inflammation, and fatty degeneration.

In H&E staining, hematoxylin stains the nuclei of cells a deep blue or purple color by binding to nucleic acids. This allows for clear identification of nuclear structure, chromatin pattern, and signs of pyknosis or karyolysis in damaged hepatocytes. Eosin, an acidic dye, stains the cytoplasm and extracellular matrix in various shades of pink or red. This contrast between nuclei and cytoplasm provides excellent differentiation of hepatic lobules, sinusoidal spaces, and inflammatory infiltrates.

After staining, the slides are rinsed, dehydrated, cleared in xylene, and mounted with a coverslip using a neutral resin. The prepared slides are then examined under a compound light microscope at various magnifications, typically 10× and 40×.

The histopathological changes commonly assessed in hepatotoxicity models include:

- Hepatocellular necrosis: visible as pale, fragmented cells with loss of nuclear staining
- Ballooning degeneration: swollen hepatocytes with clear cytoplasm
- Inflammatory cell infiltration: particularly around the central vein or portal tracts
- Microvesicular or macrovesicular steatosis: due to accumulation of lipid droplets
- Sinusoidal congestion: dilated and engorged blood spaces
- Fibrosis or collagen deposition: in chronic damage models

These changes are compared across control, toxin, and treatment groups to assess the degree of hepatoprotection provided by the test compound.

Scoring of Histological Damage

To quantify histological findings and ensure objectivity, a semi-quantitative scoring system is used. Liver tissue sections are scored by a pathologist or trained researcher in a blinded manner to reduce bias. Scoring typically involves evaluating the severity of specific parameters on a graded scale, for example:

- Necrosis:
    - 0 = none
    - 1 = mild (≤10% of the lobule)
    - 2 = moderate (10–30%)

- o   3 = severe (>30%)
- Inflammatory infiltration:
  - o   0 = absent
  - o   1 = scattered foci
  - o   2 = moderate diffuse
  - o   3 = dense infiltration
- Fatty change:
  - o   0 = absent
  - o   1 = mild (<30% hepatocytes affected)
  - o   2 = moderate (30–60%)
  - o   3 = severe (>60%)
- Congestion or hemorrhage:
  - o   0 = absent
  - o   1 = mild
  - o   2 = moderate
  - o   3 = severe

Each liver section may receive a total cumulative score based on multiple parameters, allowing for quantitative comparison between groups. Lower histological scores in the treated groups compared to the toxic control indicate a protective effect of the test substance on liver architecture.

Histological evaluation, along with biochemical markers, provides corroborative evidence of hepatoprotective activity and strengthens the overall interpretation of a compound's efficacy and safety profile in preclinical studies.

4.4.4.1 Comparison with Standard Drugs

Silymarin, N-acetylcysteine

In preclinical evaluation of hepatoprotective agents, the use of well-established standard reference drugs is essential to validate experimental outcomes and provide a benchmark for comparing the efficacy of test compounds. Two of the most frequently used hepatoprotective standards are silymarin and N-acetylcysteine

(NAC), both of which are widely studied for their protective actions against chemically induced liver injury.

Silymarin, a flavonolignan complex extracted from the seeds of *Silybum marianum* (milk thistle), is considered a gold standard in herbal hepatoprotective screening. Its mechanism of action includes antioxidant activity, free radical scavenging, inhibition of lipid peroxidation, and stabilization of hepatocyte membranes. Additionally, silymarin enhances hepatic protein synthesis and regeneration of liver cells. In most rodent studies, silymarin is administered orally at a dose of 50 to 100 mg/kg/day, often starting a day before or simultaneously with the hepatotoxin, and continued for 7 to 14 days depending on the protocol. Its efficacy is demonstrated through the normalization of liver enzyme levels, restoration of antioxidant markers (GSH, SOD), and improved histological scores.

N-acetylcysteine (NAC) is a synthetic precursor of reduced glutathione and is most widely used in paracetamol-induced hepatotoxicity models. It replenishes intracellular glutathione reserves, facilitates detoxification of reactive metabolites like NAPQI, and improves mitochondrial function. NAC also exerts anti-inflammatory effects by modulating cytokine release. In preclinical models, it is administered intraperitoneally or orally at doses ranging from 150 to 300 mg/kg, with timing of administration being critical—maximum efficacy is observed when given within a few hours of toxicant exposure. NAC treatment leads to a significant decline in ALT, AST, and MDA levels, while restoring GSH and catalase activity.

Comparison of test drugs with these standards allows researchers to classify their compound as less effective, equally effective, or superior, based on biochemical, oxidative stress, and histological parameters. A test compound that shows comparable efficacy to silymarin or NAC in reducing hepatotoxic effects may be considered promising for further development.

In any hepatoprotective screening protocol, inclusion of these standards is not only a scientific requirement but also enhances the reproducibility, reliability, and translational relevance of the study results.

4.4.4.2 Dose–Response Relationship

Selection of Effective Dose Range

In preclinical hepatoprotective studies, understanding the dose–response relationship of a test compound is critical to determine its efficacy threshold, optimal therapeutic dose, and potential toxicity. Dose–response analysis involves administering the test agent at multiple dose levels, typically low, medium, and high (for example, 50, 100, and 200 mg/kg), in parallel groups of animals exposed to a hepatotoxic agent such as carbon tetrachloride or paracetamol.

The objective is to observe whether increasing the dose of the test compound leads to a proportional improvement in hepatoprotective parameters such as:

- Decrease in ALT, AST, ALP, and bilirubin
- Restoration of GSH, SOD, and CAT levels
- Reduction in MDA
- Improved histological architecture and lower necrosis scores

The most effective dose is identified based on the dose that achieves maximum therapeutic benefit with minimum adverse effects. This is referred to as the ED_{50} (effective dose to achieve 50% of the maximal effect), which can be calculated graphically by plotting response magnitude (Y-axis) against dose (X-axis) to produce a sigmoidal dose–response curve. The steepness of the curve indicates how sensitive the biological system is to the drug.

Therapeutic Index Calculation

The therapeutic index (TI) is a numerical expression of a drug's safety margin, defined as the ratio between its toxic dose and effective dose. It is calculated as:

$TI = TD_{50} / ED_{50}$

Where:

- TD_{50} is the dose that causes toxicity in 50% of the population.
- ED_{50} is the dose that produces therapeutic effect in 50% of the population.

A higher TI indicates a wider safety margin, meaning the drug can be administered at therapeutic doses without reaching toxicity. In hepatoprotective studies, LD_{50} values may also be estimated from acute toxicity studies using methods such as the OECD 423 guideline, where single high doses of the compound are administered to determine lethality.

For example, if a compound exhibits hepatoprotective effects at 100 mg/kg (ED_{50}) and produces observable toxicity only at 1000 mg/kg (TD_{50}), then the therapeutic index would be 10, suggesting acceptable safety for further development.

Understanding the dose–response relationship and calculating the therapeutic index provide essential information for dose selection in future clinical trials, help identify safe dose limits, and assist in establishing standard therapeutic regimens in drug discovery.

Table 21: Antihypertensive Models

Model	Mechanism	Species	Measured Parameters
DOCA-Salt	Mineralocorticoid excess	Rats	Blood pressure, renal function
Renal Artery Ligation	Reduced renal perfusion	Rats	Blood pressure, renin activity

Table 22: Blood Pressure Monitoring Techniques

Method	Accuracy	Invasiveness	Use
Tail-Cuff Plethysmography	Moderate	Non-invasive	Screening
Telemetry	High	Minimally invasive	Continuous recording
Intra-arterial Cannulation	High	Invasive	Precise measurement

Table 23: Antiarrhythmic Screening Models

Inducer	Species	Readouts
Aconitine	Rats	QT prolongation, arrhythmia score
BaCl2	Rats	Ectopic beats
Electrical Stimulation	Rats	ECG patterns

Table 24: ECG Parameters in Arrhythmia Studies

Parameter	Significance
Heart rate	Chronotropic effect
PR interval	AV nodal delay
QRS duration	Ventricular depolarization
QT interval	Repolarization delay

Table 25: Antianginal Models

Model	Procedure	Measured Outcomes
Ischemia-Reperfusion Injury	Surgical ligation and reperfusion	Infarct size, ECG changes
Coronary Artery Occlusion	Permanent or temporary ligation	Histopathology, cardiac markers

Table 26: Cardiac Biomarkers

Marker	Significance
CK-MB	Myocardial injury
LDH	Cellular damage
Troponin I	Cardiac specific
Troponin T	Cardiac specific

Table 27: Antiatherosclerotic Screening

Model	Evaluation	Markers
High Fat Diet	Serum lipid profile	TC, HDL, LDL, TG
Genetic Models (ApoE-/-)	Aortic lesion scoring	Plaque area, thickness

Table 28: Lipid Profile Parameters

Parameter	Normal Range (mg/dL)	Relevance
Total Cholesterol	<200	Overall lipidemia
HDL	>40	Protective lipoprotein
LDL	<100	Atherogenic factor
Triglycerides	<150	Associated with metabolic syndrome

Table 29: Diuretic Screening Models

Test	Species	Measured Outputs
Saluretic Test	Rats	Na+, Cl- excretion
Natriuretic Test	Rats	Na+/K+ ratio
Kaliuretic Test	Rats	K+ excretion

Table 30: Anti-Diabetic Models

Model	Mechanism	Markers
Streptozotocin (STZ)	β-cell necrosis	Fasting glucose, OGTT, HbA1c
Alloxan	ROS-induced damage	Insulin level, HOMA index

Table 31: Glucose Tolerance Test Parameters

Time Point (min)	Expected Glucose Level (mg/dL)
0	<110
30	<140
60	<180
90	<160
120	<140

Table 32: Antidyslipidemic Screening

Model	Induction	Assessment
Triton WR-1339	Inhibits lipoprotein lipase	TC, HDL, LDL, TG
High Cholesterol Diet	Increased dietary cholesterol	Atherogenic index, liver fat

Table 33: Anti-Cancer Murine Models

Model	Species	Parameter
Ehrlich Ascites Carcinoma	Mice	Survival, tumor volume

Dalton's Lymphoma Ascites	Mice	Body weight, ascitic fluid
Xenograft	Nude mice	Tumor growth
Syngeneic	Immunocompetent mice	Immunological effects

Table 34: Cytotoxicity Assessment Markers

Parameter	Evaluation
Tumor Volume	Graphical curve
Tumor Weight	Excised weight
Survival Time	Days post inoculation
Cell Viability	Trypan blue exclusion

Table 35: Hepatoprotective Evaluation Models

Model	Markers	Histology
CCl4	ALT, AST, ALP	Necrosis, inflammation
Paracetamol	Bilirubin, MDA, GSH	Fatty liver, degeneration

M. Yaso Deepika, P. Naveen, A. Divya, K. Manjeera

5. Immunopharmacology and Alternative Methods in Preclinical Screening

5.1 Immunomodulators, Immunosuppressants, and Immunostimulants

5.1.1 Overview of Immunomodulation

Definition and Classification of Immunomodulatory Agents

Immunomodulation refers to the process of altering the immune response through external agents, which may either enhance (immunostimulation) or suppress (immunosuppression) the activity of the immune system. These agents, known as immunomodulators, include a wide variety of natural and synthetic substances such as cytokines, monoclonal antibodies, plant-derived compounds, synthetic drugs, and biological products. Immunomodulators do not always act directly on immune cells; some may alter the cytokine environment or antigen presentation, thereby indirectly influencing the immune response.

Broadly, immunomodulatory agents are classified into three main categories based on their functional impact on the immune system:

- Immunosuppressants: These agents reduce or inhibit immune responses. They are widely used in organ transplantation to prevent rejection and in the treatment of autoimmune diseases. Examples include corticosteroids, cyclosporine, tacrolimus, and azathioprine.
- Immunostimulants: These compounds enhance the immune response, either by directly activating immune cells or by promoting cytokine production. They are used in the

management of chronic infections, cancer immunotherapy, and immune deficiencies. Examples include levamisole, interferons, Bacillus Calmette–Guérin (BCG), and thymosin.
- Immunoadjuvants: These agents are often included in vaccine formulations to boost the immunogenicity of antigens. They do not act as antigens themselves but improve the immune system's recognition and response to the main antigen. Examples include aluminum salts, Freund's adjuvant, and MF59.

Clinical Importance in Infectious Diseases, Cancer, and Autoimmune Disorders

In infectious diseases, immunomodulators help improve host defense by enhancing innate or adaptive immunity. For example, interferon-α is used in the treatment of chronic hepatitis B and C due to its antiviral and immune-activating properties. Immunostimulants like zinc and levamisole are sometimes prescribed as adjuvants in recurrent infections where immune function is compromised.

In cancer therapy, the concept of using the immune system to fight tumors has led to the development of immune checkpoint inhibitors, cancer vaccines, and adoptive T-cell therapies. Agents such as nivolumab (anti-PD-1) and ipilimumab (anti-CTLA-4) are successful immunomodulatory drugs that have demonstrated survival benefits in malignancies like melanoma and lung cancer. Immunostimulants like IL-2 and GM-CSF are also used to activate cytotoxic T lymphocytes and natural killer cells in cancer patients.

In autoimmune disorders, immunosuppressants are vital to reduce abnormal immune responses that target the body's own tissues. In conditions such as rheumatoid arthritis, systemic lupus erythematosus, and multiple sclerosis, drugs like methotrexate, cyclophosphamide, and monoclonal antibodies targeting TNF-α or B cells help control inflammation and prevent organ damage.

Thus, immunomodulation plays a critical therapeutic role across various disease states, and preclinical evaluation of these agents involves in vivo and in vitro methods that assess changes in immune cell function, cytokine production, and antibody formation. The rising interest in personalized and precision immunotherapies has further expanded the scope of immunomodulatory drug discovery and its importance in modern pharmacology.

5.1.2.1 Cyclophosphamide-Induced Myelosuppression

Mechanism of Action and Evaluation of Bone Marrow Suppression

Cyclophosphamide is a well-established cytotoxic alkylating agent used in chemotherapy and immunosuppression. It is frequently employed in preclinical studies to induce myelosuppression, making it a suitable model to evaluate the efficacy of immunostimulant and myelorestorative agents. Upon administration, cyclophosphamide undergoes hepatic bioactivation to produce active metabolites, including phosphoramide mustard and acrolein, which crosslink DNA strands, thereby interfering with cell division and leading to cell death, particularly in rapidly dividing cells like those in the bone marrow.

The resultant myelosuppression manifests as reduced bone marrow cellularity, decreased leukocyte counts, impaired erythropoiesis, and thrombocytopenia. This immunosuppressed state mimics the clinical picture of chemotherapy-induced immune suppression or aplastic anemia, making it valuable for testing potential immunostimulants.

In a typical experimental setup using rodents, cyclophosphamide is administered intraperitoneally at a dose of 50 to 200 mg/kg, depending on the desired level of bone marrow suppression. Hematological and histopathological parameters are evaluated after 3 to 7 days post-treatment. Common observations include:

- Marked reduction in total white blood cell (WBC) count
- Decrease in neutrophils, lymphocytes, and platelets

- Histology of femur bone marrow showing hypocellularity, fatty infiltration, and reduction in myeloid and erythroid precursors

These parameters are considered as baseline suppression indices against which the effect of test agents can be evaluated.

Recovery Indices with Test Drugs

To assess the immunorestorative or immunostimulant potential of a compound, the test drug is administered either before, after, or concurrently with cyclophosphamide. Recovery is evaluated by comparing hematological parameters of the test group with those of the toxin control group and normal untreated group. Key recovery indicators include:

- Increase in WBC, neutrophil, and lymphocyte counts
- Normalization of hemoglobin and platelet levels
- Repopulation of bone marrow cells on histological analysis

Additionally, spleen index (spleen weight relative to body weight), thymus index, and reticulocyte count are sometimes measured as indirect indicators of immune system recovery. Functional assays such as phagocytic activity of macrophages, nitroblue tetrazolium (NBT) reduction, and cytokine profiling (e.g., IL-2, IL-6, TNF-α) may also be used to assess immune enhancement.

This model is commonly used for evaluating herbal extracts, synthetic molecules, and biological agents with claimed immunostimulatory properties. Agents like levamisole, ashwagandha, ginseng, zinc, and recombinant growth factors are often tested using this protocol to compare their efficacy in reversing cyclophosphamide-induced damage.

Thus, cyclophosphamide-induced myelosuppression serves as a robust and reproducible model for preclinical screening of immunomodulatory agents, particularly those intended to boost hematopoiesis and restore immune function following cytotoxic damage.

5.1.2.2 SRBC-Induced Antibody Titer Suppression

Protocol for Immunization with Sheep Red Blood Cells

The Sheep Red Blood Cell (SRBC)-induced antibody titer model is a widely used preclinical immunological assay to evaluate the humoral immune response in laboratory animals. It is particularly useful in screening immunosuppressant and immunostimulant compounds, as it directly measures the ability of a test agent to suppress or enhance antibody production against a foreign antigen.

SRBCs act as a T-cell-dependent antigen, capable of inducing a strong immune response in rodents. Upon intraperitoneal injection, they are processed by antigen-presenting cells and stimulate B lymphocytes to produce immunoglobulins, mainly IgM and later IgG. The magnitude of this response can be quantified using a hemagglutination assay, which measures antibody levels in the serum of the immunized animal.

The standard protocol is as follows:

1. Preparation of SRBC Suspension:
    - Fresh sheep blood is collected in sterile Alsever's solution to prevent coagulation.
    - The red blood cells are washed 3–4 times with sterile normal saline by centrifugation at 3000 rpm for 10 minutes.
    - A 0.1% to 1% SRBC suspension is prepared in sterile normal saline for injection.
2. Animal Grouping and Drug Administration:
    - Animals (usually rats or mice) are divided into groups: normal control, SRBC control, test compound(s), and standard immunosuppressant (e.g., cyclophosphamide 50 mg/kg IP).

- Test drug is administered for a fixed duration (commonly 7 to 14 days) either before or after SRBC sensitization, depending on whether prophylactic or therapeutic effect is studied.
3. SRBC Sensitization:
   - On day 0, each animal is injected intraperitoneally with 0.5 mL of 0.1% SRBC suspension.
   - On day 5 or 7, a booster dose is given via intravenous or intraperitoneal route to reinforce the immune response.
4. Sample Collection and Hemagglutination Assay:
   - On day 7 or 10 after initial sensitization, blood is collected by retro-orbital plexus or tail vein.
   - Serum is separated by centrifugation and serially diluted in microtiter plates.
   - Each well is incubated with an equal volume of 0.1% SRBC suspension.
   - The plates are incubated at 37°C for 1 hour and then examined for agglutination.
   - The highest dilution of serum at which agglutination is still visible is noted as the antibody titer.

A decrease in antibody titer compared to SRBC control indicates immunosuppressive activity, while an increase suggests immunostimulation. This method is sensitive, reproducible, and allows both quantitative and qualitative assessment of immune competence.

The SRBC model is routinely used in the evaluation of immunotoxicity, vaccine adjuvanticity, and immunotherapeutic screening of natural products, synthetic agents, and biopharmaceuticals.

Quantification of Hemagglutination Titer

The hemagglutination titer is a quantitative measure of the antibody concentration in serum against sheep red blood cells (SRBCs) following immunization. It is determined by assessing the antigen-antibody interaction that leads to visible agglutination (clumping) of SRBCs in a serial dilution assay. This method is simple, cost-effective, and sensitive, making it a standard approach for evaluating the humoral immune response in preclinical studies of immunomodulatory agents.

Procedure for Hemagglutination Titer Determination

1. Serum Collection: Blood is collected from animals on day 7 or day 10 post-SRBC immunization, usually via retro-orbital plexus, tail vein, or cardiac puncture. The blood is allowed to clot at room temperature, followed by centrifugation at 3000 rpm for 10 minutes to obtain clear serum.
2. Serial Dilution:
    - Serial two-fold dilutions of each animal's serum are prepared in microtiter V- or U-bottom 96-well plates using phosphate-buffered saline (PBS).
    - For example, the first well contains 25 µL of undiluted serum and 25 µL of PBS. From this, 25 µL is transferred to the next well, and so on, creating serial dilutions (1:2, 1:4, 1:8, 1:16, etc.).
3. Addition of SRBCs: An equal volume (usually 25 µL) of freshly prepared 0.1% SRBC suspension in PBS is added to each well. The plate is gently tapped to mix the contents.
4. Incubation: The plate is incubated at 37°C for 1 hour in a humidified chamber. After incubation, wells are examined visually against a light background.
5. Reading the Titer:
    - Agglutination appears as a diffuse layer of red blood cells coating the well bottom (positive reaction).
    - Absence of agglutination leads to a compact red pellet at the center of the well (negative reaction).
    - The highest dilution of serum that still shows visible agglutination is recorded as the hemagglutination titer.
    - The titer is expressed as the reciprocal of the highest dilution showing agglutination. For instance, if agglutination is seen up to the 1:64 dilution, the titer is reported as 64.

Interpretation and Relevance

A high hemagglutination titer reflects a robust humoral immune response and is indicative of effective antibody production by B lymphocytes. A reduced titer in the test group compared to the SRBC control group suggests immunosuppressive activity of the compound under investigation. Conversely, a significant increase in titer supports immunostimulatory potential.

This assay provides a direct measure of T-cell-dependent antibody production, making it valuable for evaluating B-cell function, immune competence, and drug effects on adaptive immunity in preclinical screening.

5.1.3.1 Levamisole-Based Immunostimulation

Mechanism and Evaluation in Cyclophosphamide-Suppressed Animals

Levamisole is a synthetic imidazothiazole compound originally developed as an anthelmintic agent but later recognized for its significant immunostimulatory properties, especially in restoring immune function suppressed by chemotherapy, radiation, or immunosuppressive drugs. In preclinical immunopharmacology, levamisole is commonly used as a reference immunostimulant in models where immune suppression is experimentally induced, particularly by cyclophosphamide.

Cyclophosphamide causes a profound suppression of both humoral and cell-mediated immunity by destroying rapidly dividing bone marrow progenitor cells. This leads to reduced leukocyte count, diminished antibody production, and impaired delayed-type hypersensitivity responses. Levamisole, when administered to such immunocompromised animals, enhances both T-cell and macrophage functions, restores lymphocyte proliferation, and stimulates antibody production, thereby acting as a functional immune enhancer.

Experimental Design and Evaluation Parameters

In a typical screening protocol using rodents:

1. Immunosuppression Induction:
    - Cyclophosphamide is administered intraperitoneally in rats or mice at a dose of 50 to 200 mg/kg, often given as a single or divided dose over 1–2 days.
    - After 24 to 48 hours, the animals show a marked drop in total white blood cell count, especially lymphocytes and neutrophils.
2. Levamisole Treatment:
    - Levamisole is administered orally or intraperitoneally at a dose of 2.5 to 5 mg/kg/day for 5 to 7 consecutive days, starting either before or after cyclophosphamide administration, depending on whether preventive or therapeutic immunostimulation is to be assessed.
3. Assessment of Immunostimulatory Effects:
    - Hematological Profile: Total and differential leukocyte counts are measured to assess recovery of immune cells.
    - Humoral Immunity: Antibody production is evaluated using the SRBC-induced hemagglutination test. Levamisole-treated animals typically show significantly higher antibody titers compared to the cyclophosphamide-only group.
    - Cell-Mediated Immunity: Delayed-type hypersensitivity (DTH) response is measured by injecting SRBCs into the footpad and observing swelling after 24–48 hours. A greater increase in paw thickness in the levamisole group reflects restoration of T-cell function.
    - Phagocytic Activity: The carbon clearance test or nitroblue tetrazolium (NBT) reduction assay may be used to assess the activity of macrophages. Levamisole enhances the phagocytic index, indicating stimulation of the innate immune arm.

This model is widely used to screen natural products, herbal formulations, and synthetic drugs for potential immunostimulant effects. Levamisole acts as a reliable positive control because of its well-characterized pharmacological profile. The ability of a test drug to match or exceed the effect of levamisole in reversing cyclophosphamide-induced suppression suggests promising immunorestorative potential, warranting further pharmacodynamic and clinical evaluation.

5.1.3.2 Delayed-Type Hypersensitivity (DTH) Reaction

Footpad Swelling Method

The delayed-type hypersensitivity (DTH) reaction is a widely used model for assessing cell-mediated immunity in preclinical immunopharmacology. It represents a Type IV hypersensitivity response, which is T-lymphocyte dependent, particularly involving $CD4^+$ Th1 cells and macrophages. The reaction is typically evaluated by measuring localized inflammatory swelling at the site of antigen re-exposure and reflects the strength and integrity of T-cell-mediated immune responses.

In rodents, the most commonly used antigen is sheep red blood cells (SRBCs), which are injected intradermally or intraperitoneally during the sensitization phase. The test compound is administered either before or after sensitization to assess its effect on the immune response.

Standard protocol for the footpad swelling method:

1. Sensitization Phase:
   - Animals (usually mice or rats) are sensitized by injecting 0.1 mL of 1% SRBC suspension intraperitoneally on day 0.
   - This primes the animal's immune system to recognize SRBCs as a foreign antigen.
2. Test Drug Administration:

- The test compound or standard immunostimulant (e.g., levamisole) is administered orally or intraperitoneally for 5 to 7 days, starting from the day of sensitization.
3. Challenge Phase:
    - On day 5 or 7, the animal is challenged by injecting 0.05 mL of 1% SRBC suspension subcutaneously into the right hind footpad.
    - The left hind footpad receives saline as a control.
4. Measurement of Footpad Thickness:
    - Thickness of both footpads is measured using a plethysmometer or vernier caliper before challenge and again 24 and 48 hours after challenge.
    - The difference in thickness between the challenged and control footpad indicates the extent of DTH response.

Typical results show minimal swelling in immunosuppressed animals, while animals treated with immunostimulants show significantly higher swelling, indicating T-cell activation and macrophage recruitment at the antigen site.

Cytokine and Immune Cell Profiling

To gain further insight into the mechanism of immune modulation, DTH response can be supplemented with cytokine assays and immune cell profiling:

- Cytokine Estimation:
    - Blood or tissue homogenates (e.g., footpad or spleen) are analyzed for pro-inflammatory and regulatory cytokines using ELISA kits.
    - Key cytokines include:
        - Interleukin-2 (IL-2) – promotes T-cell proliferation
        - Interferon-gamma (IFN-γ) – activates macrophages and enhances antigen presentation

- Tumor necrosis factor-alpha (TNF-α) – supports inflammation and recruitment of immune cells
- Immune Cell Profiling:
    - Flow cytometry or immunohistochemistry can be used to identify the infiltration of:
        - $CD4^+$ T-helper cells
        - $CD8^+$ cytotoxic T cells
        - Macrophages (F4/80 or CD68-positive)
        - Dendritic cells or antigen-presenting cells

An increase in cytokine levels and immune cell presence at the site of injection confirms the activation of cell-mediated immunity.

The DTH reaction, particularly the footpad swelling assay, remains a reliable and reproducible method for screening immunostimulant activity of drugs and natural products. It is particularly relevant in the context of vaccine adjuvants, immunodeficiency therapeutics, and host-directed therapies in infections and cancer.

5.2.1 Theoretical Basis of Immunoassays

Antigen–Antibody Interaction

Immunoassays are analytical techniques based on the highly specific interaction between antigens and antibodies. This antigen–antibody binding forms the foundation of most immunodiagnostic methods used for detecting and quantifying biologically important molecules, such as hormones, drugs, proteins, or pathogens. The interaction is non-covalent and involves multiple weak forces including hydrogen bonding, van der Waals forces, electrostatic interactions, and hydrophobic forces.

An antigen is any substance capable of inducing an immune response, typically a foreign protein or molecule that the body recognizes as non-self. An antibody is a glycoprotein produced by B-lymphocytes in response to the antigen and is capable of binding to that antigen with high specificity. Each antibody has two identical antigen-binding sites known as Fab regions, which recognize specific molecular patterns (epitopes) on the antigen.

The basis of all immunoassays lies in forming a stable antigen–antibody complex, which can then be detected or measured using a labeled component (enzyme, radioisotope, fluorophore, etc.). The extent of this binding reflects the concentration of antigen or antibody in the sample, depending on the type of assay used.

The antigen–antibody interaction in immunoassays can occur in various formats:

- Direct assay: where the label is directly attached to the antibody or antigen.
- Indirect assay: where a secondary labeled antibody is used to detect the primary binding.
- Sandwich assay: where antigen is "sandwiched" between two antibodies – capture and detection antibody.
- Competitive assay: where sample antigen competes with labeled antigen for limited antibody binding.

This biological recognition system is extremely specific, and therefore highly suitable for detecting even minute concentrations of analytes in complex biological samples like serum, plasma, or cell lysates.

Specificity and Affinity Principles

The specificity of an immunoassay refers to its ability to distinguish the target analyte from other substances, even those structurally related. It is primarily determined by the selectivity of the antibody used. Monoclonal antibodies, derived from a single clone of B-cells, are highly specific for a single epitope and are often preferred in assays requiring high specificity. Polyclonal antibodies, on the other hand, recognize multiple epitopes and may be used where broader detection is desired.

Affinity is a measure of the strength of binding between a single antigenic epitope and the antibody's binding site. It is usually expressed as the equilibrium constant (Ka) or its reciprocal, the dissociation constant (Kd). High-affinity antibodies form stronger and more stable complexes, which improves sensitivity and reliability of the assay. In some immunoassays, avidity (the cumulative strength of multiple binding sites) also plays an important role, especially when using polyclonal antibodies.

The sensitivity and performance of an immunoassay depend not only on the assay format but also on the kinetics and thermodynamics of the antigen–antibody binding. Optimal assay conditions such as pH, ionic strength, incubation time, and temperature are carefully controlled to ensure reproducible results.

Understanding the theoretical basis of immunoassays, particularly the principles of antigen–antibody interaction, specificity, and affinity, is crucial in designing robust analytical methods for drug quantification, biomarker detection, and pharmacokinetic studies in preclinical and clinical research.

5.2.2 Classification of Immunoassays

Competitive vs Non-Competitive

Immunoassays are broadly classified into competitive and non-competitive formats based on the binding mechanism between antigen and antibody and how the signal is generated. This classification influences the assay sensitivity, detection limits, and type of analyte that can be measured.

In a competitive immunoassay, the test analyte (usually antigen from the sample) competes with a labeled antigen (tracer) for a limited number of antibody binding sites. As the concentration of the test antigen increases, fewer labeled antigens can bind to the antibody, resulting in a decrease in detectable signal. Therefore, signal intensity is inversely proportional to the analyte concentration. Competitive assays are particularly useful for detecting small molecules such as hormones, drugs, or toxins, where simultaneous binding of two antibodies (as in sandwich format) is not feasible due to molecular size constraints.

A typical competitive assay involves:

- A fixed amount of antibody
- A known quantity of labeled antigen
- Varying concentrations of unlabeled antigen (sample)

After incubation and separation of bound from free components, the signal is measured. Examples include radioimmunoassay (RIA) and enzyme multiplied immunoassay technique (EMIT).

In contrast, non-competitive immunoassays (often called sandwich assays) do not involve competition. Instead, the antigen in the sample is captured between two antibodies:

- A capture antibody bound to a solid phase (such as a microtiter plate)
- A labeled detection antibody that binds to another epitope on the same antigen

This format produces a signal that is directly proportional to the concentration of the antigen. Non-competitive assays offer greater sensitivity and specificity and are widely used for detecting proteins, peptides, and large antigens with multiple epitopes. Examples include sandwich ELISA and chemiluminescence immunoassays.

Direct vs Indirect Assay Formats

Another classification of immunoassays is based on how the detection is performed, i.e., direct or indirect labeling of antibodies or antigens.

In a direct immunoassay, the primary antibody is labeled with an enzyme, fluorophore, or radioactive tag, and directly binds to the target antigen immobilized on a solid surface. This format is faster and simpler, as it involves fewer steps, but may have lower sensitivity due to the use of a single labeled antibody. It is suitable for detecting abundant antigens or when rapid results are needed.

In an indirect immunoassay, the primary antibody is unlabeled, and detection is achieved using a secondary antibody that is labeled and specific to the primary antibody. This two-step process amplifies the signal because multiple secondary antibodies can bind to each primary antibody, thereby enhancing assay sensitivity. Indirect methods are commonly used in ELISA and immunofluorescence assays where sensitivity is crucial.

To summarize:

- Competitive assays are suited for small molecules with single epitopes and offer a wider dynamic range.
- Non-competitive assays are more sensitive, ideal for complex or larger antigens.
- Direct formats are quick but less sensitive, while indirect formats provide signal amplification and greater flexibility in assay design.

Understanding these classifications helps researchers select the appropriate immunoassay type based on the analyte size, required sensitivity, available reagents, and time constraints of the assay.

5.2.3 Parameters for Optimization

Antibody Concentration, Incubation Time, and Temperature

Optimizing immunoassay conditions is essential to ensure maximum sensitivity, specificity, reproducibility, and low background noise. The performance of an immunoassay depends heavily on how well the experimental conditions are tailored to promote strong and specific antigen–antibody binding while minimizing non-specific interactions.

One of the most critical variables is the antibody concentration. Both the capture and detection antibodies must be used at concentrations that allow sufficient binding to the antigen without leading to excess background signal. Too little antibody may result in poor signal intensity, while too much may cause non-specific interactions or steric hindrance. A checkerboard titration is commonly used to identify the optimal antibody dilution, where varying concentrations of antigen and antibody are tested simultaneously to find the best signal-to-noise ratio.

Incubation time affects the kinetics of antigen–antibody binding. Insufficient time may lead to incomplete binding, resulting in reduced assay sensitivity, while excessive incubation may lead to higher background due to non-specific adsorption. Typically, incubation periods range from 30 minutes to overnight, depending on the assay format and reagents used.

Temperature plays a key role in the rate and strength of antigen–antibody interactions. Most immunoassays are conducted at room temperature (20–25°C) or 37°C. Higher temperatures can increase the rate of binding but may also destabilize the proteins, whereas lower temperatures reduce reaction kinetics but may improve specificity. For sensitive assays, particularly enzyme-linked methods, maintaining a controlled temperature throughout the protocol is critical for consistency.

Blocking Agents and Signal Amplification

Blocking agents are used to reduce non-specific binding of proteins or antibodies to surfaces such as microtiter plates or membranes. These agents coat the unoccupied binding sites on the solid surface to prevent background interference. Common blocking agents include:

- Bovine serum albumin (BSA)
- Non-fat dry milk
- Gelatin
- Casein

- Tween-20 or Triton X-100 (as surfactants in wash buffers)

The choice of blocking agent depends on the assay system and detection method. Inadequate blocking can lead to high background noise, whereas excessive blocking may reduce antigen accessibility or binding efficiency.

Signal amplification enhances the detectability of antigen–antibody interactions, especially when the target analyte is present in low concentrations. Several strategies are used:

- Enzyme-based amplification: Enzymes such as horseradish peroxidase (HRP) or alkaline phosphatase (ALP) catalyze chromogenic or chemiluminescent reactions, producing a measurable signal.
- Biotin–streptavidin systems: This high-affinity binding pair is used to amplify signal by adding multiple biotin molecules to antibodies and using labeled streptavidin to detect them.
- Poly-HRP conjugates or tyramide signal amplification (TSA): These are used in ultra-sensitive assays to generate enhanced chemiluminescence or fluorescence.
- Secondary antibody layering: Multiple secondary antibodies binding to one primary antibody can increase signal strength in indirect immunoassays.

Proper optimization of these parameters is essential not only for achieving high analytical performance but also for standardizing the assay for reliable, reproducible results in routine drug screening, biomarker measurement, and diagnostic applications. Each immunoassay system may require unique adjustments based on the nature of the analyte, antibody source, and detection method.

5.3.1 Heterogeneous Immunoassays

Heterogeneous immunoassays are characterized by the requirement of a separation step to remove unbound components before the detection phase. This step is essential to eliminate background noise and improve signal accuracy. These assays typically involve solid-phase immobilization of antigens or antibodies and include formats like ELISA and radioimmunoassay (RIA). Due to their high specificity, sensitivity, and reliability, heterogeneous immunoassays are widely used in preclinical screening, clinical diagnostics, pharmacokinetics, and biomarker studies.

5.3.1.1 Enzyme-Linked Immunosorbent Assay (ELISA)

ELISA is one of the most widely used heterogeneous immunoassay techniques for detecting and quantifying antigens or antibodies. The method employs an enzyme-labeled antibody or antigen and a substrate that produces a detectable signal—usually a color change—upon enzymatic reaction. Commonly used enzymes include horseradish peroxidase (HRP) and alkaline phosphatase (ALP). ELISA is performed in 96-well microtiter plates, allowing high-throughput screening and quantitative analysis.

There are three principal formats of ELISA:

- Direct ELISA: In this format, the antigen is immobilized on the solid surface, and a labeled primary antibody binds directly to it. This method is quick and requires fewer steps, but it is generally less sensitive due to the lack of signal amplification.
- Indirect ELISA: Here, the primary antibody is unlabeled, and a labeled secondary antibody (usually anti-IgG) is used for detection. This format offers greater sensitivity because multiple secondary antibodies can bind to a single primary antibody, amplifying the signal.
- Sandwich ELISA: This highly sensitive format involves capturing the antigen between two antibodies:
    - A capture antibody is coated on the plate.
    - The test sample is added to allow antigen binding.
    - A detection antibody, labeled with an enzyme, binds to a different epitope on the same antigen.
    - The amount of bound enzyme is proportional to the antigen concentration and is detected using a chromogenic substrate. Sandwich ELISA is ideal for

detecting large proteins or antigens with multiple epitopes and is widely used in hormone assays, cytokine quantification, and drug monitoring.

5.3.1.2 Radioimmunoassay (RIA)

Radioimmunoassay (RIA) is a highly sensitive technique developed in the 1960s, based on the principle of competitive binding. It uses radioactively labeled antigens or antibodies (commonly with Iodine-125 or Tritium) to detect and quantify minute amounts of substances, often in the picogram or nanogram range.

In a typical competitive RIA:

- A fixed amount of radio-labeled antigen competes with unlabeled antigen (from the test sample) for a limited number of antibody binding sites.
- After incubation, the bound and free antigen fractions are separated.
- The radioactivity of the bound fraction is measured using a gamma counter or scintillation counter.
- A standard curve is prepared using known concentrations, and the unknown sample concentration is calculated by interpolation.

RIA is particularly useful for measuring small molecules, such as hormones (e.g., insulin, thyroxine, cortisol), drugs (e.g., digoxin), and viral antigens. It has excellent sensitivity and specificity but requires stringent radioactive waste handling, short shelf life of radiolabels, and specialized instrumentation, which has led to its gradual replacement by non-radioactive immunoassays like ELISA and chemiluminescence assays in many laboratories.

Despite its limitations, RIA remains a gold standard for benchmarking the sensitivity of other immunoassays and is still in use for critical endocrine and pharmacological studies.

5.3.2.1 Enzyme Multiplied Immunoassay Technique (EMIT)

Principle and Applications in Drug Monitoring

The Enzyme Multiplied Immunoassay Technique (EMIT) is a type of homogeneous immunoassay that differs from heterogeneous systems by not requiring a separation step between bound and free antigens. It is based on the principle that the binding of an antibody to an enzyme-labeled antigen can inhibit the enzyme's activity, and that this inhibition can be reversed in the presence of the unlabeled (free) antigen from the sample.

In a typical EMIT system:

- A known amount of enzyme-labeled antigen and specific antibody are added to the test sample, which contains unlabeled antigen (the analyte).
- Both labeled and unlabeled antigens compete for binding to the limited antibody.
- When the antibody binds to the labeled antigen, the enzyme's active site is sterically hindered, and its catalytic activity is reduced.
- When more unlabeled antigen is present, less labeled antigen is bound by the antibody, allowing the enzyme to remain active.
- A substrate is then added, and the rate of enzymatic reaction (often a color change) is measured spectrophotometrically.

The intensity of the signal is directly proportional to the concentration of the analyte in the sample, making EMIT a non-competitive, direct assay format.

EMIT is widely used for therapeutic drug monitoring (TDM) due to its simplicity, rapid execution, and ability to be automated in clinical analyzers. It is particularly useful in detecting small-molecule drugs and metabolites, which are difficult to assay via sandwich formats.

Applications in drug monitoring include:

- Antibiotics: Measurement of aminoglycosides like gentamicin and tobramycin
- Antiepileptics: Monitoring of phenytoin, carbamazepine, and valproic acid levels
- Immunosuppressants: Assay of cyclosporine in transplant recipients
- Cardiac drugs: Detection of digoxin in cardiac therapy
- Psychoactive drugs: Screening for drugs of abuse like benzodiazepines, barbiturates, and cannabinoids

The advantages of EMIT include:

- No need for wash or separation steps
- Fast results suitable for high-throughput labs
- Reliable for small analytes with single epitopes

However, it also has limitations, such as being less sensitive than heterogeneous methods and being more prone to interference from structurally similar compounds.

5.3.2.2 Fluorescence Polarization Immunoassay (FPIA)

Instrumentation and Real-Time Monitoring

Fluorescence Polarization Immunoassay (FPIA) is a homogeneous immunoassay technique that relies on the principle of fluorescence polarization to measure the concentration of small molecules in biological fluids. It does not require a separation step and is based on the change in rotational motion of a fluorescent-labeled antigen when bound to an antibody, compared to when it is free in solution.

The fundamental concept of FPIA is that smaller molecules rotate faster in solution than larger ones, and this rotational speed affects how polarized emitted light is after excitation. When a small, fluorescent-labeled molecule is excited with plane-polarized light, it emits light in a depolarized manner due to rapid rotation. However, when this molecule binds to a larger antibody, the resulting complex rotates more slowly, leading to higher polarization of the emitted light.

In the presence of the analyte in the sample, competition occurs between the fluorescent-labeled antigen and the unlabeled antigen for the limited antibody binding sites. As the concentration of the unlabeled analyte increases, less labeled antigen is bound to antibody, resulting in lower polarization signal. Thus, the degree of fluorescence polarization is inversely proportional to the analyte concentration.

Instrumentation for FPIA includes:

- A light source that emits plane-polarized light, often using a mercury or xenon arc lamp.
- Polarizers placed before and after the sample to ensure only polarized emission is measured.
- A fluorometer or dedicated FPIA analyzer capable of detecting the degree of fluorescence polarization.
- A data processing unit that calculates polarization in millipolarization units (mP) and plots it against analyte concentration.

The assay can be completed within a few minutes, and the results are analyzed using standard curves generated from known concentrations of the analyte.

Real-time monitoring is one of the strong advantages of FPIA. Since the assay does not require washing steps, it allows for continuous measurement of the antigen–antibody binding reaction as it occurs. This makes FPIA highly suitable for automation and use in clinical chemistry analyzers, especially for routine monitoring of therapeutic drug levels and toxicology screening.

Applications of FPIA include:

- Quantification of drugs like theophylline, phenytoin, digoxin, and methotrexate
- Drug abuse testing for substances such as amphetamines and opiates
- Detection of hormones and antibiotics in plasma or urine

FPIA offers several advantages such as speed, simplicity, high reproducibility, and compatibility with small sample volumes, but it is generally limited to small molecules due to its competitive assay format. It remains a valuable tool in preclinical and clinical pharmacology for rapid, real-time drug analysis in biological matrices.

5.4.1 Protocol Outline and Analytical Process

Sample Collection, Reagent Preparation, Incubation Steps

A standardized and validated immunoassay procedure follows a clearly defined sequence of steps to ensure accurate, reproducible, and sensitive detection of the target analyte. These steps include sample handling, reagent preparation, assay incubation, and detection.

The first step is sample collection, which must be done carefully to avoid contamination, hemolysis, or degradation of the analyte. Serum, plasma, or other biological matrices such as urine, saliva, or cell culture supernatants may be used depending on the assay type. Blood samples are usually collected in anticoagulant-free or appropriately treated tubes, followed by centrifugation at 2000–3000 rpm for 10–15 minutes to separate the serum or plasma. The supernatant is then stored at 2–8°C for short-term use or frozen at −20°C or −80°C for longer-term preservation.

Reagent preparation involves bringing all test components—antibodies, antigens, substrates, buffers—to room temperature before use. Enzyme-conjugated antibodies or labeled antigens must be reconstituted or diluted as per the manufacturer's instructions. Wash buffers and blocking agents are freshly prepared and filtered to avoid particulate contamination. Substrates like TMB (for HRP) or pNPP (for ALP) are sensitive to light and temperature, and must be protected during use.

In most immunoassays, the incubation steps are performed in microtiter plates:

- Wells are coated with capture antibody or antigen and incubated to allow binding.
- After washing off unbound components, the sample or standard is added and incubated, typically for 30 minutes to 2 hours, depending on assay sensitivity.
- A detection antibody or labeled conjugate is then added and incubated for a specific period.
- The plate is washed again to remove excess unbound reagent.
- Finally, the substrate solution is added and allowed to react with the enzyme label.

For ELISA, color development is usually stopped by adding an acid (e.g., sulfuric acid) after a fixed time. All incubation steps should be carried out at controlled temperatures (commonly 25°C or 37°C) and with gentle shaking if required, to ensure uniform binding.

Reading and Interpretation of Signal

After completion of the reaction, the assay signal is measured using an appropriate detection instrument, depending on the label used. For colorimetric assays such as ELISA, a microplate reader is used to measure absorbance at specific wavelengths (e.g., 450 nm for TMB). In fluorescence-based assays, a fluorometer measures emission intensity, while in chemiluminescent or radioimmunoassays, luminometers or gamma counters are used, respectively.

The signal obtained from each well is directly or inversely proportional to the concentration of the analyte, depending on the assay format. A standard curve is generated by plotting the signal versus known concentrations of the analyte. Unknown sample concentrations are interpolated from this curve using software or linear/logarithmic regression models.

Key points in interpretation include:

- Consistency between duplicates or triplicates
- Acceptable background levels and signal-to-noise ratio
- Inclusion of positive and negative controls to validate the assay run
- Use of quality control samples to confirm assay performance

This systematic protocol ensures that immunoassays deliver accurate, sensitive, and reproducible measurements, critical for applications in drug development, biomarker quantification, disease diagnosis, and pharmacokinetic studies.

5.4.2 Validation Parameters

Sensitivity and Detection Limits

Sensitivity refers to an immunoassay's ability to detect even very small concentrations of an analyte. It is one of the most critical parameters in assay validation, especially when working with trace levels of hormones, drugs, or biomarkers in biological fluids. Sensitivity is usually expressed as the lowest concentration of analyte that produces a measurable signal significantly different from the background. This is also referred to as the limit of detection (LOD).

The LOD is commonly calculated by measuring the signal of the blank (zero analyte) multiple times (usually 20) and determining the mean and standard deviation. A frequently used formula is:

LOD = Mean of blank + 3 × standard deviation of blank

Another related term is limit of quantification (LOQ), which is the lowest concentration that can be quantified with acceptable accuracy and precision. LOQ is usually set at a signal corresponding to the mean of blank + 10 × standard deviation. These limits define the dynamic range of the assay and help researchers determine its utility in both low and high analyte concentrations.

Specificity and Cross-Reactivity

Specificity defines how selectively the assay detects the intended analyte in the presence of structurally similar compounds or matrix components. A highly specific assay should not respond significantly to non-target molecules. This is particularly important in drug analysis, hormone testing, or immunodiagnostics where cross-reactivity with related compounds could produce misleading results.

To assess specificity, structurally related compounds are tested at various concentrations to determine whether they bind to the assay antibodies. The degree of interference is expressed as percentage cross-reactivity, calculated as:

Cross-reactivity (%) = (Concentration of test compound producing equivalent signal / Concentration of target analyte) × 100

Cross-reactivity should ideally be below 1% for a highly specific assay, especially in clinical and pharmacological applications.

Reproducibility and Inter-Assay Variation

Reproducibility ensures that the immunoassay yields consistent results across multiple runs, different days, or operators. It is assessed using:

- Intra-assay variation (within a single run)
- Inter-assay variation (between different runs)

These are expressed as coefficient of variation (CV%), calculated using the formula:

CV (%) = (Standard deviation / Mean) × 100

Acceptable CV values are typically:

- <10% for intra-assay precision
- <15% for inter-assay precision

Multiple quality control samples at low, medium, and high concentrations are tested in triplicate or more, across multiple runs. A consistently low CV indicates the assay's robustness and reliability in real-world usage.

Proper validation of these parameters is essential before any immunoassay is accepted for regulatory, clinical, or preclinical use. It ensures the assay's accuracy, reproducibility, and trustworthiness in applications such as therapeutic drug monitoring, toxicity screening, and pharmacodynamic studies.

5.5.1 Digoxin Immunoassay

Principle and Methodology

Digoxin is a cardiotonic glycoside used in the treatment of congestive heart failure and atrial fibrillation. Due to its narrow therapeutic index and the potential for serious toxicity, monitoring of its plasma levels is essential during therapy. Immunoassays are the most widely used techniques for the quantitative estimation of digoxin in serum or plasma, with methods such as Enzyme Multiplied Immunoassay Technique (EMIT), Fluorescence Polarization Immunoassay (FPIA), and Radioimmunoassay (RIA) commonly applied in clinical and research settings.

The basic principle of the digoxin immunoassay is a competitive binding reaction where digoxin present in the patient's sample competes with a labeled digoxin conjugate (enzyme-labeled or fluorescent-labeled) for a fixed number of antibody binding sites. Since digoxin is a small molecule with a single antigenic determinant, it cannot form sandwich complexes, and hence only competitive immunoassays are used.

In EMIT, the digoxin conjugated to an enzyme such as glucose-6-phosphate dehydrogenase (G6PDH) shows reduced activity when bound to the antibody. In the presence of free (unlabeled) digoxin from the sample, fewer antibody molecules are available to bind the labeled digoxin, leaving more active enzyme available. The enzymatic activity measured by spectrophotometry is directly proportional to the concentration of digoxin in the sample.

In FPIA, the assay measures changes in the polarization of fluorescent light. When labeled digoxin binds to the antibody, the fluorescence polarization is high; when free digoxin from the sample displaces the labeled digoxin, the polarization decreases. The amount of depolarization is inversely proportional to the digoxin concentration.

Key components of the assay include:

- Calibrators and controls with known digoxin concentrations
- Specific monoclonal or polyclonal antibodies against digoxin
- Labeled digoxin reagent (enzyme or fluorophore conjugated)
- Substrates and buffers for reaction maintenance

The assay is typically automated in clinical analyzers and provides results within 30 to 60 minutes.

Clinical Importance in Cardiac Drug Monitoring

Digoxin has a therapeutic range of 0.8 to 2.0 ng/mL in serum. Plasma levels below 0.8 ng/mL may be subtherapeutic, while levels above 2.0 ng/mL can lead to toxicity, especially in elderly patients or those with renal impairment.

Common symptoms of digoxin toxicity include nausea, vomiting, visual disturbances (yellow vision), confusion, and in severe cases, cardiac arrhythmias. Co-administration of other drugs (e.g., amiodarone, verapamil, or quinidine) can increase digoxin levels due to reduced renal clearance or protein binding displacement.

Routine immunoassay-based monitoring helps clinicians:

- Adjust dosage in individual patients
- Prevent toxic accumulation
- Optimize therapeutic efficacy in congestive heart failure and atrial arrhythmias
- Evaluate patient compliance or suspected overdose

Due to its rapidity, sensitivity, and automation compatibility, digoxin immunoassay remains a cornerstone diagnostic tool in both preclinical pharmacology and clinical therapeutics.

5.5.2 Insulin Immunoassay

Differentiation of Endogenous and Exogenous Insulin

Immunoassays for insulin are essential tools in both clinical and preclinical settings for the quantification of insulin concentration in serum or plasma. These assays are widely used in diabetes diagnosis, therapy monitoring, pharmacokinetic studies, and drug development. The ability to differentiate between endogenous (pancreatic) and exogenous (injected) insulin is particularly important in diabetes research, insulin therapy assessment, and forensic investigations.

Endogenous insulin is secreted by pancreatic β-cells and is typically measured along with C-peptide, which is co-released during proinsulin cleavage. Exogenous insulin, administered via injection, does not contain C-peptide. Therefore, C-peptide levels are often used as a surrogate to assess endogenous insulin secretion, especially in patients receiving insulin therapy.

To differentiate endogenous from exogenous insulin:

- Standard insulin immunoassays may detect both forms if they recognize shared epitopes.
- Specific assays have been developed using monoclonal antibodies that either:
    - Selectively detect human insulin (to assess endogenous production)
    - Distinguish between human insulin and analogs like lispro, glargine, or detemir (used in therapeutic formulations)
- In research, mass spectrometry-based immunoassays are also used for accurate differentiation by identifying molecular weight differences between endogenous insulin and analogs.

Role in Diabetes Research and Pharmacodynamics

Insulin immunoassays play a vital role in diabetes mellitus research, especially for understanding disease progression, insulin resistance, β-cell function, and response to therapeutic agents. These assays are also key in assessing the pharmacokinetics and pharmacodynamics of new insulin formulations and oral hypoglycemic agents.

In preclinical and clinical studies, insulin levels are measured to:

- Evaluate β-cell function: Elevated fasting insulin with normal glucose suggests insulin resistance, while low insulin indicates β-cell dysfunction.
- Perform oral glucose tolerance tests (OGTT) or insulin tolerance tests (ITT): Serial measurements of glucose and insulin help determine the dynamic response of the endocrine pancreas and tissue insulin sensitivity.
- Monitor insulin therapy: Ensure therapeutic dosing, avoid hypoglycemia, and assess bioavailability of new insulin analogs.
- Study metabolic diseases: Such as metabolic syndrome, polycystic ovary syndrome (PCOS), and obesity.

Modern insulin immunoassays include ELISA, chemiluminescent immunoassay (CLIA), radioimmunoassay (RIA), and electrochemiluminescence (ECL) platforms. These assays offer high sensitivity (often in the picomolar range) and specificity, and they can be integrated into automated analyzers for high-throughput analysis.

In research and drug development, insulin immunoassays support the characterization of drug-induced pancreatic effects, facilitate screening of insulin secretagogues and sensitizers, and enable correlation of insulin levels with glucose homeostasis models.

Overall, insulin immunoassays are indispensable for precise endocrine evaluation, and their ability to distinguish between insulin sources enhances both diagnostic accuracy and scientific understanding in metabolic pharmacology.

5.6.1 Scientific Limitations

Species Differences in Physiology and Drug Metabolism

One of the most significant scientific limitations in animal experimentation arises from physiological and biochemical differences between animal species and humans. Although laboratory animals such as mice, rats, rabbits, and monkeys serve as essential models in drug discovery, their biological systems often differ in terms of organ structure, receptor expression, immune responses, and enzyme profiles. These differences can profoundly affect how a drug is absorbed, distributed, metabolized, and excreted (ADME), ultimately influencing the pharmacological or toxicological outcome.

For instance, cytochrome P450 enzymes, which are responsible for the metabolism of most drugs, vary not only in their isoforms but also in their activity between species. A compound that is rapidly metabolized in rodents may persist longer in human plasma, leading to exaggerated or prolonged effects. Similarly, some drug targets, such as neurotransmitter receptors or ion channels, show differences in binding affinity and downstream signaling across species, which may result in overestimation or underestimation of efficacy.

Moreover, renal clearance, plasma protein binding, and gastrointestinal pH also vary between animals and humans. These variations complicate the interpretation of pharmacokinetic data and may lead to inaccurate dose scaling. For example, a drug that demonstrates a short half-life in rodents due to rapid renal clearance may behave differently in humans with slower elimination kinetics.

In toxicology, species-specific susceptibility to certain toxic effects further limits the predictive value of animal studies. Some animals tolerate higher doses of a compound that would be lethal in humans, and vice versa. For instance, acetaminophen shows dose-dependent hepatotoxicity in humans but requires significantly higher doses to **produce similar liver damage in rats.**

Challenges in Extrapolating Efficacy Data

Translating efficacy data from animals to humans poses several challenges, even when the drug shows promising preclinical results. Disease models in animals often fail to fully replicate the complex pathophysiology seen in human conditions. For example, rodent models of Alzheimer's disease, cancer, or diabetes may mimic certain pathological features but not the entire clinical spectrum, leading to partial or misleading efficacy profiles.

Many animal models are developed using induced or genetically modified methods to simulate human disease, but these models may not account for environmental, genetic, or comorbid factors that influence disease progression in humans. Consequently, drugs that are effective in animal models may not demonstrate the same level of benefit in clinical trials. This limitation is one of the key reasons for the high attrition rate of drug candidates in the transition from preclinical to clinical phases.

Another challenge is the scaling of dose and response. Differences in metabolism, body surface area, and volume of distribution make it difficult to accurately calculate human equivalent doses (HED) from animal data. Even when allometric scaling is used, non-linear pharmacokinetics or inter-individual variability in humans can lead to unexpected clinical outcomes.

Therefore, while animal experiments remain a cornerstone of preclinical research, the scientific limitations underline the importance of integrating human-relevant in vitro systems, computational models, and biomarker-guided strategies to improve the translational value of preclinical data. Recognizing these limitations also encourages researchers to interpret animal results with caution and supports the ongoing development of alternative and complementary approaches to drug testing.

5.6.2 Ethical and Economic Concerns

Public Opposition and Regulatory Restrictions

The use of animals in scientific research has long been a subject of ethical debate and public scrutiny, particularly concerning their welfare, rights, and humane treatment. There is a growing societal opposition to animal experimentation, especially when procedures involve pain, distress, or long-term captivity. Many people question the moral justification of subjecting animals to invasive tests, especially in cases where the scientific gain is uncertain or when alternatives are available.

In response to these concerns, national and international regulatory bodies have introduced stringent ethical guidelines and legislative frameworks to govern the use of animals in research. In India, for example, the Committee for the Purpose of Control and Supervision of Experiments on Animals (CPCSEA) enforces rules related to the ethical treatment, housing, and use of laboratory animals. Institutions must obtain approval from their Institutional Animal Ethics Committee (IAEC) for each study involving animals, and only licensed facilities are permitted to conduct such research.

Globally, principles such as the 3Rs — Replacement, Reduction, and Refinement — are now mandatory ethical pillars in animal research. These principles require researchers to:

- Replace animals with non-animal alternatives where possible,
- Reduce the number of animals used by improving experimental design and statistical methods, and
- Refine procedures to minimize pain and distress.

Moreover, regulatory agencies like the US FDA, EMA, and OECD are increasingly encouraging the integration of non-animal models, including cell cultures, organ-on-chip systems, and in silico simulations, especially during early-stage drug development. Some agencies have already begun accepting data from validated alternatives for specific toxicity and safety assessments, reflecting a shift in global regulatory attitudes.

Financial Burden and Housing Limitations

Maintaining a facility for animal experimentation involves significant financial and logistical commitments, which can be a burden for smaller academic institutions or independent research centers. The cost includes:

- Construction and maintenance of animal houses with proper ventilation, temperature, and humidity control,
- Procurement and breeding of specific-pathogen-free (SPF) animals,
- Veterinary care, disease surveillance, and nutritional management,
- Salary for trained personnel, including animal attendants, technicians, and veterinarians,
- Compliance costs associated with ethical review processes, documentation, and inspections.

Moreover, the cost per animal can vary widely depending on species and genetic modifications. For example, transgenic or knockout mice can cost several thousand rupees per animal, while non-human primates, often used in neuroscience or vaccine research, are even more expensive to procure and maintain.

Housing limitations are another constraint. Animals require space that meets species-specific guidelines for enrichment, social interaction, and movement. Overcrowding, poor sanitation, or lack of enrichment can lead to stress, aggression, or disease outbreaks, which compromise both animal welfare and scientific data quality.

Together, these economic and ethical factors have led to increasing pressure on researchers to justify animal use rigorously and to seek cost-effective, humane, and scientifically robust alternatives. Integrating such considerations into study planning not only ensures regulatory compliance and public trust, but also promotes scientific innovation in the development of modern drug testing methodologies.

5.6.3 The 3Rs Principle

The 3Rs Principle—Replacement, Reduction, and Refinement—forms the ethical foundation of responsible animal experimentation. Proposed by Russell and Burch in 1959, the 3Rs serve as a global guideline to ensure that animals used in scientific research are treated with maximum respect, care, and necessity. Regulatory authorities and ethical committees worldwide have now made the implementation of the 3Rs a mandatory component of preclinical study design and approval.

Replacement: Use of Non-Animal Alternatives

Replacement aims to substitute animal models with non-animal methods whenever possible, without compromising scientific outcomes. This is especially important in early-phase research, toxicity testing, and routine screening studies where validated alternatives can provide equivalent or superior data.

Examples of replacement approaches include:

- In vitro methods using human cell lines, organoids, and stem-cell derived tissues
- Computer-based in silico models, including structure–activity relationship (SAR) modeling, physiologically based pharmacokinetic (PBPK) modeling, and virtual screening
- High-throughput screening platforms using biochemical or cellular assays
- Organ-on-chip technologies, which replicate human tissue architecture and fluid dynamics to study drug absorption, metabolism, and toxicity

By implementing replacement, researchers can generate human-relevant data and reduce ethical concerns associated with animal use.

Reduction: Minimizing the Number of Animals

Reduction refers to using the minimum number of animals necessary to obtain statistically valid results. This does not mean underpowering experiments but rather optimizing experimental design to extract maximum data from the fewest subjects.

Strategies for reduction include:

- Improved statistical planning to calculate minimum required sample size using power analysis
- Use of shared control groups across studies when scientifically justified
- Longitudinal study designs, where repeated measurements are taken from the same animals over time
- Data sharing and collaborative research, which avoids unnecessary repetition of similar experiments

Reduction benefits both animal welfare and research budgets while maintaining scientific validity.

Refinement: Improving Welfare and Methods

Refinement involves the modification of experimental procedures to minimize pain, distress, and discomfort experienced by animals and to enhance their overall welfare. It also includes training personnel, improving housing conditions, and using humane endpoints to reduce suffering.

Refinement practices include:

- Use of appropriate anesthesia and analgesia during and after invasive procedures
- Introduction of enrichment materials, such as nesting materials, toys, or social companions, to reduce stress
- Refined handling techniques (e.g., tunnel handling instead of tail picking in mice)
- Early euthanasia criteria to prevent prolonged suffering in toxicology or disease models
- Monitoring for non-verbal distress signals such as weight loss, abnormal posture, or aggression

These measures not only align with ethical mandates but also improve data quality, as stress and suffering can influence physiological parameters and behavioral responses.

The 3Rs principle is not only an ethical obligation but also a scientific necessity in modern biomedical research. It encourages innovation, supports regulatory compliance, and builds public confidence in the humane use of animals for scientific advancement.

5.7.1 In Vitro and Ex Vivo Models

Cell Lines: HepG2, RAW 264.7, Caco-2

In the pursuit of ethical and cost-effective research, in vitro and ex vivo models have become powerful alternatives to animal experimentation. These models help simulate biological responses in a controlled environment and provide valuable data for drug screening, toxicity assessment, and mechanistic studies. Among the most widely used tools in this domain are immortalized cell lines, which offer high reproducibility, scalability, and reduced variability compared to live animals.

HepG2 cells are a well-established human liver carcinoma cell line used primarily for evaluating hepatic metabolism, drug biotransformation, and hepatotoxicity. These cells express a variety of phase I and phase II drug-metabolizing enzymes, making them suitable for studies on cytochrome P450-mediated reactions, glutathione conjugation, and oxidative stress. HepG2 cells are frequently used in models assessing drug-induced liver injury (DILI) and are also applied in in vitro models of steatosis, fibrosis, and apoptosis.

RAW 264.7 cells are derived from murine macrophages and are extensively used in immunopharmacology and inflammation research. These cells are highly responsive to inflammatory stimuli like lipopolysaccharide (LPS) and are capable of producing cytokines, nitric oxide, and prostaglandins. Due to their robust response, they are ideal for screening anti-inflammatory compounds, studying signal transduction pathways (e.g., NF-κB, MAPK), and evaluating immune-modulatory drugs.

Caco-2 cells originate from human colorectal adenocarcinoma and are used as a model for the intestinal epithelium. When cultured for approximately 21 days, they differentiate into enterocyte-like cells with tight junctions, microvilli, and transporters that mimic the intestinal barrier. These cells are primarily used in permeability studies, such as in vitro assays for predicting oral bioavailability and absorption. Caco-2 monolayers are also used in transporter interaction studies (e.g., P-glycoprotein) and in evaluating drug–nutrient or drug–drug interactions.

These cell lines represent just a few examples of how in vitro models are tailored to replicate human organ systems. They reduce the need for animal use during the early phases of drug discovery and allow for mechanistic exploration, high-throughput screening, and preliminary safety assessments. Moreover, in vitro systems can be genetically engineered to overexpress or knock down specific genes, offering an additional level of control that is often difficult to achieve in whole animal models.

By integrating cell-based assays with modern imaging, omics technologies, and bioinformatics, in vitro models continue to advance our understanding of pharmacological and toxicological mechanisms while upholding the principles of ethical and sustainable biomedical research.

Organoid Systems and Co-Culture Models

Organoid systems and co-culture models represent advanced in vitro technologies that offer a closer approximation to human tissue physiology than traditional monolayer cell lines. These models aim to mimic the three-dimensional (3D) architecture, cellular heterogeneity, and functional characteristics of real organs, enabling more predictive and translationally relevant data in preclinical research.

Organoids are miniaturized, self-organizing tissue constructs derived from pluripotent stem cells (PSCs), adult stem cells, or primary tissue biopsies. These cells are grown in a specialized extracellular matrix scaffold, such as Matrigel, and supplemented with defined growth factors that guide their differentiation into organ-specific lineages. As a result, organoids recapitulate the cellular composition and functionality of organs like the intestine, liver, kidney, brain, and lung.

For example, intestinal organoids show features such as crypt–villus structures, tight junctions, and absorptive epithelial cells, allowing them to be used for drug absorption and toxicity screening. Liver organoids, developed from HepaRG or iPSC-derived hepatocytes, exhibit drug metabolism capacity and bile duct formation, making them suitable for evaluating hepatotoxicity, enzyme induction, and metabolic profiling.

Brain organoids are increasingly being used to study neurodevelopmental toxicity, neurodegeneration, and viral encephalitis, while lung organoids are applied in respiratory pharmacology and COVID-19 research. These models offer the ability to test long-term drug exposure, model chronic disease, and analyze patient-specific responses, especially when derived from individual human donors (personalized medicine).

Co-culture models, on the other hand, involve the simultaneous growth of two or more different cell types in the same system, allowing the study of cell–cell interactions, paracrine signaling, and drug responses in a multi-cellular environment. Common examples include:

- Caco-2 with HT29-MTX to model intestinal mucus and drug permeability
- Hepatocytes with Kupffer cells or stellate cells for inflammation and fibrosis studies
- Endothelial cells with smooth muscle cells for vascular pharmacology
- Tumor cells with immune cells to investigate immuno-oncology mechanisms

Co-culture systems can be established using Transwell inserts, which physically separate cell types while allowing soluble factor exchange, or in 3D spheroid cultures, which support cell adhesion and matrix production.

Both organoids and co-culture systems offer enhanced physiological relevance compared to conventional monolayer cultures and bridge the gap between in vitro and in vivo models. They support more accurate prediction of drug efficacy, toxicity, absorption, metabolism, and immune responses, contributing significantly to reducing reliance on animal models. With ongoing improvements in culture media, scaffold materials, and imaging technologies, these platforms are increasingly integrated into regulatory toxicology, disease modeling, and personalized drug development pipelines.

Organ-on-Chip and Microfluidics-Based Assays

Organ-on-chip (OOC) technology, a groundbreaking advancement in biomedical engineering, represents the most sophisticated evolution of in vitro modeling to date. These systems utilize microfluidic platforms to recreate the microarchitecture, dynamic environment, and physiological functions of human tissues and organs. By integrating living cells, extracellular matrix components, and controlled fluid flow within miniaturized chip-like devices, organ-on-chip models closely simulate the mechanical, chemical, and biological stimuli experienced in vivo.

An organ-on-chip typically consists of:

- A flexible polymer structure (usually made of polydimethylsiloxane or PDMS)
- Microchannels lined with tissue-specific cells to simulate organ compartments
- Microfluidic perfusion that mimics blood flow or interstitial fluid dynamics
- Sensors to monitor parameters like pH, oxygen, pressure, and electrical activity

These systems can model individual organs such as:

- Lung-on-chip: Comprising alveolar epithelial and endothelial cells, separated by a porous membrane and subjected to cyclic mechanical stretching to mimic breathing. It is used for studying inhaled drug delivery, pulmonary toxicity, and inflammation.
- Liver-on-chip: Incorporates hepatocytes and non-parenchymal liver cells under continuous perfusion, allowing accurate studies of drug metabolism, hepatotoxicity, and bile canaliculi function.
- Heart-on-chip: Utilizes cardiac myocytes and mechanical stretch to simulate electrophysiological conduction, contractility, and QT prolongation screening.
- Kidney-on-chip: Models the glomerular filtration barrier or proximal tubule epithelium for nephrotoxicity and transporter studies.

The multi-organ-on-chip approach integrates multiple tissues (e.g., liver–gut–kidney axis) into one system, enabling researchers to observe systemic pharmacokinetic and pharmacodynamic interactions, better mimicking whole-body responses. These integrated chips can be linked through fluidic circuits representing human physiological flow, forming what is sometimes referred to as a "body-on-chip".

Microfluidics-based assays, even when not fully chip-integrated, offer precise control over fluid dynamics, shear stress, and concentration gradients, which are essential for modeling vascular tissues, tumor microenvironments, and immune cell migration. They also facilitate real-time imaging, live cell tracking, and long-term culture under controlled conditions, which are difficult to achieve in static well-plate assays.

The advantages of organ-on-chip systems include:

- Use of human-derived cells for increased translational relevance
- Reduction or replacement of animal models
- Ability to study chronic and repeat-dose toxicity
- Simulation of mechanical cues such as stretch, flow, and compression
- Compatibility with high-content imaging and omics technologies

Despite their complexity and relatively higher initial cost, these models are increasingly being adopted by academic institutions, pharmaceutical industries, and regulatory agencies for toxicology studies, disease modeling, drug discovery, and precision medicine applications.

In conclusion, organ-on-chip and microfluidic models represent a transformative shift toward next-generation, human-relevant preclinical testing platforms, offering an ethical, accurate, and mechanistically rich alternative to traditional animal testing.

5.7.2 Invertebrate and Vertebrate Alternatives

Zebrafish Embryos for Drug Screening and Toxicity

Zebrafish (Danio rerio) embryos have emerged as one of the most widely accepted vertebrate alternatives for early-stage drug discovery and toxicological evaluation, offering a unique balance between biological complexity and ethical flexibility. Their transparent bodies, rapid development, and high genetic homology with humans make them highly suitable for whole-organism studies while adhering to animal welfare standards, especially when used before 5 days post-fertilization, at which stage they are not regulated as live animals in many jurisdictions.

Zebrafish embryos develop externally, and major organs such as the heart, liver, brain, pancreas, and kidneys become visible and functional within 48–72 hours. This enables real-time observation of organogenesis, morphological defects, cardiac function, circulation, pigmentation, and neurodevelopment under compound exposure.

In drug screening, zebrafish embryos are used for:

- High-throughput testing in 96- or 384-well plates
- Phenotypic assays to observe behavioral or structural changes
- Dose–response studies to determine safe and effective concentration ranges
- Cardiotoxicity and neurotoxicity assessment using live imaging and fluorescence-based tracking
- Angiogenesis and wound healing models using transgenic lines with fluorescent vascular markers
- Teratogenicity testing, including eye, jaw, and tail malformations

Zebrafish are also genetically tractable, and CRISPR/Cas9 technology allows generation of disease models to study metabolic disorders, cancer, epilepsy, or inflammatory responses. Toxicity endpoints in zebrafish include lethality (LC_{50}), hatching delay, edema formation, swim behavior alterations, and pericardial swelling, all of which are quantifiable and reproducible.

Advantages of zebrafish embryos include:

- Low cost and high reproductive rate (up to 300 embryos per mating pair)
- Reduced ethical constraints for early developmental stages
- Ability to observe whole-body responses in real time
- Fast data turnaround, with readouts typically within 3–5 days
- Amenability to automation and robotic handling

Zebrafish embryo assays are now included in OECD Test Guidelines (e.g., OECD TG 236 for acute toxicity) and are gaining acceptance in regulatory safety assessments as part of integrated testing strategies. Their use aligns with the 3Rs principle, supporting reduction and replacement of traditional mammalian models during early preclinical stages.

Thus, zebrafish embryos serve as a powerful, ethical, and cost-effective platform for initial toxicity screening, mechanism-based evaluation, and target validation in modern drug discovery pipelines.

Drosophila melanogaster for Genetic Studies

Drosophila melanogaster, commonly known as the fruit fly, has long been a cornerstone of genetic research and continues to gain importance as an alternative model organism in pharmacology and toxicology. Despite being an invertebrate, Drosophila shares approximately 75% of human disease-related genes, making it a powerful and cost-effective model for studying gene function, developmental biology, and drug response mechanisms.

Its short life cycle (around 10–12 days at 25°C), high fecundity, and ease of maintenance on simple media make Drosophila ideal for large-scale screening studies. Genetic manipulation in Drosophila is well established, with techniques like:

- GAL4/UAS system for tissue-specific gene expression
- CRISPR-Cas9 gene editing
- RNA interference (RNAi) for gene knockdown
- Transposable elements (P-elements) for gene insertion

These tools allow for the creation of models that mimic neurodegenerative diseases, metabolic disorders, cancer, cardiac defects, and developmental syndromes.

In drug screening and pharmacological evaluation, Drosophila is used for:

- Neuropharmacology studies: Models of Parkinson's, Alzheimer's, and epilepsy
- Behavioral assays: Locomotion, sleep cycles, learning and memory tests
- Metabolic studies: Obesity, insulin signaling, and lipid metabolism
- Toxicology: Lethality tests, reactive oxygen species (ROS) production, and oxidative stress responses

Because of its open circulatory system, drugs can be administered by simply mixing them with the diet, allowing for non-invasive delivery and dose standardization. Assays are designed to assess:

- Lifespan changes
- Reproductive capacity
- Morphological abnormalities
- Organ-specific toxicity (e.g., gut, muscle, or eye degeneration)

The advantages of using Drosophila include:

- Rapid and reproducible experimentation
- Low cost and space requirements

- Well-annotated genome and abundant genetic resources
- Conservation of major signal transduction pathways, including MAPK, Notch, Wnt, Hedgehog, and insulin signaling

Limitations include the lack of adaptive immune responses and vertebrate organ analogues, but for early-phase target validation and mechanism-based studies, Drosophila offers exceptional insight.

Drosophila's contributions to genetics have earned multiple Nobel Prizes, and its ongoing relevance in translational biomedical research continues to grow, making it a valuable model for preclinical screening, functional genomics, and gene–drug interaction studies.

Caenorhabditis elegans for Neurotoxicity and Lifespan Assays

Caenorhabditis elegans (C. elegans) is a small, transparent nematode worm that has become an increasingly popular non-mammalian model organism in preclinical pharmacological research. With a size of just about 1 mm in length, a fully mapped genome, and a short life cycle of 3–4 days, C. elegans offers an efficient and ethically favorable platform for studying drug effects on the nervous system, aging, metabolism, and toxicity.

C. elegans is particularly useful in neurotoxicity testing, as its nervous system is simple but highly conserved, comprising exactly 302 neurons whose connectivity (connectome) has been fully mapped. Many neurotransmitter systems—such as dopaminergic, cholinergic, serotonergic, and GABAergic—are functionally similar to those in humans. This makes C. elegans valuable for modeling neurodegenerative diseases and evaluating the neurotoxic effects of drugs, environmental toxins, or chemicals.

Neurotoxicity in C. elegans can be assessed through:

- Locomotion assays: Measurement of head thrashing, body bending, or crawling speed on agar plates

- Touch response tests: Evaluating mechanosensory neuron function
- Dopaminergic neuron integrity: Using GFP-tagged strains to monitor neuron degeneration
- Chemotaxis and olfactory behavior: To evaluate sensory neuron damage

In lifespan and aging studies, C. elegans provides a reliable model to assess how different compounds influence longevity, oxidative stress, mitochondrial function, and caloric restriction pathways. Lifespan assays involve exposing synchronized populations to test compounds and recording survival rates daily under controlled conditions.

The worm's genetic tractability supports high-throughput screening of drugs or genes involved in aging or neuroprotection. RNAi libraries, mutant collections, and CRISPR-based gene editing allow for precise functional studies.

Other notable advantages include:

- Low cost and minimal lab infrastructure requirements
- Simple compound administration via the nematode's diet or culture media
- Fluorescence microscopy compatibility for real-time imaging
- Reproducibility and scalability for automation and robotic screening

Although C. elegans lacks complex organs like lungs, bones, or a closed circulatory system, it still offers significant insights into basic cellular and molecular mechanisms of drug action. It serves as a bridge between cell culture models and higher-order animal systems, particularly in early-stage screening and mode-of-action studies.

Thus, C. elegans stands as a powerful, ethical, and genetically rich model for neurotoxicity testing, lifespan evaluation, and mechanism-based pharmacology, aligning closely with modern efforts to reduce reliance on mammalian models in biomedical research.

5.8 Extrapolation of Preclinical Data to Humans

5.8.1 Principles of Translational Pharmacology

Relevance of Animal Data to Human Biology

Translational pharmacology is the scientific discipline focused on bridging preclinical findings from animal or alternative models to clinical outcomes in humans. One of its foundational principles is ensuring that the data generated in early stages of drug development can be effectively used to predict safety, efficacy, pharmacokinetics, and pharmacodynamics in humans. This is critical for minimizing the failure rate of drug candidates during clinical trials and for ensuring ethical and economic efficiency in drug development.

The relevance of animal data to human biology depends on multiple factors, including genetic similarity, pathophysiological correlation, target homology, and metabolic comparability. For instance, while rodents are commonly used due to convenience and cost-effectiveness, their physiological responses—such as drug metabolism via cytochrome P450 enzymes—may differ significantly from those in humans. Larger mammals like dogs and non-human primates may more closely mimic human cardiovascular or endocrine responses, but ethical and regulatory challenges limit their widespread use.

A core goal in translational pharmacology is selecting an animal model that most accurately reflects the human disease phenotype, mechanism of drug action, and biomarker response. For example, a mouse model of Parkinson's disease induced by MPTP is commonly used because it mimics the selective dopaminergic neuron loss seen in humans. However, it still lacks the chronic, progressive nature of human neurodegeneration.

Furthermore, the expression and distribution of drug targets, such as receptors, ion channels, or enzymes, must be evaluated across species. If a drug targets a receptor that is nonexistent or differently regulated in the chosen animal model, the preclinical data may have limited translational value. Knock-in or humanized models, where human genes or proteins are expressed in animals, are increasingly used to improve predictability.

Understanding species-specific differences in absorption, distribution, metabolism, and excretion (ADME) is another crucial aspect. For instance, first-pass metabolism, plasma protein binding, and renal clearance rates vary between species, and these differences must be factored in when predicting human pharmacokinetics.

To enhance translational relevance, researchers often incorporate biomarkers, such as changes in blood glucose, liver enzymes, or cytokine levels, which are measurable in both animal and human studies. These biomarkers allow comparative analysis and dose extrapolation, supporting safer and more informed decisions as a drug advances to clinical trials.

5.8.1 Principles of Translational Pharmacology

Humanized Animal Models and Bridge Studies

Humanized animal models and bridge studies represent advanced strategies in translational pharmacology that aim to close the physiological and genetic gap between animal models and human systems. These approaches are particularly important when standard animal models fall short in accurately predicting human-specific drug responses, especially for biologics, immunotherapies, and precision medicines.

Humanized animal models are genetically engineered animals, typically mice, in which specific human genes, cells, tissues, or even entire immune systems are introduced. These models are designed to express human proteins or replicate aspects of human physiology that are not naturally present in the host species. This allows for a more relevant assessment of target engagement, therapeutic efficacy, and off-target effects in a human biological context, while still maintaining the systemic environment of a living organism.

Examples of humanized models include:

- Mice expressing humanized immune systems, often used for testing immuno-oncology drugs, vaccines, and monoclonal antibodies
- Liver-humanized mice, where human hepatocytes are engrafted to study drug metabolism, hepatotoxicity, and drug–drug interactions
- Transgenic mice with human receptors, such as human epidermal growth factor receptor 2 (HER2) or human insulin receptor, used to evaluate receptor-binding drugs
- Knock-in models, where mouse genes are replaced with their human orthologs, offering high translational fidelity for target validation

These models are critical when a drug targets a receptor or antigen that is absent or non-functional in traditional animal species, allowing researchers to predict human-specific responses that would otherwise go undetected until clinical trials. However, humanized models can be expensive, technically demanding, and require immunodeficient backgrounds to prevent rejection of human cells, which may limit some immune or metabolic interactions.

Bridge studies are short-term, comparative preclinical studies conducted to link data obtained in one species to another or from animals to humans. These studies are especially valuable in biologics development, where species specificity restricts the use of traditional models. For example:

- A monoclonal antibody that binds only to human antigens may first be tested in non-human primates, and then bridged to human data using surrogate biomarkers or pharmacokinetic models.

- A drug tested in rodents may require a bridge study in a more closely related species, such as dogs or minipigs, before moving to human trials.

Bridge studies are also employed during:

- Biosimilar development, to compare the reference biologic and biosimilar in at least one relevant model
- Formulation changes, where the impact of different delivery systems (e.g., oral vs injectable) is assessed
- First-in-human (FIH) dose selection, using NOAEL (No Observed Adverse Effect Level) and human equivalent dose (HED) calculations derived from bridging pharmacokinetic data

These studies are often supported by allometric scaling, PBPK (physiologically based pharmacokinetic) modeling, and biomarker correlation, ensuring a smooth transition from animal data to early-phase clinical trials.

5.8.2 PK/PD Correlation

Pharmacokinetics: ADME and Scaling Approaches

Pharmacokinetics (PK) plays a pivotal role in the extrapolation of preclinical data to humans, as it describes how a drug is absorbed, distributed, metabolized, and excreted (ADME) in the body. Understanding these processes in animal models enables researchers to estimate drug exposure, duration of action, and systemic availability in humans. However, direct extrapolation is not always straightforward due to inter-species physiological and metabolic differences, requiring the use of scaling approaches.

The four core components of ADME are studied extensively in preclinical species:

- Absorption: Measured as the rate and extent to which a drug enters systemic circulation. This depends on factors like

gastrointestinal pH, membrane permeability, and transporter activity, all of which can vary across species.
- Distribution: Influenced by blood flow, tissue binding, and plasma protein interactions. The volume of distribution (Vd) helps assess how extensively a drug spreads into tissues from the bloodstream.
- Metabolism: Primarily hepatic, involving phase I enzymes (e.g., cytochrome P450 isoenzymes) and phase II conjugation enzymes. The expression and activity of these enzymes differ between species, affecting metabolic clearance and active metabolite formation.
- Excretion: Mainly through renal or biliary pathways. Renal clearance depends on glomerular filtration rate and tubular function, which must be considered when comparing across species.

To predict human pharmacokinetics, scaling approaches such as allometric scaling are employed. Allometric scaling involves the use of body weight and surface area to extrapolate pharmacokinetic parameters like clearance (CL), volume of distribution (Vd), and half-life ($t_{1/2}$) from animals to humans.

Another approach is physiologically based pharmacokinetic (PBPK) modeling, which integrates anatomical, physiological, and biochemical data to simulate drug disposition in a virtual human system. This model accounts for organ-specific blood flow, tissue partition coefficients, and enzyme kinetics, and allows prediction of plasma concentration–time profiles, drug–drug interactions, and special population pharmacokinetics (e.g., pediatrics or renal impairment).

These PK scaling methods are essential for:

- Estimating first-in-human (FIH) dose
- Predicting steady-state concentrations
- Designing early-phase clinical trials
- Identifying potential species-specific toxicities

By understanding ADME in animals and applying robust scaling techniques, researchers can reduce uncertainty, ensure ethical compliance, and enhance the predictive power of preclinical data, ultimately improving the efficiency and safety of drug development.

Pharmacodynamics: Target Engagement and Response Biomarkers

Pharmacodynamics (PD) refers to the biological effects a drug produces in the body, including its mechanism of action, efficacy, and toxicity. In preclinical research, understanding the relationship between drug concentration (pharmacokinetics) and its pharmacological effect (pharmacodynamics) is essential for predicting how a compound will behave in humans. This PK/PD correlation allows scientists to design better dosing strategies, assess therapeutic windows, and select meaningful biomarkers for clinical monitoring.

One of the most critical aspects of pharmacodynamics is target engagement, which refers to the binding of a drug to its intended molecular target (receptor, enzyme, or ion channel) in vivo. Demonstrating target engagement confirms that the drug reaches its site of action and initiates the expected biological response. Techniques used to assess target engagement in preclinical models include:

- Receptor occupancy studies using radiolabeled ligands and autoradiography
- Biomolecular assays, such as enzyme inhibition or phosphorylation state changes
- Fluorescence or bioluminescence imaging in transgenic animal models
- Surface plasmon resonance and thermal shift assays for protein–ligand interactions

Quantifying the extent of target engagement helps determine:

- The minimum effective concentration (MEC)
- The duration of action
- The dose-response curve

- The potential for off-target effects

In parallel, response biomarkers are used to monitor the biological activity of a drug and provide measurable indicators of efficacy or toxicity. These can be molecular, cellular, or physiological readouts and are typically quantifiable, reproducible, and translatable across species.

Examples of pharmacodynamic response biomarkers include:

- Blood glucose levels in anti-diabetic drug studies
- C-reactive protein (CRP) and cytokine levels in inflammation models
- pERK or pAkt expression in signal transduction studies
- Tremor score or behavioral indices in CNS pharmacology
- Tumor size reduction or apoptotic markers in oncology

PD markers are often measured over time alongside plasma drug concentrations to create PK/PD models, which help visualize how drug exposure correlates with biological response. These models enable researchers to:

- Predict the optimal therapeutic dose
- Assess the onset and duration of action
- Define the therapeutic index by comparing effective and toxic doses
- Identify biomarkers for patient stratification in clinical trials

For translational relevance, it is vital that biomarkers used in animals have human homologs or analogs. For example, serum ALT/AST for liver toxicity, IL-6 for inflammation, or glucose/HbA1c for diabetes are used in both preclinical and clinical settings. This continuity improves confidence in predicting human outcomes and regulatory acceptance of preclinical data.

Thus, integrating pharmacodynamics with pharmacokinetics provides a comprehensive understanding of a drug's action, supports rational dose selection, and enhances the ability to translate animal data into meaningful clinical insight.

5.8.3 Regulatory Expectations

ICH S6, OECD, and FDA Guidelines

Regulatory authorities across the globe have established comprehensive guidelines to ensure that preclinical data generated from animal or alternative models are scientifically valid, ethically conducted, and translationally useful for human trials. These guidelines provide structured frameworks for assessing safety, efficacy, and quality before a compound enters clinical development.

The International Council for Harmonisation (ICH) S6 guideline is primarily focused on preclinical safety evaluation of biotechnology-derived pharmaceuticals, such as monoclonal antibodies, recombinant proteins, and gene therapy products. It emphasizes:

- Use of relevant animal species, often requiring non-human primates when rodent models lack target relevance.
- Conducting repeat-dose toxicity studies, reproductive toxicity, immunogenicity, and local tolerance evaluations.
- Selection of pharmacologically active dose levels and No Observed Adverse Effect Level (NOAEL) for defining clinical trial doses.
- Integration of pharmacokinetic/pharmacodynamic (PK/PD) data to support human dose prediction.

The Organisation for Economic Co-operation and Development (OECD) guidelines govern toxicological and environmental safety testing, and include:

- Test Guidelines (TGs) such as OECD TG 420, 423, and 425 for acute toxicity
- OECD TG 407, 408, and 409 for repeated-dose oral toxicity
- OECD TG 471, 473, 474 for genotoxicity

- OECD TG 236 for alternative models like zebrafish embryo toxicity testing

These protocols are internationally recognized and used for regulatory submissions in many countries, supporting mutual acceptance of data (MAD) among member nations.

The U.S. Food and Drug Administration (FDA) provides specific guidance through documents like:

- FDA Red Book for food and color additive safety
- Guidance for Industry: Preclinical Assessment of Investigational Drugs
- ICH M3(R2) for timing of nonclinical studies for IND and NDA submissions
- FDA GLP regulations (21 CFR Part 58) to ensure study integrity and compliance

FDA expects preclinical studies to follow Good Laboratory Practices (GLP) and to include robust documentation of all protocols, raw data, observations, and analyses.

IND-Enabling Studies and Dossier Preparation

Before initiating human trials, sponsors must conduct IND (Investigational New Drug)-enabling studies, which generate essential safety and pharmacological data. These studies support the submission of the IND application to the FDA (or equivalent agencies such as CDSCO in India or EMA in Europe).

IND-enabling studies typically include:

- General toxicity studies (acute, subacute, and chronic in two species)
- Genotoxicity and mutagenicity studies
- Safety pharmacology focusing on CNS, cardiovascular, and respiratory systems
- Reproductive and developmental toxicity
- Local tolerance studies at the site of administration

- Carcinogenicity studies for drugs intended for long-term use

These are supported by comprehensive PK/PD profiles, bioanalytical validations, target engagement data, and dose-range finding studies.

The IND dossier must include the following nonclinical sections:

- Pharmacology section: Mechanism of action, efficacy data, and biomarkers
- Toxicology section: Full study reports, histopathology, and NOAELs
- Pharmacokinetics section: Absorption, distribution, metabolism, excretion
- Justification for human starting dose: Often based on HED derived from NOAEL using allometric scaling and appropriate safety margins

Together with chemistry, manufacturing, and clinical protocols, the dossier must clearly demonstrate that:

- The drug is reasonably safe to test in humans
- The starting dose and escalation plan are justified
- The study design complies with ethical and scientific standards

Meeting these regulatory expectations ensures a smoother transition from preclinical research to human trials, enhances data credibility, and contributes to a more efficient and ethically sound drug development process.

Table 36: Classification of Immunomodulators

Category	Examples	Clinical Use
Immunosuppressants	Cyclophosphamide, Azathioprine	Transplantation, autoimmune diseases
Immunostimulants	Levamisole, BCG vaccine	Infections, cancer immunotherapy

Table 37: Cyclophosphamide-Induced Myelosuppression Model

Parameter	Details
Dosage	50–100 mg/kg
Route	Intraperitoneal
Readouts	WBC count, bone marrow cellularity

Table 38: SRBC-Induced Antibody Titer Suppression

Procedure	Details
Antigen	Sheep RBC injection
Readout	Hemagglutination titer

Table 39: Levamisole-Induced Immunostimulation

Group	WBC Count Restoration	Antibody Level
Normal Control	Normal	Baseline
Cyclophosphamide Control	Suppressed	Reduced
Test Drug + Cyclophosphamide	Improved	Restored

Table 40: Delayed-Type Hypersensitivity (DTH)

Timepoint (hours)	Footpad Thickness (mm)	Key Cytokines
0	Baseline	-
24	Mild swelling	IL-2
48	Peak swelling	IFN-γ
72	Recovery phase	TNF-α

Table 41: Competitive vs Non-Competitive Immunoassays

| Type | Signal Relationship | Use Case |

| Competitive | Inversely proportional | Small molecules |
| Non-Competitive | Directly proportional | Larger proteins |

Table 42: Direct vs Indirect Assays

Type	Primary Detection	Sensitivity
Direct ELISA	Labeled antigen/antibody	Lower
Indirect ELISA	Secondary antibody used	Higher

Table 43: Common Immunoassay Systems

Method	Detection	Application
ELISA	Enzyme-substrate	Cytokines, hormones
RIA	Radioactivity	Drugs, hormones
EMIT	Enzyme amplification	Therapeutic drug monitoring
FPIA	Fluorescence polarization	Small molecule analysis

Table 44: Immunoassay Evaluation Parameters

Parameter	Definition
Sensitivity	Lowest detectable amount
Specificity	Ability to distinguish target
Precision	Consistency of results
Reproducibility	Repeatability across batches

Table 45: Immunoassay for Digoxin

Parameter	Details
Principle	Competitive binding
Matrix	Plasma/serum
Relevance	Monitoring cardiac glycoside therapy

Table 46: Immunoassay for Insulin

Parameter	Details
Purpose	Endogenous vs exogenous differentiation
Model Use	Diabetes studies, PK/PD evaluation

Table 47: Limitations of Animal Experimentation

Concern	Impact
Species Difference	Poor predictability

Ethical Issues	Regulatory restrictions
Cost	High maintenance
Translation	Limited human relevance

Table 48: The 3Rs Principle

R	Meaning
Replacement	Use non-animal methods
Reduction	Use fewer animals
Refinement	Minimize pain and improve welfare

Table 49: Alternative Models to Animal Use

Model	Use
Zebrafish	Toxicity, screening
Drosophila	Genetics, neuropharmacology
C. elegans	Aging, neurodegeneration
Organoids	3D tissue systems
Cell lines	Mechanistic studies

Table 50: Translational PK/PD Parameters

Parameter	Significance
AUC	Total drug exposure
Cmax	Peak concentration
Half-life	Duration of action
Volume of distribution	Extent of distribution

About the Authors

Yaso Deepika Mamidisetti

Yaso Deepika Mamidisetti, M. Pharmacy (Pharmacology), is pursuing her Ph.D. at Acharya Nagarjuna University and works at SOAHS, Malla Reddy University, Hyderabad. She has over 6 years of teaching and 1 year of research experience, with expertise in pharmacovigilance, molecular docking, drug design, pre-clinical &clinical research. She has published more than 18 research papers in international journals.

Dr. Naveen Pathakala

Dr. Naveen received his B. Pharm, M. Pharm and doctoral degrees form Osmania university and having over 13 years of teaching experience. He has hands-on experience in computational molecular docking studies, animal handling techniques, behavioral analysis, and Pharmacological and toxicological screening models for various diseases.

Dr. Divya A

Dr. Divya A, Asst Prof, B.Pharm., Pharm.D (PB) has over 7 years of teaching and industry experience. She has worked in CRO and Super speciality Hospitals in Clinical data management and patient care oriented areas. She is actively engaged in conducting research projects in patient safety and disease outcomes for Pharm.D students at Anurag University, Hyderabad.

Mrs. Kuchi Manjeera

Mrs. Kuchi Manjeera, working at CMR College of Pharmacy. She has been pursuing her Ph.D from GITAM (Deemed to be University),

Visakhapatnam and about to submit her thesis shortly. She has published 17 Publications in Scopus and Web of Science Journals She has filed 3 Patents on her inventions and got published.

www.ingramcontent.com/pod-product-compliance
Lightning Source LLC
LaVergne TN
LVHW061531070526
838199LV00010B/450